Marketing Research

Marketing Research
Text and Cases

K. L. McGown

Concordia University

Winthrop Publishers, Inc.
Cambridge, Massachusetts

Library of Congress Cataloging in Publication Data

McGown, K   L   date
  Marketing research.

  Includes index.
  1. Marketing research. 2. Marketing research—Case
studies. I. Title.
HF5415.2.M22   658.8′3   79–11363
ISBN 0–87626–562–X

Cover design by Susan Marsh

© *1979 by Winthrop Publishers, Inc.*
  17 Dunster Street, Cambridge, Massachusetts 02138

10   9   8   7   6   5   4   3   2

To Nancy and Hilary

Contents

Part 3   Applications   /   293

Preface

THE INSPIRATION FOR THIS BOOK came from my personal experience in teaching marketing research at several colleges and universities in the United States and Canada. While there were numerous fine textbooks available, none seemed to be quite satisfactory. Most other marketing research texts are too complex and theoretical for the average undergraduate student.

Marketing Research: Text and Cases is written in clear and simple language, using a minimum of quantitative techniques. Whereas other major texts assume prerequisites of at least two semesters of statistics, two semesters of marketing, and substantial quantitative expertise, the only prerequisite for comprehension of this text is one semester of introductory marketing. Though other major marketing texts average at least 700 pages, *Marketing Research: Text and Cases* is considerably shorter (only 448 pages) and much easier to read, making it ideal for a one semester course.

Marketing Research: Text and Cases aims to provide basic comprehension of the marketing research process through a "how to" approach. The text is divided into three parts: Part 1, Introduction, contains Chapters 1–4, which introduce the student to the development and scope of the research process. In Part 2, The Process of Data Collection, Chapters 5–12 provide a step-by-step approach to solving research problems from how to collect data to how to write a research report. Part 3, Applications, contains chapters on the application of research techniques to various functional areas of marketing, including product and advertising research. The last chapter provides a look at the future of marketing research.

To increase the practical value of this book, "real world" cases have been included at the end of each major section. While the cases generally have been disguised, their value in reinforcing concepts and techniques found in the chapters remains undiminished. At the end of each chapter are questions and problems that can be used to assist the learning process. Every effort has been made to provide a readable and comprehensive integrated synthesis that both student and instructor will appreciate and remember.

Many people have worked to make this book a success and I am extremely grateful to all of them. For his assistance in preparing Chapters 10, 11, 13, 16, and 17, I wish to thank Professor Wilkie English of the University of Arkansas (Little Rock). A great debt is owed to the reviewers for their helpful comments on previous drafts of this manuscript: Professors Algin B. King of Christopher Newport College, Richard T. Hise of Texas A&M University, Fredrick Wiseman of Northeastern University, and Joseph P. Vaccaro of Suffolk University.

For secretarial and research assistance I am especially indebted to Judy Storen, Debbie Lawrence, Betty Tzotzis, and Maureen Scallion. My thanks go to numerous students for their assistance in preparing cases and participating in the class testing of this book. Last, I wish to thank my wife, Nancy, for her patience and understanding during the time it took to transform this book from concept to reality.

K. L. McGown
Montreal

Marketing Research

Part 1

Introduction

Chapter 1

The Marketing Research Process

LET'S BEGIN by looking at the following situations:

• A Detroit automaker wishes to bring out a new, economy, low horsepower, high gasoline mileage automobile. Such an auto might satisfy demands made by the Environmental Protection Agency (EPA) for vehicles with a minimum of pollution, but the automobile maker wonders if a small engine will satisfy North American motorists.

• The dean of the School of Business at a new and rapidly growing urban university, knowing that many undergraduate students work full-time, is considering offering more evening courses. However, the dean does not know if the demand for these extra sections will justify hiring more faculty.

• A recent university graduate with a major in marketing wishes to remain in the small town near the campus and pursue her interest in stereos by opening a hi-fi shop catering to college students. She knows students are interested in buying stereos and parts but wonders if such a small business could generate the sales needed to survive.

• Friends and acquaintances of the owner of a professional football team urge him to move his team to a new and larger home stadium on the outskirts of the city. Though the new stadium rental will be substantially higher and it will thus be necessary to raise ticket prices 25 percent, profits will be much greater if the new stadium averages at least 75 percent of seating capacity during each home game.

All the businesspeople just described face a common problem, one faced every day by planners in our society: how to make the right decision under conditions of uncertainty. Each situation presents the marketing problem of determining consumer preferences and then satisfying these preferences within the context of the organization and the environment in which it operates. Obviously, the task of determining and satisfying consumer preferences is an enormously complex one, especially if it is to be successfully and profitably accomplished by a firm in a competitive capitalistic environment. However, one fundamental and increasingly important method by which uncertainty may be reduced in dealing with marketing problems is *marketing research*.

What Is Marketing Research?

The American Marketing Association has developed the most universally accepted definition of marketing research: "the systematic gathering, recording, and analyzing of data about problems relating to the marketing of goods and services."[1] This definition has two important aspects. First, it is sufficiently broad to include all problems, including those of the *nonprofit* sector, encountered in the marketing of goods and services. Second, it explicitly recognizes the *systematic* nature of the research process in which data are gathered, recorded, and analyzed in an orderly manner.

Though this definition does not say so directly, it should be noted that the data must always be gathered, recorded, and analyzed in an *objective* and *accurate* fashion. All too often, objectivity and accuracy are missing from research investigations, and the research is designed only to support or "prove" what management wants to see. A common example of this type of research may be seen almost every day on television commercials in which research studies are cited to prove that "doctors recommend" the sponsor's particular product. Left unsaid by the sponsor is that only two medical doctors need to have recommended the product in order to make this statement technically correct, though the product may have left hundreds of other physicians unimpressed.

Properly conducted marketing research, unlike much research used to sell consumer goods or to justify top management decisions and

[1] *Report of the Definitions Committee of the American Marketing Association* (Chicago: American Marketing Association, 1961), p. 15.

ideas, is a means of acquiring needed information to aid management in making marketing decisions. As the importance of the marketing function and the cost of business decisions have increased steadily and dramatically over the years, so has the need for accurate and objective information obtained through the marketing research process. This process, therefore, provides necessary data to help executives identify and solve marketing problems within the organization.

The Role of Research in the Firm

A better understanding of the research process may be developed by examining the role of research in the firm. Accordingly, we will examine the marketing process and the role of research in the firm's marketing efforts. The location of the research department in the organizational structure, the organization of the research department, and the duties and responsibilities usually assigned to research are discussed in this chapter.

The fast-changing, dynamic nature of North American business today has dramatically increased the necessity for accurate, up-to-date information, so that executives can act immediately on profit threats and opportunities: "the executive needs specific studies of problem and opportunity areas. He may need a market survey, a product-preference test, a sales forecast by region, or an advertising-effectiveness study. These studies require the talents of skilled researchers who can apply principles of sample size, sample design, and questionnaire construction to the task. These researchers usually make up the marketing research department of the company." [2]

Marketing Research and Marketing

Twentieth-century North Americans live in an era of increasing specialization where individual self-sufficiency has become a rarity. Thus, each of us is highly dependent upon the actions of others, and we must trade with each other in order to survive. Using money as a medium of exchange, we acquire desired goods and services brought to us by a complex marketing system and enjoy a standard of living undreamed of in earlier times.

[2] Philip Kotler, *Marketing Management: Analysis, Planning and Control*, 3rd ed. (Englewood Cliffs, N.J.: Prentice-Hall, 1976), p. 425.

The Development of Marketing

Marketing activities are essential to the level of affluence and the high consumption patterns enjoyed by North Americans. Marketing may be regarded as the concomitant of an affluent society. A modern marketing system cannot exist without efficient producers and affluent consumers; without a modern, highly industrialized manufacturing sector, the marketing sector also languishes, for it is in this commercial environment that exchange flourishes, with the accompanying specialization and division of labor.

Marketing, to the American Marketing Association, is "the performance of business activities which direct the flow of goods and services from producer to the ultimate consumer or industrial user." Philip Kotler defines marketing as "human activity directed at satisfying needs and wants through exchange processes." [3] Both these definitions recognize that marketing constitutes the exchange process by which human needs and wants are satisfied through the acquisition of products. Goods and services that the consumer accepts as satisfying his needs and wants should be developed with the customer in mind. Firms whose activities begin with the customer, not with the production process, are said to be *marketing oriented*. In the past, many business firms in our society were strictly *production oriented*. That is, especially in times when goods and services were scarce, it was considered important to produce goods first and then worry about selling them. Since that time many firms moved toward *sales orientation*, where the marketing function was viewed simply as a sales function: the firms produced goods, and it was the marketing departments' duty to sell these goods; other functions of advertising or research were basically ignored or unknown. In recent years, though, a marketing orientation has become more predominant. Firms having a marketing orientation recognize that they must find needs and then fill them. This process implies adoption of the marketing concept.

One firm that has passed through all these stages is Pillsbury, the manufacturer of flour, baking mixes, and animal feeds. Founded in 1869, Pillsbury was a production-oriented firm until about 1930. The company then moved to a sales orientation, which continued basically unchanged for almost thirty years until in 1958 the firm became a total "marketing company." [4]

[3] Kotler, *Marketing Management*, p. 5.
[4] Robert J. Keith, "The Marketing Revolution," *Journal of Marketing*, vol. 24, January 1960, pp. 35–38.

The Marketing Concept and the Marketing Mix

The *marketing concept*, first implemented at General Electric, is a philosophy or a way of thinking that permeates the entire organization. This marketing concept incorporates three key criteria:

1. *Customer orientation.* That is, the objectives of the firm are stated in eternal human needs.
2. *Profitable sales.* The key objective is long-run, not short-run, profitable sales.
3. *Integrated marketing.* Top marketing management reports directly to the firm's top management.

Figure 1·1 graphically illustrates the task of marketing management in incorporating the marketing concept. The central focus of the

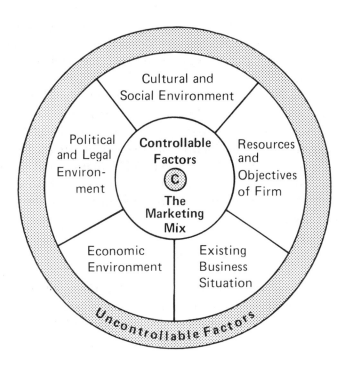

Figure 1·1
Marketing Manager's Framework

Reproduced with permission from E. Jerome McCarthy, *Basic Marketing*, 4th ed. (Homewood, Ill.: Richard D. Irwin, Inc., 1975), p. 38.

marketing concept is the customer, shown here in the center of the diagram, surrounded by the marketing mix — product, price, place (otherwise known as distribution), and promotion. These are factors that are considered generally controllable by the firm. Factors that are less controllable by the firm include the political and legal environment, the resources and objectives of the firm, the existing business situation, the economic environment, and lastly, the cultural and social environment.

The key activity that makes the marketing concept work is marketing research. If the central focus of the firm is the consumer, and if the objective of the firm is consumer orientation with profitable sales, then it is only through marketing research that the firm can ascertain what consumers desire and then satisfy these wants.

Central to the task of marketing research is research in the product policies, pricing policies, distribution policies, and promotion policies — those four basic factors in the marketing mix that are generally controllable by the firm. Research into the external and generally uncontrollable factors, diagramed in the outside circle in figure 1•1, is also necessary for firms wishing to maintain a competitive market position. For example, most large firms engage in economic forecasting; an anticipated downturn in the economy will cause the firm to forego new capital spending.

Thus, we can see that modern marketing goes hand in hand with twentieth-century industrialized society in North America. Our industrial society functions on the bases of exchange and specialization. In moving away from the production orientation of earlier times, more and more firms have adopted a marketing orientation and the marketing concept. The cornerstone of this foundation is marketing research: only through modern marketing research techniques can the marketing concept be fully implemented.

The Increasing Importance of Research

Administrators are becoming increasingly dependent upon marketing research to supply them with the quick and accurate flow of information needed to make business decisions. The increasing importance of marketing research is based on three trends: [5]

1. *The shift from local to national and international marketing.* Executives are further and further removed from their markets and

[5] Kotler, *Marketing Management*, p. 419.

therefore are more than ever dependent on accurate information flows in the decision-making process. By being so far away from the place where sales occur, the executive may lose his touch for the market and be unable to act on intuition; he must have reliable market information.

2. *The transition from consumer needs to consumer wants.* As real income (purchasing power) has risen among consumers, discretionary income (income that can be spent for nonessential items) has become increasingly important. Consumers are able to pick and choose among competing products. Because discretionary income is used for nonessentials, marketing executives will require more information on the products on which buyers wish to spend their income. Thus, not only is there the shopper's basic decision whether to spend discretionary income for a color television, a sailboat, a stereo system, or a vacation, there is a further decision concerning the style, make, and model of color television, sailboat, or stereo, or concerning where to go on vacation. Measuring the strength and direction of consumer preferences is far more complex with discretionary than with essential expenditures.

3. *The shift from price to nonprice competition.* Marketers require much information on the effectiveness of such marketing tools as branding, product differentiation, advertising, and sales promotion, since it is these tools that create in the minds of consumers differences, real or imagined, among competing products. Firms lacking this essential information are at a competitive disadvantage in relation to other firms in the same industry, and it may be expected, all other things being equal, that the firm with inadequate information flow (marketing research) will pay a severe penalty in the form of reduced sales and profits.

The Location of the Research Department

If the main purpose of marketing research is the provision of accurate and objective data about problems facing marketing management, it logically follows that research should be located within the marketing department. Firms with marketing research departments are usually organized as illustrated in figure 1•2. Figure 1•2 shows a somewhat simplified, but typical location of the marketing research department, according to which the marketing research manager reports directly to the marketing vice-president and is on the same level as sales and advertising managers. This is considered the most logical and is also the

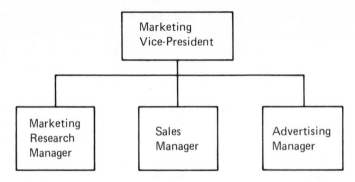

Figure 1•2
Location of the Marketing Research Department

most common location for the marketing research department within large organizations.

However, it does not necessarily follow that the marketing research manager must report directly to marketing management. Marketing research may report directly to top management — the president and executive vice-president of the organization. For example, the American Marketing Association reported in 1973 that 62 percent of marketing research managers in advertising agencies reported directly to top management.[6] Sometimes the marketing research manager reports to other corporate or general management or to engineering and development. On balance, although most marketing research managers still report directly to marketing management, an increasing number of firms have research reporting directly to top management — a reflection of the increasing importance of the research function in today's modern business environment.

The Organization of the Research Department

Like the location of the research department within the firm, the internal structure may also vary, especially in degree of decentralization. Highly centralized firms usually have just one marketing research department, while large decentralized ones may have separate research departments for each major operating division.

> Considerable shifting often continues to occur in the organization of marketing research functions. In recent years, a number of companies

[6] Dik Warren Twedt, ed., *1973 Survey of Marketing Research* (Chicago: American Marketing Association, 1973), pp. 24–25.

— about one-fourth of those surveyed — have significantly altered the placement or structuring of their research operations. A few that had previously relied on a single department at headquarters have now shifted to a strictly divisional approach, or vice versa. More often than not, a move to have all marketing research conducted at division level has been part of a major effort to decentralize all key marketing functions, thereby giving each division greater autonomy in carrying out its own integrated marketing program. When the location of marketing research has been changed from division level to corporate, the most common explanation is that this was done for reasons of efficiency or economy.

More frequently, however, divisionalized companies have changed not from one extreme arrangement to another, but to a mixed arrangement which has established marketing research activities at both levels. Usually, the addition of division-level functions has aimed at providing stronger research support for each operating function. Where marketing research was previously carried out only at division level, a recently established corporate function often serves as a research arm of a new staff unit concerned primarily with corporate development.[7]

The Duties and Responsibilities of the Research Department

The broad definition of marketing research presented at the beginning of this chapter recognizes that the duties and responsibilities assigned to research departments are seldom the same in any two organizations, especially considering that many departments have only one person assigned full-time, whereas others contain a score of full-time personnel. The duties of the research department may be limited by a lack of financial and human resources. In firms where marketing functions are given limited attention, the responsibilities of the researcher may be confined to simple surveys and sales forecasts.

As we have said, the role of marketing research tends to vary significantly from one organization to the next. The location of the research department in the organizational chart and its internal structure are seldom identical in any two organizations. The duties and the responsibilities of the marketing research managers vary considerably. Why is there so much variation? The role of marketing research in the firm is determined essentially by three characteristics of the organization: (1) the nature of the business, (2) size, and (3) top management attitudes toward the marketing function.

[7] Lewis W. Foreman and Earl L. Bailey, *The Role and Organization of Marketing Research*, no. 20 (New York: The Conference Board, 1969), pp. 18–19.

The term *nature of business* refers to the type of enterprise involved — whether the firm is engaged in the selling of consumer or industrial products, is manufacturer or middleman, is advertising agency or advertising medium, and so on. For example, firms that sell consumer products are more likely to be engaged in marketing research than are those that sell in the industrial market, though this is not to say that marketing research is unimportant in industrial firms — quite the contrary. However, firms that have a very close contact with the consumer mass market may find it necessary to rely on marketing research to a much greater extent than those who have a limited number of large customers in the industrial market. A firm like General Foods, with a multiplicity of consumer goods sold to the mass market, is in a much different position in marketing research than U.S. Steel. A large consumer goods firm is much more likely than an industrial firm of the same size to engage in such research activities as panel operations, studies of premiums and coupons, test markets, store audits, copy research, packaging research and studies of advertising effectiveness.

Size is the second major variable determining the role of research in the firm. By size we mean the annual revenue or sales of the organization. In looking at the annual sales of corporations, the American Marketing Association found that among corporations with annual sales of over $500 million, 80 percent had formal marketing research departments, 9 percent had only one person assigned the marketing research function, and just 11 percent had no one assigned. At the opposite end of the spectrum, of those corporations with annual sales of under $5 million, only 18 percent had formal marketing research departments, 19 percent had one person assigned to this function, and 63 percent had no one assigned to marketing research.[8] Results of the survey are presented in table 1·1.

This does not mean that a small company has less need for marketing research than a large company; what is indicated is rather that the small firm is unable to support its own in-house research. Therefore, the small company may do without marketing research (one of the causes contributing to the high mortality rate among small businesses), or it may decide to contract with a professional marketing research firm.

Top management attitudes toward the marketing function are critical in determining the role of research within the organization. Firms that can be characterized as marketing oriented include Philip Morris, Warner-Lambert, and virtually all the large consumer goods companies selling to the mass market. Other large organizations, even

[8] Twedt, *1973 Survey of Marketing Research,* p. 13.

Table 1·1

Organization for Marketing Research (by Company Size)

Annual Sales Millions of Dollars	No. Answering	Percent Having Formal Department	One Person	No One Assigned
Over $500	185	80	9	11
$200–500	170	77	12	11
$100–199	130	81	11	8
$50–99	147	69	16	15
$25–49	116	61	22	17
$5–24	197	38	33	29
Under $5	305	18	19	63
All Companies Answering This Question	1,250	55	27	18

From Dik Warren Twedt, *1973 Survey of Marketing Research* © 1973, p. 13. Reprinted by permission of the American Marketing Association, Chicago, Ill.

though their goods or services may be directed at the mass market, may still not be market oriented. For example, is the U.S. Postal Service market oriented?

Many large firms even today still retain an attitude best described as production oriented, not market oriented. These firms, whether through ignorance or through deliberate policy, do not fully incorporate the marketing function, and therefore marketing research is not given prominence. In such organizations, top management may view marketing simply as sales, a very low-level function existing to service production or engineering departments. Top management in these organizations may be hostile to or ignorant of the role of marketing, and thus marketing research suffers. There is little corporate willingness to invest in research, and it is quite common for no marketing research department to exist in such an environment.

Careers and Compensation

Career opportunities in marketing research have increased dramatically in recent years for both men and women. Many college graduates go directly to work for corporate marketing research departments. The continued expansion of the marketing research function has provided career avenues at the entrance level for college graduates with majors in statistics, economics, marketing, psychology, and mathematics.

Table 1•2 presents the results of an American Marketing Association survey to determine compensation levels for marketing research positions. Eleven job positions are shown in the table, though in actual practice there are considerably more positions in the marketing research field. Illustrated in the table are the mean compensation levels for these eleven positions in 1973 and the percentage of change from the 1968 mean. Annual salary levels in 1973 ranged from approximately $25,000 a year for research directors to a low of approximately $10,000 for full-time interviewers. Certainly, salary levels are much higher today, reflecting ongoing adjustments for cost of living and merit increases. In the past, women were employed primarily only in the junior professional research positions, and salary levels for women were considerably below those for men. Today, however, at the professional level, these differences have virtually disappeared.

From table 1•2 it may be seen that in corporate research departments three principal job categories prevail: research directors, analysts, and clerical staff. The research director holds the senior position and has responsibility for the entire research program. Senior analysts

Table 1·2
Mean Compensation for All Marketing Research Positions in 1973

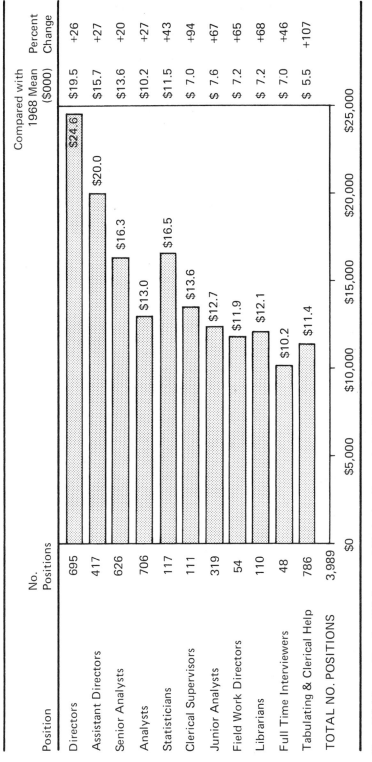

Position	No. Positions	Compared with 1968 Mean ($000)	Percent Change
Directors	695	$24.6 / $19.5	+26
Assistant Directors	417	$20.0 / $15.7	+27
Senior Analysts	626	$16.3 / $13.6	+20
Analysts	706	$13.0 / $10.2	+27
Statisticians	117	$16.5 / $11.5	+43
Clerical Supervisors	111	$13.6 / $ 7.0	+94
Junior Analysts	319	$12.7 / $ 7.6	+67
Field Work Directors	54	$11.9 / $ 7.2	+65
Librarians	110	$12.1 / $ 7.2	+68
Full Time Interviewers	48	$10.2 / $ 7.0	+46
Tabulating & Clerical Help	786	$11.4 / $ 5.5	+107
TOTAL NO. POSITIONS	3,989		

$0 $5,000 $10,000 $15,000 $20,000 $25,000

From Dik Warren Twedt, *1973 Survey of Marketing Research* © 1973, p. 57. Reprinted by permission of the American Marketing Association, Chicago, Ill.

and analysts constitute the largest professional category; it is the research analyst who has the professional responsibility for completing projects. Most people who work for a research department fall in the category of clerical staff, who usually perform clerical functions of a routine nature, such as tabulating data.

Professional marketing researchers often have graduate degrees in one or more of the five fields previously mentioned, and many research directors hold doctorates in psychology, marketing, or related fields. Although advanced degrees may make candidates overqualified for many jobs in the business world, marketing research is not an area in which the graduate degree is viewed as a handicap. A master's or doctor's degree can be of significant benefit if research methodology and problem solving have been stressed in the graduate program.

Career opportunities in marketing research have grown at a rapid rate and should continue to grow in the foreseeable future. The viability of marketing research as a professional field will be favorably affected by four factors:

1. Competitive edge in the interfirm and interbrand competition, which is intense in the business scene lies particularly in accurate marketing decisions and innovations. The complexity of these decisions has become greater and their tempo faster as new products, brands and alternatives have appeared. With more problems and a higher payoff for well-informed problem solvers, research must be stimulated.

2. Efficiency in marketing plans and decisions is sought by revamping of corporate organizations. The growing use of product, brand, and market managers and establishment of stricter profit centers are steps in this direction — and other novel organizational arrangements are being tested to improve decision competence and responsibility. Toward the same end, corporations are adopting more systematic planning companywide and for longer ranges. These trends lead to better planning and utilization of marketing research, which will enhance its value and its use.

3. Technology and data availability are opening new opportunities while also complicating the tasks of marketing research. Specifically: new data transmission media, faster and vaster electronic data processing systems, more practical and versatile decision models, and more powerful analytical methods — these too are increasing the number and the sophistication required in marketing research personnel.

4. The inadequacy of today's expenditure on marketing research provides a small base from which relatively much larger outlays readily should be possible. Consider that among consumer goods producers with over $5 million sales revenue, the average expenditure for marketing research is about 0.3 percent of sales and for very large companies (doing over $500 million in sales) the percentage is only

0.07 percent — according to the 1973 American Marketing Association survey. And similar expenditure percentages among industrial product companies are only 0.15 and 0.04 percent respectively. That is, corporations are spending ten times as much on advertising and twenty times on research and development as on marketing research, yet those functions are facing enormous risks in advertising and in new product decisions that urgently need research guidance.[9]

Summary

Marketing research is "the systematic gathering, recording, and analyzing of data about problems relating to the marketing of goods and services." We have used this definition in our introductory chapter because it is sufficiently broad to include all marketing problems, even those of the nonprofit sector. This definition implicitly recognizes that research data must always be gathered and processed in an objective and accurate manner.

Today, more and more firms have shifted from a production orientation to a marketing orientation. This shift involves adoption of the marketing concept, a way of thinking that permeates the entire organization and incorporates three basic criteria: customer orientation, profitable sales, and integrated marketing. The key factor that holds the marketing concept together and makes it work is marketing research. Without such research, how can the firm possibly be customer oriented? Marketing research is needed to help the firm find the markets and then seek to satisfy them. The marketing mix, that combination of the four key elements — product, price, place, and promotion — constituting the core of any firm's marketing program, is built directly around the customer under the marketing concept.

As an organized business activity, marketing research is primarily a post–World War II phenomenon, though the earliest commercial marketing research is considered to date from the beginning of the twentieth century. The rapidly increasing importance of marketing research information to businesspeople is a result of three major changes: 1) the shift from local to national and international marketing, 2) the transition from consumer needs to consumer wants, and 3) the shift from price to nonprice competition.

In a large firm, the manager of the marketing research department is usually on the same level with the sales manager and the advertising manager. The marketing research manager in such a firm will report usually to the vice-president of marketing but quite often to top man-

[9] David J. Luck, Hugh G. Wales, and Donald A. Taylor, *Marketing Research*, 4th ed. (Englewood Cliffs, N.J.: Prentice-Hall, 1974), p. 54.

agement. The research department may be organized on a centralized or decentralized basis, depending on the organization of the company itself. Research department responsibilities vary among firms; for example, sales research could be done by the accounting department. Three factors determine the role of marketing research in the firm: the nature of the business, the size of the organization, and top management attitudes toward the marketing function.

As the field of marketing research has increased dramatically, so have its career opportunities. University graduates with advanced degrees in statistics, economics, marketing, psychology, and mathematics can look forward to rewarding professional careers as marketing research professionals. Within the corporate research department three principal job categories prevail: research director, analysts, and clerical staff. Increasingly intense competition, greater reliance upon marketing plans and decisions, more sophisticated technology, and the extremely low level of present-day expenditures on marketing research are all factors that should cause this field to continue to grow at a rapid rate for the foreseeable future.

Questions for Discussion

1. "You cannot have an affluent, industrialized society without modern marketing." Discuss the full meaning and implication of this statement. Do you agree or disagree? Why?

2. Modern marketing research is said to be the cornerstone of the marketing concept. What is meant by this statement? Is it possible to have the marketing concept implemented without marketing research?

3. How is marketing research defined in this chapter? Explain in your own words what this definition means.

4. What is the role of marketing research in the firm? Should the marketing research manager report to the vice-president of marketing or to top management? Explain.

5. Should the marketing research function be centralized or decentralized? When might it be best to centralize and when best to decentralize it? Give examples. What about General Motors?

6. Class problem: How do career opportunities and compensation in marketing research compare with such other career areas in marketing as sales and advertising?

7. Group project: Prepare a short paper evaluating job opportunities for professionals in marketing research. What factors will you have to consider?

Chapter 2

Development of Marketing Research

JUST AS MODERN MARKETING and the marketing concept are relatively recent developments, marketing research, as an organized business activity, is not only relatively recent but is still in its infancy. The birth of modern marketing research can be traced back to 1911, when the first formal marketing research department was established. In that year Charles Parlin was appointed manager of the Commercial Research and Advertising Department of the Curtis Publishing Company. However, there were virtually no organized marketing research activities before the First World War. Research techniques were then relatively unsophisticated and consisted of firsthand observation, a few elementary surveys, and some sales and operating cost analyses.

The years between the two world wars saw the gradual development of more advanced marketing research techniques. That the users of these techniques had a long way to go, however, was well demonstrated by the 1936 *Literary Digest* election disaster: in that year, on the basis of some rather crude sampling, the now defunct *Literary Digest* forecast Alf Landon to defeat Franklin Roosevelt in the presidential election.

In 1923 the A.C. Nielsen Company, the world's largest marketing research firm, was established. In 1975, A. C. Nielsen's total revenue of over $200 million was greater than those of the other top nine U.S. marketing research firms combined. Before World War II comparatively few firms were involved in research activities.

During the years following World War II, marketing research made rapid strides. In these years probability sampling, regression methods, store panels, motivation research, regression and correlation, and other more sophisticated research techniques came into widespread use. Marketing research departments have been established at a rapid rate, and few large firms today are without at least one person assigned full-time to research.

Research Activities

The scope of current research may be grasped by looking at the activities of marketing research departments, which may be grouped under five major headings: advertising research, business economics and corporate research, corporate responsibility research, product research, and sales and market research. Table 2·1 lists thirty-one different marketing

Table 2·1
Research Activities of 1,322 Respondent Companies

	% DOING	DONE BY MARKETING RESEARCH DEPARTMENT	DONE BY ANOTHER DEPARTMENT	DONE BY OUTSIDE FIRM
Advertising Research				
Motivation research	33	18	2	16
Copy research	37	17	6	18
Media research	44	16	10	21
Studies of ad effectiveness	49	26	7	21
Other	7	5	—	2
Business Economics and Corporate Research				
Short-range forecasting (up to 1 year)	63	43	23	1
Long-range forecasting (over 1 year)	61	42	22	2
Studies of business trends	61	46	16	3
Pricing studies	56	33	25	2
Plant and warehouse location studies	47	18	28	3
Product mix studies	51	36	16	2
Acquisition studies	53	25	30	3
Export and international studies	41	19	22	3
Internal company employees studies (attitudes, communication, etc.)	45	13	29	6
Other	4	3	1	—

Table 2·1—*Continued*

	% DOING	DONE BY MARKETING RESEARCH DEPARTMENT	DONE BY ANOTHER DEPARTMENT	DONE BY OUTSIDE FIRM
Corporate Responsibility Research				
Consumers' "Right to Know" studies	18	9	7	4
Ecological impact studies	27	8	16	5
Studies of legal constraints on advertising and promotion	38	7	28	5
Social values and policies studies	25	11	12	4
Other	2	1	1	—
Product Research				
New product acceptance and potential	63	51	9	8
Competitive product studies	64	52	11	6
Testing of existing products	57	35	20	7
Packaging research: design or physical characteristics	44	23	17	9
Other	3	2	1	1
Sales and Market Research				
Measurement of market potentials	68	60	8	6
Market share analysis	67	58	9	5
Determination of market characteristics	68	61	6	6
Sales analyses	65	46	23	2
Establishment of sales quotas, territories	57	23	35	1
Distribution channel studies	48	30	19	3
Test markets, store audits	38	28	6	9
Consumer panel operations	33	21	3	12
Sales compensation studies	45	11	33	2
Promotional studies of premiums, coupons, sampling, deals, etc.	39	25	13	6
Other	2	2	—	—

From Dik Warren Twedt, *1973 Survey of Marketing Research*, © 1973, p. 41. Reprinted by permission of the American Marketing Association, Chicago, Ill.

research activities under these five headings. Also illustrated are the percentages of the research done by the marketing research department, by another department, and by an outside firm or agency. The nine most common activities for over 60 percent of the companies are determination of market characteristics, measurement of market potentials, market share analysis, sales analysis, competitive product studies, new product acceptance and potential, short-range forecasting, long-range forecasting, and studies of business trends. You will notice from the table that less than half the firms do their own advertising research: such research is often done by an outside firm, the client's advertising agency. Notice also the high percentage of business economics and corporate research done by a department other than the research department.

Table 2·1 presents combined research activities for both industrial and consumer companies. There is very little difference in the percentages of industrial and consumer companies engaged in most of the research activities listed in the table. However, the consumer companies were found more likely to undertake studies in consumer panel operations, premiums, coupons and deals, test markets and store audits, advertising copy, packaging, and advertising effectiveness. Inasmuch as all these activities are traditionally of much greater importance to consumer companies, it is logical that consumer companies are more likely to be involved than are industrial firms.

Advertising, product research, and marketing analysis are the research activities in which advertising agencies are most likely to be engaged. Publishers' and broadcasters' research activities are focused upon media research, market share analysis, determination of market characteristics, sales analyses, and measurement of market potential. Note that approximately one-fourth of the companies are involved in corporate responsibility research, an area that has received considerable attention in recent years under pressure from consumer groups and government agencies.

The Scope of Present-Day Research Activities

If we look upon marketing research activities as constituting essential information-gathering and processing activities that help top management to make critical decisions, then we can realize that these activities are not limited merely to analyses of the marketing mix. The typical questions that should be asked by marketing researchers and managers are illustrated in table 2·2. Answers to these questions can be obtained only through marketing research, and the firm that neglects to seek these answers may soon find itself out of business.

Present-day research activities do not always involve as wide a range of questions as is presented in table 2·2, but if such questions are

Table 2·2

Uses of Research to Help Marketing Management Make Decisions

I. Research to make target decisions

  1. Who are our target consumers? What are their demographics?
  2. Should we aim our promotion at more than one target market?
  3. What are the strengths and weaknesses of our competitors who court the same target consumers?
  4. Is the size of our target market likely to increase, decrease or remain the same in the near future?

II. Research to make advertising decisions

  1. What kinds of advertising appeal, slogan, and theme should we use?
  2. What media should we use? How should we allocate our advertising budget among the various media?
  3. How large should the advertising budget be?
  4. How effective is our advertising program in selling our products?

III. Research to make business and economic decisions

  1. What is the projected short-term, mid-term, and long-term demand for our products?
  2. Where should we locate inventory centers and retail facilities?
  3. Should we lease or own our real estate locations?
  4. How much money should be allocated to new product development?

IV. Research to make product decisions

  1. What modifications should be made to extend the life cycle of existing products?
  2. What products should we add or delete from our product line?
  3. What changes should be made in the packaging of specific products?
  4. Should we expand, contract, or maintain our present product line?

V. Research to make market planning decisions

  1. What should be our overall sales goal for the upcoming period?
  2. How should the market be divided into territories?
  3. What quotas should be assigned to individual salespeople?
  4. How should the sales force be compensated?

Questions

  1. In each of the above decision areas, what are some other questions marketing management may want answered through research?
  2. Can all conceivable marketing management decisions be based on research? Explain.

From *Marketing Today, A Basic Approach*, 2nd edition, by David J. Schwartz. © 1973, 1977 by Harcourt Brace Jovanovich, Inc., and reprinted with their permission.

to be answered, the marketing research function must use increasingly sophisticated techniques. If it is through competent modern marketing research that top management is ultimately able to implement the marketing concept in the firm, then techniques must go well beyond elementary surveys and analyses of internal data. In recent years we have seen far more advanced techniques incorporating test-marketing

Table 2·3
Evolving Techniques in Marketing Research

DECADE	TECHNIQUE
Prior to 1910	Firsthand observation Elementary surveys
1910–20	Sales analysis Operating-cost analysis
1920–30	Questionnaire construction Survey technique
1930–40	Quota sampling Simple correlation analysis Distribution-cost analysis Store auditing techniques
1940–50	Probability sampling Regression methods Advanced statistical inference Consumer and store panels
1950–60	Motivation research Operations research Multiple regression and correlation Attitude-measuring instruments
1960–70	Factor analysis and discriminant analysis Mathematical models Bayesian statistical analysis and decision theory Scaling theory Computer data processing and analysis Marketing stimulation Information storage and retrieval
1970–	Nonmetric multidimensional scaling Econometric models Comprehensive marketing planning models Test-marketing laboratories Multiattribute attitude models

From Philip Kotler, *Marketing Management: Analysis, Planning and Control,* 3rd ed., ©️ 1976, p. 428. Reprinted by permission of Prentice-Hall, Inc., Englewood Cliffs, N.J.

laboratories, multiattribute attitude models, Bayesian statistical analysis, and other techniques. The historical evolution of these techniques is presented in table 2•3, which clearly shows the increasing complexity of the marketing research process and indicates why research analysts must be able to use quantitative techniques. Many university students question the relevancy of quantitative courses, but marketing research is a field where the practical application of statistical techniques can be readily demonstrated in a meaningful and utilitarian context.

The Major Steps in Marketing Research

In designing and implementing the research study, it is necessary to follow carefully a designated series of steps in chronological order. This series of steps, known as the *research process*, is outlined in figure 2•1.

Problem Definition

Problem definition, the first step in the research process, is considered the most critical to the success of the project. If the problem is stated vaguely, or if the wrong problem is defined, then the rest of the re-

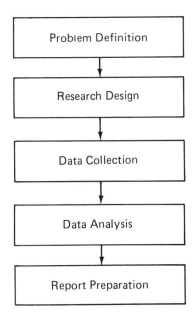

Figure 2•1
Steps in the Marketing Research Process

search is completely useless. For example, is the problem faced by the company one of declining sales, or are declining sales merely a symptom of the real problem, which could be poor product development or inadequate advertising and sales promotion? Exactly what is the specific problem that is faced?

To define the problem it is necessary to begin a process of exploratory research, in which the major emphasis is on gaining ideas or insights into the particular problem at hand. This preliminary analysis may be accomplished through a *situational analysis* and an *informal investigation* into the problem. The situational analysis is often, unfortunately, ignored, but it is vital to obtain background knowledge of the various conditions affecting the marketing operations of a business. Available information in six categories can be used in the preliminary investigation: the product; the company, industry, and competition; the market; channel of distribution; the sales organization; and advertising and sales promotion policies. The informal investigation consists of talking about the problem with customers, dealers, and persons occupying key positions within the firm. It has a twofold purpose: to develop and select the hypothesis to be used in the final study and to obtain a feel for the problems of the market.

The exploratory research steps outlined here may seem superfluous to some. However, they are of critical importance, especially in cases where the firm lacks full knowledge of the marketplace. Failure to have a proper definition of the problem at hand can well invalidate the rest of the steps.

Research Design

A clear definition of the problem at hand makes research design, the second step, easier. The research design itself serves as a framework for the study, guiding the collection and analysis of the data. The research design then focuses on the data-collection methods, the research instrument utilized, and the sampling plan to be followed.

DATA-COLLECTION METHODS

In looking at data-collection methods, the first thing that the researcher must be aware of is the distinction between primary and secondary data. Primary data have not previously existed in collected form and are gathered for the specific study at hand, whereas secondary data have been gathered for some other purpose and already exist. Secondary data may be found within the firm in its own internal records, and commercial, trade, or government publications are also major sources. The researcher can save considerable time and expense by always going to secondary data sources before attempting to collect primary data. All too often, firms have wasted immense amounts of time and money in conducting studies gathering primary data, when the same data were already available from secondary sources.

If satisfactory secondary data are not available, the researcher must rely on primary data gathered from (1) observation, (2) experimentation, or (3) surveys. Customers, middlemen and salesmen, competitors, and ultimate consumers are all sources for primary data. To gather such data from these sources, we may observe their actions in the marketplace. Experimental design, a controlled environment in which we systematically vary one factor, is another way to collect primary data; however, this method is usually not practical, because controlled laboratory experimental conditions are seldom possible in a business environment. The most common of the three methods used in gathering primary data, the survey, yields a wide range of valuable information on consumer attitudes, motives, and opinions. This kind of information cannot be readily obtained except through surveys using personal interviews or telephone or mail questionnaires.

RESEARCH INSTRUMENTS

The instrument used in research design may be mechanical, such as a tape recorder or a camera. In situations where the researcher is using the survey method, the instrument will be the questionnaire. Although in Chapter 7 we will be analyzing questionnaire construction in some detail, it is worth noting here that this research instrument must be utilized with great caution. Construction of good questionnaires is a skill that takes considerable time for a professional marketing researcher to develop. Care must be exercised in the types of questions asked, the form and wording of questions, and the choice of words and the order in which certain sensitive questions are asked.

SAMPLING PLANS

In the sampling plan the basic question concerns who is to be surveyed. Since it may not be possible to question everyone in the relevant universe (the whole collection of items studied by the researcher), especially in the case of consumer convenience goods manufacturers, we must use a sample or a subsection of people in that universe. We must determine what the sampling unit will be, how large our sample should be, what our sampling procedure will be, and, last, what sampling method should be utilized. By sampling method, we mean whether we will use the telephone, a mail questionnaire, or personal interviews in gathering our data. All three of these methods have advantages and disadvantages, which will be discussed in greater length in the chapter on questionnaire construction.

Data Collection

Data collection, the third major step in the marketing process, is also known as *field work*. Research design must have been completed before data collection can begin. As the gathering of primary data is usually considered the most expensive and the most error-prone step in the research process, great caution must be exercised at this point. Problems arise when respondents refuse to cooperate or are not at home and when there is bias on the part of either respondent or interviewer. Field work problems occur through:

> 1. *Not-at-homes.* When an interviewer does not find anyone at home, he can either call back later or substitute the household next door. The latter is the less expensive alternative because the interviewer will not have to travel back to the same block. The only problem is that there is no easy way to learn whether the adjacent household resembles the original one precisely, because no data were collected on the original. The substitution may be biasing.
> 2. *Refusal to cooperate.* After finding the designated individual at home, the interviewer must interest the person in cooperating. If the time is inconvenient or if the survey appears phony, the designated person may not cooperate.
> 3. *Respondent bias.* The interviewer must encourage accurate and thoughtful answers. Some respondents may give inaccurate or biased answers in order to finish quickly or for other reasons.
> 4. *Interviewer bias.* Interviewers are capable of introducing a variety of biases into the interviewing process, through the mere fact of their age, sex, manner, or intonation. In addition, there is the problem of conscious interviewer bias or dishonesty. Interviewers face a great temptation to fill their quota of interviews as quickly or as cheaply as possible. This can be done by not making the required number of call-backs, or by claiming refusals to cooperate, or, in extreme cases, by actually falsifying an interview.[1]

These field work problems can be reduced by carefully selecting, training, controlling, and evaluating the field force.

[1] Philip Kotler, *Marketing Management: Analysis, Planning and Control*, 3rd ed. (Englewood Cliffs, N.J.: Prentice-Hall, 1976), p. 432.

Data Analysis

Data analysis, the fourth step, is the statistical analysis of data that have been edited, coded, and tabulated. It is especially important in cases where the researcher has amassed large amounts of information from many respondents. The purpose is to determine if anything meaningful can be gathered from this mass of data, and it is to the data analysis step that the researcher must bring quantitative skills. The data may be analyzed to determine if, for example, consumers having an income of over $25,000 a year are responding differently from those consumers having an income of between $10,000 and $15,000 per year. In such instances, tests of significance, incorporating chi-square analysis, become invaluable tools to the researcher.

Report Preparation

The purpose of the research report, the fifth step, is presentation to the audience of the essential findings of the study in a clear and concise manner. The written research report follows a carefully designed format that allows the reader to ascertain the key elements immediately and to take action.

An effective research report is prepared with the level of the audience in mind. Technical sections and computer print-outs are usually reserved for the appendix.

The research report may be a source of friction between top management and research. Lengthy, highly technical, or poorly written reports may be deemed useless by top management. Chapter 12 will explore this subject in detail.

Characteristics of Good Marketing Research

By carefully following the major steps outlined in the marketing research process, the researcher reduces the possibility of making major errors and increases the probability that meaningful research results will be obtained. In evaluating the quality of a research project and in making a value judgement on the competency of the researcher, there are four key characteristics to consider: scientific method, creative research, multiple methods, and the value measured against the cost of the information.[2]

[2] Kotler, *Marketing Management*, p. 432.

Scientific Method

Effective marketing research is not based on intuition but on the scientific method, a process that calls for researcher objectivity, accurate measurement, and thorough and complete investigation, from which hypotheses are developed and tested. Consider the following example:

> A small mail-order house was suffering from a high rate (30 percent) of merchandise return. Management asked the marketing research manager to uncover the cause of the high return. The research manager proceeded to analyze various characteristics of the returned orders, such as the geographical locations of the customers, the sizes of the returned orders, and the type of merchandise. One hypothesis he formulated was that the longer the customer waited for merchandise, the greater the probability of its return. His regression analysis confirmed this hypothesis. He ventured the prediction that the return rate would fall if the company speeded up its delivery time. The company did this, and his prediction proved correct.[3]

Creative Research

Many times researchers are faced with the problem of gathering data on sensitive subjects from respondents who may be unwilling or unable to provide answers. This problem calls for creative or innovative approaches. The classic instant coffee study is described below:

> When instant coffee was first introduced, housewives complained that it did not taste like real coffee. Yet in blindfold tests, many of these same housewives could not distinguish between a cup of instant and real coffee. This indicated that much of their resistance was psychological. The researcher decided to design two almost identical shopping lists, the only difference being that regular coffee was on one list and instant coffee on the other. The regular coffee list was given to one group of housewives and the instant coffee list was given to a different, but comparable group. Both groups were asked to guess the social and personal characteristics of the woman whose shopping list they saw. The comments were pretty much the same with one significant difference; a higher proportion of the housewives whose list contained instant coffee described the subject as "lazy, a spendthrift, a poor wife, and failing to plan well for her family." These women were obviously imputing to the fictional housewife their own anxieties and negative images about the use of instant coffee. The instant-coffee company

[3] Horace C. Levinson, "Experiences in Commercial Operations Research," *Operation Research*, August 1953, pp. 220–39.

now knew the nature of the resistance and could develop a campaign to change the image of the housewife who serves instant coffee.[4]

Multiple Methods

It is usually unwise to rely exclusively upon one method in gathering data, especially primary data. Competent researchers usually use several methods at the same time to increase accuracy. For example, the A. C. Nielsen Company develops its well-known Television Index using both diaries and "black boxes" attached to sets in viewer homes. Research studies based on questioning often employ personal interviews and mail and telephone surveys.

The Value and Cost of the Information

The value of information gathered through research must be measured against its cost. In choosing which projects to undertake and what types of research design to use, the contribution of the research data must be evaluated according to value and cost.

Limitations of Marketing Research

Fundamental Limitations

Any research study will usually have several limitations, perhaps caused by financial constraints or insufficient sample, and it is necessary to emphasize these limitations in the report. Although this necessity may be well understood, it is not always well understood that there are fundamental limitations within the marketing research process itself. Basically, there are two such limitations: (1) marketing research data do not tell you what to do; and (2) the information gathered is always out of date.

Properly conducted marketing research is simply a tool, a tool that aids top management in the decision-making process. It is not an end in itself, and it does not provide final answers. Many people who are firm believers in marketing research may expect it to provide all the answers and be disappointed that it cannot. Many students, when analyzing marketing cases, tend to make the bland statement, "Call in

[4] Mason Haire, "Projective Techniques in Marketing Research," *Journal of Marketing* 14 (April 1950): 649–56.

He's doing market research. I told him we wouldn't trade eagles' feathers and beaded necklaces for 18-percent, tax-free New York City municipal bonds.

Figure 2·2
Marketing research surveys don't always solve problems!

Reprinted from *Marketing News*, Vol. 9, No. 20 (April 23, 1976), p. 11. Published by the American Marketing Association, Chicago, Ill.

the researcher," and in the business world the same thing may happen. Corporate executives may say, "Let's bring in a consulting firm," or "Let's bring in a research firm; surely these people can provide all our answers by conducting a market study." All too often management is disappointed because research is not equipped to do more than provide data that will aid in making decisions.

Tied in with this first limitation is the second. That is, information gathered through the marketing research process is always out of date. This difficulty can best be illustrated by looking at the political scene and the efforts of political pollsters (market researchers) to forecast voting patterns (consumer preferences) accurately in a given election. In the 1948 U.S. presidential election, the pollsters predicted that Dewey would defeat Truman. This report may have accurately reflected the voters' feelings at the time it was conducted; however, the last poll was taken approximately one week before the actual election. In the intervening seven days, consumer preferences changed. A still-popular photograph shows Harry Truman standing on the steps of the White House the morning after the election, holding up a newspaper with the headline claiming "Dewey Wins," when Truman had won. Was the data gathered in the research process inaccurate? No. What had happened? It was out of date, just as information gathered through the marketing research process is always out of date. The importance of this factor depends on how much the problem being investigated is affected by fast-changing consumer preferences. For example, how valid today would be a survey of consumer attitudes toward big automobiles that was taken just before the 1973 Arab oil embargo?

Cost

Despite the increasing importance and widening scope of activities, marketing research expenditures are only a tiny part of the typical firm's total budget. Marketing research accounts for less than 0.5 percent, or one-half of 1 percent, of total sales for the average firm. It is illustrative of the paucity of these expenditures that marketing research expenditures are typically only 10 percent of advertising and 5 percent of research and development spending for corporations.[5] Top management's lack of understanding of the research function is a major reason for these appallingly low percentages.

Agencies Performing and Utilizing Marketing Research

Organizations may perform and utilize marketing research for their own internal purposes. Some firms, called buyers, may use research but contract with outside agencies, called suppliers, to have the research performed. Other organizations may not utilize research themselves but may specialize in performing research for clients. Organizations supplying and buying marketing research may be grouped in the following nine major categories: [6]

1. *Manufacturers* are the principal users of marketing research, and large manufacturers usually do their own research in-house. Firms most likely to be engaged in both conducting and utilizing research are

[5] David J. Luck, Hugh G. Wales, and Donald A. Taylor, *Marketing Research*, 4th ed. (Englewood Cliffs, N.J.: Prentice-Hall, 1974), p. 54.

[6] Harper W. Boyd and Ralph Westfall, *Marketing Research: Text and Cases*, 3rd ed. (Homewood, Ill.: Richard D. Irwin, 1972), pp. 18–19.

the large consumer goods manufacturers, such as Procter and Gamble and General Foods. Nearly all these large firms have their own research departments, with one or more full-time research professionals, and they need not normally rely on independent research firms for data.

2. *Advertising agencies* have long been leading doers and users of marketing research. Much of the research done by advertising agencies is done on behalf of their clients. Traditionally, the cost of advertising research performed by agencies for their clients is included in the 15 percent fee, though large projects may be billed separately. All but the smallest advertising agencies usually have their own separate research departments. The work of these departments may be in measuring both the efficiency and the effectiveness of advertising for the agency and for its clients. Some of the advertising agencies have research departments whose activities are much more involved than measuring advertising; in these cases, the activities of the departments are similar to those of full-time marketing research agencies, and they perform a wide range of typical marketing research functions.

3. *Advertising media* are both suppliers and users of market research. Such advertising media as radio, television, newspapers, and magazines are typically quite interested in both the size and the demographic composition of their audiences. They need accurate and reliable audience measurement data to provide to their clients. Since advertising media are directly dependent on advertisers for a large portion of their income, and since media advertising rates are directly proportional to audience size, there has been a tendency in the past for some media to inflate audience size. Today, with the help of such organizations as the Audit Bureau of Circulation, most media research done by the media themselves is done in an objective and accurate manner. However, it is still advisable to have outside research agencies, rather than the media themselves, do media research, in order to convince media buyers that the figures are unbiased. Otherwise, an unethical magazine could report a 50 percent increase in circulation and raise advertising rates accordingly. That this increase might have come from an increase just in "press run" (with the extra copies of the magazine gathering mildew in a warehouse), and not in actual circulation, could only have been measured by an ethical independent research agency.

4. *Retailers and wholesalers* have traditionally been neither major suppliers nor major users of marketing research. However, a change is under way, and some of the large retail chains, such as Sears Roebuck and Safeway, who are using more and more research, now have their

own research departments. Retail chains are particularly interested in store location research and the effectiveness of their promotion programs. Had the Great Atlantic and Pacific Tea Company (better known as A & P) relied more heavily on marketing research, it might well have retained its position as the number-one supermarket retailer. Certainly, competent marketing research should have enabled A & P to avoid its postwar marketing disaster of ignoring large shopping centers and retaining small neighborhood stores. Some wholesalers conduct limited research studies, but most are too small to use extensive marketing research effectively.

5. *Independent marketing research firms* represent a tremendously diverse contribution to the field. Some of these agencies are one-person specialized consulting firms and contract to define or solve individual marketing problems. Other independent marketing research firms, such as the A. C. Nielsen Company, are quite large and employ thousands of people with offices all over the world (see figure 2•3 for a profile of A. C. Nielsen). These research firms conduct research on a continuing basis, selling their survey results to subscribers. Syndicated data services, such as Audits and Surveys, the R. L. Polk Company, and Market Research Corporation of America (MRCA), specialize in gathering and selling certain types of data to clients on a subscription basis. The data may include advertising readership or recognition, brand image studies, store audits, and consumer panel reports. Although independent marketing research firms are major performers of marketing research, they seldom conduct studies for their own internal purposes.

6. *Government agencies* at the federal level conduct a tremendous amount of marketing research for internal purposes and for the general public. Marketing research conducted by such federal government agencies as the Bureau of the Census, the Department of Commerce, the Bureau of Labor Statistics, the Department of Transportation, the Federal Trade Commission, and the Department of Agriculture provides a wealth of data, indispensable for many firms. For example, data gathered by the Bureau of the Census on population characteristics are vital to developers looking for population trends in order to locate retail shopping centers and stores wisely. Data gathered by these government research agencies are widely available, either free or at a nominal cost. Many firms have wasted a great deal of time and money seeking data already available from government research agencies.

7. *Trade and professional associations* collect much valuable market data from their members. Professional associations, such as the American Marketing Association, collect invaluable data not only on

Company and its subsidiaries provide worldwide business services which help clients to make factually-based decisions on matters relating to production, distribution, produce and package design, and sales promotional programs.

Retail Index Services include continuous measurement at point of sale of consumer sales and other vital marketing facts for makers of foods, beverages, confectionery, pharmaceuticals, proprietary drugs, toiletries, cosmetics, tobacco products, etc. and measurements of consumer awareness and attitudes by geographic area and nationally.

Neodata Services Division maintains computerized circulation lists for magazine publishers and others, magazine subscription promotion services and statistical information for publishers.

Media Research Services Division provides measurement of national and local TV audiences and identification of audience composition for advertisers, advertising agencies, networks, stations, program producers and others.

Nielsen Clearing House processes merchandise coupons for retailers and manufacturers, inquiry services for advertisers and magazine publishers, consumer promotion and other related services for advertisers.

Petroleum Information Division furnishes statistical services which make oil and gas exploration more efficient including computerized systems allowing the more practical retrieval of vitally important subsurface geological information.

Nielsen Custom Research Division does research into the marketing problems and policies of manufacturers, retailers, wholesalers, transportation companies and others usually involving custom designed surveys utilizing a variety of research techniques, and followed by personal interpretation and advice in application.

Subsidiaries and overseas branches provide similar types of consumer marketing research in numerous foreign countries. In fiscal 1975, retail index services provided 64.6% of total consolidated sales, TV audience research 11.2%, clearing house services 12.4% and other 11.8%. Foreign sales provided 43% of volume (of over $200,000,000).

Subsidiaries—wholly owned
A. C. Nielsen Co. Ltd. (U.K.)
   Television Press Agency Ltd.
Neodata Services Ltd.
   Neodata Teoranta
A. C. Nielsen Co. de Mexico, S.A.
   Inmobiliaria Zeta, S.A. de C.V.
Petroleum Information Exchange Ltd.
A. C. Nielsen (Argentina) S.A.
   Estudios de Comercios Minoristas S.A.

Figure 2·3
Profile of the World's Largest Marketing Research Firm: A. C. Nielsen Co.
From *Standard and Poor's Standard Corporate Descriptions*, February, 1976, pp. 4243–4244. © 1976, Standard and Poor. Italics added.

Company also has numerous other wholly owned subsidiaries with the name Nielsen in their titles.

Property—Co. has offices and/or production centers in 14 states and in Canada, Netherlands, Belgium, Argentina, Ireland, Germany, South Africa, Portugal, Switzerland, Spain, Mexico, Italy, Japan, United Kingdom, France, Brazil, Sweden, Australia, Austria and New Zealand.

Employees—Aug. 31, 1975, 12,604.

Incorporated in Delaware, November 14, 1958 to succeed an Illinois company of the same to carry on business founded in 1923.

Figure 2·3—*Continued*

the characteristics of their members but on industry practices. The American Marketing Associations' *Survey of Marketing Research*, conducted every five years, is one example. Data gathered by these associations can be particularly important to small member firms without the resources to undertake their own research activities.

8. *Universities and foundations* have long been engaged in marketing research, though little of it is of a commercial nature. Much university research is done by professors through bureaus of business research and is for public benefit. In many of these research studies the federal government is the client. Large foundations, such as the Ford Foundation, also fund much research. However, these studies tend to deal with broad economic or business problems and are not always directly applicable to individual firms.

9. *Other agencies* include financial institutions, and financial reporting services such as Dun and Bradstreet and Standard and Poor's. *Advertising Age* and Standard, Rate and Data Service provide statistical information on a continuous basis that is of particular value to media and advertising agencies.

Summary

In this chapter we have presented a brief overview of the development and scope of marketing research activities. In Chapter 1 we defined marketing as "the performance of business activities which direct the flow of goods and services from producer to consumer or user." Modern marketing methods go hand in hand with the affluent lifestyles that twentieth-century North Americans enjoy.

Today marketing research departments are most likely to be engaged in business economics and corporate research, product research, and sales and market research activities. Advertising research may be done by in-house marketing research departments or by the firm's advertising agency. For most research activities there is no significant difference between industrial and consumer goods companies. One very rapidly growing research activity is corporate responsibility research, a field unknown only a few years ago.

Marketing research is a valuable tool for top management in making critical decisions. Good research reduces uncertainty in the decision-making process. However, even the best marketing research suffers from two inherent limitations: research does not tell you what to do, and your information is always out of date.

The marketing research process involves following five steps, in order: problem definition, research design, data collection, data analysis, and clear and concise report writing. Good marketing research should incorporate scientific method, creative research, multiple methods, and analysis of the value and cost of information.

Some agencies are primarily suppliers of research; others are buyers of research; and some both prepare and use research. Agencies performing and utilizing marketing research include manufacturers, advertising agencies, advertising media, retailers and wholesalers, independent marketing research firms, government agencies, trade and professional associations, universities and foundations, and miscellaneous agencies. Of these nine groupings, manufacturers constitute the principal users of marketing research. The largest and oldest marketing research firm in the world is the A. C. Nielsen Company, which dates back to 1923.

Questions for Discussion

1. If modern marketing research is essential to the financial well-being of the organization, why doesn't everyone use marketing research?

2. Why, do you think, is organized marketing research of such recent origin?

3. Can you think of any possible trends that would cause a curtailment of research activities by North American firms?

4. What are the basic limitations of the marketing research process? How might you minimize them?

5. What are the major steps in the marketing research process? Which of these do you think is the most important? Why?

6. What are the characteristics of good marketing research? Is it possible to have good marketing research that is not creative? Why or why not?

7. Why do you think corporate responsibility research has been such a fast-growing marketing research activity? What conditions have caused this recent growth?

8. Why might a client firm prefer an independent marketing research agency, rather than the advertising media's own research department, to conduct research into the effectiveness of that advertising media's message?

9. In 1973 A & P was displaced as the nation's number-one super-market retailer by Safeway. How might A & P have used marketing research as a weapon in the fight to retain market leadership?

10. Class project: Divide your class into groups of four. Have each group prepare a short profile paper on an independent marketing research firm. Note: this project might be expanded to include U.S. Bureau of the Census data and activities.

Chapter 3

Marketing Research and the Scientific Method

Research and Intuition

REFER BACK TO THE EXAMPLES at the beginning of Chapter 1. In those four situations, each requiring action and a decision, how could the uncertainties have been resolved? The Detroit automaker, relying on his years of experience in servicing the North American market and his knowledge of driver preferences, could have decided not to bring out a small economy car. The dean of the School of Business, keeping in mind the often fluctuating rates of university attendance in other disciplines, could have decided not to offer the extra course sections in the evening school. Our potential hi-fi shop entrepreneur could have, without further investigation, gone ahead and opened up a small business of her own. The owner of the professional team could have moved his team to the new and larger home stadium on the outskirts of the city, basing his decision to move on the advice of friends and his personal assessment of the situation.

Would our four businesspeople have made the correct decisions? The answer to this question would not have been forthcoming until some later time, when the market reaction could be measured. What we do know is that in each of the four situations the decision would have been made without benefit of proper market research. Each decision would have been based on a certain feeling of the decision maker. Each person, faced with the problem of making the correct decision under conditions of uncertainty, would have made the decision on the basis of intuition.

Unfortunately, as in the examples just presented, most marketing decisions are made without the benefit of formal marketing research; the result is often disaster. For example, the decision to bypass a test market in the haste to get a new product directly to the mass market cost one major food processor millions of dollars and a loss of goodwill from both customers and distributors. It was discovered, too late, that the packages leaked while on retail store shelves and the product, a snack for kids, was too sweet for many customers.

All too often, business decisions and marketing decisions are made on the basis of the "gut feeling" about a certain course of action that we call intuition. We speak of someone as having "good intuition" or "bad intuition." Webster's defines intuition as "the power of knowing or the knowledge obtained without recourse to inference or reasoning." Thus, a marketing manager might say; "I don't think we should introduce this new product line; my intuition tells me that it won't succeed." Is he right? He might be, but if he is, it is only through chance. Valuable past experience may have had a hand in this intuitive feeling, but to judge by intuition is a course of action still highly prone to error and totally nonscientific.

Why, then, might managers resort to intuition instead of research? Actually, there are several conditions that may cause a manager to rely on intuition instead of more objective methods in decision making. For example, she may lack the *time* necessary to make the decision properly, by first having adequate research performed. Often answers are called for immediately, action must be taken at once, and there simply is not enough time — so she may feel — to conduct a proper research study. Another reason for using intuition, rather than formal research, is a lack of *money*. There may not be sufficient funds in the budget to conduct a research study into the problem at hand. Perhaps the manager feels that she can save money by acting on intuition. A lack of marketing research *expertise* is still another reason for relying on intuition. The executive may have no one capable and not be capable herself of conducting a proper study of the problem at hand. This lack of available expertise is a major cause for action based on intuition. A final reason why some managers depend upon intuition instead of research is *ignorance*. Some are unaware of the potential benefits from a properly conducted research study and therefore rely upon their intuitions in making decisions. For example, being unaware of Sales Management's *Annual Survey of Buying Power* could cause a manager to rely on guesswork in estimating the purchasing power of consumers in a given area, when this information has already been compiled and is currently available.

Marketing research managers are not the only people faced with this problem. A tendency to use intuition instead of research in decision making is prevalent through all levels of our society among managers in government, business, and academia. Decision making under conditions of uncertainty, without use of proper research, is sometimes referred to as "seat of the pants management." (Critics of this prevalent form of management often claim that it derives its name from the location of the brains of persons engaging in such management.)

Scientific Progress in Marketing

The question may be asked whether marketing and business activities lend themselves to serious scientific inquiry. Even the area of marketing research is sometimes subject to such questions as: Are marketing and business activities so hopelessly complex that they cannot be understood by scientific thinking? Should scientific thinking be reserved for scientists left alone in a laboratory? Is the only aid for an executive in the decision-making process years of training in actual practice rather than in techniques? Research professionals know that scientific progress has been rapid in business and that scientific thinking is invaluable in analyzing business problems, though some doubters remain.

The question whether marketing is a science or an art is also sometimes raised. The answer is that marketing activities include both science and art. Marketing research represents a relatively new area of scientific inquiry, and as a behavioral science it has not reached maturity. Many marketing research studies are not shared throughout the profession, because most research is done in secrecy and firms wish to keep results unknown to competitors. The extent of scientific progress in marketing has been described by Theodore Beckman: "Whether marketing is more of a science or more of an art is debatable, but it is certainly an area in which considerable scientific progress is being made, both in the sense of the expansion of a body of classified and systematized knowledge and also with respect to increasing application of scientific methods to basic research and in decision-making processes within firms." [1]

In spite of difficulties encountered in bringing scientific principles to such a complex area as marketing, success is gradually being achieved. The evolving sophistication in marketing research techniques and methodologies is an important contribution to the use of scientific methods in marketing. As the marketing process becomes more scientific,

[1] Theodore N. Beckman, Williams R. Davidson, and W. Wayne Talarzyk, *Marketing*, 9th ed. (New York: Ronald Press, 1973), p. 611.

marketing research becomes an increasingly valuable aid and a competitive weapon in decision making. On the other hand, poorly conducted marketing research or misuse of marketing research represents waste of the organization's time, personnel, and resources and offers no improvement over reliance solely on intuition. It is the responsibility of management to sponsor cost-effective research efforts.

The Scientific Method

Methods of Eliminating Uncertainty

The past two chapters have emphasized that the marketing research process, when properly undertaken, represents an attempt to reduce uncertainty in the decision-making process. By providing management with accurate information on which to base market decisions and by identifying new market opportunities upon which a firm can capitalize, good marketing research can lower the probability of error in decisions and thereby offer the firm a competitive edge. However, decision makers may choose to eliminate uncertainty through methods other than careful research and analysis. In evaluating problems, the decision maker may use any of four bases for reducing uncertainty: tenacity, authority, intuition, and science.[2]

THE METHOD OF TENACITY

As a method of eliminating uncertainty and avoiding a clutter of conflicting concepts in the mind, the method of tenacity is without parallel and is also the easiest to follow. The person choosing this method of eliminating uncertainty refuses to accept a new proposition if it conflicts with his existing ideas and beliefs. The mind is closed to all contradictory evidence. Frequent verbal reiteration of these ideas may strengthen the original beliefs. This manager does not like to be confused by facts; he has set views and wishes them to remain consistent and unchanged. When faced by conflicting evidence, he refuses to listen or to change.

Such a tenacious hold on beliefs is guaranteed to reduce uncertainty. The person who follows this method is not besieged by internal doubts. However, the results can be disastrous for the organization. For example, consider the case of a marketing manager who blindly

---

[2] Morris R. Cohen and Ernest Nagel, *An Introduction to Logic and Scientific Method* (New York: Harcourt, Brace and World, 1934), pp. 191–96.

believes that increased advertising expenditures will result in increased sales. Faced by evidence to the contrary (that increased advertising expenditures may have no effect on sales), she refuses to change her beliefs — clinging instead with great tenacity to her firm view that if only more money could be spent on advertising, sales would be certain to rise. The result is a waste of advertising dollars and lower morale among the marketing group.

THE METHOD OF AUTHORITY

Another highly effective method for reducing executive uncertainty is that of authority. The manager following this method, when faced with unwelcome evidence, appeals to an authority to resolve the problem favorably: a highly respected source will be sought to substantiate the manager's preexisting views. This source may be a book, an individual, company policy, or some other traditional authority figure or tribunal whose decision on such questions is considered final. In the case of the marketing manager who believes in increased advertising expenditures as a solution for all problems of declining sales, evidence to the contrary will cause her to seek out an appropriate authority to reconfirm her beliefs. In this case, the authority may be the vice-president of marketing or some other authority in the organization, it may be company policy as stated in policy manuals, or it may perhaps be a learned textbook espousing this particular strategy.

Appeal to authority is a method also commonly used to avoid accepting final responsibility for making an incorrect decision. Some executives demonstrate great skill in avoiding making decisions on their own. They take no chances and if things go wrong are quick to point out that the errors were not theirs. On the other hand, these people are adept in taking credit for successful projects. Although these decision avoiders exist in the business world, they flourish in the nonprofit sector of military and government bureaucracies.

THE METHOD OF INTUITION

Especially popular at times when quick decisions need to be made, the method of intuition is used repeatedly to guarantee stable beliefs and eliminate uncertainty. This method represents an appeal to self-evident propositions so apparently true that the understanding of their meaning becomes the conviction of their truth. According to the method of intuition, a proposition is accepted or rejected in accordance with the "gut feeling" of the decision maker in the case. Though it is often alleged that many managers have exceptionally good intuition, the cases cited usually turn out to be ones where the so-called intuition was actually the product of careful research into the problems at hand. When decisions are made solely on the basis of intuition, a "sixth sense," then the method, although it may be effective in reducing uncertainty, is neither scientific nor sound. If our marketing manager decided to increase advertising spending on the basis of her intuition, results might prove her decision to have been correct; but the results would have been left to chance, and no organization can afford to leave vital decisions to chance.

THE METHOD OF SCIENCE

The scientific method also reduces uncertainty for decision makers. However, it differs significantly from the three previously mentioned methods. Tenacity, authority, and intuition are all inflexible approaches, and none makes provision for correcting its own results, since none recognizes that there is an inherent possibility of error. The scientific method encourages and demands that the executive be skeptical in evaluating proposals. Under this method, no information is accepted as true unless it has been carefully evaluated and tested by the best available evidence. The other three methods discussed provide subjective decision making; the method of science provides objective decision making. Therefore, we may say that the proper execution of the marketing research process is accomplished through the scientific method. Marketing research incorporates the scientific method as fundamental to its viability as an effective tool for management.

Steps in Following the Scientific Method

The scientific method is an impartial, consistent, and systematic process that may be employed in solving business problems. It consists of four stages: observation, formulation of hypotheses, prediction of the future, and testing of the hypotheses.

Whereas the feasibility of applying the scientific method is taken for granted in the natural sciences, in the social sciences doubts are sometimes expressed. To the question whether the scientific method can be applied in business and in marketing, the answer is an emphatic yes. The scientific method is universally applicable:

> The scientific method of investigation and analysis is used by all scientists. The subject matter being studied does not determine whether or not the process is called scientific. It makes no difference whether the investigation is in the fields traditionally held to be sciences, such

as chemistry and physics, or as in the various areas of human relations, including business and the other social sciences. The activity of an investigator is scientific if he correctly uses the scientific method, and the investigator is a scientist if he uses the scientific method in his thinking and searching for information.[3]

Thus, our four steps may be employed in any area of scientific inquiry. Let us now look at these four steps and see how they might apply in an example.

A marketing manager for a large manufacturer of wooden tennis rackets sees that sales are stable but wants to improve the long-term sales outlook for his firm. He then takes the following steps:

1. Observation. He observes that competitors who manufacture aluminum rackets have increasing sales.

2. Formulation of hypothesis. He assumes that his firm's flat growth rate is due solely to the fact that it manufactures only wooden tennis rackets.

3. Prediction of the future. He predicts that sales will increase if his firm will start manufacturing aluminum tennis rackets of comparable quality.

4. Testing the hypothesis. The firm begins to produce some aluminum tennis rackets and puts them out to test in the market.

In this example, the market test proved the prediction correct. After going through these steps, the marketing manager found that sales increased. Had sales not increased, at least he would have been aware that the problem did not lie with the type of tennis racket the firm was manufacturing. He might then have hypothesized that other firms were spending more on advertising than was his firm, or perhaps there were differences in the price structure, quality, or channels of distribution employed by his firm. Further application of the steps in the scientific method would allow him to isolate the problem and develop a sound strategy to overcome it. Table 3•1 gives a clear breakdown of the relation of this scientific method to marketing research. The four steps involved in the scientific method provide an orderly framework in the problem-solving process.

The scientific method is not without its limitations. For example, all steps may be followed, but if the researcher is not objective the process is invalid. If the measurement techniques are not accurate, then

[3] Vernon Clover and Howard Balsey, *Business Research Methods* (Columbus, Ohio: Grid, 1974), p. 23.

Table 3·1
Relation of Scientific Method to Marketing Research

Scientific method stages	Used during the following marketing research steps
Observation	Definition of problem Situation analysis Informal investigation Formal research
Formulation of hypotheses	Situation analysis Informal investigation Formal research (Planning)
Prediction of the future (Action implications)	Situation analysis Informal investigation Formal research (Planning)
Testing hypotheses	Formal research (Unless management is satisfied with an earlier but more intuitive solution)

Reproduced with permission from E. Jerome McCarthy, *Basic Marketing*, 4th ed. (Homewood, Ill.: Richard D. Irwin, Inc., 1975).

the results will not be useful to management. The scientific method also implies that the researcher must continue to investigate the problem exhaustively, doing replication studies when necessary. Thus, in looking at research data and determining whether the scientific method has been properly followed, we not only look at the steps taken but also look to see if the researcher was objective, if measurement was accurate, and if investigation was thorough.

The Difficulty of Applying the Scientific Method in Marketing Research

As has been stated earlier, marketing is by no means an exact science. It may be considered both an art and a science, one that increasingly uses scientific methods and techniques to identify marketing opportunities and to reduce uncertainty in the decision-making process. However, there are difficulties inherent in applying the scientific method in marketing, difficulties stemming from the wide gulf between controllable laboratory conditions and uncontrollable conditions in the marketplace. We tend to conceive of the scientific method as being employed in the pure sciences, in laboratory experiments where all the variables are controllable; but this ideal is impossible in the business world, where the "laboratory" is the marketplace and it is extremely difficult to control all the variables. For example, if we wish to know the effect of increased advertising expenditures upon sales, then we need a tightly controlled marketplace situation where only one element, advertising expenditures, can be allowed to vary, with all other variables, such as competitor reaction, held constant. This is something that is virtually impossible in a marketing environment. There are several factors around which the difficulties encountered in using the scientific method in marketing revolve. Although these difficulties are being reduced as more comprehensive marketing studies are developed and as research techniques improve, they still present problems.[4]

The Complexity of the Subject

Marketing is an extremely complex and diverse subject, one that deals with human activities, attitudes, beliefs, and values as they apply in the marketplace. In looking at the almost infinite number of uncontrollable variables, the researcher must try to measure the influence of each upon consumer behavior in the marketplace. Often this is an impossible process, because human activities are so complex that it is virtually impossible to develop an exact science capable of explaining all of them. For example, the researcher might wish to know the effect of changing the price of a product on sales. However, it may well prove impossible to measure this effect because of changes in what competitors are doing at the same time.

Another illustration of the complexity involved in marketing may be seen in attempts to measure and predict consumer buying motives. Research into conscious buying motives is a difficult enough task, and subconscious buying motives present even greater challenges to market researchers. Why, for example, does a consumer prefer Schlitz over Budweiser when product taste, price, and distribution policies for the two beers are the same? Because a consumer purchases products for subconscious reasons, the buyer himself is unaware of his motivations.

The Difficulty of Obtaining Accurate Measurements

The scientific method is characterized by precise measurement, something that is often quite difficult in marketing. The question arises of how we actually measure human attitudes and opinions or values.

---

[4] Harper Boyd and Ralph Westfall, *Marketing Research: Text and Cases,* 4th ed. (Homewood, Ill.: Richard D. Irwin, 1972), pp. 37–40.

Researchers are faced with the difficulty of trying to determine the real meaning of such words as "like" or "dislike." Does "like" translate into "will buy"? The answer may be yes, but what if the product is a Corvette and the respondent is a university undergraduate with a total income of $3,000 a year? The unacquainted observer might say, "I agree with you there, but would anyone willingly buy a product she actually disliked." The answer is yes and no. Consider the sales of Listerine, a product specifically advertising the fact that it tastes bad; consumers purchase Listerine because of its other, including psychological, attributes — its reputed ability to kill germs and improve bad breath.

A problem faced by interviewers is determining whether interviewees are responding accurately. In other words, are they actually telling the truth? Many relatively sophisticated techniques have been developed to enhance the accuracy of the researcher's attempts to measure human responses. Researchers may use Thrustone or Likert-type scales to measure the relative strengths of respondents' preferences, but the process of accurately measuring consumer attitudes is full of pitfalls for unwary researchers. No legitimate research techniques can guarantee that respondents will tell the truth.

The Influence of the Measurement Process on Results

Measuring human activities and attitudes is far more difficult and complex than measuring the behavior of white rats in a cage. Humans, when they know that they are being observed and measured, often tend to react other than normally. A classic example of the process of measurement influencing the results is the case that gave the "Hawthorne Effect" its name. Studies were conducted by Elton Mayo at the Hawthorne Plant of the Western Electric Company in order to determine the effect of lighting on the output of a group of workers involved in assembling electrical components. First, the lighting was increased substantially, from 24 to 45 to 70 footcandles in intensity, and worker productivity also increased. Later the light was reduced, and output increased still more.[5] Though the results of this study caused some observers to claim that the findings confirmed that production level was greater in the dark, other social factors were present. The real issue was that the process of measurement had influenced the results. People, knowing that they were being measured, responded in unusual ways.

In marketing research the Hawthorne Effect occurs when, for ex-

[5] Henry L. Sisk, *Principles of Management* (Cincinnati, Ohio: Southwestern Publishing Co., 1969), pp. 29–30.

ample, interviewees answer questions in a manner they think will please the researcher. This leads to a question often raised in conjunction with the Nielsen ratings: "Does the presence of an Audimeter attached to the television set cause a change in viewing habits?" If so, this effect would cause error to be built in the Nielsen Television Ratings, a charge that producers of programs with low ratings sometimes level at Nielsen.

THE DIFFICULTY OF USING EXPERIMENTS TO TEST HYPOTHESES

A key component in the scientific method is establishing and testing hypotheses. In the pure sciences it is possible to establish meaningful laboratory conditions in which the researcher may control all the variables, allow one to fluctuate, and then measure the results. However, the business world is not a laboratory, and the researcher faces the virtually impossible task of establishing a controlled environment in which to conduct her measurement. Replication — reproducing the same experiment again and again — cannot be carried out completely in marketing research. If, for example, the researcher wishes to duplicate the media mix in several test markets, she will find it impossible to control all variables that might affect the sales of the product. Activities of competitors, human values, the weather, and business conditions are all factors that typically are beyond the control of the market researcher in such cases. They make it difficult to test meaningfully hypotheses developed for research purposes.

THE DIFFICULTY OF MAKING ACCURATE PREDICTIONS

Another step in the scientific method, accurate prediction, can become extremely difficult in marketing research. In a laboratory experiment the scientist can predict with a great deal of precision the behavior of a rat in a maze. However, predicting behavior of consumers in the marketplace is not nearly so exact a science. Researchers face almost insurmountable obstacles in accurately predicting future economic conditions, market demand, and human buying behavior. Too many things can happen between the prediction and the actual behavior for predictions to be made with a high degree of accuracy. Though researchers face major obstacles in accurate prediction, research can reduce the degree of uncertainty and the margin of error. Even though accurate prediction of future consumer behavior is not always possible, business is still faced with the need for forecasts. Just as meteorologists predict future weather events and are sometimes wrong, researchers who predict future market conditions are not always correct. However, just as the general public relies upon weather predictions, businesspeople must rely on market predictions.

THE PROBLEMATIC OBJECTIVITY OF THE INVESTIGATOR

A final obstacle in applying the scientific method to marketing lies in the difficulty of securing reseacher objectivity. One of the cornerstones of the scientific method is that the investigator will always be objective and report data in an impartial manner. In the pure sciences, there are cases of bias, particularly in instances where investigators seek additional research money or established professional reputations; but such cases are rare. Unfortunately, in marketing research, the investigator often is not impartial. Many times research is conducted merely to substantiate or "prove" what management wants to hear. Using research to find desired answers is not unknown in scientific investigations, but it is a particular problem in marketing research, where the research department is vulnerable to management pressure to come up with the proper answers.

Lack of investigative objectivity is not confined to deliberate attempts to induce bias. Bias may be unconscious. During the interviewing process, researchers may cause bias through the wording of questions or the use of leading questions. Bias results whether at attempt is deliberate or unconscious. This problem can become particularly acute when investigators in the field are relatively untrained and therefore ignorant of the bias they may be unconsciously introducing in the interviewing process. The answer to this problem lies in better selection and training procedures for the field force. However, time and budgetary constraints often make it difficult to prepare interviewers properly.

These problems encountered in applying the scientific method in marketing are presented, not to discourage use of this method in marketing, but to familiarize the student with the difficulties. Awareness of these problems should allow the researcher to take advance corrective action in order to avoid some of the pitfalls.

What Is a Hypothesis?

The hypothesis is an integral part of the scientific method and a key element in the marketing research process. Two of the four stages in following the scientific method are formulating hypotheses and testing hypotheses. No formal marketing research project may be called scientific and complete unless hypotheses are generated and tested.

Exactly what, then, is a hypothesis? Webster's *New Collegiate Dictionary* defines "hypothesis" as "a tentative theory or supposition provisionally adopted to explain certain facts and guide in the investigation of others." A hypothesis is a statement formulated to be tested. A good hypothesis stems directly from a clear definition of the principal problem or problems to be explored in the research study. Hypotheses should be generated during the exploratory stage in designing research projects and then tested by conclusive research. Remember that your hypothesis is a declarative statement of a very tentative nature; if found true, it is accepted, and if found false, it is rejected. Two basic types of hypotheses are *descriptive* and *relational.*[6]

Descriptive hypotheses concern the existence, size, form, or distribution of some concept subject to verification. Concepts presented in descriptive hypotheses may take on two or more values. For example, if we make the statement "The current market share for Lucky Lager beer is 10 percent," we have a statement about the size of Lucky Lager's market share. If we make the statement "Over half of Lucky Lager's sales are to undergraduate university students," we have a proposition about the form of Lucky Lager's market share. The statement "Lucky Lager's sales are concentrated along the West Coast" is a proposition about the distribution of Lucky Lager's sales. All these statements may be considered hypotheses if they are advanced as propositions to be tested by research. They are called descriptive hypotheses because they describe something — the size, the form, the distribution, or the very existence of the concept we wish to examine or test.

A hypothesis may also be stated as a question. For example, we could have said, "Do Lucky Lager customers live primarily along the West Coast?" or, "Are Lucky Lager customers primarily university students?" As a practical matter, the result is the same however the description is formulated, and in both cases the propositions must be carefully tested before they can be accepted.

Relational hypotheses are proposed in order to test the relationship or linkage between two variables. Like descriptive hypotheses, relational hypotheses may be formulated as statements or as questions. An example of a relational hypothesis would be "High consumption of Lucky Lager beer among undergraduate students is a result of heavy sales promotion on university campuses."

Researchers and statisticians commonly use various tests of significance, such as chi-square analysis, to test the relational hypothesis.

[6] C. William Emory, *Business Research Methods* (Homewood, Ill.: Richard D. Irwin, 1976), pp. 30–32.

Proving the relationship between two variables — such as the effect of each advertising dollar upon sales — can be a very complex and sometimes impossible process. The researcher is faced with the problem of determining if perhaps the increased sales of Lucky Lager on university campuses stemmed from low price more than from the advertising campaign.

Testing Hypotheses

Once formulated, the hypothesis, whether descriptive or relational, must be tested through the process of conclusive research. Testing will result in the rejection of the hypothesis if the researcher decides that it is false. There are two principal types of errors in testing hypotheses: a type 1 error stems from rejection of a true hypothesis, and a type 2 error occurs when the researcher accepts a false hypothesis. The combined chance of committing errors can be lessened by increasing the size of the sample. This topic will be examined in Chapters 9 and 10.

The critical points to keep in mind here are that sound hypotheses are vital to the scientific method and that a hypothesis is useless unless it is testable. A good hypothesis should meet two key criteria: it must be explanatory and it must be testable. Hypotheses that do not explain the facts have no value to researchers; a hypothesis with no bearing on the problem at hand is not usable. Useful hypotheses are formulated so as to be compatible with practical analytical methods for testing them. If the hypothesis calls for testing techniques that are unavailable, then it is not a testable hypothesis, and it cannot be used in a meaningful manner. Experienced researchers learn to formulate hypotheses that explain facts and can be tested through the research process.

Pseudo–Marketing Research

After absorbing the material presented so far in this chapter, the prospective market researcher might well ask, "By carefully following the scientific method, will I produce research reports that will be used by management in making marketing decisions?" Unfortunately, the answer to this question may be no.

Much research undertaken today, no matter how scientifically conducted, may actually have very little influence on marketing decisions. This is true even though conventional wisdom holds that the central function of marketing research is to provide information to aid in making decisions. It is impossible to quantify the amount of research conducted for reasons other than legitimate aid to actual decision making, as executives are understandably reluctant to admit its existence publicly.

This illegitimate use of marketing research may be called "pseudoresearch." Pseudoresearch is research that has no influence in the decision-making process; it is window dressing, undertaken for such purposes as boosting executive egos, selling advertising, and empire building. Pseudoresearch activities may be grouped in three categories:

1. Organizational politics. Research becomes pseudoresearch when it is used solely or primarily to gain power, justify decisions, or serve as a scapegoat.

2. Service promotion. Pseudoresearch is often undertaken to impress on clients and prospects the fact that the sponsor is sophisticated, modern, or sincere. In other words, the *act* of gathering information, not the information itself, is the important thing.

3. Personal satisfaction. This is a broad category that includes ego-bolstering efforts and attempts to keep up with business fads and fashions, assuage anxiety, and make use of acquired skills.[7]

Organizational Politics

Marketing research can become pseudoresearch when it falls victim to organizational politics. Pseudoresearch is used for the acquisition of power in the organization through empire building and increased visibility. Management may abuse the research function in this manner by having marketing research conduct useless studies in an effort to enhance the power and visibility of executives.

Pseudoresearch is also used to justify decisions made before the information has been gathered. Advertising media selection is one example of this practice; all too often, in the case of research conducted by advertising agencies, the researcher's goal is to sell advertising and the buyer's goal is to justify the purchase of media. Research becomes pseudo when researchers deliberately make sure that their findings are what clients wanted to see in the first place. It takes a courageous or foolhardy research manager to report that the chief executive's pet marketing project is doomed to failure. What if, in 1957, Ford Motor Company's marketing research manager had solid data indicating the

---

[7] Stewart A. Smith, "Research and Pseudo-research in Marketing," *Harvard Business Review*, March–April 1974, pp. 73–76.

likelihood of failure for the Edsel, so named for Edsel Ford of the Ford Motor Company?

Organizational politics may cause research to become pseudo when it is used as a scapegoat for marketing plans and projects that fail. Extensive research may go into a marketing plan but then be ignored regardless of its findings. In these cases, if the plan is successful, the marketing manager gets the credit. If the plan fails, marketing research is often given the blame and held responsible, even though the research manager may have warned against its implementation.

Service Promotion

Pseudoresearch enters into service promotion when service organizations, such as advertising agencies, use research in an attempt to attract new business and to impress prospective clients. Pseudoresearch undertaken for a promotional purpose often leads to heavy, highly technical research reports that are virtually unreadable and unusable. Unfortunately, it is this type of research that fosters the notion of the typical researcher as an impractical egghead; in the long run, it is damaging to the research profession.

Personal Satisfaction

Research becomes pseudo when it is undertaken primarily to provide personal satisfaction for executives by boosting egos, enhancing self-esteem, and assuring anxious executives that something is being done. An example of pseudoresearch undertaken for personal satisfaction has been provided by Stewart Smith of Lee Creative Research in St. Louis:

> A product manager once demanded that I run a market test for a new product. I had reason to suspect that he was really interested in a nationwide introduction of the product but needed a confidence-booster to take this step. The exchange between us went something like this:
>
> *Researcher*: "What if the test results are favorable?"
> *Product Manager*: "Why, we'll launch the product nationally, of course."
> *Researcher*: "And if the results are unfavorable?"
> *Product Manager*: "They won't be. I'm sure of that."
> *Researcher*: "But just suppose they are."

Product Manager: "I don't think we should throw out a good product just because of one little market test."

Researcher: "Then why test?"

Product Manager: "Listen, Smith, this is a major product introduction. It's got to have some research behind it."[8]

By carefully following the scientific method, many problems that inhibit the development of quality research can be avoided. However, adhering to the scientific method, even though it may lead to the highest quality research, is no guarantee that marketing research will be properly utilized by management. The danger lies in the fact that research, regardless of quality and utility, is still subject to abuse. Is it possible, then, to eliminate pseudoresearch in marketing? It probably is not possible; but if marketing researchers are aware that it exists, they can demand to know what use will be made of research findings.

It seems reasonable to assume that researchers may not wish to become involved in the pitfalls and dangers of corporate politics. Requiring corporate users of research to specify how they will use the information in market planning is one way in which pseudoresearch can possibly be minimized, but it is not usually practical for research to impose this requirement. In a corporate environment a marketing research manager is in no position to demand that top management reveal the plans for the research requested. For this reason, it is likely that, despite the best efforts of market researchers, much research will continue to be pseudo in nature.

Summary

Most marketing decisions are made without relying on formal research. A high percentage of these decisions are made on intuition — a "gut feeling" about something. Lack of time, money, or expertise and ignorance of the marketing research process in general are all reasons why executives may rely on intuition instead of research in making decisions. Whether marketing is an art or a science is a subject for endless debate; it is, however, definitely an area in which increased scientific progress is being made.

In evaluating problems, decision makers may use any of four bases for reducing uncertainty: tenacity, authority, intuition, or science. The method of science, better known as the scientific method, is becoming increasingly widespread in marketing research, and proper market research is the application of the scientific method. Steps in

[8] Smith, "Research and Pseudo-research in Marketing," p. 76.

following the scientific method include observation, formulation of hypotheses, prediction of the future, and testing the hypotheses. These steps are followed by all scientists in the natural and social sciences, including marketing and marketing research. There are, unfortunately, certain difficulties in applying the scientific method in marketing research. Fundamentally, these difficulties revolve around the complexity of the marketplace and the problem of treating it as a laboratory situation. These difficulties in applying the scientific method in marketing research stem from (1) the complexity of the subject, (2) the difficulty of obtaining accurate measurements, (3) the influence of the measurement process on results, (4) the difficulty of using experiments to test hypotheses, (5) the difficulty of making accurate predictions, and (6) the problematic objectivity of the investigator.

Fundamental to the application of the scientific method are hypotheses, statements formulated during exploratory research and then tested by conclusive research. Two basic types are descriptive and relational hypotheses. If in testing a hypothesis we discover it is false, then the hypothesis must be rejected. There are two principal types of error in hypothesis testing: type 1 errors stem from rejecting a true hypothesis and type 2 from accepting a false hypothesis.

Much marketing research, no matter how scientific, becomes pseudoresearch — research undertaken for reasons other than aiding the making of business decisions. Pseudoresearch may be brought about by organizational politics, when it is used to take power, justify decisions, or serve as a scapegoat. It may result from service promotion undertaken to impress clients and prospective clients, where the act of gathering information becomes the most important matter, not the information itself. It may also be used to foster personal satisfaction — boosting egos, reducing anxiety, and assuring executives that something is being done. Organizational politics will almost certainly guarantee the continuation of pseudoresearch. However, marketing research managers should be on their guard; they can try to reduce the amount of pseudoresearch by asking in advance what the purpose of the research is and how it will be applied in the process of making marketing decisions.

Questions for Discussion

1. If the scientific method is the best technique for reducing uncertainty in making decisions, then why would any other method be used? Why, for example, might a manager rely upon intuition instead of scientific research in making marketing decisions?

2. We have characterized marketing research as the application of the scientific method. Is marketing research, then, a science or an art? Why? Although there are certain difficulties in applying the scientific method in marketing research, what are some of the developments that might make it easier to apply the scientific method?

3. Ted's Texaco Service Center is a modern gasoline station located at a major intersection in a suburban city. For the past five years, Ted has been operating a profitable business, characterized by a steadily increasing monthly sales volume. However, during the past six months, sales volume has leveled off and is starting a modest downturn. Ted has asked you, the researcher, to suggest some hypotheses that might explain this downturn in sales. What would you suggest, and how might you test each of your hypotheses? Should anything be done before any hypotheses are formulated?

4. You are the marketing research manager for a medium-sized company. The vice-president of marketing has requested that you conduct a research study on consumer preferences for a new product that he says the company may introduce. You know as a fact that the company intends to introduce this new product whether or not the research indicates that it should be introduced. What do you do?

5. What is the purpose of developing hypotheses for a research study? Which is the greater error for the researcher to make, a type 1 or a type 2 error? Why?

Chapter 4

Research Design

OUR FIRST TWO CHAPTERS gave an overview of the marketing research process and the development of marketing research. These two chapters were presented to provide you, the reader, with a brief introduction to what marketing research is and how it has developed as an organized business function. In Chapter 3 we examined marketing research and the scientific method. This third chapter focused upon the hypothesis, an integral part of any formal marketing research survey. Though in Chapter 1 we outlined the major steps in the marketing research process, no overall plan in designing the research project has yet been presented. It is the function of this chapter to introduce the notion of research design.

The Importance of Research Design

Consider the following example: for the past year and a half, the market share for Blipbo, a large manufacturer of bottled soft drinks, has been declining steadily, a fact that has top management deeply concerned. The company's board of directors, seeing declining profits, recently informed the chief executive that they want the situation reversed. The chief executive in response called in the vice-president of marketing, and the resulting scene went something like this:

> *Chief Executive*: As you know, our market share has been declining, and I want to know why it has been declining and what we can do about it.

V-P Marketing: Right away, sir. We'll have our marketing research department look into it immediately.

Chief Executive: Looking into it isn't good enough. We want answers.

V-P Marketing: The answers will be forthcoming.

Chief Executive: They'd better be quick and the right ones!

V-P Marketing: They will, sir. We have a good marketing research department.

The company's marketing research department was thereby presented with a major challenge. For, as you have probably already suspected, the vice-president of marketing wasted no time in immediately summoning the marketing research manager to his office, where the same scene was reenacted, with, in this case, the research manager on the receiving end. The marketing research manager returned to his own office somewhat shaken by the encounter, having been informed that his job was on the line. The research manager mentally reviewed the situation: "Blipbo's market share has been declining, but we don't know why. Is our loss in market share caused by the aggressive promotion of our competitors? Are there differences in pricing policies? Have competitors introduced new products or package design changes? Are consumers tired of our old products? Are retailers not as aggressive in marketing our firm's soft drinks as in the past?" Faced with these and other questions, the research manager began to develop an overall strategy that would serve as a design or blueprint for conducting the research project that was to follow. What the research director was doing was formulating a *research design*.

Fundamental to the success of any formal marketing research project is sound research design. By research design we mean an overall framework or plan for the collection and analysis of data. Any good research design contains the following features: (1) it requires problem definition; (2) it specifies how the data will be gathered and analyzed; (3) it specifies a time framework, or how long the research project will take; and (4) it provides an estimate of expenses to be incurred.

The research design is an organized approach and not a collection of loose, unrelated parts. It is an integrated system that guides the researcher in formulating, implementing, and controlling the project. Useful research designs need not be complex, though often they are and sometimes they may be too complex to yield meaningful results. Often a very simple research design can produce the answers needed for management to act upon.

Types of Research Design

In this text we will classify research designs under three headings: *exploratory*, *descriptive*, and *experimental*. Exploratory research is used to define problems and develop hypotheses to be tested later. Testing uses descriptive or experimental designs that may solve the problems developed in exploratory research. Descriptive research gives an account of the frequency or the characteristics of some of the variables, whereas experimental research involves a controlled situation in which all variables are held constant except one.

It should be noted that these three types of research designs are not mutually exclusive and that a combination of all three could be used in the successful completion of a marketing research project. A clearer picture of how each works will emerge as we begin to examine them individually.

Exploratory Research

All marketing research projects of any significant scope must begin with exploratory research. This preliminary phase is absolutely essential in order to obtain a proper definition of the problem at hand. For example, in the case presented earlier in the chapter, management is faced with declining market share. However, the specific problem causing this decline is unknown and could be a combination of many different factors. For example, declining market share could be caused by changes in competitors' promotion policies or pricing policies; or some completely unsuspected problem or problems may emerge. It is the job of the investigator in this exploratory phase to define the problem and to develop hypotheses to be tested conclusively through more formal research designs.

Exactly *how*, then, does the research investigator go about the process of establishing and conducting exploratory research design? First and foremost, it must be kept in mind that there is no set way of conducting exploratory research. Key requirements for the investigator are imagination and flexibility. Exploratory research studies are not characterized by formal research design, nor are they basically very scientific in nature. Since the purpose of exploratory research is to bring the central problem into focus, the researcher may utilize any number of informal approaches in attempting to define this problem.

Although the exploratory study is characterized by its informal approach, it is nevertheless of critical importance to the study. The investigator establishes exploratory research design primarily through one or more of three approaches: (1) examining existing literature, (2) questioning people with particular expertise in the area, and (3) carefully examining a few selected cases.

EXAMINING EXISTING LITERATURE

Logically, the first place the researcher should check is existing literature on the subject. This survey of existing literature includes such relevant secondary data as trade publications, learned journals, government reports, and even newspapers. It may be desirable to examine the internal records of the firm, which would include sales records and other similar material. How could the marketing research manager for Blipbo soft drinks utilize this survey of literature in his exploratory research? A quick analysis of the firm's internal sales records might reveal sharply declining sales in certain geographical regions of the country; analysis of company financial records might indicate sharply escalating costs resulting from rising costs of labor and materials, which are causing rapidly escalating prices. Examination of journal articles and government reports might reveal that consumer tastes are turning away from the very sweet, high calorie soft drinks that Blipbo produces. Thus, after a brief study of existing data, the research manager could begin to formulate some ideas about the principal problem at hand.

QUESTIONING PEOPLE WITH EXPERTISE

Exploratory research design may adopt a second approach: the questioning of people with particular knowledge or expertise in the subject area. This process does not constitute a scientifically conducted statistical survey; rather, it represents an attempt to get additional input from people who may have some particular knowledge of the subject under investigation. Such people would include executives, sales personnel, and other relevant people within the firm, as well as others from outside the organization. The category certainly could be logically expanded to include middlemen and perhaps a few consumers. Middlemen are of particular importance, in that wholesalers, and especially retailers, are often much closer to the market and its problems than is the manufacturer. These middlemen, therefore, are in a position to provide vital information about the manufacturer's products and those of competitors.

Ultimately, the investigator may wish to question a limited number of ultimate consumers or industrial users who have familiarity with the issue or product. In this context, Blipbo's marketing research department might begin an informal survey of knowledgeable persons within the firm, including not only those within the marketing department but also some in the production department and in the financial department. Local retailers who carry Blipbo's products on their supermarket store shelves might be questioned for their opinions on the cause of Blipbo's decline in market share. Additionally, the research department might survey on a very informal basis some particularly heavy consumers of soft drinks, in an attempt to gain greater insight into Blipbo's marketing problem.

Intensive Analysis of Selected Cases

Analysis of selected cases is a final form that exploratory research design may take. The usual pattern for exploratory research is arbitrary selection of a few extreme examples and thorough analysis of these cases. For example, if the research goal is to determine the reason for varying salesperson productivity, the firm might wish to examine case histories of several of its best and worst salespeople. The research goal in this case would be to determine if, for example, there were significant educational or age variations between highly productive and highly unproductive sales personnel. Blipbo's approach in this particular instance might be to take selected retail outlets where sales have varied widely and subject them to analysis, in order to determine whether there are significant differences between retail establishments where sales are high and ones where sales are low.

Exploratory research, then, is especially important to the pattern of investigation. Exploratory research provides a relatively low-cost, low-risk form of research that may pay very high dividends. The main dividend or benefit is a much clearer picture of the problem. Unfortunately, the exploratory phase of marketing research is often skipped:

> One of the most serious defects in the current research practice of many firms is the failure to give adequate consideration to the exploratory phase of research. In many instances this step is skipped entirely or conducted in a very superficial manner. The reasons often given for this are that it is unnecessary, too time-consuming, does not justify the expense required, or else that management already knows what it wants to do and how to do it. Whenever marketing research is conducted without benefit of the exploratory phase, the consequences may well be higher cost, unnecessary or duplicated effort, or failure of the contemplated research to satisfy the needs of management. Omission of this step is rarely defensible.

The blame for not doing exploratory research can more often be placed at the feet of management than of research. Because of the pressure of other matters, or simply to avoid any decision that involves spending money on research, management often waits until the last possible moment before commissioning a study. By then, there is simply not time to do a thorough job of preliminary exploration. And often the best researchers for a particular job are tied up on other, less important work.

One large food-products firm started talking, in October of one year, about testing five new television commercials in May of the following year. Rather than laying out a research design and securing a research supplier (survey firm) in advance, the firm waited until late in April to decide upon both matters. By this time, there was no opportunity for in-depth group interviews to gain insight, for adequate pretesting of the questionnaire, and for similar exploratory matters. Understandably, the study suffered.[1]

Descriptive Research

A descriptive research design is one that, simply, describes something. That "something" could, for example, be the demographic characteristics of consumers who utilize a certain product. Thus, a descriptive study of Blipbo's consumers might describe the profile of a typical Blipbo consumer by age, sex, ethnic group, occupation, family income, and educational level.

Whereas exploratory research may be quite informal, descriptive research design is usually formal and rigid. Since descriptive research is typically utilized in problem solving, it is assumed that a clear definition of the problem has been obtained during the exploratory phase of the research design. Hyoptheses have been developed by exploratory research and now may be tested by descriptive research or, as explained in the next section, by statistical inference designs.

Most marketing research designs can be called descriptive in nature. Market data gathered from descriptive research is widely used in the making of marketing decisions. Despite the popularity of descriptive research, it suffers one important fundamental weakness: *descriptive research does not conclusively determine a direct cause-and-effect relationship.* For example, a descriptive study may show both that consumer income is increasing and that people with high incomes are purchasing expensive clothing. The investigator may *assume* that the high income causes the purchase of expensive clothing. However, a

[1] James N. Myers and Richard R. Mead, *The Management of Marketing Research* (Scranton, Pa.: International Textbook Co., 1969), pp. 66–67.

descriptive study cannot conclusively demonstrate that high income *is* the cause of such purchases. It requires carefully controlled experimental designs to measure causal relationships — a subject we shall examine later in this chapter.

There are two basic types of descriptive research designs: survey designs and panel designs. Each has relative strengths and weaknesses, so that researchers must become familiar with both types in order to make an intelligent appraisal of which to use. Let us begin by examining the more common of the two, survey research.

SURVEY RESEARCH

Survey research is the most widely used formal research design. It may be done in the field — an example would be a survey of consumer attitudes toward a new product concept — or it may take place in a library, where a survey of secondary literature is conducted.

A trait distinguishing survey research from exploratory research is the rigidity and formality of survey research designs. This formality is essential, because survey research is usually conducted in order to obtain an accurate description of the characteristics of whatever universe it purports to describe. Thus, from a survey research design we may have a description of the age characteristics of the sample, the percentage of respondents favoring a certain brand, or the number of retail stores stocking a particular product.

Survey data are usually gathered in the field through either observation or questionnaire methods. Some are obtained by observing consumers in, for example, a retail supermarket and recording their shopping habits. However, most survey data are collected through the questionnaire, a series of questions designed to elicit answers necessary to solve the problem defined earlier in the study. The use of mail questionnaires, telephone questionnaires, and personal interviews will all be discussed later in this book, in Part 2, The Process of Data Collection.

Survey data may be presented in either a one- or a two-dimensional format. A single dimension is easier to present but usually less meaningful than two dimensions. An example of a single-dimension format would be the percentage of people in certain income categories with no cross-classification. In the Blipbo case, a market research manager's data gathered through survey research could be presented to show the percentage of respondents who, for example, like or dislike the taste of Blipbo soft drinks. Descriptive survey data gathered by Blipbo in this manner could be presented in the following fashion:

Do you like the taste of Blipbo products?

Yes:	47%
No:	28%
Don't Know:	25%
Total:	100%

These unidimensional statistics, although interesting in themselves, really tell us very little. We may assume in the "don't know" category that the respondents have never tried Blipbo products, but this is only an assumption. We do not know if the percentage of respondents who indicated they like Blipbo drinks are in fact users of the product, nor do we know if they like other competing products better than Blipbo. In most instances, as here, one-dimensional survey data are of limited practical use to the researcher; at best they provide only partial answers to the questions "what," "when," and "where," and they never completely answer "why."

Descriptive survey data are of much greater value to investigators when they are presented in a two-dimensional format, otherwise known as *cross-classification* or *cross-tabulation* of data. A multidimensional format graphically shows interrelation among variables and may imply a causal relationship, though only through experimental design can this causal relationship be conclusively established. Still, two-dimensional, cross-classification survey data are quite important to researchers. Consider the data on the Blipbo Corporation presented in table 4•1, where descriptive survey data have been cross-classified on the basis of respondent age and willingness to buy Blipbo soft drinks.

From the data presented in table 4•1 the investigator can conclude that Blipbo apparently has a problem among those consumers thirty-five and under; younger respondents are much less willing to purchase Blipbo products than the over-thirty-five group. However, the researcher still does not know *why* these age differences exist; finding out why will require further investigation and more-detailed analysis. Also,

Table 4•1

A Cross-Classification of Respondent Age and Willingness to Purchase Blipbo Soft Drinks

	RESPONDENT WILLINGNESS TO PURCHASE		
RESPONDENT AGE	WOULD BUY	WOULD NOT BUY	DON'T KNOW
Over 35	52%	20%	28%
35 and under	37	34	29

the table does not conclusively establish a causal relationship between age and willingness to buy: this effect is strongly implied in the table, but a mere listing by percentages does not conclusively establish a dependent relationship. Other techniques used in cross-classification, such as chi-square analysis, are more helpful in establishing this relationship and are covered in Chapter 10, Data Analysis.

The survey format, although the more widely used of the two basic descriptive research design approaches, has several important limitations: (1) cost, (2) complexity, and (3) superficiality. Surveys may become very expensive, especially if a large survey requiring several hundred door-to-door personal interviews is desired. Such a survey might elicit only a limited amount of data, take several weeks to complete, and cost over $10,000. Survey research may become extremely complex because of the need to get a large enough number of respondents who are also representative of the full population being studied. Although sampling methods will be discussed later in the book, it is sufficient at this point to say that sampling can be a very difficult process, one that takes considerable expertise and hard work. Finally, the survey approach is superficial and does not normally specify *why* things occur; only motivational research (covered in Chapter 13) can do this. Survey research answers only "what" questions. As Fred N. Kerlinger states: "Survey information ordinarily does not penetrate very deeply below the surface. The scope of the information sought is usually emphasized at the expense of depth." [2]

PANEL DESIGNS

One of the reasons that survey research is sometimes found superficial is that data gathered are valid only for one time period, the time when the study was conducted, and do not normally reflect changes occurring over time. Thus, our knowledge of consumer attitudes toward purchasing Blipbo soft drinks is valid only for the time when respondents were asked. We do not know, for example, what changes in these attitudes might occur over a six-month period in response to changes in the Blipbo marketing mix. Measuring change over time is known as *longitudinal* analysis and is best accomplished through the use of panels.

A panel is defined as a fixed sample of respondents from which information is collected on a continuous basis. Many firms maintain continuous panels to gather data on any appropriate research topic

[2] *Foundations of Behavioral Research*, 2nd ed. (New York: Holt, Rinehart and Winston, 1973), p. 422.

that arises. Data gathered from panels have a wide use, and as a form of research design the panel has broad application beyond descriptive research. Panel data may be used in sales forecasting by measuring consumer preferences for various products, measuring audience size and characteristics for media programs, testing new products and product concepts, and testing any variable in a firm's marketing mix. Panels may be used in implementing any type of research design, but they are particularly effective in longitudinal studies, where management desires a continuous flow of information in order to measure change over a period of time.

Many companies, such as the Parker Pen Company and Procter and Gamble, maintain their own in-house panels of respondents to evaluate products, product concepts, and advertisements. Other companies may use professional marketing research panel companies. One of these, Market Research Corporation of America (MRCA), has a continuous consumer panel of 7,500 families across the United States. Members of MRCA's consumer panel record purchases of a number of consumer products on a weekly basis. Another consumer panel is Home Testing Institute (HTI), which operates on a similar basis. Perhaps the most famous consumer panel of all is the panel used by the A. C. Nielsen Company. Data from this panel is used in compiling the biweekly Nielsen Television Index, or Nielsen Ratings, as this index is better known.

The usage of panels as instruments for measuring changes over time is illustrated in table 4·2. Longitudinal data presented in the table allow Blipbo market researchers to measure the effect on sales, over a six-month period, of a new advertising campaign introduced by the Blipbo company.

As a type of descriptive research design, panels have a number of advantages over survey research designs: (1) panels measure change over time; (2) researchers have greater control over panels; (3) panel

Table 4·2
Number of Panel Respondents Purchasing Blipbo and Brand X in January and July

	BLIPBO	BRAND X	TOTAL
January	40	60	100
July	48	52	100
Total	88	112	200

members are more cooperative; and (4) panel designs allow in-depth analysis. Let us now look at each of these advantages.

The importance of the panel for measuring change over time should not be underestimated. This longitudinal characteristic of panel design makes it often much more meaningful than the one-shot research survey discussed earlier. Panels are especially useful in measuring the effects of new advertisements in changing consumer attitudes, and they are valuable when measuring changes in consumer attitudes toward the company itself, its products, or any variable. These advantages are not restricted to descriptive designs but also are highly applicable to cases of experimental research design where some panel members serve as members of a control group, while others are exposed to the variable being measured.

A second advantage of panel designs over survey designs is the degree of control they permit. In-house panels, in particular, allow the exercise of firm control; less control is possible over home panels, where respondents are recording their answers in diaries, away from the in-house premises of the firm.

Greater control is closely associated with the next advantage of panels over survey research designs — that of increased cooperation. Refusal to cooperate is a major problem in survey research. Refusal rates running as high or higher than 80 percent in mail surveys are quite common. Telephone surveys often do little better, and telephone and personal interviewers must deal with both refusals to cooperate and not-at-homes. Since panel members have voluntarily agreed to participate, 100 percent response rates are not unknown in panel design operations. This cooperativeness can be a factor in substantially holding down the costs of and the time required to complete research projects. The potential cost savings from panel design operations should not be overlooked, especially in light of rising labor costs, soaring mail rates, greater government restrictions on telephone solicitation of any type, and increased difficulty in obtaining responses from consumers in surveys.

The final and most important single advantage of panel design is its ability to provide in-depth, analytical data from respondents. This advantage grows in part out of the other three advantages described. Since panel members have voluntarily agreed to participate in a study, they can usually be expected to spend more time answering questions and filling out questionnaires than would respondents in other surveys. Researchers, accordingly, can gather a wealth of data that might not be available from survey research. Other problems can be avoided by the use of panels. For example, when panel members are asked to fill out diaries at home, indicating their use of products or viewing of certain television programs, there is none of the memory decay that would occur in a survey asking consumers what programs they watched over the past week or what brands of soft drinks they purchased over the past six months.

When we compare panel designs with survey designs, two basic disadvantages of the panel emerge: (1) panel membership may not be representative of the universe in question; and (2) responses from panel members may be biased.

As panel members are people who have voluntarily agreed to serve, the issue arises whether significant differences distinguish people who agree to serve on panels from those who decline because of lack of time, lack of interest, or some other reason. Panel members often have more time than the rest of the relevant universe; members tend to be housewives or retired people who have a great deal of time. Another question is whether panel membership adequately represents the less-well-educated segments of the population. For example, would mail panels or the diary method be biased against those who have less education or less-well-developed communication skills, the skills necessary to record responses and feelings toward a given product or issue adequately? Harper Boyd, Ralph Westfall, and Stanley Stasch comment: "It is often assumed that both the highest and the lowest social classes are under-represented in panels. The former are not interested in the small payments and the latter lack the ability to perform the reporting task." [3]

The second important disadvantage of panel design is potential respondent bias. The principal question here is whether the process of measurement influences the results. Do panel members respond differently because they know that their answers have an influence upon the acceptance of a particular program, product, or advertising theme? This disadvantage is compounded by the danger that lengthy membership upon a panel may cause respondents to begin to think of themselves as professionals or experts. They may then base responses upon their perceptions of how professionals or experts might respond and not upon their own reactions as actual consumers. For example, the question is often asked whether panel members participating in the Nielsen Index Ratings are biased in their viewing of TV programs

[3] Harper W. Boyd, Ralph Westfall, and Stanley F. Stasch, *Marketing Research: Text and Cases*, 4th ed. (Homewood, Ill.: Richard D. Irwin, 1977), pp. 89–90.

during the two-week period in which they are filling out Nielsen diaries. Would this process cause respondents to watch a better quality of television programming than otherwise? Panels also suffer from attrition as members drop out for one reason or another, leaving open the question whether the remaining members are in any way different from the dropouts.

Firms that operate commercial panels take steps to reduce respondent bias. Panel membership is kept on a rotating basis; seldom are respondents asked to remain on a panel for more than six months, lest they become to professional. The A. C. Nielsen Company usually has members of its diary panel for the Nielsen Television Index remain on the panel for only two weeks. Firms keep panel membership lists highly confidential in order to immunize the members from possible outside influence. Despite the danger of the Hawthorne Effect biasing the behavior of panel members, the evidence indicates that it is not a major problem if firms carefully monitor the selection and behavior of panel members. When careful attention is paid to the selection and control of panel membership and panel operations, this form of research design may be one of the most effective available to marketers.

Experimental Research

Experimental research is concerned with determining conclusively whether a causal relationship exists between two variables. For example, the researcher may wish to know the exact effect of a package change on sales of a product. Exploratory research might be used to define the issue and to develop some tentative hypotheses for testing. Descriptive research designs, including survey and panel data, could be used to analyze where sales have taken place or to describe the characteristics of consumers purchasing the product, the characteristics of retailers handling the product, and the attitudes of consumers toward the advertising programs. Cross-classification of data gathered in survey research might provide additional information that would lead the investigator to suspect certain cause-and-effect relationships. However, only through careful experimental design may the researcher build a conclusive case for the existence of particular causal relationships. Inferential relationships among data variables can be meaningfully determined only through experimentation.

Experimentation in marketing research was a rare phenomenon before 1960, despite its long-standing acceptance in the sciences. Since

1960, experimentation has gradually become much more widespread in marketing research. Experimentation may be regarded as one of the key aspects in the implementation of the scientific method. It is a process of manipulating one variable in a controlled environment, while holding all other variables constant, in order to establish a causal relationship. A marketing research example would be an experiment in which the investigator varies the experimental variable (package size) in order to see the effect the change may have on the dependent variable (sales). Test markets, covered in Chapter 14, may incorporate this experimental approach.

Because of the requirement of a highly controlled situation, it is often difficult to use experiments in marketing research practically. In a laboratory environment, scientists may successfully experiment with white rats by feeding only one of two groups of white rats a certain drug. The business world, though, does not offer a laboratory situation, nor can all variables be held constant while only one is manipulated. This limitation often results in less than completely satisfactory experimental research designs. Researchers are forced to accept artificial situations when building models, or they are forced to accept a less than completely controlled situation. Therefore, less confidence can be placed in data generated from market experiments than in that derived from scientific experiments.

Let us go back to the example presented at the beginning of the chapter. The marketing research manager for the Blipbo Corporation might decide to test advertising effectiveness in an experimental research design. Suppose it was decided to show a series of hard-hitting, revolutionary television commercials advertising Blipbo's products in a test market city and compare results (sales) between this city and another comparable city where conventional advertising had been used. At the end of a two-month trial period, sales figures between the two cities were evaluated, and it was found that Blipbo's sales in the area where the new advertising campaign had been conducted showed a 10 percent increase over those in the other city. Could the Blipbo researchers then infer that the increase in sales was a direct result of the advertising program? Perhaps, but a conclusive causal relationship could be established only if the conditions in the two cities were virtually identical. If, for example, one of Blipbo's competitors introduced a new product in one of the two cities, then the experiment would have been invalid. A strike among supermarket employees in one of the two cities would also have invalidated the experiment. It is necessary for investigators to exercise extreme caution in using this research design to infer causal relationships.

TYPES OF EXPERIMENTAL DESIGNS

Marketing researchers may employ any number of designs or frameworks for controlling the collection of data in experimental research. Table 4·3 presents an overview of three of the most significant types of experimental designs used in marketing research to establish causal relationships. From the table you will note that we are examining only three experimental designs used in marketing research. It should be recognized that there are numerous others, most of which are far more complex in nature and scope than the three presented here and are best reserved for more advanced courses in marketing research. We shall now examine each of these three designs.

Simple "Before-After" Design. The least complex of these three experimental research group designs is the simple "before-after" design. The "before-after" design does not conform absolutely to the definition of an experimental design used here, because there is no control group. The dependent variable is measured before and then again after subjects have been exposed to the experimental variable. Figure 4·1 graphically depicts usage of the "before-after without control group" experimental design.

Figure 4·1 shows the effect upon sales measured by the Blipbo Corporation after the new advertising format was adopted. Sales showed a modest increase, but the research manager wonders if the sales increase can be directly attributed to the new advertising campaign. Changes in competitors' marketing strategies, consumer attitudes, the

Table 4·3
Types of Experimental Research Group Designs

EXPOSURE	SIMPLE "BEFORE-AFTER"		"BEFORE-AFTER WITH CONTROL GROUP"		"AFTER-ONLY WITH CONTROL GROUP"	
	EXPERIMENTAL GROUP	CONTROL GROUP	EXPERIMENTAL GROUP	CONTROL GROUP	EXPERIMENTAL GROUP	CONTROL GROUP
Measure before exposure?	Yes	NA a	Yes	Yes	No	No
Variable exposure?	Yes	NA a	Yes	No	Yes	No
Measure after exposure?	Yes	NA a	Yes	Yes	Yes	Yes

a NA = not applicable.

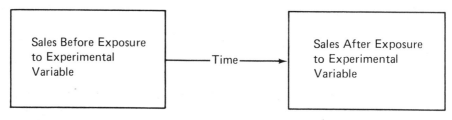

Figure 4·1
Before-After without Control Group

weather, and consumer income are factors other than the advertising program that could have had an influence on Blipbo's sales.

This simple "before-after" design is better than an "after-only" design, which measures the dependent variable only after the subjects have been exposed to the experimental variable. Since, in an "after-only" design, no measurement is made before introduction of the experimental variable, there is no measurement of the process of change. "Before-after" designs do give the investigator some opportunity to measure experimental variables. The principal weakness in "before-after" designs, represented by the arrow in figure 4·1, is one of time or history. The longer the time period between the before measurement and the after measurement, the greater danger that factors other than the experimental variable will have affected the second measurement. In order to be realistic, these research designs should be conducted in the marketplace by a field study, rather than in the laboratory with a laboratory experiment; and over a period of time respondents in the field will be exposed to influences other than the experimental variable. What is suggested is use of some technique that will allow the investigator to analyze the process of change; this technique is the use of a control group.

"Before-After with Control Group" design. "Before-after with control group" design is basically the same as the "before-after" design just described, except that a control group is added. This control group is measured at the same time as the experimental group, both before and after the experiment has been conducted. The only difference between the two groups is that the control group is not exposed to the experimental variable. Figure 4·2 illustrates the "before-after with control group" design.

The design used in figure 4·2 allows researchers to determine the effect of an experimental variable — advertising — upon the dependent variable — sales — in City *A*. An independent control group, City *B*,

Experimental Group

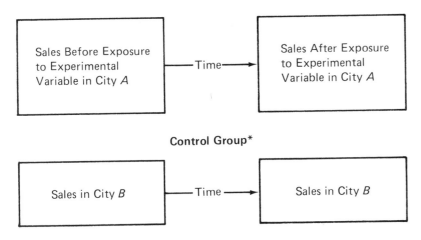

| Sales Before Exposure to Experimental Variable in City *A* | —Time—→ | Sales After Exposure to Experimental Variable in City *A* |

Control Group*

| Sales in City *B* | —Time—→ | Sales in City *B* |

*No experimental variable introduced to control group

Figure 4·2
Before-After with Control Group

is used in order to see if any changes in sales would have taken place without the introduction of the experimental variable. The time between measurements is the same in both groups. This design is sounder than the simple "before-after without control group," and in theory it closes the major loopholes in the "before-after" design by permitting analysis of the process of change over time.

However, implementation of the "before-after with control group" design involves several problems. First is the problem of selecting identical experimental and control groups. In our example, we used two cities, *A* and *B*. In reality, no two cities are exactly alike; there are variations in size, ethnic group composition, employment characteristics, geography, and personal attitudes between any two cities the researcher may select. Nor can the researcher control the actions of competitors. There is no way, for example, to prevent a major competitor from introducing a new advertising campaign in City *B* and not in City *A*. Another problem with this design arises when interaction occurs between members of the experimental group and members of the control group: some residents of City *B* might be exposed to the advertising message intended only for those in City *A*: they may visit City *A*, they may read its newspapers, or they may watch its television by a cable hookup. In some cases where firms have introduced new products in test market cities, the products have proved so popular that people have come in from outlying regions to purchase them, thus increasing their sales to unrealistically high levels (Coors beer is an example of a product that attracts buyers from considerable distances). Where panel groups are used to measure effectiveness of experimental variables, there is no guarantee that members of the experimental group and the control group will not communicate with one another and therefore bias the results. It should be recognized, therefore, that introduction of a control group does not eliminate the problem of the dependent variable being affected by things other than the experimental variable, a factor that causes much despair among marketing research professionals.

"After-Only with Control Group" Design. Numerous problems arise in using the two research designs previously presented. Both may be somewhat cumbersome, and in neither is the problem of time and possible respondent interaction overcome. The presence of a control group does not in itself adequately prevent bias in the results of the study caused by factors beyond the control of the researcher. However, the "after-only with control group" design, illustrated in figure 4·3, may be used to measure the effect of the experimental variable without a "before" measurement. This design is relatively simple to implement. In addition to simplicity, time and measurement effects are avoided, and for these reasons the "after-only with control group" design is the most widely used marketing research experimental design.

The main challenge facing the investigator who uses this research

Experimental Group

```
┌─────────────────────────────┐
│                             │
│  Sales After Exposure       │
│  to Experimental Variable   │
│  in Experimental Territory  │
│                             │
└─────────────────────────────┘
```

Control Group

```
┌─────────────────────────────┐
│                             │
│      Sales in               │
│      Control Territory      │
│                             │
└─────────────────────────────┘
```

Figure 4·3
After-Only with Control Group

design is insuring that the experimental and control groups have the same fundamental characteristics and are physically separated during the questioning process, in order to avoid any interaction. Boyd, Westfall, and Stasch have written of this research design:

> The "after only with control group" design fits many marketing problems and is easy to use. Many promotional devices can be tested this way. A dry milk company believed its biggest problem was to get consumers acquainted with its product. Therefore, it put most of its promotional money into sampling campaigns, but it had no real knowledge of their effect. An "after only" experiment was devised whereby the experimental group was given samples of dry milk. Then the experimental group and the control group were both sent coupons for purchase of the dry milk at a discount at grocery stores. The coupons were coded to indicate whether they were sent to the experimental group or control group, and the number of coupons redeemed by each group was counted.
>
> Frequently, product test are also of the "after only with control group" design. General Motors ran such an experiment to determine the desirability of nylon cord tires as compared to the traditional rayon cord tires. Nylon cord tires were more expensive than rayon cord tires and were alleged to whine and thump, but there was little evidence as to the importance of these effects if, in fact, they existed at all. Accordingly, General Motors equipped 40,000 Chevrolets with nylon cord tires and kept track of the serial numbers of the cars. Later they interviewed owners of cars with both types of tires to get their appraisals of their tires.[4]

LABORATORY AND FIELD EXPERIMENTS

Experimental research designs may be conducted in the laboratory or in the field. A *laboratory experiment* is an artificially created situation in which the researcher controls one or more variables while manipulating other variables at will. A *field experiment* occurs in a "real world" environment, the field, where the investigator *attempts* to control all other variables while manipulating the one that is the experimental variable. Thus, although the field experiment is more realistic, the laboratory experiment offers greater control. Before deciding whether to use laboratory or field experiments, marketing managers should evaluate three aspects of experimentation: (1) the type of information necessary, (2) the validity requirements of the information, and (3) the time and cost necessary to obtain needed information.[5]

[4] *Marketing Research*, p. 82.

[5] Keith K. Cox and Ben M. Enis, *Experimentation for Marketing Decisions* (Scranton, Pa.: International Textbook Co., 1969), p. 106.

Type of Information Necessary. Before deciding whether to undertake a laboratory or a field experiment, the investigator must first assess the type of information necessary for the study. If the study is attitudinal in nature, measuring consumer attitudes toward an advertisement or a product concept, then a laboratory experiment may be perfectly satisfactory. However, if information is needed on the effect of promotion change on sales, a laboratory experiment would probably be unsatisfactory, and an experiment in the field is thus necessitated.

Validity Requirements of the Information. It is at this point that the researcher must weigh the alternatives of internal and external validity for the experiment. *Internal validity* refers to the amount of control built into the experiment, whereas *external validity* refers to its realism: laboratory experiments are strong on internal and weak on external validity, and the opposite is true for field experiments (see table 4•4).

Time and Cost Necessary to Obtain Needed Information. Laboratory experiments usually take less time and cost less than field experiments. A laboratory experiment that takes a few days might take several weeks if conducted in the field. Since both time and money are usually at a premium in organizations, these factors may dictate laboratory experiments even when field experiments might be more desirable. Table 4•4 presents a brief comparison of the major characteristics of the laboratory and the field experiment.

Table 4•4
Comparison of Laboratory and Field Experimentation

EXPERIMENTAL ASPECT	EXPERIMENTAL SETTING	
	LABORATORY	FIELD
Data generated		
Basic theory	Strong	Moderate
Specific information	Weak	Strong
Validity of data		
Internal	Strong	Weak
External	Weak	Strong
Cost		
Resources	Strong	Weak
Time	Strong	Weak

Reprinted from Keith Cox and Ben Enis, *Experimentation for Marketing Decisions* (New York: International Textbook Co., 1969), p. 107.

Summary

The focus of this chapter has been on research design, the overall framework or plan used for the collection and analysis of data in the marketing research project. Incorporated in any good research design should be problem definition, a plan for the gathering and analysis of data, a time framework, and a budget estimate. The research design presents an organized, systematic approach to the formulation, implementation, and control of the research project.

Three basic types of research designs are presented in this chapter: exploratory, descriptive, and experimental.

Exploratory research is a preliminary step in which the main focus is on achieving a clear definition of the problem. Exploratory research designs are not formal but are, rather, unstructured; they may be accomplished by one or more of three approaches: (1) examining existing literature, (2) questioning knowledgeable individuals, and (3) examining a few selected cases.

Descriptive research designs, simply, describe something. They are much more formal than exploratory designs. Though descriptive research designs are far more conclusive in nature than exploratory designs, they do not "prove" cause-and-effect relationships. Survey research and panel designs constitute the two major formats for generating descriptive research data. Of the two, survey research is far the more common and is usually accomplished by a study in the field, using observation or questionnaire methods. If survey data have been cross-classified, they are more meaningful and imply causal relationships, though such relationships can only be proved through statistical inference. The effectiveness of survey research designs is limited by their cost, complexity, and superficiality. Panel designs are also used to generate descriptive research data. A panel is a fixed sample of respondents from whom information is collected on a continuous basis; this measurement of change over time is known as longitudinal analysis. As a type of descriptive design, panel design has the following advantages over survey design: (1) panels measure changes over time; (2) researchers have greater control over panel operations; (3) panel members are more cooperative; and (4) panel designs allow in-depth analysis. Two principal disadvantages arise with panel designs: (1) panel membership may not be representative; and (2) responses from panel members may be biased.

A final type of research design, *experimental research*, may be used to measure cause-and-effect relationships. Central to this design is the experiment, a highly controlled situation in which the investigator manipulates one or more experimental variables while holding all other variables constant. Marketing research experiments may be conducted in the field or in the laboratory; whereas the field experiment is more realistic, the laboratory experiment offers greater control, so that a trade-off occurs. Numerous highly complex experimental research designs are used by some professional marketing researchers and by many academics. Here, three relatively simple designs are presented: (1) simple "before-after" design, (2) "before-after with control group" design, and (3) "after-only with control group" design. Each has its advantages and disadvantages, but the "after-only with control group" is the one most commonly used by professional marketing researchers.

Market researchers must decide whether to use laboratory or field experiments, though sometimes a combination of the two is possible. In determining which to use, researchers need to evaluate the type of information required, the validity requirements of this information, and the time and cost necessary to obtain the needed information. The choice of using a laboratory or a field experiment represents a trade-off among the three factors. The greatest problem facing researchers using experimental design is one of creating a realistic and controlled environment in order to conduct the experiment and to measure its effects.

Questions for Discussion

1. What is meant by research design? Is it possible to conduct a market research study without a formal research design? How?

2. Of the three principal research designs presented in this chapter, which do you think is the most important? Why? Could a marketing research study be conducted using all three of these designs? How?

3. Can panel data be used only with descriptive studies? Can you think of any ways in which panel data could be used in exploratory or experimental designs?

4. What are some of the major advantages and disadvantages of survey research formats?

5. What is meant by longitudinal analysis? Are there any designs besides panel designs that would permit longitudinal analysis?

6. How might a marketing research manager make panels more effective? In other words, how might some of the significant disadvantages of panel designs be overcome?

7. Why, do you think, was experimentation in marketing research a rare phenomenon before 1960? Why has it become much more popular since that time?

8. Which of the three experimental designs presented in the chapter seems to you most meaningful? Why?

9. Under what conditions might a laboratory experiment be better than a field experiment?

10. Which do you think is more important in experimental designs, internal or external validity? Why?

CASE 1·1

BEST BEERS COMPANY (A)

Introduction

In recent years the brewing industry has been characterized by increasing competition among the larger companies. Competition is aimed at increasing market share, most often at the expense of smaller competitors. Best Beers has recognized the need for effective marketing research and the president of Best Beers, Sam Windstorm, is an advocate of aggressive marketing techniques to sell his products. The marketing research department provides the direction for many of the company policies developed by Windstorm.

The Company

Since its founding in 1872, Best Beers has grown from a small family operation into a publicly owned brewery with nationwide distribution. Four plants located in different areas of the country serve the North American market. In each of these plants a number of brands are manufactured, depending upon regional demand, and two different plants often produce the same brand. This overlap demands stringent manufacturing and quality control procedures to assure national uniformity. Responsibility for the uniform taste, appearance, and overall quality of a national brand lies with the master brewer of each plant: under his guidance, Best Beers is assured a quality product. However, to insure regional uniformity, the management has called upon the marketing research department — Consumer Surveys — to conduct taste tests, which perform the dual function of detecting regional disparities and evaluating the taste preferences of the beer drinker. The method used to test consumer reactions is the paired comparison technique, a technique on which the company has relied for many years with good results.

The Marketing Research Department is run by John Calendar, with the help of project coordinators for advertising and consumer research. In general, projects requiring consumer reaction are delegated to one of several competent research houses. This procedure, intended to insure a more objective experiment or survey, also gives the company access to consulting services and new developments in the field of marketing research. Recently, one of these research houses circulated a newsletter questioning the validity and reliability of the paired comparison technique.

The Brewing Industry

Beginning with the purchase of Miller Brewing Company by Phillip Morris, Inc., in 1970, the North American beer market has been experiencing a major upheaval. Phillip Morris paid $227 million for the Milwaukee brewery and by 1980 will have invested $850 million more on plant expansion. From seventh position in 1970, Miller in 1976 was challenging Pabst Brewing Company as the third largest U.S. producer. Miller beer has always had broad potential appeal, and the application of sophisticated marketing techniques and money from Phillip Morris has tripled Miller's beer sales since 1972.

The performance of tobacco executives in the brewing industry has brought a change in attitudes throughout the industry. Production efficiency and price promotion were always the key variables in brewery growth, but Miller has successfully adapted the Procter and Gamble formula to the brewing industry: beer marketing strategy is shifting to market segmentation, new product proliferation, and heavy advertising. These concepts are doctrines in many consumer product markets, but they have been ignored by most U.S. brewers.

The strong competition for market share has resulted in addition of capacity by the large brewers — a procedure bound to create overcapacity and increasing competition in the face of an unexpected decline in the growth rate of beer consumption. The number of brewers could be reduced from forty-nine today to fifteen in the next five years, which would give the major brewers almost 90 percent of the market — at the expense of the smaller regional breweries. The five largest breweries have increased their collective share of the market from 53 percent in 1971 to 69 percent in 1976.

The stronger, more aggressive, companies, like Anheuser and Miller, may look forward to increasing sales and earnings. However, increased competition has so far kept price increases to a minimum, although packaging and material costs have risen 40 percent. Correspondingly, after-tax margins of most brewers have fallen from 6 percent in 1971 to 3.5 percent in 1975. Returns on equity have fallen from 15 percent to 10 percent in the same period.

Phillip Morris's move into the brewing industry has sent the other breweries scrambling to maintain their market shares. Tobacco executives have applied the same marketing techniques that made Marlboro the leading cigarette brand in the United States. Their approach has divided up the beer market into demand segments and produced new products and packages for each segment. This process has been followed by vigorous promotional campaigns resulting in advertising expenditures of more than three dollars per barrel of beer sold, which is almost double the industry average.

It is clear that Phillip Morris's entry into the beer industry has changed the competitive framework of the business. The future looks dismal for smaller breweries that cannot adapt to more sophisticated marketing techniques.

Implications for Best Beers Company

The marketing research department of Best Beers is now forced to evaluate its position and the impact upon company procedures. John Calendar realizes that market conditions dictate that he take advantage of increasingly sophisticated marketing techniques. If the company wishes to remain among the top ten breweries in the country, research methods offering better information should be utilized. The question is whether the additional expenses can be justified.

Questions

1. In light of recent developments in the brewing industry, how can marketing research aid the Best Beers Company in reaching its objectives?

2. Best Beers makes frequent use of independent research houses to conduct specific projects. What are the implications of contracting out these projects? What are the advantages and disadvantages?

3. Assuming that Best Beers had sales of $100 million in 1974, what should the company be spending on marketing research? What do you think it is actually spending?

CASE 1·2

THE MERCHANTS' AND CONSUMERS' BANK (A)

Introduction

At the beginning of October every year, the senior and regional executives from the California Merchants' and Consumers' Bank meet to define policy and review the bank's direction for the future. The meeting is usually a four-day workshop, prepared months in advance, at which the major issues for the short- and long-term future are addressed. This year, Fred McVay, the senior vice-president of finance and investments, presented a brief in which the revenue and costs generated by the bank's operations were trended over the past ten years and results projected to the next ten years. The most revealing projection, although not a surprising one, was that the bank's spread (profit margin) will be narrowing.

Dollars deposited in the bank's coffers by business and consumers, McVay noted, have been becoming more costly to obtain, and loans less profitable, because of tight competition in the lending rate market. Therefore, the profit (or spread) made by lending out the money deposited by consumers is decreasing significantly. McVay's recommendation was that the main emphasis for the next few years be on attracting a greater volume of low-cost deposits — that is, savings accounts that offer relatively low interest rates.

The Bank

The so-called Merchants' Bank is California's oldest and second largest bank, with approximately three hundred branches located strategically throughout the state. For administrative purposes, it is divided into five regions with each regional office managing between twenty-five and forty branches. Because it is a large and rather conservative bank, it has a reputation as a solid and reliable trustee of the public's money. Consumers, however, give it higher ratings than other banks as a bank "for rich people" and "for corporations." Only four other banks, smaller ones, are as frequently associated with these images in consumer surveys.

The marketing approach at the California Merchants' and Consumers' Bank has always been, to say the least, a very conservative one. In the past, the marketing department has usually reacted to changes in the marketplace, rather than anticipating them through proper planning. Its marketing strategy has been to appeal to the total market rather than to use a target market approach. This has been true, in particular, of some of the larger advertising campaigns. However, in recent years, the research department has conducted surveys among the banking population in order to provide much-needed input into marketing decision making. Profiles of users of different banking services have been obtained, which provide some insight into financial attitudes, banking behavior, and demographics of the banking population.

The Marketing Department's Proposal

The marketing department is divided into the advertising and promotion department, the branch location department, the marketing research department, and the various service departments — deposit services, automated services, and the new services development department (see exhibit 1). When the new goal of generating low-cost deposits was announced, the deposit services department and the new services development people began actively reviewing past research results, seeking to uncover target segments or undeveloped needs in the marketplace.

Peter Graham, the manager of the new services development department, was particularly eager to uncover new ideas and opportunities to meet this latest request from top management. He came across a memo referred to him a few months ago by the marketing director.

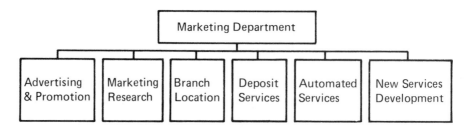

Exhibit 1
Organization of the Marketing Department at the Merchants' and Consumers' Bank

The memo had come from Jim Johnson, the regional manager of a wealthier southern California region. Johnson mentioned that a local one-branch bank in his region had come out with a special type of deposit account for senior citizens, offering a higher rate of interest than most other banks. They also offered free bill-paying privileges to this group of customers. What had happened was a significant loss of low-cost funds from the Merchants' Bank in that region, because some older customers had taken their money out and deposited it into the competitor's bank.

In essence, Johnson was asking the head office to consider providing senior citizens with a comparable service, so that he could regain or at least retain his share of this age group. In fact, only four customers left the one branch in Johnson's region to switch to the other bank. However, these four customers had deposits sizable enough to make him notice the difference. A few months ago, Graham let Johnson know that his office was looking into the matter but that it was not expected to be resolved in the near future. The Merchants' never introduces a service in one branch or region only; it usually introduces it in all three hundred branches at once. In addition, Graham had other priorities more important at the time. As he read through the memo this time, however, he saw a possibility beginning to take shape in his mind; he started to think that the timing might just be right for a special service for senior citizens.

Graham tracked down all the information he could get on this group of customers.

The state government statistics bureau provided a population distribution by various age groups based on the 1970 census, which indicated that:

• Of the total population, 11 percent is sixty-five years old and over.

• Approximately 14 percent of the population aged sixty to sixty-four years is disabled to some extent, and this figure increases to 21 percent among the sixty-five to seventy year olds and to 42 percent of people over seventy years of age.

• The number of Californians aged sixty to sixty-five years is equally distributed among the two sexes; however, the proportion of women increases and that of men decreases after the age of sixty-five, so that, among people aged seventy-five years or over, 66 percent are women.

- Of the population aged sixty-five years and over, 74 percent lives in the cities of California; the remaining 26 percent lives in smaller towns and rural areas.

The marketing research department of the bank conducted a statewide financial service study last year and had the information broken down by different age groups. The last two subgroups were people aged between sixty and sixty-four years and those aged sixty-five years or more. It was these two last groupings that interested Graham.

His first observations were of the demographic distributions:

- *Education*: People aged sixty and older are less likely to have completed college or university than younger population segments.

- *Marital status*: 55 percent are presently married and 33 percent widowed.

- *Income*: Average family yearly income is very low, since few senior citizens are working and earning income.

- *Residence*: A majority (77 percent) own their own homes.

- *Banking service profile*: They make greater use than other age groups of savings accounts, term deposits, and safe deposit boxes and safekeeping services. However, they write fewer checks per month and pay fewer bills at the bank than other age groups.

- *Balances in accounts*: Although they represent a relatively small percentage of the total population, they control a disproportionately large percentage of personal savings deposit business.

Graham suspected that these older customers do not switch banks very often, so that whatever the Merchants' offered to them had to have a strong drawing power to succeed in increasing the bank's market share and volume of deposits. Consequently, he decided that the bank should not only give these people a better rate on savings accounts but should consider developing a package of services especially designed to meet their needs.

The timing for this type of service would also be appropriate, in that it would improve the bank's lagging public image: recent criticism from pressure groups and social agencies charged that the big Merchants' Bank is so intent on reaping profits that it neglects the small saver and charges unfair prices for some of its services.

However, the bank's primary consideration would be to make

the service for senior citizens profitable. For this to happen, the service had to appeal above all to the wealthier among them. If this subgroup did not apply for the service, then the program would fail, since they had the largest deposits of low-cost funds in bank savings accounts.

Graham's idea was to combine a number of services, many of which involved service-charge payments by customers, and offer them to this market either at no cost or at a very nominal fee.

The features under consideration were:

- Checking accounts in which customers would not have to pay service charges. Previous research indicated that they wrote few checks, so that the bank's income loss on this feature would be minimal.

- Special checks that were extra large, easy to read, and easy to fill out. Each check and deposit slip would have a duplicate copy, providing customers with duplicate records of all transactions.

- No service charges on payments of utility bills (such as telephone and electricity) at the bank.

- No commission on traveler's checks.

- Five-year term deposits that would pay interest at the end of the term.

- A no-charge direct deposit to savings accounts of pension checks, dividends, and so on.

- A special subscription to a monthly periodical on retirement living.

- A free financial calendar and diary for the convenient recording of investments, interest payment dates, and dividends.

The only requirement was to be that the customer be sixty-five years old or over and have some type of savings account at the bank.

Graham then went over each item with the cost analyst and projected the total cost of the package to the bank's customer base of people over sixty-five. The projection was based on this group's current level of use of individual services. Surprisingly, because of the low usage of some of the features by senior citizens, the total cost was reasonable and even insignificant, compared to the total benefit derived from the use of their low-cost funds.

The initial costs, as well as the promotion and staff training, would be substantial but, if amortized over the next few years, also fairly reasonable. The service would begin to pay for itself after the third year of operation.

The ideas for this package of services all came from Peter Graham himself and not from the potential consumers. He realized that this was a missing link and went to speak to Ellen Walett of the marketing research department. He provided her with the background, the marketing problem, and his proposed solution.

Questions

1. According to the problem definition stated above, what were Graham's marketing objectives?

2. In going to see Ellen Walett from the marketing research department, what would be Graham's research objectives?

3. What topics should be covered in any consumer research on this subject?

4. Propose a research design to secure the information requirements developed in question 3.

CASE 1·3

SAM'S SNAPPY SUPERMARKETS (A)

Introduction

Sam's Snappy Supermarkets is a regional chain of supermarkets operating in the Southwestern Sunbelt. Samuel S. Snodgrass, Sr., founder and largest shareholder of the chain, has always followed an intuitive, "seat of the pants" approach to running the operation, which currently grosses $75 million annually and produces a net after-tax profit of $750,000. With twenty-five stores and approximately 300 employees, Sam has never established a marketing research department, nor does Mr. Sam, Sr. (as the founder is known), have any intention of doing so.

The Problem

Recently, Samuel S. Snodgrass, Jr., Mr. Sam's son, has joined Sam's, after graduating in marketing from State University. A quick examination of the firm's operating strategies revealed to him that marketing decisions are being made on the basis of Mr. Sam's intuition and experience. Furthermore, careful analysis showed that Sam's growth rate is tapering off and profit margins have been narrowing for the past three consecutive years.

Samuel, Jr., is convinced that some basic marketing research is necessary to pinpoint the causes of the slowing down, but he is not sure what to do. He wonders if perhaps the company should establish its own marketing research department, though he is sure that Mr. Sam, Sr. will oppose the idea.

Questions

1. Should Sam's establish a marketing research department? Defend your answer.

2. What kind of research design would you recommend to solve Sam's problem? Why?

Part 2

The Process of Data Collection

Chapter 5

Secondary Data

IN THE PREVIOUS CHAPTER we explored the issue of research design, which was defined as an overall framework or plan for the collection and analysis of data in the marketing research project. Whether the research design is exploratory, descriptive, inferential, or a combination, it will have as its purpose the generation of useful data that can then be analyzed for the solving of business problems. Data analysis, the subject of Chapter 11, converts a mass of data into useful information presented in a concise and orderly format, in order to facilitate decision making.

Modern business in North America can be characterized as becoming increasingly information-dependent, by which we mean that, in the fast-changing, complex business world of today, managers are more than ever in need of up-to-date information on which to base decisions. Since the task of gathering and disseminating this information falls to the marketing research department, researchers must have substantial familiarity with the sources and types of information. The researcher must know when and how to go to the library or into the field for needed information, as the cost and time trade-offs between the two can be of critical importance. In order to obtain information efficiently, marketing researchers must have considerable knowledge about both primary and secondary data-collection techniques, as well as understanding of the appropriate times to use and gather one or the other, or both.

Primary and Secondary Data Sources

It is very important to understand the nature and use of primary and secondary data sources. That is, information may be characterized as being either primary or secondary in nature, depending on the purpose for which the data were originally gathered. The terms "primary" and "secondary" are somewhat confusing, as they in no way assess priority of importance. Primary data, the subject of our next chapter, are original data gathered by the researcher for the project at hand. Secondary data are data already existing in printed form, having been previously gathered for some project other than the one presently in question. Neither type of data is more important than the other, though they have relative advantages and disadvantages.

An example will illustrate the use of primary and secondary data. If Safeway Stores, Inc., the largest North American food retailing chain, wanted to know what percentage of consumer family income was spent for grocery products, this information could be secured from either primary or secondary research. Primary research might involve conducting a survey among consumers in order to gather the information; a thorough survey might take weeks to complete and cost well over a million dollars. On the other hand, the researcher could go to external secondary research, such as published government reports, and secure the same information. This case illustrates two benefits of secondary over primary data: economy and speed. By using secondary data, Safeway would have gathered the required information much faster and more cheaply than by the lengthy, costly, and often cumbersome process of surveying consumers in a primary data-gathering field research project.

There is one cardinal rule to be followed in beginning a marketing research study: *Always begin by exhaustively searching through all secondary data before attempting to gather primary data.* Many students, as well as some professionals who should know better, invariably reverse the procedure. When presented with a research problem to be solved, they make the mistake of rushing to gather primary data through survey research, when adequate and full information to solve the problem already exists in published secondary form. The end result is that, by failing to search exhaustively through secondary information, the researchers waste extensive time and money in collecting primary data.

This bypassing of secondary information often results from the aspiring rasearcher's ignorance about the existence and location of this information in a gloomy and unfamiliar place — the library. And it also results from the assumption that research for primary data has more "sex appeal" than does that for secondary data. Some researchers have a bias against using secondary material, holding the mistaken belief that primary, or survey, research is what marketing research is all about. Unfortunately, this attitude has caused firms to lose much time and money in research projects. Many firms have spent several months and many thousands of dollars in gathering primary data, when the same data were available in published secondary form and could have been gathered by a relatively short search in the library at little cost.

Primary and Secondary Sources

It is sometimes easy to confuse primary and secondary data with primary and secondary sources; therefore, it is important to be aware of the distinction between the two.

Secondary data may be gathered from either primary or secondary sources.[1] A primary source is the source that originated the data, whereas a secondary source is a source that secured the data from the original source. The U.S. government's *Census of Population,* conducted every ten years, is an example of a primary source. A local newspaper that published certain census population characteristics would be regarded as a secondary source, since the newspaper would be quoting a primary source, the *Census of Population.*

Are both primary and secondary sources equally acceptable? The answer is no! In using secondary data, researchers always should go first to the primary source, not the secondary source, of the secondary information. The two main reasons for using primary sources before secondary sources are that primary sources are (1) more complete and (2) more accurate than secondary sources. The primary source is more complete because it is the source that contains the full amount of information in an unabridged form. Also, the primary source will usually describe the process by which the data were gathered, thus allowing the researcher to make an assessment of the quality of the information.

Primary sources are considered more accurate than secondary sources because of the likelihood that secondary sources may have misinterpreted the original sources. The possibility of typographical errors is increased in using secondary sources, just as in the case of passing information by word of mouth: the more people who repeat a given

[1] Gilbert A. Churchill, *Marketing Research: Methodological Foundations* (Hinsdale, Ill.: Dryden Press, 1976), p. 129.

message, the more apt the message is to become distorted. Secondary sources may omit significant footnotes or key textual elements and therefore change the meaning of the primary source. The danger of overreliance upon secondary sources may be illustrated by examining the field of history, where secondary sources are used and reused in the rewriting and updating of history books. This process often allows and perpetuates distortions or inaccuracies. However, it is not always possible to use primary source material; in these cases the investigator must rely upon secondary source information.

Sources of Secondary Data

When beginning a secondary data search, the researcher may become confused in looking at the vast array of secondary data source material. The question becomes, "Where do I go for secondary data?"A maze of sources are available to the researcher, including trade association data, government publications, trade publications, research foundations, commercial information, other business firms, one's own organization, and last, but not least, libraries. Simplicity and logic permit us to divide the sources of secondary data into two groups: internal and external data sources.

Internal Data Sources

Internal secondary data are found within the organization where the research is being conducted. Internal secondary data have been gathered for some purpose other than the project at hand. Sources of such data include (1) sales and accounting data and (2) internally generated research reports.

Sales and accounting data may include information about customer billings, sales activities, inventory turnover, and cost of new and existing products. By examining these internal data on a product, customer, or inventory basis, the researcher is in a position to measure and determine why variations exist among sales territories, products, and customers over a period of time. This examination may be used in establishing sales quotas, selling efforts, or a need to tighten credit granted to customers. Properly evaluated, these data allow the researcher to perform a cost/benefit analysis of the marketing expenses incurred within the company — an area often neglected.

Previously conducted research studies and published reports constitute the second principal source of internal secondary data. These are a significant source of data, especially in large firms where the research function and report writing are well established. Giant, monolithic organizations, such as the Bell System, have a well-established research and report writing system that results in the publication of numerous detailed reports and studies, which may be used as secondary data sources for future studies and reports. For example, the Bell Business Planning Group of Bell Canada has produced a series of internal research reports dealing with such diverse areas as the Impact of Communication Services in the Eastern Arctic, Exploration in the Future of Educational Technology, Cross-Impact Matrix Applications in Technology and Policy Assessment, Cross-Impact Analysis in Bell Canada, Exploration of the Future in Medical Technology, Group Judgemental Data in Cross-Impact Analysis and Technology Assessment, and numerous others. Obviously, not every firm, especially not smaller ones, will have access to such a wealth of internal secondary data; however, even in medium-sized firms there often exist a substantial amount of internal cost and accounting data that are often overlooked.

Though internal secondary data may be somewhat limited, they do provide the most logical place for the researcher to begin the investigation. Research projects should begin with a careful review of internal secondary data, because these data are the least expensive to gather of any type in marketing research. Also, since these are data that have been generated within the organization, they are the most easily accessible of all types of information.

External Data Sources

External secondary data are those *outside* the organization. Although external data sources may not be the originating sources for secondary information, they are of such importance that no intelligent information system can afford to overlook them. An almost unlimited amount of secondary information is available to the marketing researcher, making proper use of external data sources a formidable task. This vast amount of available secondary information presents to research professionals the major problem of determining which sources are useful and where they are located. Lack of knowledge of external secondary sources causes decision makers to act without complete information in attempting to solve marketing problems. The end result may be lost sales and lower profits.

External secondary sources provide data that can be used in two basic ways: (1) as general references in helping firms to be in contact with their outside environments, and (2) as an aid in solving specific problems.[2]

MAJOR CLASSIFICATIONS OF SECONDARY DATA SOURCES

What, then, are the major external sources of secondary information? Though no clearly defined classification system exists, because of the large number of different sources, for purposes of simplicity we may classify external sources as four in number: (1) publications of government agencies, (2) syndicated commercial information, (3) trade and professional association publications, and (4) other miscellaneous published sources. However, the sources classified here may also contain internal secondary information. Each of these four general categories of external secondary information is described below.

Government Agencies. The continually expanding role of government, especially at the federal level, into virtually all phases of business and consumer activity generates enormous amounts of secondary data available to the public. One important by-product of this constant government expansion is that, in its efforts to oversee the activities of individuals and organizations, the federal government has compiled a wealth of statistical data. In commenting upon this mass of government data Bertram Schoner and Kenneth Uhl write: "Governments collect and disseminate more information than any other source. To the uninitiated, the various types of information that are available can be almost unbelievable. It ranges, for example, from estimates of the number of wild horses (or, if you prefer, whooping cranes) in the United States to the number of retail food stores in each county to the number, breeds, and even names of dogs registered in various counties." [3]

Nearly all federal government agencies collect and disseminate statistical data of interest to marketing research professionals. Accordingly, a complete listing of all federal government information-collecting activities would be well beyond the page constraints of this text; indeed, it could fill at least a complete textbook itself. The information-collection and -dissemination activities of the federal government are well known to people outside the research profession and would include activities of such diverse agencies as the CIA, whose information-collection activities, though of great interest to many people, are

[2] Bertram Schoner and Kenneth P. Uhl, *Marketing Research,* 2nd ed. (New York: John Wiley and Sons, 1975), p. 174.

[3] *Marketing Research,* p. 181.

beyond the limits of traditional marketing research. Let us then examine the data-collection and -distribution activities of some of the most significant of the government agencies whose activities are of special importance to marketing researchers.

The Bureau of the Census is the single most important source of marketing information within the federal government and the single largest gatherer of statistical data in the country. Established in 1790 by an act of Congress, this agency is a vital source of published statistical information. By definition, a census is a complete enumeration of each any every item in a given universe. Typically, marketing researchers find it impractical to try to conduct a census of large populations, preferring instead to take a sample from the population, for two reasons. First, in a large universe, such as the total population of the United States, only the federal government has the resources to undertake a counting of every item in the universe. Second, the federal government has the authority to require respondents to reply to census questions, something private industry does not have.

The federal government conducts censuses at periodic intervals on population, housing, business, manufacturing, agriculture, transportation, governments, and mineral industries. The oldest, best known, and most important of these is the *Census of Population*. Conducted every ten years since its beginning in 1790, the *Census of Population* has been modified many times over the years. Not only does this census give the total number of people living in the United States and within state, county, metropolitan area, city, and census tract areas, but also it makes available detailed breakdowns of the demographic traits of the population. Ethnic, social, educational, and occupational characteristics are all presented in substantial detail by the census. For example, by examining the *Census of Population* for Dallas County, Texas, one can find out the average number of years of schooling completed by residents of that county; should the researcher prefer, the average number of years of schooling for people within the state of Texas is given. The *Census of Population* even includes a detailed breakdown of occupational characteristics of population in a given geographical area. Putting together information on occupations and information on income characteristics, the market researcher is in a position to make educated guesses about the purchasing power of residents in a geographical area, something that is very important in locating specialty shops and shopping centers. Unfortunately, as the *Census of Population* is conducted only every ten years (1970, 1980, 1990, and so on), this information is often considerably out of date. For example, in 1979, market planners using census data may be forced to make decisions based on data developed on the basis of the 1970 *Census of Population*. However, since all respondents surveyed by census are required by law to answer all the questions asked, the census provides data that might otherwise be unavailable to private industry.

Examine figure 5•1, "Using Census Data." Population is reported on the basis of Standard Metropolitan Statistical Area (SMSA), Census Tract, Block Group, and Block. As relatively permanent, homogeneous areas with populations of approximately 4,000, Census Tracts are especially convenient for market surveys. The SMSA, which contains a central city of at least 50,000 people and surrounding metropolitan area, is useful to retailers in measuring market potential (total sales by all competitors) and sales potential (one firm's share).

Like the *Census of Population*, the *Census of Housing* is also conducted every ten years on the turn of the decade. This census provides researchers with information concerning details of housing conditions throughout the United States by type of dwelling, specifying whether a house is owned or rented, how many bathrooms it has, and other similar characteristics. Thus, for example, if a manufacturer of plumbing supplies wanted to know the number of homes with outdoor toilets in a particular rural area, he could immediately find the information by consulting the *Census of Housing*. An air-conditioning supply firm could determine what percentage of homes were equipped with air-conditioning in a given market. In both cases, census data would enable the vendor to estimate the potential for the product in that market.

Some censuses are taken more frequently. The *Census of Manufacturers*, the *Census of Business*, and the *Census of Agriculture* are taken every five years. Included in the *Census of Agriculture*, which is taken in the years ending in four and nine, is information on the numbers and sizes of farms, the value of acreage, crops, facilities and equipment, farm labor, fertilizers used, and characteristics of farm families.

The *Census of Business*, conducted in the years ending in 7 and 2, is divided into three sections: retail sector, wholesale sector, and service sector. This census provides extensive data about business establishments and their employees, which are reported on a state, county, metropolis, and city basis. In addition to the main *Census of Business*, current surveys are furnished by this department on annual, monthly, and even weekly bases in the retail sector.

Census of Business data classify retailers, wholesalers, and service firms by number of establishments, type of operation, products sold, gross sales, and number of employees. Thus, from *Census of Business* statistics, a firm can often make a reasonably accurate estimate of its

CENSUS GEOGRAPHIC AREAS

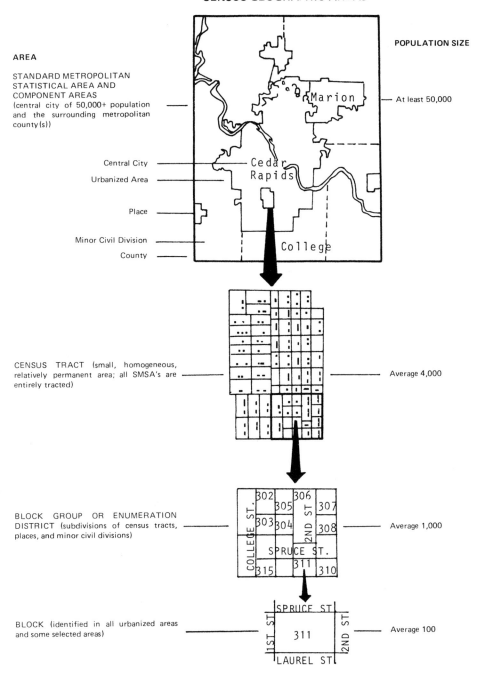

AREA

STANDARD METROPOLITAN
STATISTICAL AREA AND
COMPONENT AREAS
(central city of 50,000+ population
and the surrounding metropolitan
county(s))

Central City

Urbanized Area

Place

Minor Civil Division

County

CENSUS TRACT (small, homogeneous,
relatively permanent area; all SMSA's are
entirely tracted)

BLOCK GROUP OR ENUMERATION
DISTRICT (subdivisions of census tracts,
places, and minor civil divisions)

BLOCK (identified in all urbanized areas
and some selected areas)

POPULATION SIZE

At least 50,000

Average 4,000

Average 1,000

Average 100

Figure 5·1
Using Census Data

Reprinted from U.S. Bureau of the Census, *Data Access Description,* no. 33, p. 4.

share of the market in its industry. For example, *Census of Business* data report total retail supermarket sales; this information permits a firm like Safeway Stores, Inc., to know what its share of retail supermarket sales is. These census data provide information from which a firm can determine what its market potential is and what its sales potential should be on a nationwide or local basis.

Although the Bureau of the Census is considered the most important of the government agencies in providing useful information to marketing managers, numerous others also publish significant information. The Department of Commerce, which includes the Bureau of the Census, publishes a monthly *Survey of Current Business and Business Cycle Developments.* The Department of Agriculture gathers data concerning consumer preferences and merchandising methods associated with agricultural products and also publishes information on retail and wholesale market practices in merchandising agricultural products. A measure of insight into the number of federal government publications can be gained by going to the *Monthly Catalog*, which lists nearly thirty-five thousand federal government publications, but even this figure represents only a small fraction of the total.

Syndicated Commercial Information. The second major external source of secondary data is syndicated commercial information. Syndicated commercial information is marketing research data sold on a continuing subscription basis by private firms for a profit. Syndicated commercial information, unlike special reports prepared solely for one firm, may be purchased by a number of buyers, since such syndicated information is not tailored to any one firm. Because it is not collected for a particular project at hand, syndicated commercial information is not considered primary data but is included in secondary data sources. Suppliers of syndicated commercial information may be divided into two groups: (1) those who supply financial data and (2) those who supply market data.

The two best-known syndicated sources of *financial data* are Moody's Investors Services, Inc., and Standard and Poor's Corporation. These two firms supply up-to-date financial information about large, publicly held corporations. For example, Moody's publishes *Stock Survey, Bond Survey, Handbook of Common Stocks, Industrial Manual, OTC Industrial Manual, Bank and Finance Manual, Transportation Manual, Public Utility Manual,* and *Municipal and Government Manual.* Standard and Poor's Corporation publishes *Industry Survey* and *Standard Corporation Records.* The latter provides detailed financial and operating data about medium- and larger-sized firms trading on the major stock exchanges in North America. Poor's *Register of Corporations, Directors and Executives* is an annual publication listing the products, sales, officers, and employees of approximately thirty thousand U.S. and Canadian firms. Both Moody's and Standard and Poor's syndicated services constantly send updated information to subscribers.

Numerous other sources of financial data are also available to marketing managers, depending upon the kind of information desired. For example, if the firm needs an estimate of the credit worthiness of potential customers, a common method is to employ the services of Dun and Bradstreet, the international credit-reporting firm. While Moody's and Standard and Poor's services are reported and available in university libraries, other firms, such as Dun and Bradstreet or Retail Credit, do not publish their information but, rather, sell it on an individual basis.

A second group of commercial information firms supply *market data*. Professional research firms are involved in collecting channel information and then selling it on a syndicated basis. Manufacturers of consumer products are particularly interested in securing additional information on sales activities of middlemen, wholesalers, and retailers in their channels of distribution. Two firms, A. C. Nielsen Company and Market Research Corporation of America (MRCA), specialize in gathering channel information and making it available to subscribers, particularly manufacturers.

The A. C. Nielsen Company [4] provides a variety of syndicated services of interest to marketing researchers. Nielsen's Retail Index Services is conducted every two months in a sample of approximately two thousand food and drug stores, where Nielsen representatives audit complete sales and inventory levels of each store in the sample during that time period. As an incentive, each store is given a copy of the report plus some small monetary awards. Information derived from this Retail Index is available to subscribers, who receive bimonthly reports on total sales by product class, brand, price, and stockturn (merchandise turnover). A series of six Retail Index reports may cost a subscriber in excess of $100,000 yearly, but manufacturers receive valuable data, not only about their own sales but about sales of competitors. Thus, though a firm such as General Mills would know its own sales, it could learn what General Foods' sales were in a given product class. Nielsen's Television Index, which operates on a similar basis, is discussed more fully in the chapter on advertising research.

[4] See Chapter 2 for a more complete description of the A. C. Nielsen Company.

A second firm supplying syndicated channel information is Market Research Corporation of America (MRCA). Using a panel of approximately 7,500 families, MRCA collects much the same information as is in Nielsen's Retail Index, except that MRCA's information is collected at the *consumer level*. Members of the MRCA consumer panel, using diaries supplied to them by that firm, report their experiences in using new consumer products that the firm may wish them to try free of charge. MRCA also operates the Metropolitan Supermarket Audit. Every three months, MRCA representatives go to a sample of large supermarkets and check product, prices, availability, shelf space allotment, and location for various consumer products. Subscribers to MRCA's Metropolitan Supermarket Audit receive information on such things as the relative shelf location and selling price of their and their competitors' products. The alternative, for a firm desiring this type of product information, would be sending its own representatives into a supermarket. This would necessitate considerable time and expense, assuming the individual firm could secure retailer cooperation. MRCA provides reliable data secured more cheaply than if the firm undertook the data collection itself. Other firms similar to MRCA include National Family Opinion (NFO) and Household Testing Institute (HTI), to name but two.

Trade and Professional Associations. Trade and professional associations provide an excellent external secondary data source, a source often overlooked. A main objective of trade and professional associations is to provide information about the industry and its environment to members. To accomplish this objective, these associations publish books, magazines, journals, and newspapers, which are sent to members and libraries. For example, publications of the American Marketing Association include the *Journal of Marketing*, the *Journal of Marketing Research, Marketing News*, and many others. In the advertising field, there is *Advertising Age*, a weekly publication of Crain Communications, Inc., and the *Journal of Advertising Research (JAR)*, published by the Advertising Research Foundation.

Other important publications are the magazines *Supermarketing* and *Progressive Grocer*, trade publications in the retail grocery field. Still others would include *Sales Management* and the *Journal of Retailing*.

These are only a few of the many publications prepared by trade, professional, and learned organizations. Many of these publications are quite specialized, like *Supermarketing*, whereas others, such as the *Journal of Marketing*, are of much more general interest. Virtually all these periodicals should be available in any good university library, and these, as well as others, would be cross-referenced in an index called the *Business Periodicals Index*, or *BPI* (see fig. 5·2 for a sample page).

Miscellaneous Published Sources. By no means do government agencies, syndicated commercial sources, and trade and professional associations constitute the only sources for published external data. There is an almost unlimited number of other published sources of various types that are of relevance to marketing researchers. Of this enormous array of periodicals, newspapers, special published reports, dissertations, books, and monographs, it would be impossible to list or otherwise describe more than a very few.

One particularly useful external source is the *Annual Survey of Buying Power* published by *Sales Management* magazine. This annual issue contains statistical information, arranged in geographical categories, on effective buying income, population, and retail sales for various types of retail outlets.

These miscellaneous published sources are referenced in a library's card catalogue and in published collections of abstracts and indexes. The card catalogue provides a reference to all books in the library by author, title, and subject heading. Collections of abstracts include, among the most useful, *Dissertation Abstracts*, *Psychological Abstracts*, and *Sociological Abstracts*. Indexes provide a comprehensive cross-classification of newspaper articles and published articles; some of the most important are the *Business Periodicals Index*, the *Wall Street Journal Index* (*WSJI*), the *Social Science Citation Index*, the *Readers' Guide to Periodical Literature*, and the *New York Times Index*. No review of external published secondary data is complete without having consulted these major indexes.

A guide to some of these miscellaneous published sources follows:

1. *Dissertation Abstracts* (Ann Arbor, Mich.: University Microfilms). Published monthly by subject field and author. All doctoral dissertations accepted by American and Canadian institutions of higher learning are listed.

2. *Business Periodicals Index* (New York: H. W. Wilson Co.). Indexes by subject all the articles appearing in approximately 160 periodicals covering all aspects of business.

3. *Readers' Guide to Periodical Literature* (New York: H. W. Wilson Co.). Indexes by subject over 100 popular periodicals. These periodicals tend to be less useful than those listed in *BPI* for most marketing research projects.

MARKET research—*Continued*

Mathematical models

Some methodological alternatives in the analysis of life style data. P. E. Green and F. J. Carmone. tabs J Econ & Bus 30:158-61 Wint '78

MARKET research firms

Audience research debate: who's got the answer. Media Decisions 13:72-5+ My '78

Can you count on the numbers? Media Decisions 13:59-63+ Ap '78

MARKET segmentation

New approach to industrial market segmentation. J. M. Choffray and G. L. Lilien. bibl tabs Sloan Mgt R 19:17-29 Spr '78

Target groups and advertising messages. K. Grønhaug and L. Røstvig. bibl tabs J Adv Res 18:23-8 Ap '78

Mathematical models

Some methodological alternatives in the analysis of life style data. P. E. Green and F. J. Carmone. tabs J Econ & Bus 30:158-61 Wint '78

MARKET share

Imports from US up, market shares down in most nations. Comm Am 3:11-12 My 8 '78

Market share model of rural telephone service. J. G. Church and I. M. Gordon. bibl Omega 6 no 1:59-64 '78

Oligopoly pricing in the world wheat market. C. M. Alaouze and others. bibl tabs Am J Agric Econ 60:173-85 My '78

Right size: an organizational dilemma. R. L. Cason. il tabs Mgt R 67:24-8+ Ap '78

Xerox is trying too hard. B. Uttal. Fortune 97:84-6+ Mr 13 '78

MARKET structure

See also

Competition

MARKET surveys

See also

Consumers—Attitudes

Consumers' preferences

MARKET testing. See Test marketing

MARKET value

Key to value estimation: highest and best use or most probable use. D. Scribner, jr. bibl Real Estate Appraiser 44:23-8 My '78

MARKETING

Advertisers lick marketing problems with newspaper ads. Ed & Pub 111:18 Ap 22 '78

From sales obsession to marketing effectiveness. P. Kotler. Harvard Bus R 55:67-75 N '77

Marketing or metamarketing? G. Wasem. Bankers M 95:32-5 My '78

Marketing when things change. T. Levitt. Harvard Bus R 55:107-13 N '77

Should government programs have marketing managers? J. D. Claxton and others. tabs U Mich Bus R 30:10-16 My '78

Structural constraints, consumerism, and the marketing concept. R. W. Stampfl. MSU Bus Topics 26:5-16 Spr '78

See also

Advertising

Bank marketing

Diffusion of innovations

Distribution of goods

Education market

Franchise system

Industrial marketing

Manufacturers agents

Market segmentation

Market share

Marketing managers

Merchandising

Metropolitan market

Old age market

Price discrimination

Product differentiation

Product planning

Retail trade

Sales management

Sales promotion

Salesmanship

Test marketing

also subhead Marketing under the following subjects

Airlines

Printing industry

Real estate business

Savings and loan associations

Securities

Semiconductor industry

Service industries

Small business

Soft drink industry

Tea industry

Telephone companies

Telephone equipment industry

Toilet goods

Travel

International aspects

See also

Export-import trade—Promotion

Laws and regulations

See also

Advertising laws and regulations

Mathematical models

Role of business economists in marketing. N. K. Dhalla. tabs Bus Econ 13:47-51 My '78

Study and teaching

How to teach marketing [editorial] C. Ramond. J Adv Res 18:51 Ap '78

Marketing: who should teach what to whom? S. Marshak and J. DeGroot. J Adv Res 18:17-20 Ap '78

MARKETING (home economics)

See also

Consumer education

Consumers

MARKETING, Foreign. See Export-import trade—Promotion

MARKETING channels

Sources of power: their impact on intrachannel conflict. R. F. Lusch. bibl tabs J Mkt Res 13:382-90 N '76; Discussion. 15:273-6 My '78

See also

Distribution of goods

MARKETING managers

Managerial style and the design of decision aids. M. De Waele. bibl Omega 6 no 1:5-13 '78

Should government programs have marketing managers? J. D. Claxton and others. tabs U Mich Bus R 30:10-16 My '78

MARKETING research. See Market research

MARKETING service by advertising agencies. See Advertising agencies—Service

MARKETS

Morocco

Bazaar economy: information and search in peasant marketing. C. Geertz. Am Econ R 68:28-32 My '78

MARRIAGE

Towards a marriage between economics and anthropology and a general theory of marriage. A. Grossbard. bibl Am Econ R 68:33-7 My '78

See also

Divorce

Husband and wife

MARRIED women in the labor force. See Women—Employment

MARS flights. See Space flight—Mars flights

MARSH & McLennan, Inc.

Lloyd's ban hit by M&M chairman [J. M. Regan, jr] Nat Underw (Prop ed) 82:2+ My 26 '78

Lloyd's rebuffs US brokers, fears control. E. Simon and J. H. Miller. Bus Insur 12:1+ My 1 '78

MARSCHAK, Jacob

Jacob Marschak contributions to the economics of decision and information. K. Arrow. Am Econ R 68:xii-xix My '78

Jacob Marschak, 1898-1977. T. C. Koopmans. Am Econ R 68:ix-xi My '78

MASS communication. See Mass media

MASS feeding. See Food service

MASS media

Business and the media: how to get along. Nations Bus 66:74+ Ap '78

Haldeman, Encounters, Super Bowl, Bee Gees,

Figure 5·2

Sample Page from the *Business Periodicals Index*

From *Business Periodicals Index*, © 1976. Reprinted by permission of the H. W. Wilson Company, New York, N.Y.

4. *New York Times Index* (New York: New York Times Company). Indexes by subject all articles appearing in the *New York Times.*

5. *Wall Street Journal Index* (New York: Dow Jones and Co.). Arranged in two sections (corporate news and general news). Corporate news is indexed by firm and general news by subject, alphabetically.

6. *Public Affairs Information Service Index* (*PAIS*) (New York: Public Affairs Information Service). Organized by subject area. Various types of English-language publications in economics and public affairs are indexed.

Organizations find external secondary information useful in making long-term plans. Changes in demographic characteristics of the population, retail sales, and consumer-disposable personal income are examples of the types of information firms may find useful as general references obtained from external secondary data. In this case, the primary source of the data would be federal government census data and the secondary source would be a periodical, such as *Business Week* or the *Wall Street Journal,* that reported the government census statistics.

Specific problems may be solved with the aid of external secondary information. In research projects, such information is most often used as an aid in developing hypotheses in exploratory research, though it is also used in solving problems through conclusive research. For example, a retail firm wishing to know the demographic and income characteristics of consumers living in a certain geographic area needs only to consult external secondary information, in this case published government census reports, to be able to find the information and avoid costly primary data-gathering surveys. If the manager of a newly created marketing research department wanted to know the salary level at which employees in that department should be paid, she could, by examining the American Marketing Association's *Survey of Marketing Research,* determine the average salaries for research employees in a number of different categories by size of organization.

Using the Library

By now it should have become obvious that there is no lack of external sources of secondary published information. The sources noted above provide a mass of data on virtually any subject imaginable. However, knowing about the existence of these sources and knowing *how to* locate and use them are two fundamentally different matters. The answer to the question of locating these external sources of marketing information is the library. Most college and university students, as well as many marketing research professionals, have only the vaguest idea of proper utilization of library facilities in secondary research. Libraries may be perceived as musty, dim, foreboding places to be avoided at all costs. Despite this (often inaccurate) perception, the ability to use library facilities successfully is an absolute necessity for marketing researchers.

Although many large firms maintain in-house library facilities, the most up-to-date and complete collection of external secondary information will be found in good college, university, or large city libraries. University libraries are especially useful, since most of them have been designated official depositories for federal government statistical data, which means that all census and other similar information is automatically sent to them.

The thorough search through secondary data that should initiate any research study means a comprehensive library search. In figure 5•3 a library search flow diagram is presented, to show the researcher how to proceed systematically in locating secondary material on an unfamiliar topic.

If the researcher has selected or been assigned a research project on a totally unfamiliar topic, a good place to begin is with a search through appropriate elementary textbooks, encyclopedias, and reference works. These sources should provide basic familiarity with the subject.

Then a comprehensive bibliography on the subject should be located: a bibliography facilitates the quick acquisition of a complete inventory encompassing all materials on the research topic.[5] It is recommended that the researcher go first to the *Bibliographic Index: A Cumulative Bibliography of Bibliographies* (New York: H. W. Wilson Co., 1937–). Organized by subject, the *Bibliographic Index* indexes books, magazine articles, and other printed materials containing bibliographies. This index therefore makes it easier to locate publications in which authors have listed their own reference sources on the particular subject. Another valuable bibliography has been published by the AMA: *A Basic Bibliography on Marketing Research*, comp. Robert Ferber et al., 3rd ed., 1974 rev. (Chicago: American Marketing Association, 1974).

[5] C. William Emory, *Business Research Methods* (Homewood, Ill.: Richard D. Irwin, 1976), p. 182.

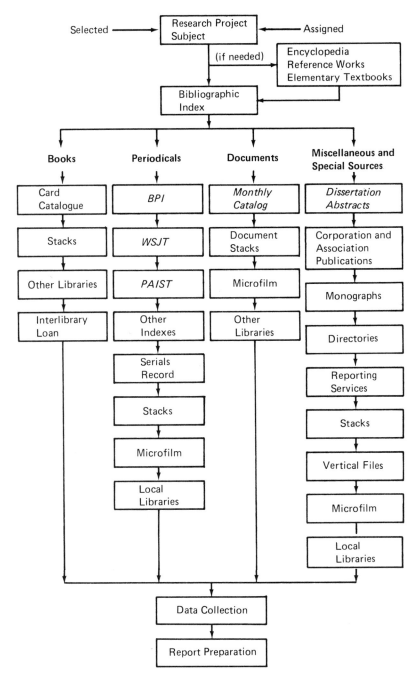

Figure 5•3
Library Search Flow Diagram

Adapted from C. William Emory, *Business Research Methods* (Homewood, Ill.: Richard D. Irwin, Inc., 1976), p. 183.

The library search procedure outlined in figure 5•3 indicates that the next step is to examine books, periodicals, government documents, and then other miscellaneous or special sources. When searching for books in a particular area, the researcher should begin by going to the card catalogue. Books will be referenced in a card catalogue under author, title, or subject. Often problems arise in looking for a particular topic in the subject catalogue. For example, if one looks under the subject heading "Marketing," there will be such an endless array of titles that it might prove more time-consuming than worthwhile.

A more fruitful source of material for most marketing research projects will be periodicals. In this case, the proper procedure is first to consult the appropriate indexes: the *Business Periodicals Index*, the *Wall Street Journal Index*, the *Public Affairs Information Service Index*, and the *Readers' Guide*. These indexes cross-reference hundreds of magazines and newspapers that may be utilized by marketing researchers.

Government documents, especially at the federal level, represent an excellent source of secondary data found in the library. The best place to begin in a search for the appropriate government document is the *Monthly Catalog*, a full citation to which reads: U.S., Superintendent of Documents, *United States Government Publications*: *Monthly Catalog* (Washington, D.C.: Government Printing Office, 1893–). The *Monthly Catalog* is a constantly updated comprehensive listing of public documents issued by all branches of the U.S. government. Figure 5•4 illustrates a sample page from this publication. Note that a complete description of each government document is given, including author name, title of the report, a brief discussion, length of the report, cost, and where the publication may be obtained.

Lastly, the researcher is directed to numerous miscellaneous and special sources. These include *Dissertation Abstracts*, various publications of corporations and trade associations, monographs, directories, and such reporting services as Standard and Poor's or Moody's.

If at this point the researcher is still unable to locate all the secondary information considered necessary, the reference librarian should be consulted and asked for additional suggestions. It may be that this information is on microfilm in the university library, or perhaps it is available in other local libraries. Especially in the case of books unavailable in the library, it may be necessary to use interlibrary loan services, whereby the needed publication may be borrowed by the library from another library.

Upon completion of the library search, the next task is to determine how much of the information collected can be used in prep-

AGRICULTURE DEPARTMENT
Washington, DC 20250

76-1434   A 1.2:An 5/4/973

United States. Dept. of Agriculture. Office of the Secretary.
Animal welfare enforcement 1973 : report of the Secretary of Agriculture to the President of the Senate and the Speaker of the House of Representatives. — [Washington] : U.S. Dept. of Agriculture, 1974.
ii, 30 p. : ill. ; 26 cm.
Cover title.
Item 10
pbk.
1. Animals, Treatment of — Law and legislation — United States. 2. Laboratory animals I. Title.
OCLC 1491919

76-1435   A 1.9:2148/6

Reid, William J.
Aphids on leafy vegetables : how to control them / [by W. J. Reid, Jr., and F. P. Cuthbert, Jr.] — [Rev. Feb. 1976] — [Washington] : U.S. Dept. of Agriculture, Agricultural Research Service : for sale by the Supt. of Docs., U.S. Govt. Print. Off., [1976]
14 p. : ill. ; 24 cm. — (Farmers' bulletin ; no. 2148)
Cover title.
Item 9
S/N 001-000-03478-1
pbk. : $0.35
1. Plant-lice — Control. 2. Insecticides. I. Cuthbert, Frank P., joint author. II. United States. Agricultural Research Service. III. Title. IV. Series: United States. Dept. of Agriculture. Farmers' Bulletin ; no. 2148.
S21.A6 rev. no. 2148 1969   72-604400
632/.7/52
OCLC 0084699

76-1437   A 1.9:2257

Soderholm, L. H.
Selecting and using electric motors / [by L. H. Soderholm and H. B. Puckett ; North Central Region, Agricultural Research Service] — [Washington] : U.S. Dept. of Agriculture : for sale by the Supt. of Docs., U.S. Govt. Print. Off., [1974]
56 p. : ill. ; 24 cm. — (Farmers' bulletin ; no. 2257)
Cover title.
"This publication supersedes Farmers' bulletin no. 2177, Single-phase electric motors for farm use."
Item 9
S/N 0100-03178
pbk. : $0.85
1. Electric motors. I. Puckett, H. B., joint author. II. United States. Dept. of Agriculture. III. Title. IV. Series: United States. Dept. of Agriculture. Farmers' bulletin ; no. 2257.
OCLC 2181164

76-1438   A 1.34:535/supp.

Jones, Mildred V.
Supplement for 1976 to statistics on cotton and related data, 1920-73 / [prepared in the Fibers Program, Commodity Economics Division, Economic Research Service, by Mildred V. Jones] — Washington : U.S. Dept. of Agriculture, Economic Research Service, Commodity Economics Division, Fibers Program, 1976.
viii, 93 p. ; 26 cm. — (Statistical bulletin ; no. 535)
Cover title.
Chiefly tables.
"This publication serves as a statistical handbook to the Cotton and Wool Situation."
Item 15
pbk.
1. Cotton — United States — Statistics. I. United States.

Figure 5·4
Sample Page from the *Monthly Catalog*

113

aration of the research report. As a general rule, only a very small proportion of the total amount of data collected in a library search will be incorporated directly into the report itself. This problem presents the researcher with one of the major tasks in report writing: synthesizing the mass of data into a useful and readable format. This process will be covered in some detail in Chapter 12, "The Research Report."

Evaluation of Secondary Data

At the beginning of this chapter we identified secondary data as data already existing in printed form. Since secondary data have been gathered for some project other than the one presently being considered, there are unique advantages and disadvantages associated with their use in lieu of primary data. Marketing researchers must be aware of the merits, as well as the demerits, of using secondary data sources, so that the best combination of secondary and primary can be incorporated in the research project.

Advantages

In comparing primary data and secondary data, three major advantages of secondary data emerge. First, secondary data can be gathered much more quickly than primary. For example, a library search of a few hours, if conducted properly, will often reveal information that would have taken the researcher months to collect using survey research to gather primary data.

A second advantage of secondary data is their relative low cost: most secondary data are available at little or no cost. Data found in libraries such as journal articles, may be secured at the cost of photocopying the required pages. Even in cases where secondary information is gathered by commercial firms and syndicated for a fee to subscribers, such as Nielsen's Retail Index, the cost is still appreciably lower than if the individual firm had gone out to collect the same primary information: all the subscribers help to bear the cost, thus reducing the expense for each firm.

A final reason dictating use of secondary data is that certain types of information may be available *only* from secondary data sources. That is, some types of information may be impractical or virtually impossible to gather through primary research, no matter how thoroughly conducted. One example is census information.

Disadvantages

When comparing secondary data with primary data we must recognize that secondary data have limitations. The two main problems associated with their use are: (1) the data may not be appropriate for the needs of the project, and (2) the data may not be accurate.[6]

By appropriateness, we mean the degree to which the data conform to the information requirements of the problem. Secondary data may not be appropriate in solving the particular research problem under consideration for various reasons. First, the information may be completely out of date. Often, it has been so long since the secondary data were originally gathered and published that they are no longer useful. An example is census data: though the *Census of Population* is conducted every ten years, 1970 *Census of Population* figures are not very meaningful in 1979 because of population increases and decreases in states, counties, and census tracts. Rapidly changing attitudes, values, and demographic characteristics of the population quickly make secondary data in marketing obsolete and no longer appropriate as a source of reliable information.

The second reason that secondary data may not be appropriate is a lack of standard classifications. Despite attempts to establish uniform classifications in market research by such groups as the American Marketing Association, there are still substantial variations in defining classes of, for example, demographic data. One research study may classify respondents in the age brackets 20–29, 30–39, 40–49, and so on, whereas another project breaks down consumer age groupings into the brackets 15–25, 26–35, 36–45, and so forth. It becomes difficult to compare meaningfully distinctions and similarities between responses or data gathered in the two studies.

Lastly, all too often there is a significant difference in units of measurement in secondary data. For example, there are many different measurements of consumer income reported in different projects. Is consumer income measured on the basis of median income, individual income, family income, reported income, or some other unit? Obviously, there are some differences among these units. To take another example, consider a retail store whose customers come from a certain trading area (the geographical territory from which the firm's customers are drawn). The firm's management, in attempting to make marketing decisions based upon available population statistics, may find these

[6] Donald S. Tull and Del I. Hawkins, *Marketing Research* (New York: Macmillan Co., 1976), p. 116.

data available only by census tract, city, county, or state — all units that will be of little use to the firm if they do not match the trading area from which customers are drawn.

The second major disadvantage often encountered in attempting to utilize secondary data is its lack of accuracy. Unfortunately, much secondary information suffers from this limitation. There is a particular problem, as indicated earlier in this chapter, when using secondary instead of original sources. Even in original sources, data may be inaccurate because of simple errors made by the researcher who collected and published the information. Worse still, data may have been made inaccurate by deliberate attempts to manipulate them to suit the needs of the original research project. Thus, the issue often becomes one of credibility. If one is attempting to assess the cost involved in producing and marketing prescription drugs, does one believe *Consumer Reports* or the Pharmaceutical Manufacturers Association (PHA)? Another example involves mileage of automobiles. Again, the question is which source, if either, is to be believed: claims made by Detroit automobile manufacturers based upon their research studies or claims by the Environmental Protection Agency based upon its research studies?

What all this means is that researchers must exercise caution in accepting the accuracy of secondary data. Professional researchers should always be skeptical when evaluating such data and should be looking for simple or deliberate errors in published reports. Researchers should always seek to ascertain the identity of the person or persons who published the information and to uncover possible motives for publishing it. It is also desirable to evaluate data for evidence of careful research, the method of data collection utilized, and the purpose of the research. The question that should always be asked is, "Why was this published?" Failure to be critical may compound original errors and extend them over time.

Summary

The subject of this chapter is secondary data — data that already exist in published form, having been previously gathered for some project other than the one presently under consideration. Primary data are original data gathered by the researcher for the project at hand. In no way do the terms "primary" and "secondary" infer any hierarchy of importance in the two types.

Some researchers have an unfortunate tendency to begin a data search with primary data. A cardinal rule to be followed in any marketing research study is always to begin by exhaustively searching through all relevant secondary data, before attempting to gather primary data. The reason for this procedure is that secondary data can be secured much more cheaply and quickly than primary data.

Secondary data may be gathered from either primary or secondary sources. A primary source is the source that originated the data, whereas a secondary source is a source that secured the data from the original publication. Primary sources are distinctly preferable for research use because they tend to be (1) more complete and (2) more accurate than secondary sources.

Useful secondary data can be found both internally and externally. Internal secondary data are located within the organization where the research is being conducted but have been gathered for some project other than the one at hand. Internal secondary data include (1) sales and accounting data and (2) internally generated research reports. The researcher should search internal secondary data thoroughly before going to external data.

External data are those outside the organization. They can be used as general references in maintaining contact with the outside environment and as an aid in solving specific problems. Four principal external sources for secondary data exist: (1) publications of government agencies, (2) syndicated commercial information, (3) trade and professional association publications, and (4) other miscellaneous published sources. The single most important source of secondary information is the U.S. federal government; within the government the most important source is the Bureau of the Census.

Virtually all sources of external secondary information mentioned in this chapter can be found in any good college or university library, though relatively few people know how to use library facilities. A library search flow diagram is presented in the chapter (fig. 5·3) to aid the student in using library facilities in preparation of research reports. One of the first things to do in the library in beginning a research project is to check the indexes, particularly the *Business Periodicals Index*, which gives references to all major business periodicals. The card catalogue provides a starting place in the search for appropriate books, and the U.S. government's *Monthly Catalog* provides references to government documents.

Secondary data have both strengths and weaknesses when compared with primary data. Advantages of secondary data are (1) speed, (2) economy, and (3) the difficulty or impossibility of obtaining the information through primary research. The disadvantages of secondary data are that (1) it may not be appropriate for the needs of the project and (2) it may not be accurate.

In conclusion, as Claire Selltiz et al. have written: "The positions for which social science students are likely to be preparing themselves — teaching, administration in government or business, community consultation, social work — increasingly call for the ability to evaluate and to use research results: to judge whether a study has been carried out in such a way that one can have reasonable confidence in its findings and whether its findings are applicable to the specific situation at hand." [7]

Questions for Discussion

1. A new brand of beer that will appeal mainly to women and upper-income consumers is being planned for introduction by a major brewer. Your client, the brewer, wants to estimate the sales potential for this new product. Your task is to identify at least five specific sources of external secondary information (not indexes) that could be consulted to estimate sales potential for the new beer.

2. Go to the library and, using census data, locate the most recent U.S. figures for total wholesale trade and percentage of total sales by type of wholesale operation. Specifically, you are to find out (a) the number of wholesale establishments and their most recent gross sales and (b) sales for (1) Merchant Wholesalers, (2) Manufacturers' Sales Branches and Offices, (3) Merchandise Agents and Brokers, (4) Petroleum Bulk Plants and Terminals, and (5) Assemblers of Farm Products.

3. Can you identify a research problem where *only* secondary information would be available? Explain why or why not.

4. What is the best single source for locating U.S. government documents? What information does it contain?

5. As a researcher, how might you overcome some of the limitations or disadvantages associated with using secondary data?

6. Go to the library and find the following: (a) the name of the chief marketing executive for Ford Motor Company, (b) the title of a recent doctoral dissertation in marketing, (c) the median number of years of school completed for male adults in New Orleans, Louisiana, and (d) the most recent total food retailing sales for the state of Nevada.

7. Explain the difference between primary sources and secondary sources of secondary information. Which is better? Why?

8. What are the factors you should be looking at when examining the reliability of secondary information?

[7] *Research Methods in Social Relations,* rev. ed. (New York: Holt, Rinehart and Winston, 1959), p. 6.

9. A local department store manager has asked you to use census data in estimating the average income of consumers living in the store's trading area. What problems might you encounter in following this suggestion?

10. What is the difference between internal secondary data and external secondary data? Which of the two would you examine first in a research project? Why?

Chapter 6

Primary Data

By now, it should be evident not only that information requirements of marketing managers are extremely complex but also that marketing researchers — to whom, regardless of the research design chosen for the project at hand, the task of gathering and assembling the necessary data will fall — must develop substantial expertise in securing required information. The need for expertise becomes especially obvious when one considers that information requirements and data-collection conditions will vary substantially from one problem to the next. For example, locating a retail site and determining probable consumer acceptance of a new soft drink will necessitate radically different research designs and types of data.

In the previous chapter it was noted that the proper way to begin the process of collecting needed marketing information is by a thorough review of secondary data. Many marketing research questions can be answered and problems solved merely by going to existing data sources. However, in other cases, the needed material may not be available, or what is found may prove inadequate. In cases where information requirements cannot be satisfied from secondary sources, the researcher must gather primary data.

What Are Primary Data?

Primary data are original data gathered by the reseacher expressly to solve the problem under consideration at that time. These data have not been previously collected or assembled for any other known project and therefore cannot have been already published in any form. In short, they are data that did not previously exist in any organized fashion.

Sources of Primary Data

Where can researchers go to collect primary data? The four major sources are: (1) the organization, (2) middlemen, (3) customers and potential customers, and (4) the competition.

The Organization

Although the organization provides a source for internal secondary data it also is an important source for primary data. For example, Procter and Gamble uses its own employees when testing new products and product concepts and reports that these employees are some of the most objective and critical evaluators the company has. Procter and Gamble employees are used to evaluate the performance of detergents, toothpaste, mouthwash, and even new deodorants.[1] Salespeople, as well as executives, often provide valuable input to decisions on marketing forecasting, especially in industrial goods firms, where salespeople have close contact with industrial customers and their needs.

Middlemen

Members of the manufacturer's channel of distribution are often very good sources of primary data. Wholesalers and retailers, because of their closeness to the market, are often much more knowledgeable about current market trends and customer preferences than is the manufacturer. For example, the major breweries have their wholesalers provide market information on sales to retailers; this procedure allows a firm like Schlitz or Anheuser-Busch to have a good record of the retail beer sales in any area of the country.

Customers and Potential Customers

Customers are the most important of the four major sources of primary data identified in this chapter. From the marketing concept of attempting to assess customer wants and needs it logically follows that market-

---

[1] Peter Vanderwicken, "P & G's Secret Ingredient," *Fortune,* July 1974, p. 79.

ing managers must be directly concerned with what consumers think of existing products and what they would like in new products. In their attempts to attract and hold customers, firms seek to secure information about consumer attitudes, knowledge, behavior, and purchase intentions. A firm like Schlitz might conduct a survey among potential customers (beer drinkers) in order to find out what their purchase intentions might be if Schlitz were to introduce a new brand of super premium beer to compete with Anheuser-Busch's Michelob. Information gathered from such a survey would be important, though it would not guarantee market success for the new Schlitz product.

The Competition

In a market with pure competition, competitors might be a very poor source of any kind of marketing information. However, most market competition in our economic system is not "pure"; in most markets, competitors are usually large enough to influence each other. Especially in industries dominated by a few large competitors, firms tend to exchange market information. The information most commonly available concerns pricing policies: it is not unusual to find competing firms exchanging information about prices and price policies, including planned price increases — although these practices, which may be viewed by the Federal Trade Commission as acting in restraint of competition, are best avoided. To expect a competitor to reveal much marketing information would, however, be unrealistic. Some friendly exchange of nonsensitive information may occur, but as a practical and ethical matter, competitors are not usually reliable sources of primary data.

Other, more devious, approaches hold attractions for some market rivals bent on securing market information from competitors by less-than-ethical means. Industrial espionage (the theft of trade secrets from competitors) is an illegal method of obtaining market information. The folly in this method of securing primary data from competitors was well demonstrated by the Watergate misadventure.

Types of Primary Data

A question common to marketing researchers attempting to secure primary data from respondents is *what types* of primary data may generally be obtained. For instance, if a firm such as McDonald's, the international hamburger chain, wanted to conduct a marketing research study in order to gain better in-depth analysis of customers and their buying habits, what types of primary data would be wanted? The firm might be interested in getting a detailed profile of the average customer in a McDonald's retail outlet, or it might want information concerning *why* people come to McDonald's instead of Burger Chef or Dairy Queen. In the first instance, the needed information could be secured from brief questionnaires filled out on location by the respondents; in the second case, a complete and accurate answer to the question "why" would be likely to involve personal interviews and quite possibly the usage of motivation research techniques, such as in-depth interviewing. The needs of each particular data-collection survey will dictate the types of primary data the researcher will collect.

Though specific primary data requirements will vary substantially with almost every survey conducted, certain general types of primary information are widely available and may be wanted in almost any major survey. Four main types of primary data may be secured from respondents: (1) purchase intentions, (2) attitudes and opinions, (3) activities or behavior, and (4) demographic characteristics.

Purchasing Intentions

Marketing managers are keenly interested in measuring consumers' purchase intentions. A specific research survey might be commissioned, for example, in order to find out what consumer purchasing intentions would be toward a new type of dog food, in which case potential customers would be asked if they would be willing to buy this product. A broader type of survey of purchasing intentions is conducted by the Survey Research Center at the University of Michigan.[2] Consumers are asked about their purchasing intentions for such consumer durables as automobiles, major appliances, and even housing. The Survey Research Center then reports four responses: (1) a definite intention to buy, (2) a probable intention to buy, (3) undecided, and (4) a definite intention not to buy. This type of data not only indicates consumer willingness to purchase big-ticket items but also is regarded as a general measure of consumer confidence in the economy and as a key variable in forecasting future economic up- or downturns.

A word of caution against overreliance on surveys of consumer purchasing intentions should be included at this point. It is true that

[2] Gilbert A. Churchill, *Marketing Research: Methodological Foundations* (Hinsdale, Ill.: Dryden Press, 1976), p. 161.

a great deal of time and effort is expended in marketing research in attempting to determine what probable purchasing behavior will be. However, no matter how scientifically obtained, survey results must be treated with a measure of caution. There is *no* guarantee that purchase intentions will be translated into purchase actions. In other words, a consumer reporting a definite intention to purchase a new automobile when the new models come out could change this intention for any number of reasons: changes in general economic conditions (a rise in interest rates, for example), the consumer's own economic conditions (such as the loss of a job), or some change in buyer preferences (perhaps the decision to buy a camper trailer instead of a new car).

Attitudes and Opinions

Marketing managers want to know the level of consumer awareness of the firm and its products and the attitudes or opinions held about them. Attitude-research issues and measurement techniques are more fully discussed in subsequent chapters of this text. At this point it is important to note that a firm will often conduct studies of such issues as brand awareness and corporate image, not only to learn what consumers think about the firm and its products, but also to locate any need for a campaign to change consumer attitudes and opinions. Recent studies revealed that most consumers had a totally unrealistic conception of oil company profits, thinking profits were much higher than they really were. In an attempt to change this misconception, petroleum companies undertook a massive advertising and public relations campaign directed at improving industry image and consumer perception of petroleum industry profit margins.

Activities or Behavior

Many primary data-gathering studies are concerned with finding out what consumers are doing. That is, how long do you, the average shopper, spend in the retail supermarket? Who usually does the family grocery shopping? How often does your family take holidays? How much do you usually spend for an evening's entertainment? What brand of beer do you drink? All of these are examples of the types of primary data that may be gathered about consumer activities; they concern the "who," "what," "when," and "where" of consumer behavior. Research into consumer motivation is conducted to answer the "why" aspect of buyer behavior and will be examined in more detail in Chapter 13.

Demographic Characteristics

The types of primary data discussed thus far provide the researcher with good information concerning consumer intentions to purchase a particular product and consumer attitudes toward the product or the firm, and perhaps also with a good indication of overall shopping activities or habits. But the picture obtained so far would not identify, for example, the age category of consumers most likely to shop in the early morning as opposed to the evening, or the consumers most likely to purchase a Cadillac Seville. This is why almost every major primary data-gathering survey of consumers includes a section gathering demographic data about the respondents.

Demographic characteristics include the respondent's educational level, income, ethnic group, age, sex, occupation, marital status, and other related variables. These types of primary data are gathered for purposes of cross-classification, so that marketers can determine, for example, the profile of the consumer most likely to read *Playboy* or *Sports Illustrated*. If major television network research finds that the average viewer from 1:00 to 3:00 o'clock in the afternoon is a middle-aged housewife with limited education, then the research will suggest developing programs to appeal to this individual's interests; the outcome is the television soap opera, a successful product developed for a specific market segment.

Primary data gathered in this fashion can be used in segmenting consumer markets. Table 6·1 illustrates the major demographic segmentation variables used by researchers. Regarding the use of demographic variables in market segmentation, Philip Kotler has written:

> In demographic segmentation, the market is subdivided into different parts on the basis of demographic variables such as age, sex, family size, income, occupation, education, family life cycle, religion, nationality, or social class. Demographic variables have long been the most popular bases for distinguishing significant groupings in the marketplace. One reason is that consumer wants or usage rates are often highly associated with demographic variables; another is that demographic variables are easier to measure than most other types of variables.[3]

[3] *Marketing Management: Analysis, Planning and Control*, 3rd ed. (Englewood Cliffs, N.J.: Prentice-Hall, 1976), p. 145.

Table 6·1
Demographic Segmentation Variables

Variable	Categories
Age	Adults: 18–34, 35–49, 50–64, 65+
Sex	Male, female
Income	Under $5,000, $5,000–$7,999, $8,000–$9,999, $10,000–$14,999, $15,000–$19,999, $20,000+
Family size	1–2, 3–4, 5+
Education	Grade school or less, some high school, high school graduate, some college, college graduate
Occupation	Professional and white collar, including managers, officials, proprietors, clerical personnel, salespeople; technical and blue collar, including foremen, operators, maintenance people; retired persons; farmers; students; housewives; unemployed
Social class	Lower-lower, upper-lower, lower-middle, middle-middle, upper-middle, lower-upper, upper-upper
Religion	Catholic, Protestant, Jewish, other, none
Race	Black, White, Oriental
Nationality	American, British, French, German, Eastern European, Scandinavian, Italian, Latin American, Middle-Eastern, Japanese

Source: Adapted from Philip Kotler, *Marketing Management: Analysis, Planning, and Control*, 3rd ed. (Englewood Cliffs, N.J.: Prentice-Hall, 1976) p. 146.

The use of demographics in market segmentation confronts researchers with certain risks. Often psychological variables are more important in influencing consumer purchases than are actual demographic variables. Consider the following:

A seller must be careful in his use of demographics because their influence on consumer product interest does not always operate in the expected direction. For example, Ford Motor Company utilized buyers' age in developing its target market for its Mustang automobile; the car was designed to appeal to young people who wanted an inexpensive sporty automobile. Ford found, to its surprise, that the car was being purchased by all age groups. It then realized that its target market was not the chronologically young but those who were psychologically young.[4]

Nor is income altogether reliable as a predictor of buyer behavior, though in many instances it is considered an acceptable indicator of *ability*, if not willingness, to buy. "Income is another demographic variable that can be deceptive. One would think that working-class families would buy Chevrolets and managerial-class families would buy Cadillacs. Yet many Chevrolets are bought by middle-income people (often as a second car), and some Cadillacs are bought by working-class families (such as high-paid plumbers and carpenters)." [5]

After this introduction to the sources and types of primary data, we are now ready to examine the basic methods used in gathering these data.

The Basic Methods of Gathering Primary Data

Three basic primary data-gathering methods exist: (1) experimentation, (2) surveys, and (3) observation. These three methods are *not* mutually exclusive; research design could allow for a project to incorporate two methods, or all three. Since experimentation was covered in Chapter 4, our discussion of experimental primary data-gathering methods will be limited to a brief recapitulation of their main features.

The Experimental Method

The experimental method is comparatively new to the marketing field and is extremely difficult to apply. Briefly, it is a tightly controlled method, where the researcher holds all variables constant while systematically manipulating one. In a crude sense, this manipulation might involve experimenting with the advertising budget, while attempting to keep all other factors of the marketing mix constant. Philip Kotler provides a brief summary:

> The experimental method consists of introducing selected stimuli into a controlled environment and systematically varying them. To the extent that extraneous factors are eliminated or controlled, the observed effects can be related to the variations in the stimuli. The purpose of control is to eliminate competing hypotheses that might also explain the observed phenomena. Marketers have applied this data collection method to such marketing problems as finding the best

4 Kotler, *Marketing Management*, pp. 145–47.
5 Kotler, *Marketing Management*, p. 147.

sales-training method, the best incentive scheme, the best price level and the best ad campaign.[6]

The remainder of this chapter is focused on an examination of the two principal methods of collecting primary data: surveys and observation. Not all aspects of these two methods are covered in this chapter; more details will be included later.

The Survey Method

The marketing manager of a large motel chain, such as Holiday Inn, wants to know what features of that motel chain guests find most attractive. A manufacturer of stereo equipment wants to know if customers would buy a more expensive model were it added to the product line. The manager of a large department chain would like to know whether extending operating hours into the evening would efficiently accommodate customers who have to work during the day. Although partial answers to these questions may be obtained from secondary data, the best way to secure answers is through survey research.

Survey research is the systematic gathering of data from respondents through questionnaires. The purpose of survey research is to facilitate understanding or enable prediction of some aspect of behavior of the population being surveyed.

A *questionnaire* is a formal list of questions to be answered in the survey. Questionnaires may be administered by mail, telephone, or personal interview.

Involved in survey research are questionnaire construction, survey administration, sampling, and data analysis — topics covered in the next four chapters. Telephone or face-to-face contacts enable respondents to complete the questionnaire with the aid or assistance of an interviewer. Survey research may take place without any personal contact between researcher and respondents by the use of a mail questionnaire.

SURVEY TECHNIQUES

Once the investigator has decided to use the survey approach in securing primary data from respondents, the next question to be answered is which method of communication will be used in the resulting interview. Will the personal interview, the telephone interview, or the mail questionnaire be most appropriate for the survey?

[6] *Marketing Management*, pp. 429–30.

Unfortunately, no clear-cut answer to this question exists; if any one method were always the best, all researchers would undoubtedly be using that one alone, and not all three.

When collecting information from respondents, marketing researchers strive to utilize methods that will secure accurate information in the shortest period of time with the least cost. The ideal survey would be characterized by flexibility — allowing the maximum amount of data to be gathered; providing accuracy, control, a high response rate, and speed; and requiring a minimum amount of supervision and cost. All of these characteristics, however, do not apply to any one single method of communication. Each method is appropriate some of the time, depending upon the nature of the survey and the requirements of the investigator. Before discussing the relative strengths and weaknesses of each of these methods, let us briefly describe them.

Personal Interview. In the personal interview, the investigator asks questions of the respondents in a face-to-face meeting. Personal interviews may be conducted on a door-to-door basis or in public places, such as shopping centers. The usual approach is for the interviewer to identify herself to a potential respondent and attempt to secure the respondent's cooperation in answering a list of predetermined questions. These answers may be tape-recorded or written down by the interviewer.

Telephone Survey. In a telephone survey, prospective respondents are telephoned, usually at home, and asked to answer a series of questions over the telephone. This form of survey communication has become more popular in recent years, as home telephone ownership has become almost universal and costs of personal interviewing have rapidly escalated.

Mail Survey. The usual procedure followed in mail surveys is to mail to each potential respondent a questionnaire, complete with instructions and a self-addressed stamped envelope. No personal interaction occurs between respondent and interviewer. Respondents fill out mail questionnaires and return them at their convenience. Sometimes mail questionnaires are distributed to respondents by personal delivery or newspaper and magazine inserts, but in most instances the entire process relies upon the mail system.

DETERMINING WHICH SURVEY METHOD TO USE

What are the criteria that may be used in judging which of these methods of communication will be most effective for the research problem at hand? There are seven specific factors that should be examined before a decision is made: (1) cost, (2) speed, (3) accuracy, (4) amount of data desired, (5) response rate, (6) flexibility, and (7) control. It should be noted that these factors do not constitute a completely exhaustive list of all criteria that may be used in selecting a proper survey method, nor are they mutually exclusive. Recognize, too, that there may be cases where specific conditions of the research project under consideration provide an exception to the general rules.

Cost. Cost is a major consideration in any research undertaking and is usually the most important reason why telephone or mail interviews are used instead of the personal interview. Costs will vary, depending upon the necessary response rate, the length of the questionnaire, the quality and quantity of information desired, and the location of the interviews. Still, the personal or face-to-face interview is nearly always much more expensive than the other two methods. If the questionnaire is administered on a door-to-door basis, then cost considerations include the total time of the interviewer, the amount of time devoted to each completed interview, and transportation expenses. Rapidly escalating postal rates have driven up the cost of the mail questionnaire substantially, but this form of communication still remains the least expensive where a large sample on a national basis is required.

Speed. The speediest method of communication, as defined here, is the one that allows the survey to be completed in the shortest period of time. The telephone interview is generally considered the fastest method of completing a survey. Typically, professional telephone surveys are conducted by dividing a room into cubicles, each equipped with a telephone that can be monitored by a supervisor sitting in a central control room. In each cubicle a telephone interviewer sits and calls the numbers on a given list. The ensuing interview seldom takes over ten minutes, as it is difficult to retain respondent interest longer. A supervisor manning the central control board can listen in on any conversation to verify that the interview is indeed taking place. Conducted in this manner, a complete telephone survey may take only two days. A typical mail or personal interview survey may easily take two weeks or longer to complete. Interviews conducted on a door-to-door basis are usually considered the slowest of the three methods. The mail interview occupies an intermediate position in speed, although in recent years U.S. mail efficiency and speed have been questioned.

Accuracy. Accuracy refers to freedom from mistakes in the data. Inaccurate information may be the fault of either the interviewer or the respondent, or both. Inaccuracies result from simple errors in misinterpreting questions and from deliberate attempts by respondents to provide incorrect replies. The accuracy of the information obtained is also a function of the interviewer: inaccuracies may result from interviewer bias, cheating, or misinterpretation of responses.

Inaccurate responses from consumers may stem from unwillingness to provide information, inability to remember answers to questions asked, or misinterpretation of the questions. The anonymous nature of the mail questionnaire makes this survey method best for information of a sensitive nature, such as questions about usage of deodorants, drinking habits, and use of credit. Note the differences in answers to the same questions from personal interviews and mail questionnaires in table 6·2. Inaccuracies caused by a respondent's misunderstanding or misinterpreting a question can best be minimized by personal interview. In this case, interviewers can explain questions, provide additional interpretation, and can make certain that respondents do indeed understand what is wanted. The mail questionnaire has proved the least effective method of securing accurate responses, since there is no interaction between interviewer and respondent.

The interviewer may also be responsible for inaccurate data in survey research. Interviewer bias, which occurs when the interviewer consciously or unconsciously distorts or otherwise influences responses to questions, is a major source of inaccuracy in survey data. Poorly trained or motivated interviewers may make errors in asking questions or in interpreting or recording responses, or they may deliberately falsify interview results, a process called "cheating." A simple variation in tone of voice in asking certain questions among certain respondents

Table 6·2
Responses to the Same Questions via Personal Interview and Mail Panel

Question	Personal Interview % Yes	Mail Panel % Yes
Have you ever used a hair rinse?	37	51
Have you ever used eye shadow?	46	59
Have you ever purchased margarine?	75	82
Has anyone in your family ever borrowed money from a regular bank?	17	42
Has anyone in your family ever borrowed money from a credit union?	16	22
Has anyone in your family ever borrowed money from a small loan company?	11	13

Source: William F. O'Dell, "Personal Interviews or Mail Panels," *Journal of Marketing* 26 (October 1962): 36.

will produce different answers. This problem, as well as ways to overcome it, will be covered in greater detail in Chapter 8, "Survey Administration." Since there is no direct interviewer-interviewee interaction, the mail questionnaire does reduce problems associated with poorly trained or unmotivated interviewers. The personal interview has the greatest likelihood of interviewer error, a factor that necessitates careful selection and training of and control over interviewers in field operations.

Amount of Data Gathered. Which of the survey approaches is capable of collecting the most information from respondents? Although there are long mail questionnaires and short personal interviews, the personal interview usually elicits the greatest amount of respondent data. Whereas the respondents' commitment to complete a mail questionnaire or telephone interview is limited, respondents usually feel obligated to answer all the questions in a personal interview because of the presence of the interviewer. The face-to-face nature of the personal interview permits at-home interviews of forty-five minutes in many instances, and interviews of an hour are not at all unknown.

The telephone is not a good approach if lengthy interviews are required. The telephone interview competes with other interviewee home activities, making it difficult to hold an interview longer than five minutes. Each question in a telephone interview must be read to the respondent and then often reread or explained. Therefore, the very process of asking questions consumes an enormous part of the telephone interview, leaving relatively little time for responses; this approach is best used, accordingly, only when limited amounts of information are required.

Response Rate. Response rate refers to the percentage of planned interviews that are successfully completed. In other words, it is sample size divided by completed interviews. Nonresponse is derived from two basic factors: refusals and not-at-homes.

Survey response rates can vary tremendously, from nearly 0 to almost 100 percent. Characteristics of the population from which the sample was drawn, interviewer skill, and respondents' interest in the subject, as well as the survey instrument used, are all factors affecting response rate. Response rate is also influenced by increased public concern over privacy and security, the increasing participation in the labor force by married women, and the gradual shift to housing patterns (such as high-rise apartments) that discourage door-to-door interviewing.

Which survey method yields the highest response rate? The answer to this question is not an easy one, as marketing research literature yields conflicting answers, and most marketing research textbooks neatly avoid even attempting to give an answer. The issue is complex in that there are differing types of telephone surveys, mail questionnaires, and personal interviews, which, in turn, yield different response rates.

Still, it appears that the highest response rates can be achieved through personal interviews using ongoing panels as interviewees. Even though some mail questionnaires have had extremely high response rates, the fact remains that "the major disadvantage of mail surveys are generally believed to be their low response rates." [7] In general, response rates from mail surveys are the lowest of our three methods, mainly because call-backs can be made with personal and telephone interviews.

Flexibility. Of the three methods, the personal interview is the most easily adjusted to changing conditions. Skilled interviewers can rephrase questions when necessary to ensure that respondents understand. The length of the personal interview may be varied at the discretion of interviewer. Also, the personal interview allows the interviewer to use both sight and hearing, whereas the telephone and the mail survey permit only one sense. The rigid nature of fixed written questions renders a mail interview the least flexible approach.

Control. There are three aspects of control useful in evaluating these three methods of communication. The first, *sample control,* or sample validity, refers to control over sample membership — the degree to which the sample reflects the universe. Although nearly all households have telephones, an increasing percentage have unlisted telephone numbers, especially single women. Lower-income families are also underrepresented among telephone owners, as many cannot afford the monthly charges. Since everyone has a mail box, mail surveys are considered the best source of sample control. However, one caution should be exercised: an incomplete or out-of-date mailing list will severely hamper the effectiveness of a mail questionnaire. Thus, a good mailing list is a prerequisite for sample control.

The second aspect of control is *interview control,* or the researcher's degree of control over the interview taking place. The absence of personal contact causes the mail questionnaire to be subject to the least amount of interview control; the personal interview is characterized by the greatest amount of interview control. Interview control is important because it assures the researcher that the respondent is responding accurately to the questions asked. The face-to-face interview

[7] Leslie Kanuk and Conrad Berenson, "Mail Surveys and Response Rates: A Literature Review," *Journal of Marketing Research* 12 (November 1975): 440–53.

allows the interviewer to explain questions, making sure that respondents understand them, and to determine if flagrantly inaccurate replies are being given. For example, if a respondent in a tar-paper shack claimed an income of over $30,000 a year, the interviewer might be suspicious, but the claim might go unquestioned with a mail questionnaire. Another reason why the interviewer has the least control over mail questionnaires is that the person who filled out the questionnaire may not have been the one for whom the questionnaire was intended. For example, a questionnaire sent to the head of the household might conceivably be filled out by the head of the household's eleven-year-old son, with inaccurate or misleading data as the result.

The third aspect of control, *administrative control*, refers to the degree of control of the research manager over the interviewer. The least amount of administrative control is provided with the personal interview conducted in the field. The research manager often does not know whether the interviews were conducted properly or, in some cases, conducted at all. Good administrative control may be maintained over telephone interviewing, but the best is over the mail questionnaire; this survey form eliminates the middleman, the nonprofessional interviewer, between research professional and respondent. The research manager knows that the mail questionnaire has definitely been sent out; he also knows that the questions have been asked in a uniform and consistent manner, something that is not possible when questions are being asked orally by various people.

Choosing the Right Survey Method. Which of these three survey methods, then, is the best one to use? The answer to this question depends simply upon the needs of the particular research project at hand. The requirements and constraints placed upon the research will dictate which method will be chosen. The selection can be made only after careful evaluation of the strengths and weaknesses of each of these techniques in each of the seven categories just discussed; see table 6·3 for a summary. Recognize that no one technique is always superior and that the criteria or goals may conflict.

The Observation Method

Often the information requirements of the research project are such that survey data, questions, are not satisfactory. In other cases, even though the survey method is used, it may be supplemented by observation techniques. *Observation* is a method of gathering primary data by

Table 6.3
Determining Which Survey Technique to Use

	TECHNIQUE		
CRITERIA	PERSONAL INTERVIEW	TELEPHONE SURVEY	MAIL SURVEY
Cost [a]	Most expensive	Intermediate	Least expensive
Speed	Slowest	Fastest	Intermediate
Accuracy	Most accurate	Intermediate	Least accurate
Amount of data generated	Most	Least	Intermediate
Response rate	Highest	Intermediate	Lowest
Flexibility	Most flexible	Intermediate	Least flexible
Control			
Sample control [b]	Intermediate	Worst	Best
Interview control	Best	Intermediate	Worst
Administrative control	Worst	Intermediate	Best

[a] Where the sample is scattered on a nationwide basis.
[b] Assumes an accurate mailing list.

physically or mechanically recording some designated aspect of consumer behavior.

In some instances, observation may be the only way in which research information can be collected. In one research study where the problem was to analyze information content in television advertising, the researchers were obliged to rely solely upon observation.[8] A sample of 378 commercials, randomly selected from all times during the week on the ABC, CBS, and NBC networks, was color-videotaped and then later played back, so that each advertisement's content could be carefully reviewed. This mechanical observation approach, videotaping, permitted the researchers to evaluate the informational content of the commercials carefully and accurately, something that would not have been possible using any other method.

Observation may at times be the most practical method for gathering needed market information. Traffic counts are commonly employed in the site-location process for fast food retailers. In this process traffic patterns are recorded visually or mechanically, as in the case of the automobile counter used on highways to count the number of cars passing a certain location.

[8] Alan Resnick and Bruce L. Stern, "An Analysis of Information Content in Television Advertising," *Journal of Marketing*, 41 (January 1977): 50–54.

OBSERVATION VERSUS SURVEY

The two most basic ways in which primary data can be collected are *questioning* and *observing*. These two approaches lend themselves to two basic methods of collecting data: the survey method and the observation method. The method of observation has both advantages and limitations.

First among the advantages, the need for respondent cooperation can be eliminated. Subjects need not, as with the survey approach, be asked to reply to oral or written questions. Consequently, refusals, not-at-homes, and incorrect responses from consumers are all avoided. Observation is used instead of questioning quite commonly when suburban shopping center or supermarket owners want to measure the trading area, the geographical territory from which customers are drawn. This measurement can be made easily by observing and recording license plate numbers of automobiles in the parking lot. State automobile registration data permit researchers to secure quickly the desired information, consumer home addresses, from which they can determine the distances shoppers have traveled. Subjects are unaware that a research study has been conducted, and there is no need to ask for their cooperation.

The second advantage is that the observation method is more objective; it avoids interviewer-interviewee bias, thus permitting more accurate information collection. Also, questioning is impractical if we wish to study the behavior of infants, companies, or animals. In the previously discussed case in which the information content in television advertising was analyzed, researchers could have conducted a survey of television viewers' attitudes toward the subject, but it was thought that more objective results could be obtained by observation.

Consumer unwillingness to divulge purchases of "off brand" or nonprestige items makes questioning an unreliable approach to collecting objective information on private brand merchandise and cut-rate gasoline. In fact, one research study in which automobile license numbers had been recorded at an independent gasoline service station revealed a reluctance by owners of prestige cars — Cadillacs and Lincolns — to admit purchasing such gasoline.

At least two limitations emerge in an evaluation of the observation method. First, the method is limited to measuring overt behavior or external factors. It cannot measure motives or such internal factors as attitudes, beliefs, and values. Therefore, this method misses one of the most important aspects of consumer action — the "why" of human behavior. By observing consumers in a supermarket check-out line, the researcher is able to determine *what* consumers bought, but it is impossible to determine *why* these items were purchased.

The second limitation of the observation method is that subjects cannot be observed or otherwise measured at all times. While the trained observer can faithfully record what is purchased in the supermarket, it is impossible to observe when and how the items are consumed in homes. Or, to present another instance, it could be observed that women over fifty years of age are much more likely to purchase cold cream than women under age thirty; however, usage patterns or application techniques cannot be observed: no researcher is likely to be permitted into private bedrooms or bathrooms.

OBSERVATIONAL METHODS

There are three major methods of observation: (1) direct, (2) contrived, and (3) mechanical. Each of these is discussed separately.

Direct Observation. The most frequently employed method is direct observation, in which respondents' actions are observed and recorded by a trained observer. Direct observation takes place in a real, not contrived or artifically created, setting, and no mechanical recording devices are used. It is a method of data collection especially useful in cases where survey techniques might yield inaccurate responses. For example, a manufacturer of milk cartons might want to know if shoppers would actually use labeling information, such as unit pricing or open code dating, before purchasing the product. By asking shoppers whether they would actually use such a service, the researcher is posing a motherhood-type question: few, if any, respondents would admit purchasing a product without utilizing all the information available. By stationing a trained observer in the local supermarket near the milk counter, however, the researcher is able to record by observation how many subjects actually read the labeling information before selecting the product for purchase.

This example illustrates two problems associated with using direct observation. First, misinterpretation of respondent actions is a problem. The researcher is unable to determine for certain if the consumer actually reads the labeling information. That is, though the subject may be observed looking at the label, there is no guarantee that the labeling information is being read. Second, direct observation may result in wasted time. It may be an inefficient method of observation, because the researcher may waste a great deal of time waiting until the next shopper comes along. This second limitation is among the major reasons for use of contrived observation.

Contrived Observation. Contrived observation involves the creation of an artificial situation in order to allow more efficient and effective observation of the action being measured. In some cases it may become necessary to create a situation artificially in order to reduce the lengthy waiting time asosciated with direct observation. In other cases, contrived observation may be necessary because direct observation is impractical or impossible. Consider the following example. The manager of a large department store has received reports that sales personnel have been ignoring poorly dressed prospective customers. Directly observing or questioning sales clerks would be impractical. Therefore, both shabbily dressed and well-dressed researchers, posing as customers, are sent in to record salespeople's reactions. In this manner, measurements can be quickly and accurately obtained, thus answering the research question, although not solving the problem. Many companies commonly use contrived observation to measure employee courtesy by having trained interviewers, pretending to be customers, confront sales personnel with complaints or difficult questions.

Mechanical Observation. In some cases, personal observation, whether direct or contrived, may not be the best method. It may be found that mechanical devices, such as cameras or other recording instruments, can be used with greater efficiency and precision than can personal observers. Data secured in this fashion are generally considered more objective than data obtained using personal observation. Four mechanical devices are described here.

1. *The Audimeter.* Created by the A. C. Nielsen Company, the Audimeter is the famous black box attached to the television set for Nielsen's television index. This device, made famous by the Nielsen Ratings, records when the family television set is on and to what channel and program the set is tuned. Unfortunately, the Audimeter does not record who, if anyone, is watching the set during programs or commercial breaks. The Audimeter is discussed in greater detail in Chapter 15, "Advertising Research."

2. *The Perceptoscope.* The perceptoscope is a camera used in advertising research in a laboratory setting. It measures pupil dilation. The use of this instrument is based on the premise that pupil dilation is an indication of interest and may help in evaluating advertising copy — the more the consumer's pupil dilates, the greater the interest. Presumably, such an instrument would be most interesting in evaluating respondents' reactions in reading the latest edition of *Playboy* or *Playgirl* magazine.

3. *The Eye Camera.* This instrument, first developed in 1890, was not actually utilized in a research situation until almost fifty years later, when *Look Magazine* made a practical application of it in 1938. The eye camera measures movement of the eye and is considered useful in measuring which parts of advertising copy are most attractive or appealing to readers.

4. *The Psychogalvanometer.* This device measures galvanic skin responses and perspiration in determining emotional reactions of respondents exposed to products or product concepts. Researchers then ascertain whether respondents react emotionally to various advertisements or brands. Unfortunately, the device provides little other information to researchers.

It should be noted that of the four mechanical methods, none is without a substantial body of critics. The perceptoscope, the eye camera, and the psychogalvanometer are instruments sometimes used in advertising research in a laboratory setting. Their practical value is questioned by many researchers, but, primarily because of the inexact and uncertain nature of advertising research, they continue to be used.

Regarding pupil size and eye direction, Albert S. King has written:

> Enlarged pupil size is indicative of favorable attitudes towards others and covertly influences consumers' interests and attitudes toward the communicator.
>
> Message communication appears to be influenced by the direction of the eyes, and whether their angle is consistent with the appeal of the message and the receiver's attitude toward the message.
>
> When eye direction is to the right, rational and objective thoughts are reinforced; eyes directed toward the left reinforce emotional and subjective expressions.
>
> How an advertiser treats eye size and eye direction in his advertisements may enhance the effectiveness of the advertising appeal.[9]

Since it cannot measure whether a television program or commercial is actually being viewed, or by whom, the Audimeter is also subject to criticism.

In general, then, mechanical observation devices are inferior to personal observation, though there are specific situations where they may be appropriately used.

[9] "Pupil Size, Eye Direction, and Message Appeal: Some Preliminary Findings," *Journal of Marketing* 36 (July 1972): 57.

Evaluation of Primary Data

Nearly all professional marketing research reports contain both primary and secondary data. Although the two types of data are of equal importance, researchers should always first go to secondary data.

Because primary data are generated by original research to answer specific questions that cannot be answered by secondary data, primary data have two advantages: (1) they are specific, and (2) they are relevant. *Specificity* means that the information is collected specifically for the project at hand; data tailored to the particular problem under consideration are more desirable. *Relevance* refers to the data's appropriateness for the problem under consideration. Primary data are more relevant than secondary because they are more up-to-date; primary data are also more likely to provide specific solutions to the research problem.

The two principal limitations of primary data are (1) *cost* and (2) *time* requirements. Regardless of which method is used to collect primary data, first-hand information is almost always expensive. No matter how desirable primary data may be, if the firm's research budget will not allow for this expense, then it cannot be undertaken. Since many marketing decisions must be made extremely quickly, collecting primary data may not be possible. The length of time required to collect, tabulate, code, and analyze firsthand information may make it impractical to obtain such data if the firm is to keep ahead of competitors.

Summary

Basically, there are two types of information used by market researchers: (1) primary data and (2) secondary data. Secondary data, the subject of the previous chapter, are data that already exist, having been previously collected for some purpose other than the one under consideration. Primary data are original data collected or developed by the researcher. Typically, the solution to a given research problem will call for both primary and secondary data. Primary data should be collected only after secondary data sources have been thoroughly researched.

Four major sources of primary data exist: (1) the organization, (2) middlemen, (3) customers and prospective customers, and (4) competitors. Of these four sources, customers and potential customers represent the most important source of information. Four major types of primary data can be obtained from consumers: (1) purchase intentions, (2) attitudes and opinions, (3) activities or behavior, and (4) demographic characteristics. Demographic characteristics provide a rich source of information useful in marketing segmentation.

Observation, experimentation, and surveys constitute the three basic methods of gathering primary data. The survey method is the most common of these three. Three survey techniques exist: personal interview, telephone survey, and mail survey. Before attempting to decide which of the three should be used, the researcher should consider the following factors: cost, speed, accuracy, amount of data desired, response rate, flexibility, and control. Observation techniques include direct observation, contrived observation, and mechanical observation, of which direct observation is by far the most popular. Many of the methods used in mechanical observation, such as the eye camera and the perceptoscope, are useful primarily in a laboratory setting and have limited practical applicability.

Researchers much carefully evaluate both the strengths and weaknesses associated with using primary data. The two principal strengths are specificity and relevance, and the major limitations are cost and time requirements.

Questions for Discussion

1. In your own words, distinguish between primary and secondary data. Give an example of a research problem that could be solved by using both primary and secondary data.

2. There are at least two major reasons for not using competitors as a source of primary information. What are they?

3. Four main types of primary data can be secured from respondents. Design a research project that requires all four types.

4. Design the part of a mail questionnaire that will secure the necessary demographic information from consumers for a manufacturer planning to introduce a new organic cereal priced above the market.

5. What is the problem associated with using conventional demographic variables as a basis for segmenting consumer markets?

6. Compare the relative efficiency of the survey and the observational methods in: (a) cost, (b) accuracy, (c) time requirements.

7. Design three simple research problems, each of which could be best solved by a different one of the three types of survey: personal interview, telephone questionnaire, and mail questionnaire.

8. Assuming time and cost considerations were of relatively minor importance, which type of survey would you recommend? Why?

9. Which method of communication is best if the primary consideration in the survey is control? Be sure to cover all aspects of control.

10. Some people assert that contrived observation is an unethical practice. Do you agree or disagree with that statement? Why or why not?

Chapter 7

Questionnaire Construction

THE PREVIOUS CHAPTER pointed out the two principal ways of gathering primary data: observing and questioning. Methods of observation have already been discussed; here, we turn to the questionnaire. A *questionnaire* is a formal list of questions designed to gather responses from consumers on a given topic. Questionnaires are the major instrument used in obtaining primary data from respondents through the survey approach. As previously stated, a questionnaire can be designed to secure any or all of four types of primary data from consumers: (1) purchase intentions, (2) attitudes and opinions, (3) activities or behavior, and (4) demographic characteristics.

How often have you been exposed to questionnaires? Probably you have seen many more than you realize. You may be thinking only of mail questionnaires, which might include such questions as your income or what kind of toothpaste you use. Have you ever been stopped by an interviewer in a shopping center and asked to answer a few questions? If so, then you participated in completing a questionnaire. Have you been called on the telephone by someone saying he was doing "marketing research" and asked to answer a few questions? If so, whether it was legitimate marketing research or a sales promotion effort, you participated in answering a questionnaire.

A questionnaire can be viewed as a means of communication, a method of communicating between interviewer and interviewee. Not all questionnaires are equally successful in securing desired information from respondents. Often clarity is lacking, and the respondent fails to understand precisely what the researcher wishes to communicate. In other cases, respondents are unwilling to provide necessary information, or they may be influenced by the questioning process. Careful structure and disguise may be needed in questionnaire construction in order to help overcome some of these difficulties.

Questionnaire Structure and Disguise

Questionnaire studies may be classified by structure and disguise. *Structure* refers to the degree to which the questionnaire is standardized. A structured questionnaire requires respondents to give an exact answer and does not, as do unstructured questionnaires, allow respondents to answer freely in their own words. Often a highly structured questionnaire allows respondents to answer only "yes" or "no" to certain questions. Consider the following structured question:

Which brand of mouthwash do you normally use?

_____	Cepacol	_____	Micrin
_____	Colgate 100	_____	Listerine
_____	Lavoris	_____	Scope

This example illustrates the advantages of a structured questionnaire: ease of administration and of tabulation of data. It also illustrates the main disadvantage of rigid structure: since responses are predetermined, they must embrace all possible alternatives. In the example just presented, if the respondent used no mouthwash or used another brand, there would not have been an appropriate category to check.

Questionnaire *disguise* refers to the degree to which the purpose of the research study is known to the respondent. Undisguised questionnaires make the purpose of the study clear, because the questions are direct. Undisguised questionnaires are much more common than disguised, because of the difficulty of administering the latter. Disguised questionnaires usually require highly trained personnel, such as psychologists, to interpret responses correctly, especially if the study is also unstructured.

Questionnaires classified according to structure and disguise fall into four categories: (1) structured-nondisguised, (2) unstructured-nondisguised, (3) unstructured-disguised, and (4) structured-disguised. Let us examine each of these in turn.

Structured-Nondisguised

By far the most common type of questionnaire, the structured-nondisguised, is so named because not only are the questions and the allowed responses predetermined, but the purpose of the study is obvious to the respondent from the beginning. The popularity of the structured-nondisguised questionnaire is explained by ease of administration. This questionnaire can be administered by relatively unskilled interviewers, such as college students or other part-time or temporary workers, using the telephone, the mail, or the personal interview approach. Another advantage associated with this type of questionnaire is ease of tabulation and interpretation of responses. Since all replies have been placed in a predetermined category, the questionnaire may be so coded that keypunchers can directly punch out cards for computer analysis.

Two types of questions are found in the structured-nondisguised questionnaire: dichotomous and multiple-choice. A *dichotomous* question allows for only two possible answers. For example, the interviewer might ask, "Do you usually smoke at least one cigar a week?" The responses are either "yes" or "no"; no other answer is possible. Students are usually quite familiar with the dichotomous question, having experienced this format many times on examinations under the guise of true-false questions. *Multiple-choice* questions, also quite familiar to students, permit the respondent to select from several answers the one that is most suitable. The problem with multiple-choice questions is that none of the answers may appear entirely appropriate, and the respondent may wish for other choices.

Structured-nondisguised questionnaires are most effective when the possible replies are definitely known, clearly understood, and limited in number. Multiple-choice and dichotomous questions work best in securing factual information, such as age, income, and car ownership. They are less, though still somewhat, useful in securing information on buyer behavior, purchase intentions, and motivation. Example: imagine the difficulty in listing all possible vacation places in North America!

Unstructured-Nondisguised

Like the structured-nondisguised questionnaire, the unstructured-non-disguised makes no attempt to conceal the true objectives of the study from the respondent. What does differ is the structure of the questions themselves: they are usually *open-ended*. No dichotomous or multiple-choice questions are used, and the interviewer may not even have a list of formal questions to ask, since the approach is to get the respondent to talk as freely as possible. Rather than ask a question like "What brand of toothpaste do you normally use?" the researcher is apt to ask, "Why do you use Crest toothpaste?" This is an open-ended question, one that permits the respondent to express himself freely, without forcing answers into predetermined categories.

The unstructured-nondisguised questionnaire is often associated with depth interviewing, where respondents are encouraged to talk at length on the subject being probed. The researcher normally does not have a list of predetermined questions, though a rough outline is usually followed. The time period for an in-depth interview will vary, though one or two hours is not unusual. In-depth interviews may be held individually or in groups. One such type of interview is the *focus group* interview, which is conducted among small groups of people; the interviewer asks the group as a whole for opinions on a product concept, an advertisement, or a television program. Proponents of the focus group interview claim it is better than individual interviews, where information flows one way, because with focus group interviews, "the group setting causes the opinions of each person to be considered in group discussion. Each individual is exposed to the ideas of others and submits his ideas for the consideration of the group."[1]

Though the focus group usually contains no more than eight to twelve people, the interviews are especially helpful in developing hypotheses in the planning stage of the marketing research process. Not only do the interviews provide information for developing additional research, but they are quite useful as a source for new product ideas, advertising themes, and packaging concepts. Consider the following actual example:

> The Harris meat company had declining sales of its luncheon meat wieners and franks in one region during the previous year and needed to identify and isolate reasons for the lack of sales growth. In this case, the focus group interviews exposed a serious packaging problem and minor problems in shelf space allocation and competitive pricing. The packaging problem had extensive ramifications for the product's image, the ease of using the product, the quantity and quality of the shelf space exposure it received, and the consumer's decision to buy certain sizes of the product. The interviews produced very clear hypotheses for explaining consumer behavior and brand penetration in particular market segments. Housewives in the focus groups explained clearly why the packaging was a problem to them. Therefore, the quantitative study was narrowed to specific alternatives for improving the packaging strategy, communicating brand attributes, and increasing distribution penetration.[2]

[1] Alfred E. Goldman, "The Group Depth Interview," *Journal of Marketing* 26 (July 1962) : 62.

[2] Keith K. Cox, James B. Higginbotham, and John Burton, "Applications of Focus Group Interviews in Marketing," *Journal of Marketing* 40 (January 1976): 79.

Whether individual or group interviews are used, the advantages of the unstructured-nondisguised questionnaire are in the *information* that it yields. Usually, a much better quality and a greater quantity of information can be collected from nonstructured than from structured interviews. Open-ended questions allow respondents to talk freely and bring out information that would not have surfaced in a more structured questionnaire. Just as some university students prefer essay examinations, so that the full range of their knowledge can be displayed to the professor, many market researchers prefer this unstructured-nondisguised approach because of the additional information it secures.

The greatest disadvantages associated with this approach are the *high costs* involved and the difficulty of tabulating and analyzing the responses. Highly skilled market researchers must be found to conduct depth interviews. Not only are the salaries of these people much higher than those of interviewers administering the typical structured-nondisguised questionnaire, but the time and expense involved in conducting and analyzing the information secured from each interview will be substantially greater. Lengthy personal, not telephone or mail, interviews are required, and the attendant expense often becomes prohibitive. This cost consideration affects all phases of marketing research, and the researcher always faces the problem of a trade-off between expense and the quality of information desired.

Unstructured-Disguised

In an earlier chapter it was observed that one recurring problem with direct questions to respondents, especially on sensitive subjects, is the unwillingness of many respondents to provide answers to certain questions. Age, income, and consumption patterns are examples of this problem. When asked "How many beers did you drink last night?" the respondent may be inclined to answer, "Only one or two," when in fact he or she actually consumed one or two six-packs. Such problems lead to the usage of the disguised questionnaire, which seeks to obscure the true objectives of the study from the respondent.

Unstructured-disguised questionnaires are particularly important in motivation research, where researchers are exploring the "why" of buyer behavior. The use of *projective techniques*, commonly associated with this type of questionnaire, is based upon the assumption that a person describing a situation will describe it according to his own frame of reference: a respondent will "project" himself into the situation and thus reveal his own true feelings. Thus, for example, in reply to the undisguised question "Will you buy a new car this year?" he might respond very rationally, "No, I won't; my old car runs just fine." However, the researcher might ask, using the projective method, "Do you think your next-door neighbor will buy a new car this year?" The respondent might then answer, "Well, I don't think my neighbor has any business buying a new car, since her present car is adequate and she probably can't afford a new one, but she will probably break down and buy a new car anyway." According to the theory of projective techniques, the respondent has unwittingly projected himself into his neighbor's situation and has revealed his own interpretation or probable action in the particular instance described. Various projective techniques will be described in more detail in Chapter 14.

The foremost advantage of the unstructured-disguised questionnaire approach is that it is able to secure data that respondents might be unwilling or unable to provide in a more structured or in an undisguised format. High cost is the main disadvantage of this method. There are other limitations, as well: problems in securing highly skilled interviewers, lengthy time requirements for conducting interviews, the difficulty of interpreting responses, and the questionable validity of the extremely small samples on which results are based.

Structured-Disguised

Like the unstructured-disguised questionnaire, the structured-disguised questionnaire approach also seeks to conceal the true objectives of the study from respondents. Here again, projective techniques may be employed by the researcher. The main difference between this approach and the previous one is that the questions are asked in a more structured format. Asking structured questions in a disguised manner makes a questionnaire fairly easy to administer, but the range of replies is limited by the more rigid format.

Carrying over the projective technique example used earlier, we could give the question a structured-disguised twist by rephrasing it:

What kind of car do you think your neighbor will buy this year?

_____ General Motors
_____ Ford
_____ Chrysler
_____ American Motors
_____ Other

Of the four methods discussed here for classifying questionnaires by structure and disguise, the structured-disguised approach is the least commonly used by market researchers. Logically, if a questionnaire is to be disguised, it follows that it should also be unstructured, allowing respondents to provide more and better-quality information. The principal advantage derived from the structured-disguised approach is the ease in administration and interpretation of results.

Characteristics of a Good Questionnaire

Constructing a good questionnaire is a great deal more difficult than it may appear to be at first glance. Questionnaire construction is a process that cannot be completed in an hour or two but is much more likely to require a week of hard work. It is also a task that is never complete: there is no such thing as a "perfect" questionnaire. Questionnaire construction is an inexact art, not an exact science. Even after numerous revisions and extensive pretesting, a questionnaire will still have some undetected flaws.

The foregoing paragraph is not designed to cause the would-be questionnaire developer to give up in despair before ever attempting the task. Rather, it is designed to instill a bit of caution into a delicate and complicated undertaking, which all too often receives insufficient attention. In constructing and evaluating questionnaires, there are certain characteristics, found in all professional questionnaires, to keep in mind. The requirements of a good questionnaire are:

1. Completeness
2. Conciseness
3. Clarity
4. Cooperation of the respondents
5. Careful construction

Completeness

To be complete the questionnaire must include questions on all subject areas relevant to the project. There is no direct connection between the length of a questionnaire and its completeness. Some questionnaires can be complete with only a very few questions; others may require several pages of legal-size paper in order to cover the research problem adequately. A project designed simply to find out whether consumers would prefer longer shopping center hours will necessitate far fewer questions than one designed to give a comprehensive assessment of ethical standards and practices of professional marketing researchers. The key to completeness is whether the questionnaire adequately covers the objectives of the research problems.

Conciseness

A good questionnaire should be as short as possible, containing only questions relevant to the subject and asking nothing that is not absolutely necessary. The questions themselves should be as short as possible to make them easily understood. The more concise the questionnaire, the less time respondents will need to complete it, and the lower the cost of administering it. Unless the information is essential to the completion of the project, the researcher should avoid questions on such sensitive subjects as age and income.

Clarity

Researchers must ensure that questionnaires contain no vague or ambiguous questions. Questions must be so designed that they will not be misunderstood. Consider the question "Do you watch television?" How is the respondent to reply? Should she answer in the affirmative if she has not watched TV in six months? What if she watches only the CBS evening news, once every two or three weeks, and does not consider herself "a television watcher"? A clearer question might have asked, "Do you usually watch at least one hour of television each week?"

Cooperation of the Respondents

Every good questionnaire should include all possible means of ensuring respondent cooperation. Cooperation is important because it increases response rate, thus helping to increase the validity of the survey. With mail questionnaires, a cover letter or advance letter should be sent to explain the objectives of the study and assure the anonymity of respondents. Offering respondents copies of the results of the questionnaire, tendering small monetary incentives for completed mail questionnaires, and carefully explaining the objectives and purposes of the study are three ways to help increase cooperation. In general, the respondent should be made to feel that it is important to participate in completing the questionnaire.

Careful Construction

Whether the questionnaire is to be administered by mail, telephone, or personal interview, it should be constructed in a manner that facilitates tabulation and analysis of the data obtained. It should be a simple matter to process the results by computer. Careful construction of the questionnaire not only can result in better quality data but also helps save money. Careful construction implies, too, that a questionnaire will be pretested extensively before it is used in an actual survey.

Now that we have looked at these five characteristics of a good questionnaire, carefully examine figure 7·1, a questionnaire that appeared in Montreal newspapers after the 1976 Olympics. Questions 1 and 2 are dichotomous, and 3 and 4 are open-ended. Do you see anything wrong with this questionnaire? How well does it meet the requirements of a good questionnaire?

Format Design of Questionnaires

There is as yet no systematized body of knowledge establishing an exact method in designing questionnaires. However, there are certain established rules and principles to follow in developing a good questionnaire. Before we begin to consider these rules, let us examine the main components of a questionnaire.

Components

The major components of a questionnaire fall into three basic categories: (1) explanation information, (2) basic information, and (3) classification information.

EXPLANATION INFORMATION

Explanation information is provided by the researcher to the respondent to explain the purpose of the questionnaire. Explanation information, usually given at the beginning of the questionnaire, is designed to reduce respondent errors and to improve response rates. In the case of mail surveys, this information may take the form of an attached cover letter or directions for answering the questions properly. Explanation information common to most questionnaires includes

HOW SHOULD THE OLYMPIC STADIUM BE COMPLETED?

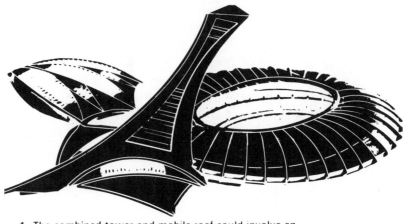

1. The combined tower and mobile roof could involve an additional expenditure of up to $100 million. Should it be completed according to the original plan of the architect, Taillibert?   yes ☐ no ☐

2. If the tower were not finished, should the authorities still proceed to construct another type of roof but at a lesser cost?   yes ☐ no ☐

3. If you agree, what kind of roof would you suggest, an inflatable one, a geodesic dome, or what?

4. Within the Stadium, there remains about 200,000 square feet of space whose use has yet to be determined. What would you propose be done with it?

Name:

Send us your replies and suggestions BEFORE MARCH 15, 1977 to:
THE ADVISORY COMMITTEE ON THE FUTURE OF OLYMPIC INSTALLATIONS
600 Fullum Street, 8th floor Montreal, P.Q.   H2K 2L6

Figure 7•1
Aftermath of the 1976 Montreal Olympics

From the *Montreal Star*, © February 25th, 1977. Reprinted by permission of the Government of Québec (La Régie des Installations Olympiques).

152

Over the years, we have asked you many questions about yourself and about your travels. We ask for your help this time in streamlining the many aspects of customer service which you meet in arranging for and making your flight. You encounter as many as eight or nine types of Air Chance people by the time you pick up your baggage at the end of your flight. Each encounter can affect how you feel about us as an airline and influence your decision on whether to use us again.

By completing the following questions, you will be telling us what you like and what you want changed. We value you as a customer, and realize that only by listening to what you want and providing it will we keep you as a customer.

The following questions about service are divided into sections in the same order that you probably encounter them in making a flight. For each service, please tell us whether or not you used or were exposed to it and, if you were, what you thought about it, by "x'ing" the appropriate space.

A number of questions have been set up as pairs of statements with six spaces in between each pair. The space closest to a statement indicates that the statement is very close to what happened.

As an example:

When the plane took off:

| It was very sunny outside | — — — — — — | There was no sun outside |

If you took off in bright sunshine you would place an "X" in the space beside "it was very sunny outside" or if it was somewhat cloudy, you would put your "X" in, say, the second or third space away from "there was no sun outside."

Please read each statement carefully as the positive statements are sometimes on the left and sometimes on the right.

In answering this questionnaire, please think about *only* the flight on which you were given this questionnaire.

Figure 7·2
Example of the Explanation Information Section of a Questionnaire

promises to keep respondent identity anonymous and assurances that no attempts will be made to sell anything to respondents. Figure 7·2 is an example of explanation information in a questionnaire used by a major airline seeking information from passengers (although the name is disguised, both the airline and the market survey are real). Notice that the explanation information identifies the purpose of the survey, makes an appeal for respondent cooperation, and provides instructions to assist respondents in filling out the questionnaires.

BASIC INFORMATION

The largest and most important part of a questionnaire is the basic information sought by the researcher, the real purpose of the questionnaire. The basic information section may be only a few questions in length or it may be several pages, depending upon the amount of data sought.

In the basic information section should be questions to cover all necessary subjects adequately, but researchers must take pains to avoid asking unnecessary questions and thereby making this section longer than is necessary. Figure 7·3 presents an example of a basic information section in a questionnaire designed to find out what automobiles the respondents personally own or plan to acquire within the next year.

This section deals with automobiles that you personally own and/or plan to acquire. Please check the appropriate space.

Now currently own:

It was purchased: New _____   Used _____

Manufacturer:

_____ AMC	_____ Fiat	_____ Peugot	_____ Volvo
_____ BMW	_____ Ford	_____ Renault	_____ Other
_____ Br. Leyland	_____ GM	_____ Saab	
_____ Chrysler	_____ Honda	_____ Toyota	
_____ Datsun	_____ Mazda	_____ VW–Audi	

In the next 12 months, plan to acquire or change to:
It will be: New _____   Used _____

Size preferred:

_____ Sports	_____ Subcompact	_____ Compact	_____ Mid-size
_____ Full-size			

Manufacturer preferred:

_____ AMC	_____ Fiat	_____ Peugot	_____ Volvo
_____ BMW	_____ Ford	_____ Renault	_____ Other
_____ Br. Leyland	_____ GM	_____ Saab	
_____ Chrysler	_____ Honda	_____ Toyota	
_____ Datsun	_____ Mazda	_____ VW–Audi	

Figure 7·3
Example of the Basic Information Section of a Questionnaire

Note the briefness of this part of the questionnaire. Is it too brief? Are all possible alternatives listed? Are too many alternatives listed?

CLASSIFICATION INFORMATION

At the end of most questionnaires will be a section designed to gather relevant classification information, such as marital status, sex, education, occupation, family income, and family size. Classification information enables researchers to analyze the data obtained, through cross-classification, in order to determine if there are significant differences between groups of respondents. For example, though we may find that most respondents are negatively oriented toward a new product concept being tested, there may be a certain group of respondents favorably disposed toward the product, and this group may be large enough or significant enough to constitute an identifiable and viable target market. Classification information allows the researcher to develop a profile of the consumer most likely to use the product or service in question.

Figure 7·4, entitled "A Little about Yourself," illustrates the classification section of a questionnaire used in a market survey of Air Chance passengers (again, though the name is disguised, the airline and the market survey are both real). Information obtained from this part of the questionnaire allowed the airline to develop a customer profile, identify target segments not well represented among Air Chance customers, and devise marketing strategies to increase market share.

Steps to Follow in Designing Questionnaires

Having examined the principal sections of a questionnaire, we are now in a position to consider some of the rules for questionnaire construction. In designing or constructing a proper questionnaire the researcher has to consider such things as what *information* is desired, what *types of questions* will be asked, questionnaire *length*, question *wording*, *order* of questions, and *pretesting* the questionnaire. By carefully considering these six design problems or steps, the researcher can minimize questionnaire problems. However, remember that the flawless questionnaire does not exist: even extensive pretesting will not remove all the problems, though they can be reduced. Let us examine each of these steps for questionnaire design.

A Little About Yourself

Have you ever flown on Air Chance before?   Yes _____   No _____

Where are you now living?   City/Town   _____
                              State/County _____
                              Country   _____

What is your occupation,   In what kind of business is the
that is, what kind of work   company you work for?
do you do?

_____   _____

Which age group are you
in? If under 18 years,
please write in age _____   Are you:

    18–21   _____   Married   _____
    22–29   _____   Single   _____
    30–39   _____   Divorced/Separated   _____
    40–49   _____   Widow/Widower   _____
    50–64   _____
    65 and over _____

Are you: Which language do you speak most
                                        often at home?
    Male   _____
    Female _____   _____

What is your approximate yearly income before taxes? Also, if you are
married, what is your approximate yearly family income, that is, your income
plus that of your spouse or children living in your home?

	Your Income	*If Married,* *Your Family Income*
U.S. Dollars		
No Income		
Under $4,000	_____	_____
$ 4,000–$ 4,999	_____	_____
$ 5,000–$ 5,999	_____	_____
$ 6,000–$ 6,999	_____	_____
$ 7,000–$ 9,999	_____	_____
$10,000–$14,999	_____	_____
$15,000–$19,999	_____	_____
$20,000–$24,999	_____	_____
$25,000–$29,999	_____	_____
$30,000 and over	_____	_____

Residents of other countries

_____   _____   _____
 Type of Currency   Personal Yearly Income   Family Yearly Income

Figure 7·4
Example of the Classification Information Section of a Questionnaire

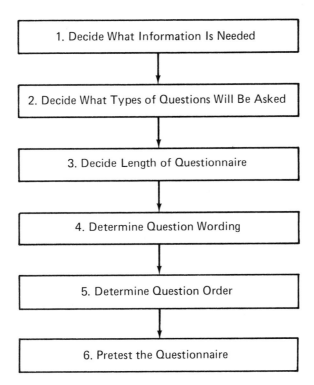

```
┌─────────────────────────────────────────┐
│  1. Decide What Information Is Needed     │
└─────────────────────────────────────────┘
                     │
                     ▼
┌─────────────────────────────────────────┐
│  2. Decide What Types of Questions Will Be Asked │
└─────────────────────────────────────────┘
                     │
                     ▼
┌─────────────────────────────────────────┐
│  3. Decide Length of Questionnaire        │
└─────────────────────────────────────────┘
                     │
                     ▼
┌─────────────────────────────────────────┐
│  4. Determine Question Wording            │
└─────────────────────────────────────────┘
                     │
                     ▼
┌─────────────────────────────────────────┐
│  5. Determine Question Order              │
└─────────────────────────────────────────┘
                     │
                     ▼
┌─────────────────────────────────────────┐
│  6. Pretest the Questionnaire             │
└─────────────────────────────────────────┘
```

Figure 7·5
Steps in Questionnaire Design

INFORMATION DESIRED

The very first thing to be done in designing a questionnaire is to determine just what information is desired. The researcher should sit down and write out a statement of the objectives of the study, listing what she seeks to accomplish. A plan must be made if the number of questions is to be kept manageable, as there is always a tendency to add more questions to get more data, which may be interesting but not actually necessary.

If the information requirements of the project are substantial, then use of the telephone may be undesirable, and personal interviews or mail questionnaires may be essential. If the information required is not only lengthy but complex, then use of the personal interview may be dictated.

A final item to be considered at this point is whether respondents possess the information desired. For example, it would probably not be advisable to ask men what brand of laundry detergent is used in their homes, as laundry is still the province of women in most North

American households. The researcher should also keep in mind that most people have a fairly short memory span; the average respondent, if asked, "What television program were you watching at 9:00 o'clock last Saturday night?" will have difficulty in remembering. Firms involved in surveying television viewing habits often use the telephone to make on-the-spot surveys during the program, rather than wait and ask the question a week later. When determining what information is desired, the researcher should always try to keep the number of questions, and hence the length of the questionnaire, to a minimum.

TYPES OF QUESTIONS

At this point the researcher must decide what types of questions will be used in the questionnaire. As discussed earlier in the chapter, there are three basic types: (1) open questions, (2) dichotomous questions, and (3) multiple-choice questions. The open question usually begins with such words as "why," "how," or "what," which are quite useful in getting the respondent to open up. Consider the following open-ended questions:

What brand of vodka do you usually drink?
Why do you drink this particular brand?

Open-ended questions are safer than multiple-choice questions, because, in the above example, had brands of vodka been listed in a multiple-choice format, the researcher might have omitted certain possibilities. Regarding this problem Paul Erdos has written: "Often the researcher has no way of knowing what the answers to his questions will be, and therefore he cannot list them. What is worse, he may *think* he knows and be wrong, and in that case he may never find out that he *was* wrong." [3] Unfortunately, the open-ended question adds difficulty in the recording and analysis of responses, a time-consuming, expensive process.

Difficulties in using and administering open questions lead many researchers to favor the simpler approach of using multiple-choice or dichotomous questions in questionnaire construction. Use of such questions is associated particularly with the structured-nondisguised questionnaire format, discussed earlier.

[3] Paul L. Erdos, *Professional Mail Surveys* (New York: McGraw-Hill Book Co., 1970), p. 50.

LENGTH

The issue of length in questionnaire construction has two aspects. The first is the length of individual questions. It is advisable to keep each question as short as possible, in order to minimize respondent confusion or misunderstanding. If the interviewer is asking a long and involved question in a telephone interview, the respondent may forget the first part of the question by the time the last part has been asked. Consider the following example of a too-lengthy telephone question:

Please rank in order of preference the following things you might do on a vacation:

Watch a movie being made	_____
Live with a foreign family	_____
Hunt big game	_____
Watch a bull fight	_____
Swim in a pool	_____
Fish in the ocean	_____
Backpack	_____
Go to a dog show	_____
Visit relatives	_____
Sail on a lake	_____

Obviously, all but the most unusual respondents would have great difficulty in remembering the entire question from start to finish. The only possible way to ask this type of question in its present form is by visual means — in writing.

On the other hand, the researcher should avoid questions that are too brief to be meaningful. Consider, for example, the question

Do you smoke?

This question is so brief that it can mean different things to different people. The respondent has no idea exactly what kind of information the researcher is seeking. Does the person who smokes a cigar once a month answer in the affirmative? A better way of asking this question might have been

Do you usually smoke at least one pack of cigarettes each week?

In this case, the question, though a bit longer, should be clear to the respondent and there is much less chance of misinterpretation.

The second aspect of length, total questionnaire length, is more complicated and controversial. Conventional wisdom holds that questionnaires should be kept as short as possible, or respondents will become bored filling them out and response rate will suffer. One authority on mail surveys has written that a "questionnaire containing too many pages of small type will draw very few replies." [4]

Though it might seem logical for lengthy questionnaires to cause lower response rates, this is not the case. Questionnaire length and response rate are independent variables; that is, there is no direct correlation between the two. "It seems logical that response rate would decrease with an increase in questionnaire length, but most of the evidence to date has failed to support this hypothesis. In fact, the opposite result has been found in a number of studies." [5]

If there is no proved direct correlation between questionnaire length and response rate, should the researcher still try to keep a questionnaire as short as possible? The answer is yes. Though questionnaire length may not affect response rate, it does affect *cost*. The longer the questionnaire, the more it costs to administer and to interpret the data obtained. For example, it has been estimated that each question included in the U.S. Bureau of the Census questionnaire "adds approximately $1,000,000 to the cost of the census." [6]

WORDING

Of the five design problems covered in this section, the way in which individual questions are formulated presents the researcher with the most difficult task. A major objective of wording is formulation of questions in a way that will not bias responses. Each question must be as neutral as possible.

The problem with questionnaire wording is twofold: both ambiguous and leading questions must be avoided. Ambiguous questions are those that do not convey a clear meaning to respondents. The "Do you smoke?" question presented earlier was an example of ambiguity. Since questions may seem perfectly clear to the researcher, but not to many respondents, extensive pretesting of questionnaires is needed, in order to clarify potential ambiguities. To avoid ambiguous questions, researchers should avoid such vague words as "sometimes," replacing them with more precise phrases, such as "about half the time." Ques-

[4] Erdos, *Professional Mail Surveys*, p. 39.

[5] A. Marvin Roscoe, Dorothy Lang, and Jagdish N. Sheth, "Follow-up Methods, Questionnaire Length, and Market Differences in Mail Surveys," *Journal of Marketing* 39 (April 1975): 20.

[6] Harper W. Boyd, Jr., Ralph Westfall, and Stanley F. Stasch, *Marketing Research: Text and Cases*, 4th ed. (Homewood, Ill.: Richard D. Irwin, 1977), p. 227.

tions should also use simple words that are easily understood by people of any educational or cultural background.

The second wording problem concerns leading questions, or questions that bias answers. Leading questions are often used when the researcher is trying to influence the results of the survey. For example, if interviewers in a shopping center ask, "Do you use Crest toothpaste?" there will be a high affirmative response, and such a study will be able to report a more widespread use of Crest than will a study asking respondents to name their brands.

Question wording should always avoid identifying the sponsor of the survey, because this identification may bias answers. Questions should be worded in as neutral a manner as possible, never beginning, for example, with such phrases as "Don't you think. . . ." A better way of wording the question of the previous paragraph might have been "What brand of toothpaste do you use?"

ORDER

The order in which questions are asked is extremely important. Usually the questionnaire will begin with general questions and then lead to specific ones. Potentially sensitive questions, such as age or income, should always appear in the classification section of the questionnaire at the end.

Question order is especially important when multiple-choice questions are to be used. Two aspects of question order must be considered here. First, it is often advisable, before asking a multiple-choice question, to use a *filter question*. The filter question is designed to reduce respondent bias by "filtering out," in advance, respondents who belong in none of the appropriate categories. Rather than immediately asking respondents which brand of automobile they own, the filter question would ask first, "Do you own an automobile?" This filter screens out those respondents who might, if asked directly which automobile they owned, be inclined to check one of the categories. Those answering no to the filter question are directed to the next section of the questionnaire.

The second aspect of question order in multiple-choice questions involves the order of the choices. It is a phenomenon well known to politicians that respondents have a tendency to check the first category presented. Thus, for example, if a survey asked:

At which supermarket do you usually shop?

_____ A & P
_____ Kroger

_____ Safeway

_____ Other

a disproportionately high number of respondents would check the first item presented, A & P. This problem of *order bias* is eliminated when researchers design questionnaires so that the order of multiple-choice questions is *rotated*. Thus, only on one-fourth of these questionnaires would A & P appear first. Candidates for public office resolve this problem by drawing lots for first place on the election ballot, a position that often guarantees a substantial number of extra votes.

Order bias can also be present with dichotomous questions. For example, the question "Do you prefer shopping in a shopping center or downtown?" will result in a disproportionately high number of people answering "shopping center." Again, the answer is rotation. Half the questionnaires should have "downtown" first and the other half "shopping center" first. Otherwise the results will be biased and misleading.

Pretesting the Questionnaire

No questionnaire design is ever complete if the questionnaire has not been pretested. A pretest involves trying out the questionnaire under field conditions in order to find and attempt to eliminate problem spots. The trial run offers the researcher the opportunity to change and clarify the wording of questions and make final revisions.

The best pretests are done by conducting personal interviews with respondents similar to those to be surveyed in the final study. The number of interviews need not be large, nor must the sample of respondents be scientifically selected. Usually a dozen interviews with respondents roughly similar to those sought in the final survey will be sufficient.

What the researcher really wants to know from a pretest is whether respondents properly understand the questions, so that no communication gaps exist. If confusion emerges, the researcher has the opportunity to change or eliminate the question or questions. Researchers should review whether all five design problems have been adequately resolved in the questionnaire design. The importance of the pretest is that it represents the researcher's final opportunity to make changes and revisions in the questionnaire before actually submitting it in the field for survey research (but several pretests should be made, if necessary, to iron out all the apparent problems).

Summary

The subject of this chapter has been questionnaire construction. A questionnaire is a formal list of questions designed to gather responses from consumers on a topic being researched. The questionnaire is the main instrument used in obtaining primary data from consumers and represents the principal means of communication between respondent and researcher in survey research.

The extent of questionnaire structure and disguise is important. *Structure* refers to the degree to which the questionnaire is standardized; *disguise* indicates the degree to which the purpose of the research study is known to the respondent. Questionnaires classified on the basis of structure and disguise are of four types: (1) structured-nondisguised, (2) unstructured-disguised, (3) unstructured-nondisguised, and (4) structured-disguised. The structured-nondisguised questionnaire is the most common because it provides ease of administration, tabulation, and interpretation of the questionnaire and the data obtained. The least commonly employed approach is the structured-disguised questionnaire, because of the time, cost, and difficulty involved in interpreting responses.

Three types of questions are normally employed in questionnaires. The first is the open-ended question, which allows respondents to make free responses, without confining answers to any predetermined categories. Second is the multiple-choice question, which allows respondents to check the appropriate categories or answers. Third is the dichotomous question, which permits only two choices, usually "yes" and "no." The open-ended question offers researchers the best quality and quantity of data but also is most difficult to tabulate and interpret. Multiple-choice and dichotomous questions are easier to tabulate and interpret, but they are criticized for limiting respondent answers, and they may omit listing some of the possible choices.

Questionnaire construction, which may be viewed as more an art than a science, is a process that is never complete. Requirements of a good questionnaire include (1) completeness, (2) conciseness, (3) clarity, (4) cooperation of the respondents, and (5) careful construction. Every good questionnaire should meet all five of these requirements. Questionnaires may be divided into three parts: (1) explanation information, (2) basic information, and (3) classification information. Explanation information states the purpose of the questionnaire, makes an appeal for responses, and provides information on completing the questionnaire properly. Basic information is the real purpose of the questionnaire, the data sought by the researcher in the survey. Classification information appears at the end of the questionnaire; it includes personal information on respondents for purposes of cross-tabulation.

When designing or constructing a questionnaire the researcher must consider the following five questions: (1) What information is desired? (2) What types of questions should I ask? (3) How long should the questionnaire be? (4) How should the questions be worded? and (5) In what order should the questions be asked? Careful adherence to these first five steps in questionnaire construction does not guarantee a finished questionnaire; only a rough draft will have emerged at this point. The questionnaire must then be pretested in the field to detect flaws in design or wording. The pretest process should also be extended to include a trial tabulation of data gathered, because difficulties in coding pretest data can point the way to improvements in the design of the questionnaire. Only then can the final version be administered to respondents.

Questions for Discussion

1. Questionnaires may be classified on the basis of structure and disguise. What is meant by these two terms?

2. What are the advantages associated with using an unstructured-disguised questionnaire instead of a structured-nondisguised approach? Compare and contrast these two approaches according to cost, ease of administration and tabulation of data, and quality of data obtained.

3. What is a focus group interview? With what types of questionnaire design is this approach associated?

4. Discuss the relative advantages and disadvantages of each of the following: (a) dichotomous questions, (b) multiple-choice questions, (c) open-ended questions.

5. The owner-operator of a major gasoline station at a busy urban intersection wants to know more about his customers. Specifically, he wants to know why they purchase gasoline at his station and what improvements in service he can make. Construct a short questionnaire using dichotomous, multiple-choice, and open-ended questions to secure this information.

6. a. Evaluate the questionnaire constructed in answer to the previous question for completeness, conciseness, clarity, cooperation of the respondents, and careful construction. How well does it meet all these requirements of a good questionnaire?

b. Is your service station questionnaire divisible into three parts? Is the basic information section the longest?

7. Though research studies indicate that questionnaire length has no direct bearing on response rate, the questionnaire should still be kept as short as possible. Why?

8. The following five questions might be found on any questionnaire. Evaluate each and discuss why you think it is or is not a good question. Assume that no filter questions are required; judge each on its own merit.

a. Are you familiar with the *Journal of Marketing Research?*

b. Do you believe that public officials should be more responsive to the wishes of their constituents?

c. Do you prefer Schlitz or Budweiser beer?

d. What is your annual discretionary income?

e. Do you normally pay for merchandise using cash or credit cards?

9. What is the purpose of a filter question? Provide an example.

10. a. What is the purpose of a questionnaire pretest? What size sample and how much sample control are necessary?

b. What kind of pretesting would you recommend for the questionnaire developed in question 5?

Chapter 8

Survey Administration

IN THE PREVIOUS CHAPTER we examined the various aspects of a good questionnaire and looked at steps or guidelines to be followed in questionnaire design. However, formulating a good questionnaire is only one step, granted a very important one, in the marketing research process.

No matter how well designed it may be, the research questionnaire itself is incapable of securing the needed information for the study. In a field survey the questionnaire is merely one part of a triangle; the other two are the *interviewer* and the *respondent*. When a survey is administered by personal and telephone interview, this interview may be viewed as a social process: social interaction and communication occur between interviewer and respondent. This process directly influences the three components of survey administration, the relationship among which is diagramed in figure 8·1.

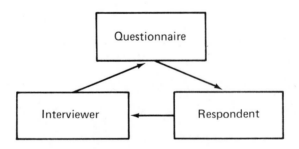

Figure 8·1
Components of Survey Administration

Administering Mail Questionnaires

Although this chapter focuses primarily on the personal interview, some unique problems are presented by administration of the mail questionnaire. Basically, these problems revolve around sample control and response. *Sample control* refers to obtaining representative samples to be used for the mail questionnaire, whereas *response* refers to the response rate, or percentage of usable questionnaires returned by respondents. Since a discussion of methods for dealing with response rates is included later in this chapter, the discussion here is confined to the issue of sample control.

The biggest problem in sample control for mail surveys is obtaining a satisfactory sampling frame (the complete list from which the sample will be selected). Unfortunately, satisfactory sampling frames may not be readily obtainable. Telephone books and city directories are often used to secure samples from the general population, but these sources may not be representative: some people do not have telephones, others have unlisted telephone numbers, and the lists themselves are quickly outdated in our highly mobile society.

Quite often researchers purchase mailing lists, especially for sales solicitation purposes. For example, at one time or another you may have taken out a subscription to a magazine like *Time* and then noted an increase in the "junk mail" arriving at your address over the next several months. This increase occurs because publications, such as *Time* and virtually all others, regularly sell their subscription lists.

Another option available to researchers wanting to secure representative mail survey sampling frames is mail panels. A *mail panel* is a commercial firm's listing of persons who have agreed to answer mail questionnaires. Consumer Mail Panels, Inc.; National Family Opinion (NFO), and Home Testing Institute (HTI) are but three of these. At any one time several thousand American families are members of these firms' panels. Usually they serve without significant compensation, but with the assurance that their panel membership will not be divulged to sales solicitors. For a fee, the mail panel firm will send out mail questionnaires (and new consumer products) to members of its panel. Advantages of using this approach are its simplicity and high response rate. The major disadvantage is the impossibility of knowing whether the mail panel is truly representative of the consumers the researcher is seeking to contact.

Interviewer Problems

When a survey is not administered by mail, the research manager must be aware of and able to anticipate potential problems with the people involved, the interviewers and respondents. We begin with an examination of the first of these problem areas.

Interviewer problems faced by the marketing research professional are often personnel management problems, that is, problems of attracting, holding, and motivating competent personnel. Since most field interviewers are relatively unskilled, poorly paid nonprofessionals, it is the responsibility of the market research professional to see that they do a competent job, and here problems often occur. Even if a very good questionnaire has been constructed and sound sampling techniques have been followed, poor questionnaire administration, stemming directly from interviewer problems, will severely limit the validity of the study. Problems of this sort center around (1) obtaining interviewers, (2) training interviewers, (3) interviewer error, and (4) cheating.

Obtaining Interviewers

Who are the people typically involved in personal interviewing? Interviewers have traditionally tended to be university students and housewives, two categories of people who are often willing to work on a part-time basis at the minimum wage level. Where skilled interviewing techniques are required, as for in-depth interviews or motivation research, interviewers are usually paid much more than minimum wages. However, most interviewing in the field does not require highly skilled personnel, since the structured format permits questionnaires to be administered by people without extensive training or education in the social sciences.

Obtaining personnel for field interviews is usually not too difficult a task. Most large research firms have available an ongoing list of people used in previous field surveys who may be called upon to participate in the next project. Additional interviewers may be obtained by newspaper advertising or by contacting university placement offices for part-time student help. As with most jobs, there is little difficulty in securing personnel; the difficulty is in securing personnel with the characteristics necessary for successful job performance.

The ideal interviewer is one with whom the respondent can readily identify. Interviewers should have an agreeable personal appearance and be somewhat extroverted. Housewives are very suitable because they are often available for part-time daytime work. Also, it is common procedure to use female instead of male interviewers, especially in door-to-door interviewing, as male interviewers are more apt to encounter refusals if only women are at home. It is absolutely necessary that interviewers be able to speak with total strangers and have no qualms about approaching people whom they do not know. In summarizing the native characteristics essential for good interviewers, Robert Ferber has written:

> Good health is essential! Field interviewing is a tiring job, and an interviewer is likely to be on her feet much of the day, walking from house to house or office to office. The incessant repetition of battling resistance and establishing rapport is exhausting in itself. Sometimes there are cumbersome or heavy displays to carry, tape recorders to haul from car to respondent and other such impediments. Strong feet, steady nerves, and sensitivities as invulnerable as possible are interviewer essentials. Interviewers should be of prime age, that is, over 18 if they are to be taken seriously and under 55 for health stamina.[1]

Training Interviewers

A poorly trained or motivated field force can ruin any good research study. It is the responsibility of the marketing research professional to ensure that field interviewers are properly trained on procedures to be used in the project and to see that interviewers are properly motivated to do a good job. Training, as opposed to education, is job-specific and is designed to enable the worker to perform the job at hand successfully. Interviewer training may be accomplished through three methods: (1) written instructions, (2) training in person, or (3) on-the-job training. Any good training program should give prospective interviewers exposure to both written and oral training instructions, along with the opportunity to ask questions and engage in practice interviewing or role playing.

Written instructions include textbooks, manuals, or other materials that can be sent to the interviewer through the mail. Written instructions are best used as the primary phase of interviewer training, followed by personal training or on-the-job training (on the principle that the best way to learn how to do something is by actually doing it, not reading about it).

[1] Robert Ferber, ed., *Handbook of Marketing Research* (New York: McGraw-Hill Book Co., 1974), p. 2–125.

Personal training is considered an improvement over the study of written instructions at home. Training classes held on the premises of the research house are the usual means of conducting personal training, which may last only a few hours or, in some cases, a week or more. Though personal training classes are conducted by most large research companies, they vary a great deal in details of both form and content.

Field training, or on-the-job training, is probably the best of the three methods, but it should not be undertaken unless the interviewer has had some previous training. In this method, the interviewer accompanies a more experienced supervisor on the first assignment in the field. The supervisor may conduct the first interview while the trainee watches. During the second interview the trainee interviews while the supervisor watches; after the interview, the instructor provides feedback to the trainee. This procedure may be repeated for subsequent interviews until the supervisor is assured that the trainee is competent to proceed alone. This method of training is the best of the three but is much more expensive than the others.

Many items are covered in a good training program. Interviewers are taught, among other things, how to establish rapport with respondents, how to accept refusals graciously, how to phrase questions properly, and how to record answers properly. In figure 8•2 you will see a list of dos and don'ts often given to interviewers in a training program. This list is by no means exhaustive, but it should give you a sense of the general content of a training program. These dos and don'ts may sound simplistic, but they are the keys to successful interviewing.

Interviewer Error

Despite careful selection and training procedures, there will usually be some interviewer error present in the research study. Such error is a sadly neglected area in marketing research. Great effort may be expended in questionnaire construction, proper sampling, data analyses, problem formulation, and other related areas, but all this effort may be wasted by errors in field work. Professional researchers must be aware of interviewer errors and take corrective action to keep these errors to a minimum. Without this control, interviewing becomes the weak link in the research process. Too many errors can destroy the usefulness of the survey; in fact, it has been estimated that "one out of every four surveys may contain serious errors." [2]

[2] Peter B. Case, "How to Catch Interviewer Errors," *Journal of Advertising Research* 11 (April 1971): 39–43.

Do's

1. Always carry proper identification.

2. Interview strangers, not friends, unless specifically told to interview people you know.

3. Sell yourself to the respondent — make her like you!

4. Conduct the interview in a relaxed, friendly way. Remember that you set the tempo and, in a way, are your respondent's hostess even though you are in her home.

5. Read the questions, word for word, exactly as written.

6. Follow the order of questions on the questionnaire.

7. Give the respondent plenty of time to think each question through.

8. Record replies verbatim except when otherwise instructed, or when the length of the reply prevents doing so.

9. Make your entries accurate and legible.

10. Unless otherwise instructed, record unsolicited comments that pertain to the subject matter.

11. While on the premises, check your interviews for completeness and legibility.

12. Start early in the day while people are still at home.

13. Meet your deadline . . . beat it if possible.

Don't's

1. Don't ever compromise with quality. If you can't complete an assignment, notify your supervisor, but don't rush interviews.

2. Don't let personal problems interfere with your work.

3. Don't deviate from a business attitude while calling on your respondents. Don't accept alcoholic drinks.

4. Don't do anything but the survey at hand. Don't try to combine one survey with another, or with sales or other activities.

5. Don't take anyone with you when you interview.

6. Don't deviate from prescribed sampling in order to seek "good" respondents. Don't reuse the same respondents.

7. Don't interpret questions. If they are not understood, reread them, and ask the respondent to interpret them herself.

8. Don't concentrate your interviews in one or two neighborhoods unless told to do so. Don't work near your own home.

9. Don't allow the respondent to read over your shoulder. Don't ever let her read the questionnaire or the responses you have recorded unless specifically instructed to do so.

10. Don't ever begin work unless fully equipped.

Figure 8·2
A Few Do's and Don't's Given to Interviewers

From *Handbook of Marketing Research* by Robert Ferber, p. 2–128. Copyright 1974, McGraw-Hill Book Co. Used with permission of McGraw-Hill Book Co.

What kinds of errors do interviewers make? Two major kinds are (1) errors in asking questions and (2) errors in recording responses.

Errors in asking questions occur when interviewers do not ask questions exactly as they are worded, when they omit certain questions, when they change the question sequence, and when they fail to ask all questions in exactly the same manner. An example of this last error would be the use of a disdainful manner in asking respondents whether they had watched an X-rated movie; the interviewer's tone would reduce the likelihood of affirmative answers. This is an example of interviewer bias — an interviewer's distortion of or influence on respondent answers.

Multiple-choice questions are particularly susceptible to interviewer bias if the interviewer places too much emphasis on one alternative when stating the question. Interviewer bias may be detected and sometimes reduced by including a tape recorder to record both questions and answers given in interviews. One difficulty encountered here is getting both interviewer and respondent to accept the presence of this control without the recorder itself introducing bias (the bias in this instance would be a Hawthorne Effect caused by the presence of the tape recorder).

Errors in recording answers also come from simple computational mistakes made by the interviewer, from misinterpretation or misunderstanding of respondents' answers, and from failure to demonstrate that a suspect response is not correct. For this final reason, one of the ingredients of the interviewer training program should be instructions to press for additional comments when incomplete or questionable answers are given.

Interviewer errors may also be caused by social distance between interviewer and respondent. When the two come from radically different socioeconomic backgrounds, the chance of the interviewer making an error is substantially increased. Cultural differences may compound this problem. For example, a Mexican-American respondent may be easily misunderstood by a unilingual Anglo interviewer. This type of interviewer error can be reduced by providing interviewers from the same social and cultural background as respondents, something that is particularly desirable in door-to-door neighborhood interviewing. Using this approach not only will increase accuracy but will help increase response rate, by reducing the number of refusals.

The Advertising Research Foundation has developed the Field Audit and Completion Test (FACT), an interview verification service to catch interviewer errors. About 10 percent of respondents are reinterviewed, usually by sending a postcard or by random telephone calls, in which questions are asked in order to verify whether interviews took place under proper conditions:

1. Did the interviewer actually interview the person she claims to have interviewed? Even when probed, an occasional respondent will deny ever having been visited by an interviewer.

2. Was the person interviewed a qualified respondent as designated by the study? Interviewing a teenage daughter when the study calls for housewives would constitute an error on this item.

3. Does the respondent reside at the address reported? Substituting neighbors or friends for designated respondents can distort the sample.

4. Was the interview conducted according to study specifications? If the study specifies personal interviews, those conducted by telephone are not accepted.

5. Was the interview conducted at the place indicated? Interviews conducted on street corners or at parties are not accepted if the study calls for at-home interviews.[3]

The answer must be yes to all these questions in order for the interview to be verified. An additional four questions, tailored to each interview, may then be asked to determine how well the interviewer performed. Questions are asked to find out whether the interviewer asked all the questions, recorded answers correctly, and followed directions. FACT has been shown to be an important verification service for catching interviewer errors. (For verification checks to be made, of course, the questionnaire must include spaces for the respondent's name, address, and telephone number.)

Cheating

Cheating is deliberate falsification of data by the interviewer. It is a major interviewer problem, not an interviewer "error." The full extent to which cheating occurs is generally unknown, probably because no one involved in cheating is likely to report it and because cheating is most likely to occur when no controls are present and there is hence little likelihood of detection.

Cheating may take several forms. The most glaring example of cheating is the "street corner method," in which an interviewer, rather than conducting actual door-to-door interviews, sits down on a street corner and fills out a stack of questionnaires. Friends or relatives, instead of the intended respondents, may be used to fill out questionnaires. A milder form of cheating occurs when interviewers fail to ask

[3] Case, "How to Catch Interviewer Errors," pp. 39–40.

all questions on the questionnaire. Cheating means that interviewers have to do less work, and many data gatherers have a natural inclination in this direction. Cheating is much more apt to occur when adequate controls or supervision are not present.

Cheating can probably never be completely eliminated. However, it can be controlled. Proper control will minimize the amount of cheating by discouraging it in the first place and detecting it when it does occur. Controls include (1) good training, (2) proper field supervision, and (3) verification checks, such as the FACT method. Where interviewer cheating is detected, a more intensive verification audit must be taken to determine the full extent of cheating in the survey. If extensive cheating is found to have taken place, the cheater should be fired and the survey redone. Otherwise, cheating will continue, and the reputation of the research firm will be damaged.

Respondent Problems

We come now to a second major group of problems, those dealing with the respondent. Two major types of respondent problems, known collectively as *nonsampling* errors, can be identified: (1) *response error* and (2) *nonresponse error*. The first is a communications problem in which inaccurate responses are given to the researcher; the second stems from not-at-homes and refusals to cooperate. These problems are of critical importance to researchers, because such nonsampling errors bias results and can distort a study. Let us examine each of them separately.

Response Error

Of the nonsampling errors covered in this chapter, response error, which occurs when a respondent gives an incorrect answer to a question, is the most difficult to detect. The difficulty of detecting response error is increased if neither interviewer nor respondent is aware that error has occurred. For example, the respondent may misinterpret the question and, accordingly, give a misleading response. See Figure 8·3 for an overview of respondent problems.

CAUSES OF RESPONSE ERROR

Sources of response error have been covered briefly in previous chapters. Two major sources or causes can be identified as (1) *semantics* and (2) *deliberate falsification*.

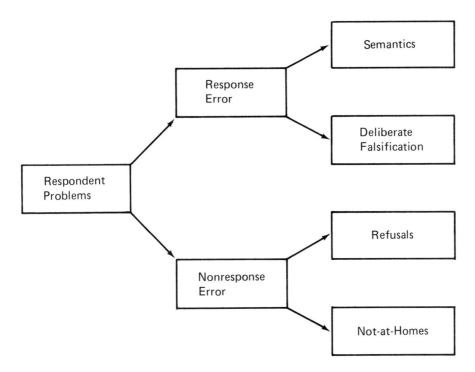

Figure 8·3
Sources of Respondent Problems

Semantics. Semantics, which refers here to the misinterpretation of questions by respondents, is probably the greatest cause of response error. Semantic errors may be caused by poor wording of questions, interviewer error in reading or explaining the questions to the respondent, or a lack of understanding resulting from differing educational or cultural backgrounds.

Consider the question "Do you often drink coffee?" What does "often" mean? Daily? Weekly? "Often" may be interpreted differently by each respondent. Errors in semantics, or question misunderstandings, can be controlled by proper interviewer training and extensive questionnaire pretesting to ensure that questions are clearly understood by respondents. Where personal interviews are to be conducted, it is desirable to have interviewers from the same ethnic or cultural background as the respondents, especially in cases where respondents may not be fluent in English.

Deliberate Falsification. Deliberate falsification of responses is believed to be less of a problem than question misinterpretation. People are usually honest, and if they have consented to respond to a questionnaire, it is unlikely that they will falsify their answers.

Three conditions under which respondents will knowingly give incorrect answers to interviewers can be identified, however. First, some respondents may deliberately attempt to mislead the interviewer, out of a conscious desire to "play games" in answering questionnaires. This is most likely to happen when someone other than the intended respondent is replying to the questionnaire — for example, a twelve-year-old child, rather than the head of the household.

A second reason why a respondent will knowingly provide incorrect answers is a desire to "help" the interviewer. This problem can occur if respondents know the purpose or the sponsor of the study. In this instance they will identify themselves as users of that sponsor's products in a disproportionate number of cases.

Thirdly, inaccurate replies are likely to result when interviewers ask potentially embarrassing questions. For example, consumers typically report beer consumption patterns considerably lower than sales by brewers. Asking questions about beer *purchases* instead of beer *consumption* is one way to get around this problem, as consumers are likely to be more truthful when responding to a less direct or less incriminating question.

Although it can never be completely avoided, response error can be held to a minimum by establishing certain procedures. Interviewers should be carefully trained so as to be able to detect inconsistent answers. Questionnaires should be constructed to minimize embarrassing questions and to avoid identifying the purpose of the survey or the name of its sponsor. Survey control should be exercised to ensure that only the intended respondent replies to the questionnaire, not a child or a neighbor. In general, the influence of the questioning process itself must be carefully controlled; otherwise, respondents may supply answers contrary to the facts.

Nonresponse Error

The second major type of nonsampling error, nonresponse error, occurs when consumers do not respond to a study. Nonresponse error, also known as nonresponse bias, is error caused by a difference in characteristics between those who do and those who do not respond to a survey. Nonresponse error is an extremely important problem in marketing research, though it is often unrecognized and extremely difficult to measure. How, for example, do you know if people who do not respond are different from those who do, when no information is available on the nonrespondents?

Importance of Nonresponse Error to Research Data

Why is nonresponse error considered so important by marketing researchers? What is wrong with a 50 percent response rate in a survey, provided that the sample size obtained is large enough to be statistically significant? The answer to this question is response bias; though great pains may be taken to ensure that a sample is selected in a random manner to be representative of the universe being surveyed, nonresponse bias can ruin this careful planning. (See the following chapter for a discussion of probability sampling.)

How do respondents differ from nonrespondents in a typical survey? In general, the response rate tends to be higher among older people than among young people; the lowest response rate is from young males. Older people, especially retired people, have more time to fill out questionnaires and are more likely to be at home than are younger, working-age people. In the case of questionnaires sent through the mail, response rate is higher among the better-educated segments; people with little education may not have literary skills sufficient to interpret and fill out written questionnaires properly. Women are more likely to respond to telephone and door-to-door surveys than are men, as more women than men are found at home during the daytime. Nonresponse bias in telephone surveys is found among people in the highest and the lowest income brackets; the former may have unlisted telephone numbers, and the latter often cannot afford telephones. Researchers need to plan studies carefully to minimize nonresponse bias. Ways of reducing this type of error will be covered later in the chapter.

Causes of Nonresponse

Refusals and *not-at-homes* constitute the two main sources of non-response error. Not only are both these types serious, they are also on the increase. Today, more people than ever before are refusing to co-operate with researchers or are otherwise unavailable to participate in survey research. Regardless of methods used, whether telephone, mail, or personal interview, nonresponse is on the upswing for many reasons.

Refusals. A refusal occurs when a respondent declines to participate in a survey. Refusal rates vary widely from survey to survey. The number of refusals is influenced by such things as the personality of the interviewer, the type of survey being conducted, respondent interest in the survey material, the personality of the respondent, and the circumstances surrounding the interview itself.

The refusal rate is in general increasing. Figure 8•4 illustrates one

WALL STREET JOURNAL

"Sorry, sir, I'm not going to open up seven locks and disconnect the burglar alarm just to tell you what shampoos I favor."

Figure 8•4
An Example of a Refusal

Reprinted with permission of Herbert Goldberg.

reason for the increasing refusal rate in personal interviews — crime. Many people, especially women alone at home during the daytime, will refuse to allow a stranger into their homes. Given the crime rate in North America, this reluctance to open doors to strangers is understandable. Obscene telephone callers, masquerading as legitimate marketing researchers, have compounded the difficulties of getting people to respond to telephone interviews.

Another reason for the increasing refusal rate has been the abuse of marketing research by sales and solicitation agents. Sometimes respondents are called and asked to participate in "marketing research" studies, when, in fact, they are being asked to purchase some item, such as encyclopedias. This kind of abuse has naturally made many people reluctant to participate in studies. If respondents suspect that a study is not legitimate, refusals will soar. Consumer confidence can be gained by giving interviewers proper identification and by notifying respondents in advance.

Interest in the survey itself affects response rate. A survey conducted by the American Medical Association among member doctors regarding attitudes toward socialized medicine would almost certainly achieve a much higher response rate than would a general consumer survey designed to find out what kind of soap powder or bleach is used in the home. In the latter case many respondents would find themselves too busy, too tired, or too generally uninterested to fill out the questionnaire.

A good cover letter is invaluable in creating interest in mail surveys. In figure 8·5 you will see an example of a cover letter, one used by the American Marketing Association in its 1973 *Survey of Marketing Research*. Usable replies totaled 1,322, or 39 percent, a respectable response rate for a mail survey.

Lastly, both the method of survey communication and the characteristics of the respondent interviewed have an effect on the response rate. Generally speaking, personal interviews have the highest response rate and mail questionnaires the lowest. Respondents differ from nonrespondents in age, marital status, occupation, geographic region, income, and education. Of these characteristics, education is the most significant, especially in mail surveys; the better-educated consumer is more likely to respond.[4] In personal interviews and telephone surveys, refusals tend to be concentrated at both extremes of the population — the highest and the lowest socioeconomic groups.

Not-at-Homes. As a cause of nonresponse, not-at-homes are on the increase. This type of nonresponse occurs when the respondent either is not at home when the interviewer calls or cannot otherwise be located. This definition also includes, then, those who have moved recently — a particularly acute problem in today's mobile society.

The problem with not-at-homes is that they quite likely have characteristics that differentiate them from those who are at home. It has been demonstrated that not-at-home respondents are often younger, better educated, more likely to live in urban areas, and higher in income than those who are at home.[5] The not-at-home problem is further aggravated by the increasing rate at which women participate in the labor force. Today there are many more families with both husband and wife working than only a generation ago, and it is therefore increasingly difficult for researchers to find anyone at home during the

[4] Leslie Kanuk and Conrad Berenson, "Mail Surveys and Response Rates: A Literature Review," *Journal of Marketing Research* 12 (November 1975): 440–53.

[5] W. C. Dunkleberg and G. S. Day, "Nonresponse Bias and Callbacks in Sample Surveys," *Journal of Marketing Research* 10 (May 1973): 160–68.

June, 1973

Will You Please Help
Update the AMA Survey
of Marketing Research?

Five years have elapsed since the last "Survey of Marketing Research" sponsored by the American Marketing Association. The AMA Board of Directors asks your help now in filling out and returning this questionnaire, even if your company has no formal marketing research department.

Briefly, it is a study of the organization, functions, budgets, and compensation levels of the marketing research departments in companies represented in the American Marketing Association.

Your replies will be kept *entirely confidential.* The accounting firm of Price Waterhouse & Co. will receive your returned questionnaire and remove the cover letter bearing your name and that of your firm. No one else will be able to connect any questionnaire with any company or any individual respondent. (A telephone survey may be made later among nonrespondents to determine possible sources of bias, hence the need to know who has not replied.) The unidentified questionnaires will then be tabulated by the University of Missouri's Computer Center. Dik Twedt, who planned and reported the 1963 and 1968 studies, will also prepare a report of the current study.

The American Marketing Association plans publication of these results in October, 1973. Your help is urgently needed now to make this survey most useful to you and your marketing colleagues.

Won't you please complete the questionnaire today? Remember, *even if you don't do any marketing research*, please answer the first three questions and return the questionnaire to Price Waterhouse & Co., 1 South Memorial Drive, St. Louis, Missouri, 63102.

Sincerely,

David K. Hardin
President

P.S. If this questionnaire should be completed by someone else in your company, we would appreciate your passing it along. If there is a problem as to how the questions should be answered, please communicate with Dik Twedt, Professor of Marketing, the University of Missouri-St. Louis (314) 453-5115.

Figure 8•5
An Example of a Cover Letter
From Dik Warren Twedt, *1973 Survey of Marketing Research,* © 1973. Reprinted by permission of the American Marketing Association, Chicago, IL.

daytime. Such two-career families may also be reluctant to grant an interviewer time to conduct a survey during the evening, as their at-home time is quite limited.

Should the researcher fail to consider not-at-homes, survey results may be biased. Since some segments of the population may be less likely than others to be at home at certain times, underrepresentation of these respondents can invalidate survey results: the results may be distorted by having too many retired people in the sample and too few young, employed males or too few high-income families.

METHODS OF REDUCING NONRESPONSE

Fortunately, there are techniques and methods that can increase response rates. Though even the best survey is extremely unlikely to gain a 100 percent response rate, nonresponse can be substantially reduced in personal interviews and telephone and mail surveys. In all cases, careful planning and execution is necessary to increase response rate and hold nonresponse bias to a minimum.

Increasing Response in Telephone and Personal Interviews. Nonresponse may be reduced in both telephone and personal interviews by using advance notification and call-backs. Advance notification means informing the respondents in advance that they are being asked to participate in a survey. This preliminary notification may take the form of letters or, in the case of personal interviews, advance telephone calls.

If the first attempt to contact a respondent is not successful, call-backs must be made. Usually at least three call-backs are recommended, at different times of the day and week, to contact respondents missed in the first round. Researchers have found that a second call-back can double the response rate.[6] As might be expected, housewives and retired people are the groups most likely to be home during the weekdays, whereas it may be necessary for the researcher to use evenings and weekends to contact working couples or people otherwise absent from the home during the day. Care must be taken, however, to avoid calling too early in the morning, too late in the evening, or on religious holidays.

Increasing Response in Mail Surveys. A major cause of poor response rates in mail surveys is lack of respondent interest in the research problem. Who, for example, can be highly motivated to fill out

[6] Dunkleberg and Day, "Nonresponse Bias and Callbacks in Sample Surveys," pp. 160–68.

a lengthy questionnaire describing supermarket buying behavior? Respondent interest and motivation can be increased in the following three ways: (1) *follow-ups*, (2) *preliminary notification*, and (3) *selective concurrent techniques*. All of these may be used at the same time; that is, respondents may be notified in advance that they will be receiving questionnaires, and call-backs and repeat mailings can be used to remind respondents that they have not yet replied. Such concurrent techniques as identifying the survey sponsor, guaranteeing anonymity, and using monetary incentives may all be used.

Follow-ups, or reminders, are almost universally successful in increasing response rates. Since each successive follow-up results in added returns, the very persistent (and well-financed) researcher can usually achieve an extremely high total response rate. As with all market research, however, the value of additional information obtained must be weighed against the cost of successive contacts. In other words, is the additional time, effort, and expense worth it?

Advance notification, particularly by telephone, is effective in increasing response rates; it also serves to accelerate the rate of return. However, follow-ups appear to be a better investment than preliminary notification.

Concurrent techniques that may be employed include:

1. *Adjusting questionnaire length.* Although common sense suggests that short questionnaires should obtain higher response rates than longer questionnaires, research evidence does not support this view.

2. *Stating survey sponsorship.* Official or "respected" sponsorship tends to increase response.

3. *Including return envelopes.* Inclusion of a stamped return envelope does encourage response because it facilitates questionnaire return.

4. *Including postage.* Special delivery is very effective in increasing response rates. Findings do not show a significant advantage for first class over third class, for commemorative stamps over ordinary postage, for stamped mail over metered mail, or for multiple denomination stamps over single, larger denomination stamps.

5. *Personalization.* Personalization of the mailing has no clear-cut advantage in improved response rates. For example, neither personal inside addresses nor individually signed cover letters significantly increase response rates; personally typed cover letters have proved somewhat effective in most cases cited, but not in all. One study testing the use of a titled signature versus one without a title did show a significant advantage for the title.

6. *Using cover letters.* The cover letter appears to be the most logical vehicle for persuading individuals to respond, yet the very few reported studies offer no insights about its formulation.

7. *Guaranteeing anonymity.* The promise of anonymity to respondents — either explicit or implied — has no significant effect on response rates.

8. *Varying size, reproduction, and color.* Questionnaire size, method of reproduction, and color have no significant effect on response rates.

9. *Using money incentives.* A twenty-five-cent incentive sent with the questionnaire is very effective in increasing response rates. Larger sums tend to bring in more responses but at a cost that may exceed the value of the added information.

10. *Stating deadline dates.* Deadlines do not increase the response rate; however, they do serve to accelerate the rate of questionnaire return.[7]

Although response rates may "range from below 20% to 100%, there is still no reliable evidence identifying the factors responsible for this enormous variation."[8] Follow-ups, preliminary notification, and the concurrent techniques noted above are all used to improve response rates in mail surveys, but with varying degrees of success. The best results have been found to result from the use of follow-ups and monetary incentives. Still, careful usage of all these techniques will increase the efficiency of mail surveys by reducing costs and improving predictive validity.

How to Treat Nonresponse Bias

So far, we have identified what nonresponse error is, how it is caused, and some ways of reducing it. Since nonresponse error can almost never be completely eliminated in any survey, however the problem facing the professional market researcher is how to treat the remaining nonresponse error in each survey. Several methods, varying in sophistication and validity, are used by researchers. They include (1) substitution, (2) weighting, (3) call-backs, and (4) ignoring the problem.

[7] This section on improving response rates has been adapted from Kanuk and Berenson, "Mail Surveys and Response Rates," p. 450.

[8] Kanuk and Berenson, "Mail Surveys and Response Rates," p. 450.

Substitution. A common way of treating nonresponse is substitution of someone other than the intended respondent. In the telephone survey, substitution may take the form of calling the next number in the phone book if there is no answer at the first. In personal interviews, substitution may be accomplished by having another member of the household complete the questionnaire or by going next door. However, substitution is not practical in mail surveys.

Although substitution may facilitate the completion of the survey, it does not reduce nonresponse error, which may still be present because the units substituted may differ from those originally selected in the sample. Substitution is only valid if nonrandom sampling techniques, which involve no attempt to obtain a representative sample, are being used. In some cases it may be possible to question members of the household other than the designated respondent. This method has been reported successful in cases where "the questions are relatively objective, when informants have a high degree of observability with respect to respondents, when the population is homogeneous, and when the setting of the interview provides no clearcut motivation to distort responses. . . ." [9]

Weighting. A second approach to treating nonresponse bias is weighting the nonresponses. Segments of the sample that the researcher considers underrepresented, such as inner-city blacks, can be adjusted by weighting "the results of the central city interviews that are secured in order to give them full representation in the results." The weakness of this approach is that weighted returns often differ from those that would be secured if call-backs were made. [10]

Call-Backs. Otherwise known as follow-ups or reminders, call-backs are the best approach to the problem of nonresponse. If the first attempt to contact the respondent fails, then at least three call-backs should be made at different times of the day and week. Call-backs may take the form of postcard reminders, telephone calls, or personal visits: all have been shown reliable in increasing the response rate.

The main drawback of call-backs is that, though they may increase response rate and thus reduce nonresponse bias, they do not solve the nonresponse problem. Call-backs serve only to diminish the magnitude of nonresponse; they do not provide a solution. Still, they are perhaps

[9] Eleanore Singer, "Agreement between Inaccessible Respondents and Informants," *Public Opinion Quarterly* 36 (Winter 1972–73): 603–11.

[10] C. William Emory, *Business Research Methods* (Homewood, Ill.: Richard D. Irwin, 1976), p. 276.

the most effective way to deal with nonresponse bias and, when effectively used, can decrease it substantially.

Ignoring the Problem. By far the most common way of dealing with nonresponse bias is to ignore the problem completely, hence not dealing with it all. In most instances, researchers do not attempt to treat nonresponse bias; they assume instead that there is no difference between respondents and nonrespondents.

Ignoring response bias is certainly the easiest method of treating it. However, this method should perhaps more appropriately be called *nontreatment*, because nothing is being done about the problem. What may result from ignoring the problem is invalidation of the survey results, though the researcher may not be aware that this has occurred. Thus, whereas ignoring the problem represents the most common and easiest way to deal with nonresponse, it is the worst possible course of action (or nonaction).

Probably nonresponse bias can never be completely avoided. Callbacks, or reminders, are the most effective way of holding it to a minimum, but lack of time and research funds may make call-backs problematic. Still, if the nonresponse problem is ignored, marketing researchers must be prepared to accept the consequences — consequences that have been described as "the very weak foundations upon which so many research reports and subsequent management decisions are based." [11]

Summary

Survey administration is a social process that takes into account the relationship and interaction among the interviewer, the questionnaire, and the respondent. In the previous chapter we examined the first of these components, the questionnaire itself. In this chapter we have examined the other two components, the interviewer and the respondent, and the problems associated with each.

Interviewer problems are often personnel management problems of attracting, holding, and motivating competent employees. Four principal interviewer problems exist: (1) obtaining interviewers, (2) training interviewers, (3) interviewer error, and (4) cheating. The last of these problems, cheating, occurs when interviewers deliberately falsify some aspect of the interviewing process. Cheating can be controlled

[11] Kanuk and Berenson, "Mail Surveys and Response Rates," pp. 450–51.

through proper training, supervision, and such verification checks as the FACT method.

Two major types of error stem from respondents: *response error* and *nonresponse error.* The first is a communications problem, in which inaccurate responses are given; the second stems from not-at-homes and refusals to cooperate.

Response error is more difficult to detect than nonresponse error. Both interviewer and respondent, in fact, may be unaware that an error has been made. Usually, response error is caused by semantics, or a misunderstanding; occasionally, it is caused by a deliberate false answer from a respondent who wants to mislead the interviewer or avoid answering embarrassing questions.

Both refusals and not-at-homes are increasing, and researchers are becoming more and more concerned with nonresponse errors. Changing lifestyles and fear of crime have made it more difficult to find people at home and to get them to participate in answering questionnaires. Although nonresponse error can never be eliminated completely, it can be reduced by using follow-ups, preliminary notification, and, in mail surveys, selective concurrent techniques.

Researchers have developed various ways of treating, or not treating, nonresponse error, including substitution, weighting, call-backs, and ignoring the problem. Ignoring the problem is the most commonly used approach, though it does not really represent an attempt to deal with the problem at all. Call-backs are usually the best way to increase response rates, though occasionally substitution may be used for objective questions.

Questions for Discussion

1. What is meant by social distance between the interviewer and the interviewee? What are the problems associated with social distance? Suggest ways of overcoming social distance.

2. A verification check reveals that one of your field interviewers has been arbitrarily substituting next-door neighbors if intended respondents are not at home. What is wrong with this procedure? What course of action do you take?

3. What is nonresponse bias? Why is it so important?

4. What is response error? How can it be minimized?

5. You are conducting a mail survey of housewives' grocery shopping habits. Develop a plan for ensuring the highest possible response rate.

6. You are in charge of a research project in which it is necessary to interview consumers at home. Devise a plan for ensuring the highest possible response rate.

7. What is the most common type of response error? How would you hold it to a minimum?

8. What are the four methods used by researchers to treat non-response bias? Which of these is best? Which is the most commonly used? Why?

9. What factors beyond the control of researchers affect response rate and personal interviews? How can researchers overcome these problems?

10. Since the personal interview usually gets the highest response rate, this is the most desirable method of communicating by questionnaire. Do you agree or disagree with this statement? Defend your answer.

Chapter 9

Sampling Concepts

THUS FAR WE HAVE STRESSED the qualitative aspects of the marketing research process, not the quantitative. We have used this procedure in order to introduce marketing research without getting you bogged down in a maze of formulas and complex mathematical symbols. However, some basic understanding of statistics *is* necessary to the marketing research process. It need not be great; in this text we assume you have had only a minimum of preparation in statistics, and we make no attempt to turn you into an expert in multivariate techniques — these can be covered in a more advanced course.

Here we begin with a discussion of basic sampling concepts.

What Is a Sample?

Each of us is constantly engaged in sampling. We take a few sips of Coors beer and perhaps become brand-loyal at that moment. We go for our first ride in a Corvette; it breaks down and we decide at that point never to buy a Corvette. We form our impressions of another country from contact with only a very few people from that country. In each case we are sampling, though our sampling methodology is hardly scientific and may lead us to completely incorrect conclusions.

A *sample* is a collection of observations from a parent population or universe. In the case of information, a sample is a portion of the total amount of information that can conceivably be gathered. The *universe* or *population* is the entire collection of items the researcher wishes to study, from which he or she plans to draw conclusions. If every item in the universe is studied, we have a *census*. With large populations, it is usually much too expensive and time-consuming to conduct a census (the U.S. government's *Census of Population* being a notable exception); such cases necessitate the use of samples, by which certain items from the parent populations are studied.

Sampling Problems and Procedures

The first step in any sampling procedure is to define the universe being studied clearly, so that a proper sample can then be drawn. Two kinds of populations exist: finite and infinite. A *finite population* is one containing a finite or fixed number of elements. Examples include the number of Corvettes manufactured by General Motors in the week's production, the number of full-time students currently enrolled in Utopia University, and the number of seats in a football stadium.

Finite populations have definable limits; *infinite populations* are without measurable limits of any kind and are therefore indeterminate. The number of mosquitoes in South Louisiana and the number of illegal immigrants into the United States within the past twenty-five years are examples of infinite populations: they cannot be measured with any degree of precision. Whereas a census might be impractical with a finite population, it would be impossible with an infinite one.

It is often necessary in marketing research studies to make accurate predictions on the basis of samples selected from both finite and infinite populations. Making generalizations about the characteristics of a large population on the basis of a small sample creates many problems. For instance, if we want to forecast accurately the average amount of money people spend on their summer vacations, we would not use for our sample only amounts spent by U.S. university students in Europe. However, it is difficult to determine just *which* vacationers should be included in our sample and *how many* of them should be surveyed.

Since a sample is only a part of a whole, it is not always a reliable indication of the characteristics of the population from which it is drawn. Many researchers have found to their dismay that inferences drawn from samples can be incorrect. There is no certainty that the characteristics of a sample will be the same as those of the universe from which the sample is drawn. Why, then, are samples so widely used by marketing researchers?

Reasons for Sampling

The basic idea behind the use of sampling methodology is that a sample can be more quickly, easily, and cheaply secured than a census of every item in the population. This premise is based upon the assumption that sample characteristics will accurately represent universe characteristics. In order for a sample to represent its population accurately, it must be large enough and must be so taken that it does not overrepresent some elements in the population while underestimating others.

There are at least six good reasons why a researcher would prefer to use a sample instead of a census. Let us examine each of these six.

FINANCIAL CONSTRAINTS

Seldom, if ever, in the case of survey research does the research professional have the funds available to do everything he or she would like to do in a given project. Operating under strict budgetary conditions, the typical researcher simply does not have the money to survey each item in the population. Limited funds mean that only a certain number of people can be employed for a limited time period to collect required information, whether the research is conducted by telephone survey, personal interview, observation, or mail questionnaire. Financial constraints also help determine sample size by placing a limit on the number of consumers to be surveyed or observations made. Though a nationwide census of all consumers might be desirable in certain cases, financial constraints may limit the geographical size of the area that can be covered.

TIME CONSTRAINTS

Information on which to base marketing decisions is usually needed immediately. Gathering information from the entire population can be an enormously time-consuming process, one that may be totally impractical when market information is needed as soon as possible. For example, in the 1970 U.S. *Census of Population*, there was a three-year time lag between the beginning of data collection and the publication of the full results. Seldom can a private organization afford to spend three years conducting a full census in a large universe. Even the U.S. Bureau of the Census must resort to sampling at periodic intervals in order to have current population statistics.

UNIVERSE SIZE

Where the researcher is faced with the task of surveying a large universe, sampling is usually more feasible than taking a complete census. A complete census of the universe may be impossible even where time and money are not the most important considerations. At any given point, some people are out of the country; others are institutionalized in jails or asylums; still others, such as miners, sailors, and hunters, are inaccessible. Generally speaking, the larger the population, the greater the likelihood of resorting to sampling. Where the population is relatively small — for example, U.S. manufacturers of steel — a complete census becomes practical; but with large populations, such as the total number of ultimate consumers of Coca Cola, the researcher is more likely to sample.

THE DESTRUCTIVE NATURE OF SAMPLING

Especially in many quality control situations — examples would be testing the useful life of light bulbs and fuses, tensile strength of steel bars, resistance to heat of materials — the sampling process is of a destructive nature. Naturally, taking a census is out of the question. What good is it for the sales manager to receive accurate information about the tensile strength of all steel bars produced last week? Even if the results show a very high quality, all the bars have been "tested" to the extent that none are left to fill orders from customers. Performing functional tests on every item produced is impossible if it destroys the item; in other cases, such as testing light bulbs to see if they work, though a census may be possible, it is hardly practical.

THE SUFFICIENCY OF AN APPROXIMATION

Quite often an exact description of a characteristic or an exact value of a population parameter is not really necessary for the researcher to make a decision. Sample information will suffice and no census need be taken. It is not necessary for an instructor to know exactly how many students will take a certain course next year in order to decide how many textbooks to order. If too many books are ordered, then the book store may return part of the order to the publisher at no cost. Nor is it necessary to know exactly how many pints of beer are consumed per week to decide what the production level will be, though having fairly precise knowledge might well be desirable.

ACCURACY

It is possible for sample results to be more accurate than the results obtained from a census: in a census, there is a greater likelihood of computational errors in the handling and processing of the much greater volume of data obtained. For example, the U.S. Bureau of the Census conducts a sample survey to check the accuracy of its own census. The smaller number of people required to collect sample data can be rigorously trained in the necessary techniques, and survey instruments can be much more complex in a sample than in a census. Finally, statistical controls for achieving greater accuracy are more useful and efficient when the amount of data is small.

Sampling Problems

Although sampling has a number of clear advantages over census taking, sampling does present problems. Four principal problem areas can be identified: (1) sample design, (2) the skilled personnel required for administering surveys and interpreting sample data, (3) sampling error, and (4) bias. Certainly researchers must contend with many other problems involved in sampling, but careful attention to each of these will eliminate many potential problems.

SAMPLE DESIGN

In designing a sample the researcher must consider three things: (1) the sampling frame, (2) selection of sampling items, and (3) sample size. The *sampling frame* is the list of items in the universe from which the sample is selected. Thus, it may be all the students at Utopia University, names in the phone book, or credit card customers of a department store. After determining the sampling frame, the researcher must decide how sample items will be selected. Basically, this choice involves selection of probability or nonprobability techniques, both of which will be discussed later in this chapter. Finally, the size of the sample must be determined. Should ten or one hundred people be interviewed? Though accuracy is greater with larger samples, so are costs. This matter will be covered later in greater detail.

SKILLED PERSONNEL

For the decision maker to have any faith in sample data, a great deal of the study's time and expense must usually be spent on sampling methodology. Therefore, personnel highly skilled in administering surveys and interpreting sample data must be employed throughout this phase of the research project. People possessing these skills are often difficult to find and expensive to hire. However, if the administering of surveys and interpreting of sample data are left to people with inadequate skills, the reported results may be more confusing and misleading than if a complete census had been undertaken.

SAMPLING ERROR

No sample is guaranteed to be exactly representative of the universe from which it was drawn. Generally, the larger the sample, the smaller the likelihood that it will differ from the universe, but differences are sometimes found. In such cases we have *sampling error*, the difference between characteristics of the sample and those of the population from which the sample was drawn. Sampling error can occur purely by chance and can be especially difficult to detect when the characteristics of the total population are unknown in the first place. For example, when political pollsters say that a candidate will win with 55 percent of the vote, adding that this prediction is accurate within two percentage points in either direction, nineteen times out of twenty they will be right; the one chance in twenty that they will not be right is caused by sampling error. Treatment of sampling error will be discussed later in this text.

BIAS

When an error is made in the selection or measurement of respondents, we have bias. Should the sampling methodology cause one population element to have a systematically higher or lower probability of being selected than other elements in that population, the researcher has induced bias. Bias results from such systematic variance, something that does not happen with an accurate sample.

Consider the following case. A sample survey was conducted in order to find out the average age of students at Utopia University. If the sample had been drawn from students attending evening classes, would we have bias? Certainly we would: evening students tend to be older than those attending day classes, and they would not be representative of the full student body.

The most famous example of sample bias occurred in the 1936 U.S. presidential election. In that year the now extinct *Literary Digest*, a relatively highbrow journal, predicted that the Republican candidate, Alf Landon, would win over the Democrat, Franklin D. Roosevelt.

Sampling error had a negligible impact in this case, since approximately two million voters participated in this sample. What happened?

The *Literary Digest* made the mistake of drawing its sample primarily from the telephone directory. During the height of the depression of the 1930s, many voters were not able to afford the luxury of having a telephone at home, and these voters tended to be Democrats more often than Republicans. The sample was biased toward the more affluent members of society, those who were most likely to vote Republican. Because of bias in sample selection, a tremendous error in forecasting the winner of the 1936 election was made — an error of such magnitude that it is still regularly reported in almost all elementary statistics books.

Types of Samples

Samples can be divided, according to the method used to select them, into two broad categories: *probability* samples and *nonprobability* samples. In the case of probability sampling, all items in the universe have known and equal chances, or probabilities, of being selected. With nonprobability sampling, sometimes referred to as "researcher-controlled sampling," all items in the universe do *not* have known and equal chances of being selected. Figure 9•1 classifies these two basic types of samples and their variations. Let us examine each in greater detail.

Probability Sampling

In probability sampling, also referred to as random sampling, every elementary unit of population has some known element of chance of being selected in the sample. The selection of units is determined purely by chance, using some random device, such as a table of random numbers. On this basis, therefore, we should expect different samples to be selected if the procedure were repeated a number of times. Four main types of probability samples can be identified: (1) simple random, (2) stratified random, (3) cluster, and (4) systematic. Though this is not an exhaustive listing of the types of probability samples, these are the four main ones used by researchers.

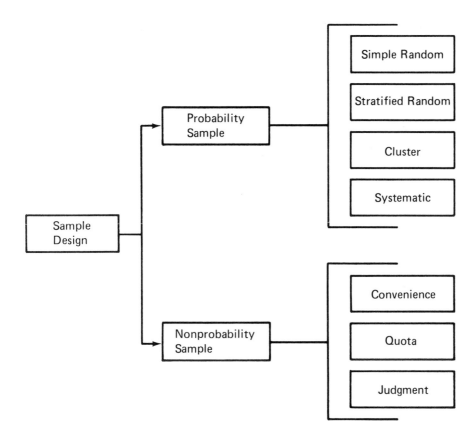

Figure 9·1
Classifying Sample Designs

SIMPLE RANDOM SAMPLING

The easiest probability sampling concept to grasp is that of simple random sampling. Basically, in a simple random sampling scheme, all units of the population being surveyed have equal probabilities of being selected. An example of the most basic form of a simple random sample would be a lottery draw where ten thousand tickets valued at one dollar each have been sold to ten thousand different individuals, who have written their names and addresses on the ticket stubs. The ticket stubs are placed in a squirrel cage and thoroughly mixed. A blindfolded person then draws ten tickets from the squirrel cage and the winners each receive a one thousand dollar prize. In this simple random sample, all ten thousand entrants had known and equal probabilities of being selected: one in one thousand.

Although drawing names from a squirrel cage or numbers from a hat constitutes an acceptable and relatively simple method of taking a simple random sample, perhaps the easiest way of taking such a sample is by using a table of random numbers. Tables of random numbers, often known as tables of random digits, consist of rows and columns in which the decimal digits zero through nine appear. These tables of random numbers are generated by a computer so that each decimal digit has the same probability of being selected as all the others.

Table 9·1 is a partial table of random numbers. Though this table is of four-digit random numbers, any combination can be used and the gaps need not appear, as they do here, between the columns. Any series of numbers read across, up, or down the table is considered random. The only effective restraint is the size of the population being surveyed, which dictates how many digits should be used. A sufficient number of digits must always be selected so that the highest numbered item in the population can be included.

To illustrate the use of such tables, let us assume that a bank has 9,999 depositors. The marketing researcher is planning a survey of 100

Table 9·1
Partial Table of Random Numbers

Rows	COLUMNS									
	1	2	3	4	5	6	7	8	9	10
1	5852	9739	1457	8999	2789	9068	9829	1336	3148	7875
	0440	3769	7864	4029	4494	9829	1339	4910	1303	9161
	0820	4641	2375	2542	4093	5364	1145	2848	2792	0431
	7114	2842	8554	6881	6377	9427	8216	1193	8042	8449
	6558	9301	9096	0577	8520	5923	4717	0188	8545	8745
2	0345	9937	5569	0279	8951	6183	7787	7808	5149	2185
	7430	2074	9427	8422	4082	5629	2971	9456	0649	7981
	8030	7345	3389	4739	5911	1022	9189	2565	1982	8577
	6272	6718	3849	4715	3156	2823	4174	8733	5600	7702
	4894	9847	5611	4763	8755	3388	5114	3274	6681	3657
3	2676	5984	6806	2692	4012	0934	2436	0869	9557	2490
	9305	2074	9378	7670	8284	7431	7361	2912	2251	7395
	5138	2461	7213	1905	7775	9881	8782	6272	0632	4418
	2452	4200	8674	9202	0812	3986	1143	7343	2264	9072
	8882	3033	8746	7390	8609	1144	2531	6944	8869	1570
4	1087	9336	8020	9166	4472	8293	2904	7949	3165	7400
	5666	2841	8134	9588	2915	4116	2802	6917	3993	8764
	9790	2228	9702	1690	7170	7511	1937	0723	4505	7155
	3250	8860	3294	2684	6572	3415	5750	8726	2647	6596
	5450	3922	0950	0890	6434	2306	2781	1066	3681	2404
5	5765	0765	7311	5270	5910	7009	0240	7435	4568	6484
	8408	1939	0599	5347	2160	7376	4696	6969	0787	3838
	8460	7658	6906	9177	1492	4680	3719	3456	8681	6736
	4198	7244	3849	4819	1008	6781	3388	5253	7041	6712
	9872	4441	6712	9614	2736	5533	9062	2534	0855	7946

of the bank's customers to see what they think of the bank's service. A random sample is to be drawn, using a table of random numbers like table 9·1. The researcher could arbitrarily select the numbers in columns two, four, six, and eight, which would give the required random sample of 100. Thus, the first item to be surveyed would be account number 9,739, the second would be account 3,769, and so on.

What if the bank had between 10,000 and 100,000 depositors? In this case, the researcher could have simply added the last digit of each number in columns one, three, five, and seven in the table of random numbers, so that the first number selected would have been account number 29,739, the second account number 3,769, and so forth. Similar adjustments could be made for a larger or smaller universe.

STRATIFIED RANDOM SAMPLING

Seldom is the researcher faced with a homogeneous population from which to sample; populations in most consumer surveys tend to be heterogeneous. When the population can be divided into distinguishable strata that differ significantly from other strata, but have considerable internal homogeneity, stratified sampling may give more precise results than simple random sampling. In stratified random sampling, the population is divided into subgroups and a simple random sample is taken from each subgroup.

Let us examine an oversimplified example. A researcher needs to estimate the average weight of six persons gathered in a room. The weights of the six, individually, are 120, 116, 110, 160, 175, and 190 pounds. However, an average of the six will not be a very meaningful figure if we recognize that the first three people are females and the second three males. By dividing our sample into two strata, **male and female**, we get a much more significant figure for the average weight of each group — 115 pounds and 175 pounds — showing the substantial difference between the groups.

The use of stratified random sampling is desirable from a marketing point of view when we wish to engage in *differentiated marketing* [1] — developing different products and promotional appeals for different market segments. In such cases it is imperative to have accurate data on identifiable and measurable segments of the market, rather than aggregate population statistics.

Two techniques commonly used for stratifying consumer popula-

[1] For a more detailed treatment of differentiated marketing see Philip Kotler, *Marketing Management: Analysis, Planning and Control*, 3rd ed. (Englewood Cliffs, N.J.: Prentice-Hall, 1976), pp. 152–53.

tions are (1) classifying consumers by age and sex and (2) classifying by social and economic criteria. Classifying consumers by age and sex is a relatively simple stratification technique, assuming that there are no problems in obtaining these basic demographic data. This procedure can be particularly valid if the researcher, for example, wishes to find out what teen-age girls think about a new cosmetic product. Drawing a stratified random sample from different social or economic classes is more difficult when we attempt sampling based upon income, residence, car-ownership, marital status, or membership in social organizations. For example, marital status, in recent years, has become a constantly changing phenomenon.

As Charles T. Clark and Lawrence L. Schkade have noted, there are two conditions under which stratified sampling is not possible:

1. There may not be available any frame, or list of items in the universe from which the sample might be drawn. For example, if we wish to interview a sample of farmers in a particular state, it might be impossible to find a list of them.

2. Even with a frame available, if the units in the universe are widely scattered it may be cheaper to use a large sample of units that lie close to one another than to use a small sample of widely scattered units. For example, it might be cheaper to interview fifty farmers in one county than thirty farmers in thirty different counties.[2]

In such cases, the researcher turns to cluster sampling.

CLUSTER SAMPLING

Cluster sampling, which involves groups of sample items chosen at random, is best used when stratified sampling is not possible. It is often referred to as a multistage sampling technique; that is, the random selection of primary sampling units can be either a two-stage or a three-stage exercise. For example, the selection of census tracts would be a first stage, the selection of city blocks within the census tract would be a second, and selecting individual families would be a third. Much cluster sampling is, like this example, *area sampling*, where each cluster comes from a different or separate geographic area. Ideally, each cluster should be selected in such a way that every cluster is heterogeneous, though in practice this is often not possible.

Figure 9·2 illustrates how a two-stage area cluster sample, using

[2] *Statistical Methods for Business Decisions* (Cincinnati, Ohio: Southwestern Publishing Co., 1969), p. 359.

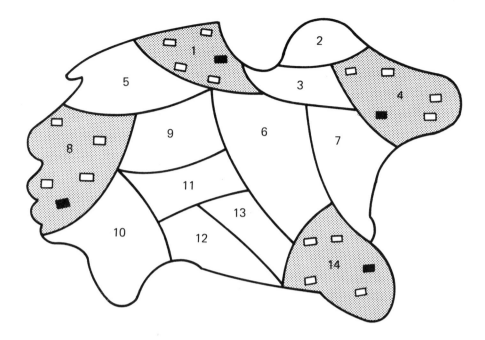

Number of primary units in the population = 14 census tracts
Number of primary units in the sample = 4 census tracts (shaded)
Number of items in each primary unit = 5 blocks
Number of items sampled from each primary unit = 1 block from each tract

Figure 9•2

Illustration of a Hypothetical Two-Stage Cluster Sample of 14 Census Tracts with 5 Blocks in Each Tract

Adapted from Charles T. Clark and Lawrence L. Schkade, *Statistical Methods for Business Decisions* (Cincinnati, Ohio: Southwestern Publishing Co., 1969), p. 363.

census tracts and city blocks, could be taken. Study this simplified example carefully. Can you see how cluster sampling would be easier and cheaper than random sampling? What would be the next step if three-stage sampling were desired?

Researchers are often partial to cluster sampling because it is usually cheaper than simple random sampling from the same population. For example, a national survey using simple random sampling might require data collection from all parts of the country, at considerable expense. By using cluster sampling techniques, the researcher is able to limit traveling for data collection to only one or a few states. John E. Freund and Frank J. Williams have written: "It may well be possible to obtain a cluster sample several times the size of a simple random sample at the same expense. It is much cheaper to visit and interview families living closer together in clusters than families selected at random over a wide area." [3]

In most cases, cluster sampling is not as statistically efficient as random sampling, given the same size samples. That is, cluster sample estimates are usually less accurate than the same size estimates derived from simple random sampling. For the same budget, however, a cluster sampling plan may yield more efficient results, as the savings in traveling expenses and time can be devoted to increasing sample size within each cluster.

> The lower cost per unit and higher sampling error potential of a cluster sample is illustrated by considering a sample of 100 households to be selected for personal interviews. If the 100 households are selected on a single unit basis they will most likely be scattered around the city. This will increase the chance of getting a representative cross section of the various ethnic groups, social classes, and so on. In contrast, a cluster sample in which ten blocks are selected and ten households interviewed on each block will be likely to miss more of the social groups. The reason for this is that members of social groups tend to live in neighborhoods where others of the same group live. The within-cluster variability is likely to be low since the family backgrounds are similar. The costs of personal interviews per unit in a cluster sample will be low, however, because of the close proximity of the units in- each cluster.[4]

In summary, two general advantages of cluster sampling are: (1) it permits random sampling where a sampling frame is not present; and (2) it is often much cheaper than other probability sampling designs.

Cluster Sampling versus Stratified Sampling. It is sometimes not immediately clear just exactly how cluster sampling differs from stratified sampling, since in both cases we are dividing our population into strata or subgroups. Table 9·2 provides a concise comparison of these two sampling techniques.

SYSTEMATIC SAMPLING

Systematic sampling involves the random selection of the first item and then the selection of a sample item at every nth interval. Many times systematic sampling is the simplest as well as the most prac-

---

[3] *Elementary Business Statistics*, 2nd ed. (Englewood Cliffs, N.J.: Prentice-Hall, 1972), p. 419.

[4] Donald S. Tull and Del I. Hawkins, *Marketing Research: Meaning, Measurement, and Method* (New York: Macmillan, 1976), pp. 163–64.

Table 9·2
Stratified Sampling Versus Cluster Sampling

STRATIFIED SAMPLING	CLUSTER SAMPLING
1. The population is divided into a few subgroups, each containing many elements.	1. The population is divided into many subgroups, each containing a few elements.
2. Homogeneity is secured within subgroups and heterogeneity between subgroups.	2. Ideally, heterogeneity is secured within subgroups and homogeneity between subgroups; usually, however, the opposite breakdown is found.
3. Elements from within each subgroup are chosen at random.	3. A number of subgroups are chosen at random to be studied in their entirety.

Source: Adapted from C. William Emory, *Business Research Methods* (Homewood, Ill.: Richard D. Irwin, 1976), p. 160.

tical way to draw a sample. It is used in quality control: perhaps every one-hundredth unit leaving the assembly line is subjected to a detailed quality control inspection. A table of random numbers may be used to generate the first number and thereby identify the first sampling unit.

Systematic sampling is often utilized when the researcher is taking the names listed in a large city telephone directory as the universe. The telephone directory may have 500 pages with four columns of names on each page. Suppose that a sample of 250 is to be drawn from this directory. The easiest way to proceed is to select a name from every other page systematically, using a table of random numbers to generate a number for the selection process. Perhaps the first number is 322; the researcher could take the twenty-second name from the third column of every other page in systematically drawing a sample of 250. In cases where the random number was greater than the number of names on the page, the next random number could be used.

Is systematic sampling as valid as simple random sampling? The answer depends on the arrangement of items from which the sample was drawn. In some cases systematic sampling is better than simple random sampling, because the sample is more evenly distributed from the full population.

The main problem in systematic sampling occurs if we have *hidden periodicities*.[5] That is, does some systematic variance occur at every interval we have selected? In our previous example of the tele-

[5] Freund and Williams, *Elementary Business Statistics*, p. 416.

phone directory, hidden periodicities would probably not have occurred. However, what if we had decided to poll systematically the residents of every twelfth house along the street? Probably no systematic variance would occur, but we might find that every twelfth house was on a corner. Houses on corner lots are usually more expensive than those in the middle of the block and are occupied by people with higher incomes, who may hold opinions and attitudes different from those of their less affluent neighbors.

Nonprobability Sampling

In the previous section, four main probability sampling designs were discussed: simple random, stratified random, cluster, and systematic. We call them probability samples because all items in the population have equal chances of being selected.

However, in actual practice, probability sampling is not always used. Some investigators are not very scientific in their sampling techniques. In other cases, precise accuracy in sampling may not be necessary. For example, the cost factor of test marketing a new product on the national scale is such that most new products are test marketed only in one or a very few cities. These cities are not selected through probability sampling techniques but rather because the researcher thinks they represent "typical" American cities. Consequently, when marketers opt for full-scale national distribution based on sales results in a few test-market cities, this decision is being made on the basis of a nonprobability sample. It is not that the large consumer goods manufacturers, such as General Foods and General Mills, are unscientific in their research methodology; it is simply that a probability sample is not practical in this instance.

Exactly what do we mean by nonprobability sampling? Any sampling technique in which the selection of sample items is *not* determined by chance, but rather by personal convenience, expert judgment, or any type of conscious researcher selection, is called nonprobability sampling. Three principal types of nonprobability, or nonrandom, sampling may be identified: (1) convenience, (2) judgment, and (3) quota.

CONVENIENCE SAMPLING

Convenience sampling is so named because it is convenient for the researcher to select the first few sample items quickly, rather than to go through the laborious process of obtaining a probability sample.

When approximations will suffice, and both time and money are seriously limited, convenience samples are widely used. Selecting sample units from the population solely on the basis of personal convenience to the researcher is widely found in man-on-the-street interviews conducted by television newspeople. If it is convenient to do the sampling during lunch hour, the researcher may well draw the sample from a cafeteria or neighboring tavern. Often pretests of questionnaires use convenience sampling; in these cases the researcher wants only a trial run of the questionnaire itself.

Convenience sampling is a widespread practice, one in which all of us are participants in one form or another. Since our private convenience samples usually include only our close friends, family members, and people within our social class, we are often surprised when we find that a political candidate whose views are directly opposite to ours and those of nearly all our friends is elected by a large majority.

Although convenience sampling is not very scientific, it is not likely to disappear as a sampling technique. Its speed and ease ensure its long-term existence. The important thing to recognize is that projections for the entire population should not be based on a convenience sample; yet it may be a perfectly valid technique in exploratory research, questionnaire pretesting, and any other case where a representative sample is not considered necessary.

JUDGMENT SAMPLING

Slightly more scientifically selected than a convenience sample, the judgment sample is determined by the researcher's idea of a representative sample. Judgment samples are selected through researcher intuition or on some other subjective basis. Therefore, sample representativeness is highly dependent upon the good judgment of the researcher, and possibly upon a good bit of luck, also.

As in the case of convenience samples, judgment samples can be very misleading if they are interpreted as accurate reflections of universe characteristics. Probably the most valid usage of judgment sampling is to obtain expert opinions. Thus, the *Wall Street Journal* might select a sample of twelve of the most influential economists to estimate next year's rate of inflation. Certainly the judgment of these experts is much superior to a convenience sample that might arbitrarily be limited to the estimates to the first twelve people found on the street or in a neighborhood bar. Of course, the problem with expert opinions is first determining who the experts are and then recognizing that expert opinion is not necessarily representative of the general population.

Nor will the views espoused by the "experts" always be well received by the population. William Buckley, for example, is alleged to have said, "I'd rather be led by the first 100 people in the phone book than the entire Harvard Law School faculty."

QUOTA SAMPLING

The most sophisticated of our three nonprobability sampling techniques is quota sampling. In this method, the population is divided into a number of segments, and the researcher arbitrarily selects a quota of sample items from each segment, or cell. Taking a quota sample is therefore a three-step operation: (1) deciding how many segments or cells the population will be divided into, (2) deciding what percentage of sample items should be in any one cell, and (3) actually selecting the sample items.

Carefully examine table 9•3, a somewhat simplified illustration of a six-cell quota sample. Here all three steps in drawing a quota sample have been followed. First, the universe was divided on the basis of age and sex, with three cells allocated to age categories and two to sex. Second, the appropriate percentages to be included in each cell (49 percent male and 51 percent female and so forth) were determined. Third was the actual selection of sample items for each cell. For a total sample size of one hundred, accordingly, a field worker would be assigned an interview quota of twelve male subjects aged eighteen to twenty-five — hence the name *quota sampling*.

How, then, does quota sampling differ from stratified random sampling? In both sampling techniques, a universe is divided up into strata or segments; but there the similarity ends. In stratified random sampling a random sample is taken within each strata or cell, whereas in quota sampling the researcher arbitrarily selects items from each cell. Look back at table 9•3; the twelve male subjects aged eighteen to

Table 9•3
Illustration of a Six-Cell Quota Sample

		AGE		
SEX	18–25	26–49	50 AND OVER	TOTAL
Male	12%	21%	16%	49%
Female	13	21	17	51
Total	25%	42%	33%	100%

twenty-five would be chosen at random in a stratified random sample, whereas in a quota sample they would be selected arbitrarily.

Although quota sampling is the most systematic and scientific of our three nonprobability sampling techniques, it does not ensure the selection of a representative sample. As with stratified random sampling, there is difficulty in determining the appropriate percentages to be assigned to each cell and in determining in which cell sample items properly belong. For example, mistakes could be made by researchers in determining respondent age quotas in table 9•3. Why should 25 percent of our sample be selected from the eighteen to twenty-five age group? However, the principal drawback of quota sampling is the arbitrary nonrandom selection of items in each cell by the researcher. This arbitrariness reduces the likelihood of obtaining a representative sample. Still, cost and time constraints sometimes make quota sampling an attractive alternative to stratified sampling.

Summary

This chapter has dealt with sampling concepts. A *sample* is defined as a subgroup of observations from a larger population or universe (the terms *universe* or *population* are used interchangeably to refer to every item of the whole that is being studied). Thus, a sample is only a portion of the total amount of information that can conceivably be gathered. If we have counted all the items in the universe, we have taken not a sample but a census.

A critical first step in sampling is to define clearly the limits of the population being studied. Depending on the nature of the study being undertaken, we could have a population consisting of all university students in North America, all business students in North America, all business students at Utopia University, all marketing majors at Utopia University, and so forth. Populations may be finite or infinite. A *finite* population is one containing a fixed number of elements, whereas an *infinite* population is one without limits of any kind. Although it is possible to draw samples from both finite and infinite populations, it is impossible to take a census of an infinite population; from the latter only a sample may be drawn.

Sampling is based on the premise that a relatively small number of items drawn from a universe will provide an accurate representation of the characteristics of that population. Although this theory does not always hold true in actual practice, we do know that a sample can be more quickly, easily, and cheaply taken than a census. Six main reasons have been identified for sampling instead of census taking: (1) financial constraints, (2) time constraints, (3) universe size, (4) the destructive nature of sampling, (5) the sufficiency of an approximation, and (6) accuracy. Despite these advantages, sampling does present problems. Four main problem areas are identified here: (1) sample design, (2) the skilled personnel required for administering surveys and interpreting sample data, (3) sampling error, and (4) bias. Each of these problems, however, is controllable.

Depending on the selection method used, samples are either *probability* or *nonprobability*. In the case of probability sampling, all items in the universe have known and equal chances, or probabilities, of being selected. Nonprobability sampling, quite simply, means that all items in the population do *not* have equal chances of being selected. When classifying sample designs, four major types of probability samples can be identified: (1) random, (2) stratified random, (3) cluster, and (4) systematic. Nonprobability samples include (1) convenience, (2) judgment, and (3) quota samples. Though probability sampling techniques are generally clearly superior, researchers sometimes find it advantageous to use nonprobability sampling when it is not necessary to have a representative sample or when time and cost constraints make probability sampling impractical.

Questions for Discussion

1. A manufacturer of men's clothing has approximately one hundred retail outlets concentrated in the southwestern United States. The manufacturer needs to begin production of a new line of men's trousers within the next four weeks but thinks it might be a good idea to survey the store managers in order to get their opinions on how well this new line will sell. In answering each of the following questions, give your rationale.

a. Should the manufacturer conduct a census or take a sample among his dealers?

b. If a sample is taken, should it be probability or nonprobability?

c. If a sample is taken, which type of probability or nonprobability sample do you think would be best?

d. Is the survey necessary in the first place?

2. Explain the difference between a convenience sample and a judgment sample. Which is better?

3. Your marketing research professor has assigned you the task of selecting a probability sample of one hundred students from among the five thousand enrolled at Utopia University. Describe the sampling procedure you have elected to follow.

4. Give a research problem that would favor the use of a cluster sample and one that would favor a stratified sample.

5. Why does the U.S. Bureau of the Census have to resort to sampling in addition to taking censuses?

6. You are asked to survey at random twenty-five people identified in your city's telephone directory. How would you go about selecting this probability sample?

7. A manufacturer of dietetic soft drinks is considering adding a new low-calorie carbonated beverage to her firm's product line, but first she wants to take a survey to find out what potential customers think of this product concept.

a. What is the manufacturer's relevant population or universe?

b. How should the sample be selected?

c. What kind of sample should be selected?

8. A radio station wants to find out what local people think about a forthcoming school bond election. The station manager has his disc jockeys request listeners to phone in with their opinions concerning the proposed bond offering. What are some of the things that might be wrong with this type of sample?

9. Design a two-stage area sample using your own hypothetical data.

10. In order to measure neighborhood opinion of a proposed city ordinance, you are to survey the occupants of every fifth house in a residential neighborhood. Is there anything wrong with this systematically drawn sample?

Chapter 10

Data Analysis

THE PURPOSE OF THIS CHAPTER is to give an introduction to the mechanics of data analysis. We will look first at some of the problems of data editing and data coding that must be addressed before data tabulation and testing can begin. Then, in the latter sections of the chapter, we will investigate several tabulation methods commonly used for the analysis of numerical data.

Editing

Beginning researchers often have the impression that once a set of responses is collected, the job of tabulating and analyzing those responses should be very straightforward. Experienced researchers know that, in most cases, the job will be anything but simple; they realize that the coding of questionnaires is far from mechanical, that much subjective editing and interpretation are necessary before the analysis can be completed. No mere description of the process can suffice; only after one has waded through several hundred survey forms, each with a variety of errors, omissions, and inconsistencies, does one realize the magnitude of the task that coding, and editing in preparation for coding, can present. Some researchers estimate that approximately 25 percent of the time and resources of a survey project goes into the process of coding the questionnaires into a format suitable for numerical tabulation. Therefore (and 25 percent may be a conservative figure), the coding of the data, which is usually viewed as a quick, automatic process of inconsequential cost, must be seen in its true perspective as one of the most expensive and most crucial parts of the entire research project.

Thus, one of the researcher's considerations is to prepare a survey instrument that will produce results amenable to coding. Too many open-ended or ambiguous questions can quickly cause the coding to become prohibitively expensive. Furthermore, the coding can be done improperly, thereby distorting or even negating the results of the entire project. Even when the editing and coding process is carefully monitored and supervised, because of the large amount of detail work countless "little" errors can enter into the calculations. Quality control studies indicate that for every one hundred human calculations, five are incorrect; and studies of data coding and editing often reveal that upwards of 10 percent of all material has been misprocessed in some manner. Market researchers deal with this problem in two ways: first, they try to provide intensive supervision and support to eliminate as many of the errors as possible; then, they simply assume (hope) that those undetected errors that are bound to get through will be self-canceling — that is, that the errors made in one direction will be offset by those made in the other. Although this is a reasonable enough assumption, there is yet another source of nonsampling error.

Problems Caused by Respondents

Even when the researcher has taken pains to produce what should be a very codable questionnaire, and even when he has taken pains to supervise the careful work of trained coders vigorously, the respondents themselves can still create a host of problems against which there are actually very few defenses.

Many times, while working on a set of questionnaires, a researcher gets the distinct impression that the answers are just not making sense. For instance, a respondent may say that he prefers hamburgers from Wendy's over hamburgers from McDonald's, only to say later in the questionnaire that he has never tried a Wendy's hamburger. Or perhaps the respondent has written down a number of replies, but they are so illegible that they cannot be deciphered. Or perhaps, in a dichotomous question, the respondent has checked both "yes" and "no" and written a series of qualifiers. In cases such as these, what is the researcher to do?

Perhaps the respondent has left a number of the questions blank, or certain questions are producing a large number of "don't know" responses, or the respondent gives other, similar responses, indicating that she really does not know what she is talking about. Again, what is the researcher to do? What value does the researcher assign in these situations?

Missing Data

All the situations just described fall into the basic category of missing data. Missing data represent the single most severe problem for the researcher trying to edit, code, and tabulate numerical data. The researcher can attempt to deal with this problem in several ways, although none of them is entirely satisfactory as a replacement for the actual data that has been omitted. Four approaches that can be tried are: (1) predicting the individual respondent's probable response, (2) substituting the overall group average or distribution, (3) randomly inserting a replacement value, and (4) leaving that question blank in the coding.

The Individual Approach. In some cases, it may be possible to predict the respondent's probable response. For instance, if a respondent said that she was retired and living on social security, but did not put her age, we could assume with reasonable safety that she was at least sixty-five years old. In the case of personal interviews, the interviewer might have obtained a good impression of the respondent during the conversation and might feel qualified to predict the respondent's answers for some questions.

The Group Average. In cases where information is lacking on the individual respondent, then the group average of those respondents who did answer the question might be substituted for the missing item. In the case of a frequency distribution, the blanks might be distributed among the classes in the ratio observed in the completed items.

Arbitrary Substitution. When the number of missing items is small, the difficulty of computing group averages, making individual predictions, and so forth can be avoided by substituting arbitrarily assigned values in place of the missing items. Although there is very little in this technique to recommend it statistically, it does fill in the blanks in an efficient and economical manner.

Leaving the Question Blank. It may seem strange to the reader that so much effort is being made to fill in these missing responses. After all, if the respondent left the question blank, why not simply record that answer as a nonresponse? Of course, this is exactly what is done in many situations; however, there is a very good reason why the researcher is anxious to have as few blanks as possible in the final set of numbers. The reason is that in some types of numerical calculations, including virtually all computer analyses, blanks are treated like zeros. Thus, if someone was embarrassed about his age and left that question blank, then his age would become zero by default. You can see that, if the data contained a sizable number of these zeros, the results would soon become worthless. Correlations between age and income, between age and buying patterns — even the average age of the group — would be greatly distorted by the presence of such zeros. It is for this reason that the researcher usually tries to provide some response, if at all possible.

A related problem is that, because of the computer's inability to differentiate between zeros and blanks, it is inadvisable to use zero as a valid code: a coding format such as *yes* = 1 and no = 0 will not differentiate the "no" responses from the nonrespondents.

Coding Numerical Data

Before beginning the discussion of numerical tabulation techniques, it is important to emphasize that all numbers are not alike. In other words, that symbol which looks like the number 5 may not actually represent what we consider the quantity five. Therefore, much of the data you encounter, especially in marketing, may not be numeric at all, simply symbolic.

As a matter of fact, there exist several different kinds of data, each of different strength. It is important that you realize the differences between the various kinds of data, because not all are appropriate for all types of analysis.

Types of Data

Most marketing researchers note four types of data:

- *Nominal.* From nominate, to name, to classify. The numbers in nominal data have no intrinsic value; they are used only for classification. For example, football jerseys might be coded male = 1, female = 2.

- *Ordinal.* To order. The numbers indicate position or order but not distance. Knowing, for example, that the finish order was first, second, third, one still doesn't know whether it was a close race or a lopsided victory.

• *Interval*. Like ordinal but with constant intervals. The numbers tell both position and distance. The distance between positions is assumed to be equal in most interval scales, and there is no fixed zero point. Temperature is an example.

• *Ratio*. Can form meaningful ratios. The most powerful kind of data, ratio data have a fixed zero point. Examples are money and length.

These types of data are presented in order of their strength, starting with the weakest and proceeding to the strongest. The type of data is very important to the marketing researcher, because the type of statistical analysis that can be performed on the data is theoretically dependent upon the type of data that was collected. The dependence is theoretical because, in actuality, once the numbers have been punched on cards the computer will perform any type of analysis desired. However, unless the data are of the proper strength, the results may be as meaningless as an average of the numerals of a football team or, at best, misleading in that they may overstate or understate the true differences between groups of numbers.

It is also important to note that, by changing the format of the question, the researcher can ask essentially the same question but obtain different types of data. For instance, consider a question regarding income:

Ordinal	*Interval*	*Ratio*
What is your income?	What is your income?	What is your income?
_____very low	_____less than $5000	
_____low	_____$5000 to $9,999	
_____average	_____$10,000 to $14,999	My yearly
_____high	_____$15,000 to $20,000	income is
_____very high	_____more than $20,000	$_____.

Note, also, that data can always be broken down from the higher forms into the weaker forms. Thus, a researcher could form interval data from ratio data, and ordinal data from interval data. The reverse does not hold; strong data can be downgraded into weak data, but weak data cannot be upgraded into strong. For this reason, the survey instrument should seek to obtain the highest level of data possible.

Coding Nominal Data

When coding, it is necessary to guard against accidentally coding nominal data into the form of some higher data. Consider the following coding of a question regarding marital status:

```
Single  . . . . . . . . . . . . .1
Married  . . . . . . . . . . . .2
Separated  . . . . . . . . .3
Divorced  . . . . . . . . . .4
Widowed  . . . . . . . . . . .5
```

Notice that the nominal data has been inadvertently converted into ordinal data. Although it is true that steps 4 or 5 would have to follow steps 1 and 2, and that 1 must precede 2, the scale as a whole breaks down as ordinal data. Being now improperly coded as ordinal data, the answers to this question cannot be statistically related to answers to any other questions in any meaningful way. Any analysis (correlation, regression, even averages and dispersions) using such a batch of data will be perfectly useless.

In order to code such a question so that it will be significant in conjunction with other questions, each category of the question must be coded as a separate question, turning one question into five:

```
Marital status:
Single  . . . . . . . . . .Yes = 1,  No = 2
Married  . . . . . . . .Yes = 1,  No = 2
Separated  . . . . . . .Yes = 1,  No = 2
Divorced  . . . . . . . .Yes = 1,  No = 2
Widowed  . . . . . . .Yes = 1,  No = 2
```

Although this may seem like a lot of extra work, it represents the only way of handling nominal data in a valid fashion, and the technique should be used whenever nominal data are encountered.

Maintaining Logical Consistency

It is quite common to see *yes* = 1 and *no* = 2, but a better coding would be *yes* = 2 and *no* = 1. In this way the more positive reply will be associated with the higher number. In the example above, therefore, the coding should be:

```
Single  . . . . . . . . .Yes = 2,  No = 1
Married . . . . . . . . Yes = 2,  No = 1
Separated . . . . . . . .Yes = 2,  No = 1
Divorced  . . . . . . .Yes = 2,  No = 1
Widowed  . . . . . . .Yes = 2,  No = 1
```

A researcher should always try to arrange the coding so that an increasing amount of the quantity gets a higher value in the code. Consider the original coding in the example on marital status (*yes* = 1, *no* = 2): if the respondents were divided into two groups and the researcher averaged the replies to the "single" question, that coding would indicate that the group with the *higher* average had the *lower* number of singles. Such logical flips can become quite confusing, especially when there are many variables to consider. Therefore, it is important to keep the intuitive meanings of the answers consistent with the coding.

Tabulating the Data

The simple forms of descriptive statistics — percentages, averages, dispersions, and classification tables — are by far the most used and the most useful of all statistical tools. Senator Patrick Moynihan has expressed the importance of these simple measures: "There is simply nothing so important to a people and its government as how many of them there are, whether their number is growing or declining, how they are distributed as between different ages, sexes. . . . I have often wondered whether government pays so little seeming attention to these issues for the simple reason that when it does, Behemoth must confront the fact that the great decisions of the world are made by solitary couples — male and female — and are made in bed to boot." [1]

In the next chapter we will investigate a number of statistical techniques to analyze averages and percentages, but the fact remains that the averages by themselves, or the percentage breakdowns by themselves, devoid of any further analysis, remain the business planner's most useful tools.

Percentages

Surely the most widely used statistic for reporting and summarizing data is the percentage. We are constantly bombarded with reports stating that such and such percentage does this, and so and so percentage does that. Yet despite the disarming simplicity of the percentage, its use is often fraught with pitfalls; it is sometimes misused, at other times underused, and at still other times overused.

Underuse of the Percentage as a Rate

One of the most useful features of the percentage is that it can reduce everything to a common base and thereby allow meaningful comparisons to be made. For instance, suppose that teacher Eezy

[1] Quoted from the *Wall Street Journal*, 15 August 1977.

flunked two students last semester, whereas teacher Grimm flunked four. Which teacher is the more demanding grader? Actually, the information given tells us virtually nothing. We need to know how many students were involved in each case, so that we can determine the *rate* at which students were being flunked. If, for instance, we discover that Eezy had five students and Grimm had eighty, we see that Eezy's rate of failures was $2/5 = 0.40$ or 40 percent, whereas Grimm's was $4/80 = 0.05$ or 5 percent.

Yet the percentage is still underused in this regard. The single most valuable thing that can be done for most numerical presentations is conversion of all the numbers into percentages so that the reader can tell at a glance their relative magnitudes.

A Word of Caution on Overuse of the Percentage as a Rate

There is a time, however, when it is best *not* to convert numbers into percentages. This is when the absolute number of entries is very small. For instance, suppose a candidate claims that a survey shows 60 percent of the voters favoring his platform, but then it is discovered that he talked to only five people, three of whom were for his platform. As the example shows, reporting by percentages can be used to camouflage a small base and make a small sample sound more authoritative. For this reason, many researchers advise against the use of percentages unless the group numbers at least fifty. Of course, the best way to present data is to provide both the absolute numbers and the derived percentages.

Percentages on a Declining Base

Another problem with the use of percentages involves interest rates. Suppose that you borrow $100 for a year at 6 percent, the sum to be paid back with interest in monthly installments. The loan merchant computes the payments in this way: principal ($100) + interest ($6) = $106/12 = $8.34 per month. The question now is, will you really be paying 6 percent interest on that loan? The answer is no, because you did not have the use of the entire $100 for the entire year. Since by the end of the year the sum was down to nothing (see fig. 10•1), on the average you had the usage of only $50, which means that your effective rate of interest was approximately $6/$50 = 0.12 or 12 percent.

We do not wish to get too carried away with these financial formulas and their calculations. Our purpose here is to point out that it is very easy to play all kinds of games with percentages and percentage rates. The reader or user of statistical information expressed in per-

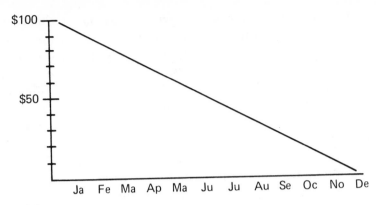

Figure 10·1
Percentages on a Declining Base

centage form must be very careful to understand exactly what is being figured, which numbers are being used, and where they came from.

Pitfalls of Percentage Increases and Decreases

In the discussion of interest rates given above, we saw the effect upon interest rates of a change in the base. The same effect accompanies percentage increases and decreases. Suppose that you were forced to take a 20 percent cut in pay. If you were later given a 20 percent pay raise, would that raise restore your pay to its original amount? The answer is no, because the base would have changed. It would take an increase of 25 percent to restore the cut of 20 percent (the reciprocal of 4/5 is 5/4; thus, a reduction of 20 percent, cutting your pay down to 80 percent of its original amount, would require an increase of 25 percent to regain the original figure). Although the mathematics involved here are not terribly sophisticated, it is extremely easy to become careless and make an error. Constant vigilance is required to avoid mistakes.

Averages

Measures of Central Tendency

There are three forms of central tendency commonly used in marketing research: the arithmetic mean, the median, and the mode. Though there are other measures of central tendency, these three cover most marketing usages. The usual order of presentation — mean, median, mode — aside from being alphabetical, also gives the approximate magnitude of usage of each and even indicates their position in a

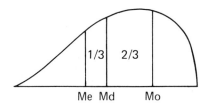

Figure 10·2
Skewed Distribution

skewed distribution (fig. 10·2), one which has a more pronounced "tail" on one end. Theoretically speaking, the mode will always occupy the highest point in a skewed distribution, with the mean the farthest out along the tail and the median in between, twice as far from the mode as from the mean. In a symmetric distribution all three will be right in the middle.

The Mean (abbreviated Me or μ). The arithmetic mean, or what most people consider "the average," is the sum of all items divided by the number of items. Of the three measures, the mean is the one most affected by extreme values. It has the form

$$\mu = \text{mean} = \frac{\Sigma x}{\eta}$$

No more than a different formulation of the arithmetic mean, the *expected value* has the form

$$\mathrm{E}(\mu) = \Sigma x_i p_1$$

and is used in many kinds of marketing analysis. It is sometimes referred to as the *weighted mean.*

The Median (abbreviated Md.) The median is the middle value of an *ordered* or arrayed set of numbers (see fig. 10·3). The median is quite popular in population and income studies, since it is not overly affected by extreme values. Each member of the population has one vote in determining where the middle of the group will be, and for this reason the median is sometimes cited as the most democratic measure of central tendency.

The Mode (abbreviated Mo). The mode is the most frequently occurring value of a group of values. It is the least frequently used measure: not only is it neither a consistent nor a sufficient estimator,

Data Analysis · 217

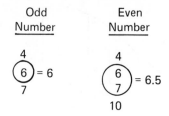

Figure 10·3
The Median

it also suffers from the problem that computation is basically a matter of inspection rather than formula and therefore is not usually amenable to computer manipulation.

SLANTED STATISTICS AND OTHER PROBLEMS

One of the biggest problems with these three measures of central tendency is that they all can qualify as "averages," and yet, as shown in figure 10·2, they will all be different if the distribution is skewed. Unfortunately, many of the variables of critical concern to marketing researchers have just such skewed distributions (sales, income, travel, consumption, and so on). Because of the different averages involved, there is always the opportunity for "slanting" the statistics in a given direction, and the researcher must be on guard for this slanting. Aside from possible misrepresentations caused by reporting the various averages from a skewed distribution, there are other pitfalls involved with the use of the average.

The Nonexistent Average. If the population has some unusual distribution, the average (mean and median anyway) may be nonexistent, or at least of minimal importance (see fig. 10·4). It is like the story of the statistician who has his head in the refrigerator and his feet in the oven; asked how he was feeling, he replied; "Well, on the average, I feel

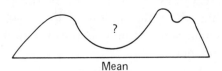

Figure 10·4
The Nonexistent Average

218 • Marketing Research

pretty good." This problem can be critical to marketing strategies because the average frequently obscures significant market segments.

Nobody Is Average. More technically, from a theoretical standpoint *nobody* is average, because the average represents only a single point on the number line (see fig. 10•5), and a point has no area. The probability of any person's being average is therefore zero. Even as a practical matter, the chance of being precisely average is also zero. For example, though a child-care book may state that the average youngster begins to walk at one year, that figure is only approximate: no child will walk precisely as he blows out the candles on his first birthday cake. Every child will be either a little bit early or a little bit late. The question of whether a child is significantly early or late can be answered only through the use of some measure of dispersion (the variation within a set of values), yet many a parent has overreacted to these average figures and worried needlessly.

Spurious Precision. Because of the manner in which the average is computed, it is very easy to develop an average that appears much more precise than the data from which it was composed. Consider this example:

```
$ 5,000
$ 3,000
$ 2,000
‾‾‾‾‾‾‾
$10,000
```

$10,000/3 = 3,333.333333333$. Thus, the average can be said to be $3,333.33, instead of $3,000 or, at most precise, $3,300. Although it is always apparent where the increase in decimal places came from, the final answer is overly precise and as such is very misleading. It gives a feeling of exactness and certainty that is unwarranted. This is but another version of the familiar GIGO (Garbage In, Garbage

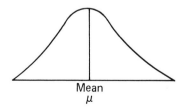

Mean
μ

Figure 10•5
Nobody Is Average

Out) — a final answer, like a chain, is no stronger than its weakest link; the final answer can be no more precise than the most imprecise figure used as input. For instance, a study recently reported that fathers spent only 37.1 seconds per day with their infants under one year of age. Certainly, however, the estimates supplied by the individual fathers were not accurate to the tenth of a second and probably not even to the second. The researcher simply went ahead with the estimates he had, totaled them up, divided by the number of respondents, and then cranked out the quotient to a ridiculous specificity. A more appropriate conclusion would have been that the average time fathers spent with their infants was under one minute per day.

SAMPLE PROBLEMS INVOLVING MEASURES OF CENTRAL TENDENCY

1. For the following set of numbers (which features an even number of elements), compute the median, the mode, and the arithmetic mean, using the expected value formula:

Initial Data Set	Ordered to Compute Median	Arithmetic Mean	Expected Value
6	1	1	$1 \times 2/8 = 2/8$
5	1 ⎱ mode = 1	1	$1 \times 2/8 = 2/8$
7	2	2	$2 \times 1/8 = 2/8$
8	4	4	$4 \times 1/8 = 4/8$
2 ⎱ median = 4.5	5	5	$5 \times 1/8 = 5/8$
1	6	6	$6 \times 1/8 = 6/8$
1	7	7	$7 \times 1/8 = 7/8$
4	8	8	$8 \times 1/8 = 8/8$

$$\mu = \Sigma x / \eta \qquad \Sigma x = 34 \qquad E = \Sigma p_i x_i = 34/8 = 4.25$$
$$\mu = 34/8 = 4.25$$

2. For the following set of numbers (which features an odd number of elements), compute the median, the mode, and the arithmetic mean, using the expected value formula:

Initial Data Set	Ordered to Compute Median	Arithmetic Mean	Expected Value
5	6	6	$6 \times 1/7 = 6/7$
4	5	5	
5 median = 5	5	5	
5	5	5	$5 \times 3/7 = 15/7$
6	4 ⎱ bimodal 4 and 5	4	
4	4	4	
4	4	4	$4 \times 3/7 = 12/7$

$$\Sigma x = 33 \qquad E = \Sigma x_i p_i = 33/7 = 4.71$$

Dispersions

Most of the problems concerning averages that were presented in the last section could have been solved if the exact nature of the distribution had been known. This section will focus primarily on the measures of dispersion, which tell the amount or the magnitude of the spread. Measures that tell something of the shape of the distribution will also be discussed.

Note, however, that the only way to know the exact shape of the distribution is to use a graph showing shape and percentages. Such a picture can convey more important information in a single glance than can be conveyed in pages of numbers — numbers that probably are not going to be read or remembered anyway.

MEASURES OF DISPERSION

Range. The crudest measure of spread, the range is often the most useful. It is simply the difference between the highest value and the lowest value.

Interquartile Range. One of the problems with the range is that it can be unduly influenced by an unusually high or low end value. To avoid this problem, the interquartile range is sometimes used. The interquartile range is the range of the middle 50 percent. To derive it, subtract the value at the end of the third quarter (75 percent) from the value at the end of the first quarter (25 percent) (see figure 10•6).

Average Deviation. Just as its name implies, the average deviation is the average (arithmetic mean) of the deviations of the various items in the group from the mean. The problem of the negative signs is handled by the use of the absolute value; that is, we ignore the positive or negative values of the deviations from the mean and measure the

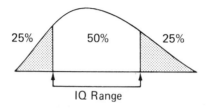

Figure 10•6
Interquartile Range

absolute difference. Without the absolute value, the total of the sum would be zero. The formula for the average deviation is

$$\frac{\sum\limits_{i=1}^{\eta} |x_i - \mu|}{\eta}$$

Standard Deviation. The standard deviation is just like the average deviation except that, instead of taking the absolute value of the numbers to eliminate the negative signs, the standard deviation takes the square of the deviations of individual values from the arithmetic mean. The magnitude of the numbers is altered by this process, so the result is then brought back into line by taking the square root of the resulting sum. Despite the increased difficulty of computation caused by the squaring process, the standard deviation is the generally preferred measure of dispersion. The reason for this preference is that the standard deviation is one of the parameters of the normal curve (discussed below). The formula for the standard deviation is

$$\sigma = \begin{matrix} \text{standard} \\ \text{deviation} \end{matrix} = \sqrt{\frac{\sum\limits_{i=1}^{\eta} (x_i - \mu)^2}{\eta}}$$

There is an alternate standard deviation formula, which is easier to compute by hand:

$$\sqrt{\frac{\Sigma x^2}{\eta} - \left(\frac{\Sigma x}{\eta}\right)^2}$$

The squared difference before the square root is taken is called the *variance*; its formula is

$$\frac{\sum\limits_{i=1}^{\eta} (x_i - \mu)^2}{\eta}$$

Note that the value of the standard deviation will not be equal to the value of the average deviation; as a rule it will be about 15 percent to 20 percent larger. To be specific, the range plus or minus one standard deviation around the mean is expected to take in 68.2

percent of a normally distributed population, whereas the range plus or minus one average deviation around the mean is expected to take in only 57.5 percent of a normally distributed population.

The Standard Deviation and Its Relationship to the Normal Curve

As mentioned above, the principal reason for the importance of the standard deviation is that it is one of the parameters of the normal curve (the other parameter being the mean). In practice, this means that if you know the standard deviation, and if you know (or assume) that the population is normally distributed, you can determine what percentage of the population falls between selected intervals (as measured in standard deviations). As shown in figure 10•7, 68 percent of the population will lie within one standard deviation of the mean (taken from both directions). Since many population characteristics can be assumed to have a normal distribution, the use of the standard deviation in this manner is quite important in marketing research, as in many other disciplines.

Sample Problems Involving Measures of Dispersion

1. Using the following data set (the same set used in the first of the problems involving measures of central tendency), compute the range, the average deviation, and the standard deviation (here the

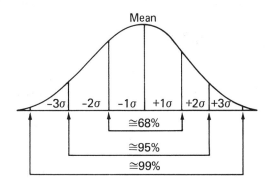

Figure 10•7
Standard Deviation and Normal Curve

standard deviation is computed using both formulas; formula 2 is easier to use):

Initial Data Set	Ordered to Compute Range
6	1
5	1
7	2
8	4 range = 1
2	5 or 8 $\longleftrightarrow$ 7
1	6
1	7
4	8
$\Sigma x = 34$	

$$\mu = \frac{34}{8} = 4.25$$

Average Deviation	Standard Deviation	Standard Deviation (alternate formula)
$\|1 - 4.25\| = 3.25$	$(1 - 4.25)^2 = 10.5625$	$1^2 = 1$
$\|1 - 4.25\| = 3.25$	$(1 - 4.25)^2 = 10.5625$	$1^2 = 1$
$\|2 - 4.25\| = 2.25$	$(2 - 4.25)^2 = 5.0625$	$2^2 = 4$
$\|4 - 4.25\| = 0.25$	$(4 - 4.25)^2 = 0.0625$	$4^2 = 16$
$\|5 - 4.25\| = 0.75$	$(5 - 4.25)^2 = 0.5625$	$5^2 = 25$
$\|6 - 4.25\| = 1.75$	$(6 - 4.25)^2 = 3.0625$	$6^2 = 36$
$\|7 - 4.25\| = 2.74$	$(7 - 4.25)^2 = 7.5625$	$7^2 = 49$
$\|8 - 4.25\| = 3.75$	$(8 - 4.25)^2 = 14.0625$	$8^2 = 64$
18.00	51.000	$196 = \Sigma x^2$

$$\text{average deviation} = \frac{\Sigma|x - \mu|}{\eta} \qquad \begin{array}{c}\text{standard}\\ \text{deviation}\\ \text{(formula 1)}\end{array} = \sqrt{\frac{\Sigma(x - \mu)^2}{\eta}} \qquad \begin{array}{c}\text{standard}\\ \text{deviation}\\ \text{(formula 2)}\end{array} = \sqrt{\frac{\Sigma x^2}{\eta} - \left(\frac{\Sigma x}{\eta}\right)^2}$$

$$\text{A.D.} = \frac{18.00}{8} \qquad \sigma = \sqrt{\frac{51.50}{8}} \qquad = \sqrt{\frac{196}{8} - \left(\frac{34}{8}\right)^2}$$

$$\text{A.D.} = 2.25 \qquad \sigma = \sqrt{6.437} = 2.537 \qquad = \sqrt{24.5 - (4.25)^2}$$

$$\sigma = 2.5 \qquad = \sqrt{24.5 - 18.0625}$$

$$= \sqrt{6.437} = 2.537$$

$$\sigma = 2.5$$

2. Using the same data set used in the second of the problems involving measures of central tendency, compute the range, the average deviation, and the standard deviation:

	Initial Data Set		Ordered to Compute Range
	5		6
	4		5
	5		5
	5		5
	6		4
	4		4
	4		4

$$\Sigma x = 33$$

5 range = 2
$$6 \longleftrightarrow 4$$

$$\mu = \frac{33}{7} = 4.714$$

Average Deviation	Standard Deviation	Standard Deviation (alternate formula)
$|6 - 4.71| = 1.29$	$(6 - 4.71)^2 = 1.6641$	$6^2 = 36$
$|5 - 4.71| = 0.29$	$(5 - 4.71)^2 = 0.0841$	$5^2 = 25$
$|5 - 4.71| = 0.29$	$(5 - 4.71)^2 = 0.0841$	$5^2 = 25$
$|5 - 4.71| = 0.29$	$(5 - 4.71)^2 = 0.0841$	$5^2 = 25$
$|4 - 4.71| = 0.71$	$(4 - 4.71)^2 = 0.5041$	$4^2 = 16$
$|4 - 4.71| = 0.71$	$(4 - 4.71)^2 = 0.5041$	$4^2 = 16$
$|4 - 4.71| = 0.71$	$(4 - 4.71)^2 = 0.5041$	$4^2 = 16$
4.29	3.4287	$159 = \Sigma x^2$

average deviation	standard deviation (formula 1)	standard deviation (formula 2)
$A.D. = \dfrac{\Sigma |x - \mu|}{\eta}$	$\sigma = \sqrt{\dfrac{\Sigma(\chi - \mu)^2}{\eta}}$	$\sigma = \sqrt{\dfrac{\Sigma x^2}{\eta} - \left(\dfrac{\Sigma x}{\eta}\right)^2}$
$A.D. = \dfrac{4.29}{7} = .612$	$\sigma = \sqrt{\dfrac{3.4287}{7}}$	$\sigma = \sqrt{\dfrac{159}{7} - \left(\dfrac{33}{7}\right)^2}$
	$\sigma = \sqrt{0.4898}$	$\sigma = \sqrt{22.714 - 22.2218}$
	$\sigma = 0.6999$	$\sigma = \sqrt{0.4922} = 0.7016$

Summary

The purpose of this chapter has been to provide an introduction to the mechanics of data analysis. The data analysis process consists of several stages: editing, coding, tabulation, and perhaps statistical testing.

The first step involves editing and coding the data into a format suitable for numerical processing. Although this may seem like a very straightforward, mechanical step, it often demands much more effort and supervision than one might at first anticipate. Such questionnaire deficiencies as illogical answers, illegible answers, incomplete answers, insufficient answers, and missing answers can cause the researcher great amounts of worry and concern. It should also be realized that even very straightforward coding can be extremely expensive and quite time-consuming, often usurping a major part of the funds available for the project.

All the coding problems discussed above fall into the basic category of missing data. The researcher generally tries to reduce the amount of missing data by utilizing one of three methods: (1) predicting the individual respondent's probable response, (2) substituting the overall group average or distribution, or (3) randomly inserting a replacement value. A fourth possibility is simply to code the missing data as a blank; this procedure can create problems, however, since most types of numerical analysis treat blanks like zeros.

The coding process must also take into consideration the type of data that has been collected. Of the four types of data discussed here — nominal, interval, ordinal, and ratio — ratio is the strongest type and nominal the weakest. Although data can be downgraded from strong to weak, weak data cannot be upgraded into strong; hence, special care must be taken not to code nominal data in an improper form.

Three types of tabulation have been discussed here: percentages, averages, and dispersions. The percentage is the easiest form of summary statistic to use and compute, but care must be taken, in that changes in the base (changes that are often very subtle and can go virtually unnoticed) can cause significant changes in the resulting percentages.

There are three forms of averages — measures of central tendency — that are commonly used in marketing research: the arithmetic mean, the median, and the mode. Although all three classify as measures of central tendency, they will all be different in a skewed distribution; the mean will be the measure farthest out in the tail, the mode will be the point of maximum concentration (the center of the "hump"), and the median will lie between the other two.

Four measures of dispersion have been discussed: the range, the interquartile range, the average deviation, and the standard deviation. The standard deviation is the preferred measure of dispersion, because it is one of the parameters of the normal curve. With a normally distributed population, use of the standard deviation will permit determination of the percentage of the population that falls between selected intervals. Even without normal distribution of the population, measures of skewedness and kurtosis can be used to determine the shape of a curve.

Questions for Discussion

1. Why is the coding of data from questionnaires not a straightforward mechanical task? Some editing and coding errors are bound to slip through; what do marketing researchers assume about these errors?

2. What are the four things that the researcher can do to cope with missing data? Explain. Why is the researcher so anxious to fill in a missing or omitted response, instead of entering it as a blank?

3. What are the four types of data discussed in this chapter? Define them. Give an example of a question with different answer formats, causing the same basic question to produce data of different strengths.

4. What problems can be encountered in the coding of nominal data? Give an example and show how the data should be coded.

5. How can the three measures of central tendency all give different answers if the distribution is skewed?

6. How does the problem of spurious precision relate to the arithmetic mean?

7. How can measures of central tendency, including the arithmetic mean and the median in particular, often obscure important market segments?

8. Why is the median often referred to as the most democratic measure of central tendency?

9. Why is the standard deviation the preferred measure of dispersion?

10. For the following data set, compute the arithmetic mean, the median, the mode, the expected value, the range, the average deviation, and the standard deviation: data set = 6,2,8,7,5,4,7,7.

Chapter 11

Statistical Evaluation of Sample Results

In Chapter 9 two principal sampling problem areas were identified: (1) sampling error, and (2) nonsampling error. A brief review of these two terms is advisable, since they and their somewhat unexpected meanings are confusing to many novice researchers.

Sampling error is a *quantitative*, or mathematical, problem. Whenever you take a sample, there is going to be some scatter of the sample results around that universe value the sample is trying to estimate. Because this is a mathematically defined problem, the amount of sampling error present in a given sample design can be estimated. Furthermore, this error can be controlled by manipulation of the sample size and other aspects of the sample design.

Nonsampling error is a *qualitative* problem. Nonsampling error includes everything that can go wrong in a sample with the exception of that natural scatter of the sample estimate discussed above. Thus, nonsampling error includes selection bias, nonresponse bias, improper questionnaire design, interviewer bias, and all the other qualitative problem areas discussed heretofore in this text. Because nonsampling errors are nonquantitative by definition, there is usually no way to estimate their size.

Survey Errors in Marketing

The total error present in a survey is the total of the sampling and nonsampling errors. Since the nonsampling error cannot be estimated, the only way in which an estimate of the total survey error can be made is by assuming that the nonsampling error is zero. The estimate of sampling error alone then becomes the estimate of total error.

There are many fields of research in which such an assumption is quite valid. For instance, consider the testing of products as they come off a factory production line. The products could be sampled and tested for certain desired characteristics, and the nonsampling error would probably be zero: there would be no problem with selection bias, since all the units would be ready and available for sampling; there would be no problem with nonresponse bias, no questionnaire, no subjective interface between interviewer and respondent, no problems of wording, or order, and so forth. In this case the total error would be the sampling error alone, and that error could be easily calculated.

Usually the marketing researcher has a much more variable situation. In general, marketing involves people, and the processes of measuring and interviewing people bring into play all the problems noted above. This was what happened in the *Literary Digest* survey discussed in Chapter 9. The sampling error alone, which is primarily a function of sample size, should have been 0.035 percent (0.0035). The researchers should therefore have been more than 99 percent sure that their estimate was within 0.1 percent of being correct. Because their sample estimate said that Landon would get 69.6 percent of the electoral votes, *statistically* speaking they should have been 99 percent sure that he would actually get between 69.5 percent and 69.7 percent of the votes, a very precise estimate indeed. Of course, this estimate was off, not by one or two tenths of a percent, but by tens of percentage points. The reason was the huge nonsampling error.

The potential for nonsampling errors of enormous magnitude in the execution of marketing surveys hangs like a Damoclesian sword over the heads of marketing researchers. Since nonsampling error is nonquantitative by definition, it can never be estimated, and very often it cannot even be identified. Although marketing analysts frequently give estimates of the probable survey error based upon the statistical sampling error, the presence of nonsampling error should always be suspected. Extreme care and vigilance must be given to the design and execution of the survey in hopes of keeping the nonsampling error to an absolute minimum.

The Concept of Statistical Confidence Intervals

In dealing with statistical sampling error in a survey, the marketing researcher basically wants to know how much confidence she can have in an estimate. She wants to know the probability of an estimate falling within a certain range. For instance, if a survey has produced results showing that 60 percent of the people favor a certain new product, how confident can she be in those results? How sure is she that the universe really has about 60 percent favorable responses? (Keep in mind that we are talking about statistical confidence, so that only the sampling error is being considered). A similar question might arise if two new products were tested, one gaining the favor of 62 percent of the sample and the other gaining the favor of 58 percent of the sample. How confident can the manager be that the observed difference of four percentage points represents a true difference and is not within that normal range of scatter we identify as "sampling" error?

Probability Levels

Suppose that you had tested a gun and you were of the decided opinion that the gun was indeed shooting off target. How would you convey that belief to someone else? Well, you might express your opinion in the form of a bet, saying, "I'll bet that gun isn't shooting on target," to which your friend might reply, "Oh yeah? How *much* do you want to bet?"

If you decide to take him up on the bet, the amount that you bet indicates your confidence, the strength of your belief that you are right; it also gives a measure of the probability with which you are betting. Thus, if you are willing to bet only $.50, then you are probably not very confident; you feel that the probability of being right is rather low. On the other hand, if you are willing to bet $300,000, you are very confident and feel that you have a high probability of being correct.

In marketing, we express belief that there is a difference (note that we never say how much difference, only that the difference is not zero) as a probability. The commonly used probability levels are 10 percent, 5 percent, and 1 percent, which represent bets of 90 percent confidence, 95 percent confidence, and 99 percent confidence, respectively.

The Probabilities Involved in Confidence Intervals

Where does marketing usually get the probability levels it uses — 90 percent, 95 percent, and 99 percent — and how is the level of confidence for a given sample estimate determined?

Unfortunately, the answer to these questions can involve some rather tricky mathematics, depending upon the precise situation in question. As discussed in the example involving the target rifle, four distinct factors are involved:

1. The magnitude of the difference. For instance, in judging between two brands, the strength of your confidence will depend upon the magnitude of the difference between the brands. The larger the difference, the greater confidence you will have in concluding that one brand is better than the other.

2. The number in the sample (the sample size). The larger the sample, the greater confidence you will have in your results and in your conclusions (other things being equal).

3. The dispersion of the sample (the standard deviation). Some situations have intrinsically more scatter, because of the nature of the phenomena. The greater the dispersion (i.e., the more unstable the population), the less confidence you will have in your results (other things being equal).

4. The conditions affecting the test (the specifics of the sample). The actual calculation of the degree of confidence varies, depending upon the type of data, type of sample, and so forth. Perhaps an example would be appropriate. If you are cooking some meat, the question arises, how *long* should you cook the meat? The answer to that question depends upon a variety of factors: how big is the piece of meat? how done do you want it? how hot is the oven? will it be roasted in an open pan or a closed pan? and so forth; but how *long* to cook the meat also depends upon what *kind* of meat you have. Every kind of meat has its own distribution of cooking times. As with meat, so with samples: there are different types of sample numbers — there are percents, averages, frequency distributions, and so forth. And each different kind of number has its own particular sampling distribution.

SAMPLING DISTRIBUTION

As explained above, the precise determination of the sampling error depends upon the shape of the relevant *sampling distribution*; this aspect of the estimation of the sampling error is what makes that estimation such a complex subject. Unfortunately, the sampling distribution and its corresponding shape change with each change in the sample design. Thus, the sampling error of an estimate from a stratified sample is computed differently from that of an estimate from a cluster sample, because the relevant sampling distributions are different.

However, it is not our intention (and probably not yours either) to become expert in the gamut of these sampling distributions. In this book we focus upon only two sampling distributions, the normal distribution and the chi-square distribution. Most of our effort will be spent on the chi-square distribution; we will here pay passing notice to the normal distribution.

Sampling Errors for Percentage Estimates

The Normal Distribution and Sample Size

The statistics involved in computing the precision of an estimate (that is, the sampling error) can become quite difficult, and we intend in this text to avoid as many of those statistical complexities as possible. Later in this chapter we will present one simple test (the chi-square) that can be used for almost every type of problem.

At this point we will make use of the normal curve as it relates to the calculation of the sampling error of a percentage estimate. Such an application is easy to understand, and we can use it to illustrate the importance of sample size in obtaining precise estimates. Sample size is of critical importance to the marketing researcher for several reasons. First of all, a look back at the list of factors that have a bearing upon the researcher's confidence in a sample will show that only one of those factors, namely, the sample size, is under the control of the researcher. Furthermore, since precision can be increased by increasing the sample size, sampling error can be reduced by whatever amount is desired simply by increasing the sample. Finally, since it is possible to compute the required sample size for any specified level of precision, the researcher can determine the necessary sample size before embarking upon a project. Doing so gives a good idea of the task and the costs that lie ahead.

The Central Limit Theorem

The crucial law of sampling statistics is embodied in what is known as the central limit theorem. This most important theorem states that for almost all populations (finite, infinite, and virtually without regard to shape of the distribution), the sampling distribution of the means observed will be approximately normal if the sample size is sufficiently large.

Table 11·1
95 Percent Confidence Level

	APPROXIMATE PLUS-OR-MINUS SAMPLING TOLERANCE FOR PERCENTAGED SURVEY RESULTS AT OR NEAR						
SIZE OF SAMPLE OR SUBSAMPLE	5% OR 95%	10% OR 90%	15% OR 85%	20% OR 80%	30% OR 70%	40% OR 60%	50% OR 50%
50	7	9	11	12	13	14	15
100	5	6	8	8	10	10	10
200	4	5	5	6	7	7	8
300	3	4	5	5	6	6	6
400	3	3	4	4	5	5	5
500	2	3	4	4	5	5	5
750	2	3	3	3	4	4	4
1,000	2	2	3	3	3	4	4
1,200	2	2	3	3	3	3	3
1,500	2	2	2	3	3	3	3
1,600	1	1	2	2	2	2	2

Increases in the precision of estimates derived from sample data can only come with comparatively large increases in sample size. Thus, if you wanted to decrease the magnitude of a given sample error by half, you would have to take a sample four times as large as your original. This relationship is seen in table 11·1. Because of this relationship, further increases in precision can soon become cost ineffective.

The Required Sample Size for Percentage Estimates

The sample size required to achieve a specified level of precision is quite predictable in the case of an estimate of a universe percent — that is, a sample in which the result of the question will produce a percentage (for example, "What percent of the voters favor a certain candidate?"). Questions involving percentage estimates are quite common in marketing research, and as a result, such tables as table 11·1 have been developed to show the sampling error (sometimes called the sampling tolerance) that can be expected for various sample sizes. A researcher can tell from the table that, for example, if a survey among a sample of 400 showed that 80 percent had telephones, the chances are 95 in 100 that the true percentage is within 4 percent of 80 percent (between 76 percent and 84 percent). Notice that the precision de-

Table 11·2
95 Percent Confidence Intervals

SAMPLE SIZE	SAMPLE ERROR AT OR NEAR				
	10%/90%	20%/80%	30%/70%	40%/60%	50%
100	5.88	7.84	8.98	9.60	9.80
400	2.94	3.92	4.49	4.80	4.90
900	1.96	2.61	2.99	3.20	3.26
1,600	1.47	1.96	2.24	2.40	2.45

creases as the percentage being estimated moves toward 50 percent. Accordingly, we can say that a sample of 200 has a 95 percent probability of being within ±8 percentage points when the percent being estimated is around 50 percent. But if the percent being estimated is around 10 percent, a sample of 100 should be 95 percent sure of being within ±5 percentage points.

Notice also that, as discussed in the section involving the central limit theorem, the sampling tolerances are lowered only as a function of rapidly increasing the sample size. For instance, look at the estimate for 15 percent or 85 percent: as the sample size goes up in multiples of 4 from 100 to 400 to 1,600, notice that the sampling error drops from 8 percent to 4 percent to 2 percent, or drops in half. Some of the columns may not appear to be following this rule, but that apparent variation is caused only by rounding. Table 11·2 is a slightly condensed version in which the sampling errors have not been rounded; you can see that increases in precision come exactly with large increases in sample size.

Notice also that these sample estimates begin achieving very respectable precision quite rapidly. As is evident from table 11·2, even under the worst of conditions (estimating a probability near 50 percent), by the time the sample size is around one thousand the researcher is 95 percent confident that his estimate is within three percentage points of the correct answer. Thus, marketing surveys tend to be fairly small in size, involving usually less than a thousand consumers. Critics unskilled in sampling methodology are often skeptical about the small samples involved in marketing: "How can you hope to estimate a country the size of the United States with a sample of only one thousand?" But from sampling tolerances we can see that a sample of one thousand is a very strong sample indeed. The size of the population does not figure into these sampling tolerances (as a matter of fact, these tolerances were computed on the basis of a universe population of infinity).

The concepts behind tables 11·1 and 11·2 can be further clarified by using the following formula in computing the necessary sample size for percentages:

$$Ns = \frac{pq}{\left(\frac{AE}{z}\right)^2}$$

where,

Ns is necessary sample size

p and q are responses expressed in percentages (Note: If percentages are unknown, they may be arbitrarily set at .5 each).

AE is allowable sampling error or desired accuracy between sample percentage and universe percentage.

z is desired confidence interval for the study; it is expressed in standard deviations (Appendix B).

Example: An initial research study found 50 percent of respondents preferred Brand X, while the other 50 percent preferred Brand Y. The researcher wants to know at the 95 percent confidence level that the final results of the sample will be plus or minus 5 percent of the true universe mean (μ). Calculate the necessary sample size.

$$Ns = \frac{(.5)\,(.5)}{\left(\frac{.05}{2}\right)^2} = \frac{(.25)}{\left(\frac{.0025}{4}\right)} = \frac{1.00}{.0025} = 400$$

Had we been willing to double our allowable error to ±10 percent, we could have cut our necessary sample size by 75 to 100 percent. (Note these same data are in tables 11·1 and 11·2.)

$$Ns = \frac{(.5)\,(.5)}{\left(\frac{.10}{2}\right)^2} = \frac{(.25)}{\left(\frac{.01}{4}\right)} = \frac{1.00}{.01} = 100$$

Obviously, the greater the allowable error or sampling error we are willing to tolerate, the smaller the sample necessary. However, the smaller the sample, the less certain we can be that sample data accurately reflect universe data.

Sample Size versus Representativeness

Of course, the critic concerned about the sample size of one thousand may still have a point. A sample of one thousand people from a country as large and as diverse as the United States leaves open the serious question whether that sample is *representative* of the population as a whole. Remember, however, that the question of the representativeness of the sample is a function of the specifics of the sample selection and is hence a qualitative problem, a nonsampling error. Though there may be doubts about the representativeness of a sample of one thousand, statistically the sampling error has been quite well controlled.

This distinction between sampling error and nonsampling error brings us to one final point. Another reason why samples in marketing are seldom larger than about one thousand is that experienced marketing researchers are always aware that the possibility exists for appreciable amounts of nonsampling error. Marketing researchers generally feel that to try to estimate a percentage much more closely than within two or three percentage points is probably a waste of time and money, since most marketing situations are sufficiently imprecise that the nonsampling error will be at least that great.

The Chi-Square Test

The chi-square test is one of the most useful statistical tests, as well as one of the easiest to use. It differs from most of the other statistical tests in that it can work with nominal data.

As discussed previously, nominal data are data in which the numbers do not have mathematical properties in the usual sense but rather can be used only to classify an item into a designated category. In working with the chi-square test, the focus will be upon the classifications, or to phrase it another way, upon the frequency distributions produced by a classification.

Any type of data can be converted into some type of frequency distribution. Data can always be downgraded, and since nominal data is the lowest form, any data can be converted into nominal data. Therefore, the chi-square test (unlike other statistical tests) is always appropriate.

Examples of Conversions to Nominal Data

The following examples will help illustrate the way in which other types of data can be downgraded into nominal data. For instance, suppose you had income figures from two groups, people living in Ohio and people living in Iowa. You could run a statistical test between the arithmetic means of the two groups. Or you could take these income figures and break them down into a frequency table like figure 11·1. The chi-square test could be run upon the frequency counts found in that table.

Another example might be a comparison of the percentages of persons favoring each of two candidates. You could run a statistical test comparing the two percentages, or you could break those "percentage" responses into a frequency table like figure 11·2. The chi-square test could then be run upon the frequency counts found in that table.

The purpose of the chi-square is to examine (mathematically) a given frequency distribution and to decide (mathematically) if there is anything unusual about that distribution. In performing this test, the mathematical process will be looking for a *significant difference* between the classification frequencies that have been observed and those classification frequencies that were expected.

Statistical Difference Reviewed

Before beginning the discussion of the actual mechanics of the chi-square test, let us review exactly what is meant by "statistically significant difference."

Figure 11·1
Frequency Table

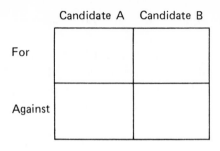

Figure 11·2
Frequency Table

Observed Difference. This difference is always present. Any time a sample is taken, there will be some variation in the numbers within the classifications. If the sample is large enough, this observed difference, no matter how small it is, can become a statistically significant difference.

Significant Difference. This is a statistical term. The presence of a significant difference is largely a function of sample size. The idea behind the concept is that the term *statistically significant difference* represents a bet: one is betting at a certain level of probability that the true difference between the observed frequencies and the expected frequencies is not exactly zero.

The Common Objective and Procedure

All the statistical testing in this chapter has a common objective, and in it all the tests follow a common format.

The Common Objective: Statistic versus Parameter

The objective in each test is to compare the value (often referred to as the statistic) computed from the observed data with a value (often called the parameter) obtained from the theoretical distribution of values. Thus, the actual value of chi-square (the statistic), which is computed from the observed frequency distribution, is compared with the theoretical chi-square value (the parameter) obtained from the tables in the back of the book. In this process, a sample statistic is compared with a population parameter.

The Common Procedure

For all problems involving any type of statistical test, this book follows a five-step process:

1. First we set up the hypothesis; that is, we state clearly the proposition that is to be statistically tested.

2. We obtain the values for the parameters from the theoretical distribution shown in the tables. These figures tell us within what ranges we can have an "allowable" difference and at what point we have an "excessive" difference.

3. Using the observed data from the problem, we compute the "actual" value of the statistic. More simply, using the data from the problem we compute the statistic.

4. We compare actual with theoretical. Or, if you prefer, we compare statistic versus parameter, or the observed with the expected.

5. From that comparison, we reject or do not reject the hypothesis stated at the beginning of the problem.

The Distribution of the Chi-Square

As mentioned earlier, the chi-square test is designed to work with nominal data, usually in the form of classification tables showing the frequency of occurrence of the various classifications in the breakdown. The chi-square test provides us with a mathematical way of examining a classification table to see whether the arrangement of values within that table is unusual in some way.

In performing the test, we will be comparing a computed with a theoretical value of chi-square. The theoretical distribution of chi-square is a skewed distribution that varies in shape according to the number of cells in the classification table. More precisely, the chi-square varies in shape according to "degrees of freedom," which in the case of the chi-square equal (the number of rows minus one) multiplied by (the number of columns minus one) (see fig. 11•3). Because the shape of the distribution varies with degrees of freedom, we will use the degrees of freedom to guide us to the proper values in the chi-square table. Degrees of freedom also represent the expected value or mean for the chi-square distribution.

The chi-square test looks at the distribution, by comparing the observed distribution against some expected distribution, to determine

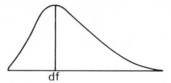

df = (number of rows – 1) (number of columns – 1)

Figure 11·3
Degrees of Freedom

if a statistically significant difference is present. These expected distributions usually take one of two forms:

   1. Goodness-of-fit. In the goodness-of-fit test, the observed distribution is compared with an arbitrary distribution, to see how well it fits.
   2. Independence-of-classification. The purpose of this test is to determine whether the arrangement of values in the classification table is independent of the factors according to which the data were classified.

An Example Involving Degrees of Freedom

Let us go through a sample problem illustrating the use of the degrees of freedom in obtaining the chi-square parameters. The specifics of the solution to the problem will be explained later.

   Suppose that we had a classification table such as the one in figure 11·4, which has three rows and four columns. The degrees of freedom in this case would be 6: df $= (3 - 1) \times (4 - 1) = (2) \times (3) = 6$. Therefore, using the tables in Appendix A at the back of the book and using 6 degrees of freedom, we develop a picture of the distribution of chi-square values from a classification table with 6 degrees of freedom.

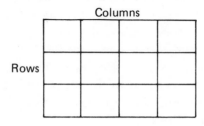

Figure 11·4
Classification Table

Because df $= 6$, if the numbers classified on the rows had no significant relationship to the numbers classified on the columns, we would nevertheless expect to generate an *average* chi-square value of 6. (Note that if there is absolutely no relationship among the numbers in the table, we would expect the value of chi-square to be 0. However, we expect to find some scatter, even among variables with no intrinsic relationship to one another. In this case we expect the average scatter to be 6.)

Furthermore, if there is indeed no significant difference, no relationship (as, by analogy, a gun being on target), then on the basis of the picture developed (fig. 11·5), we would know that only 5 percent of the time should we get a value of chi-square greater than 12.54, and only 1 percent of the time should we find a value of chi-square greater than 16.81.

To rephrase, because this chi-square distribution is computed on the assumption that there is no significant relationship, no difference, between the values in the classification table, an actual value of chi-square (the statistic) *outside* that 5 percent cutoff of 12.59 (the parameter) shows a 95 percent probability that there is a relationship. (You may need to reread the preceding sentence several times.) Likewise, if the actual value of chi-square is outside the 1 percent cutoff of 16.81, then we are 99 percent sure that there is a relationship.

Since this material is probably still quite confusing, let's work a few sample problems.

An Example of a Goodness-of-Fit Test

As noted earlier in the chapter, the chi-square can be used to test any two frequency distributions against each other. Here we will test an observed distribution against an arbitrarily derived "expected" distribution.

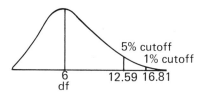

Figure 11·5
An Example Using 6 Degrees of Freedom

	F_o
Winter	30
Spring	25
Summer	25
Fall	40

	F_e
Winter	30
Spring	30
Summer	30
Fall	30

Figure 11·6
Observed and Expected Frequencies

Figure 11·6 shows observed sales over the seasons of the year (frequency observed, F_o) and an assumption of equal sales from each quarter (frequency expected, F_e). If the 120 total sales were divided equally among the four quarters, we would get the expected frequency distribution shown.

With these distributions in hand, we can test for significant difference, following the five steps of the common procedure.

1. The hypotheses to be tested are:

H_0 The seasons are equal ($F_o = F_e$)
H_1 The seasons are not equal ($F_o \neq F_e$).

2. The theoretical distribution is based upon 3 degrees of freedom (df = 4 − 1). Therefore, if there is no real difference, just scatter, we can expect an average chi-square value of 3 as a result of our comparison of F_o with F_e. Furthermore, if there is no real difference, only scatter, we can expect to see a value of chi-square as large as 7.81 only 5 percent of the time and a value of chi-square as large as 11.34 only 1 percent of the time (see fig. 11·7).

3. The actual value of chi-square (the statistic), which summarizes

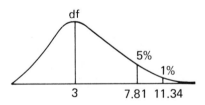

Figure 11·7
The Theoretical Distribution

the amount of difference (or scatter) between the two frequency tables, is computed according to the formula

$$\chi^2 = \Sigma \frac{(F_o - F_e)^2}{F_e} \ .$$

The computation here is:

F_o	F_e	$F_o - F_e$	$(F_o - F_e)^2$	$(F_o - F_e)^2/F_e$
30	30	30 − 30	0	0/30 = 0.00
25	30	25 − 30	25	25/30 = 0.83
25	30	25 − 30	25	25/30 = 0.83
40	30	90 − 30	100	100/30 = 3.33
				$\overline{4.99} = \chi^2$

4. Figure 11·8 shows the comparison of the statistic with the parameter, or of the actual value of chi-square, which is 4.99, with the cutoffs from the theoretical distribution.

5. Conclusion: the actual value of chi-square is inside the theoretical cutoffs. Therefore, we do not reject H_0; we do not declare that there is a statistically significant difference among the seasons.

Note that we have not proved that the seasons are equal; we have simply been unable to show that they are not equal. In other words, we have concluded that differences of the magnitude observed in this problem may be attributable simply to "random" scatter.

Note also that we are always implying rejection or nonrejection at a certain probability level. A chi-square value of 4.99 happens to be significant at the 25 percent level. Thus, we are 75 percent sure that we have a significant difference, although we did not obtain the 95 percent or 99 percent levels that are considered "traditional" in most statistical testing.

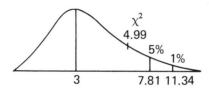

Figure 11·8
Statistic versus Parameter

An Example of an Independence-of-Classification Test

The most frequent use of the chi-square test is to perform what is known as an independence-of-classification test. The purpose of this test is to see if the arrangements of values within a group of cells is independent of the factors by which they were classified. Thus, in a table in which data are classified by age and sex, the chi-square test will determine whether there appears to be a relationship between age and sex for that set of data. In this test, the expected frequency distribution is not derived arbitrarily, as in the goodness-of-fit test; rather, the expected distribution is derived from the observed distribution, using the row and column totals of the observed distribution.

We will illustrate this process using the classification table in figure 11•9, which gives a breakdown between sex and test scores. In this test we will be trying to determine whether the males have the higher scores. Although it appears from the table that they do, we wish to test that conclusion mathematically. (Note: do not jump to conclusions about an example showing higher scores for males. The example does not say what those scores are concerned with; it might be that the males scored higher on an alcoholic tendency test. The point is that one must always look behind the scenes when analyzing numerical data and avoid making assumptions that may prove to be false.)

To test this table, we will develop the expected distribution from the observed distribution using the row and column totals, or the totals of items shown around the *margins* of the table in figure 11•10. Because of this procedure, this method is sometimes called the *method of marginal products*. To compute the expected cell values using the method of marginal products, we will use the formula

$$\text{cell value } (F_e) = \frac{\text{row total} \times \text{column total}}{\text{grand total}}$$

	Scores	
	High	Low
M	14	7
F	12	23

Figure 11•9
Classification According to Sex and Test Scores

244 • Marketing Research

Sex	Scores: High	Scores: Low	
M	14	7	21
F	12	23	35
	26	30	56

Figure 11•10
***F_o* Scores**

The cell values for the expected table are (fig. 11•11):

$$\text{cell } (1, 1) = \frac{\text{rt} \times \text{ct}}{\text{gt}} = \frac{26 \times 21}{56} = 9.75$$

$$\text{cell } (1, 2) = \frac{\text{rt} \times \text{ct}}{\text{gt}} = \frac{30 \times 21}{56} = 11.25$$

$$\text{cell } (2, 1) = \frac{\text{rt} \times \text{ct}}{\text{gt}} = \frac{26 \times 35}{56} = 16.25$$

$$\text{cell } (2, 2) = \frac{\text{rt} \times \text{ct}}{\text{gt}} = \frac{30 \times 35}{56} = 18.75$$

Notice that we actually did not need to compute all four cell values separately. We needed to find only one of the four cell values, and from there we could have found the remaining three by subtracting from the appropriate row and column totals (this process further illustrates what degrees of freedom mean).

Sex	Scores: High	Scores: Low
M	9.75	11.25
F	16.25	18.75

Figure 11•11
***F_e* Scores**

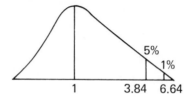

Figure 11·12
The Theoretical Picture

With F_o and F_e now computed, let us begin the statistical test.

1. The hypotheses are:

H_0 Classifications independent, score not related to sex $(F_o = F_e)$
H_1 Classifications not independent, score related to sex $(F_o \neq F_e)$.

2. The theoretical picture (fig. 11·12): in this case df $= 1$; if sex and score are not related, then we can expect an average scatter of chi-square equal to 1, with a chi-square greater than 3.84 only 5 percent of the time and a chi-square greater than 6.64 only 1 percent of the time.

3. The calculations, using the formula

$$\chi^2 = \sum \frac{(F_o - F_e)^2}{F_e}$$

are:

F_o		F_e		$F_o - F_e$	$(F_o - F_e)^2$	$(F_o - F_e)^2/F_e$
				$14 - 9.75$	18.0625	1.85
14	7	9.75	11.25	$7 - 11.75$	18.0625	1.61
12	23	16.25	18.75	$12 - 16.75$	18.0625	1.11
				$23 - 18.75$	18.0625	0.96
						$5.53 = \chi^2$

4. When the statistic is compared with the parameter, the actual value of 5.53 falls between the 5 percent cutoff and the 1 percent cutoff (fig. 11·13).

5. Conclusion: we are 95 percent sure that there is a statistically significant difference, although we are not 99 percent sure. Thus, we reject the null hypothesis that the classifications are independent at the

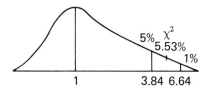

Figure 11·13
Statistic versus Parameter

95 percent level but do not reject the null hypothesis at the 99 percent level.

Another Example of a Goodness-of-Fit Test

In this example, an observed distribution is tested against an arbitrary distribution. Suppose that the director of the student union dance committee claims that twice as many lowerclassmen attend the dances as upperclassmen. A random sample of 120 people is selected from those attending the dance, and their classification is recorded. The test for significant difference is conducted at *alpha* equal to 10 percent — a confidence level of 90 percent.

1. Hypotheses:

H_0 Number of upperclassmen half number of lowerclassmen ($F_o = F_e$)
H_1 Number of upperclassmen not half number of lowerclassmen ($F_o \neq F_e$)

2. Theoretical picture — df $= (2 - 1)(4 - 1) = 3$:

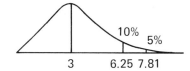

3. Calculations:

F_o	F_e	$F_o - F_e$	$(F_o - F_e)^2$	$(F_o - F_e^2)/F_c$
24	20	24 − 20	16	16/20 = 0.80
29	20	29 − 20	81	81/20 = 4.05
36	40	36 − 40	16	16/40 = 0.40
31	40	31 − 40	81	81/40 = 2.03
				$7.28 = \chi^2$

4. Comparison:

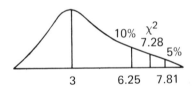

5. Conclusion: at 10 percent level, actual x^2 of 7.28 is outside cut-off of 6.25; .. reject H_0 : 90 percent sure $F_o \neq F_e$. However, at 5 percent level, actual x^2 is inside cutoff. At 5 percent level, do not reject H_0. Although 90 percent $F_o \neq F_e$, not 95 percent sure.

Another Example of an Independence-of-Classification Test

Suppose that the manager of a grocery store wants to see if there is a relationship between the size of the eggs customers buy and the amount of bacon they buy. To determine if there is indeed a relationship, he monitors one hundred customers and makes a chart of his findings. The test for significant difference is conducted at the 95 percent confidence level (5 percent alpha).

1. Hypotheses

H_0 Classifications independent $(F_o = F_e)$
H_1 Classifications not independent $(F_o \neq F_e)$

2. Theoretical picture — df $= (3 - 1)\ (3 - 1) = 4$:

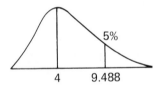

3. Calculations:

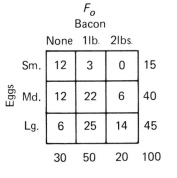

F_o
Bacon

	None	1lb.	2lbs.	
Sm.	12	3	0	15
Md.	12	22	6	40
Lg.	6	25	14	45
	30	50	20	100

Eggs

F_e
Bacon

	None	1lb.	2lbs.
Sm.	5	7	3
Md.	12	20	8
Lg.	13	23	9

Eggs

$F_o - F_e$	$(F_o - F_e)^2$	$(F_o - F_e)^2/F_e$
12 − 5	49	$49/5 = 9.80$
3 − 7	16	$16/7 = 2.28$
0 − 3	9	$9/13 = 3.00$
12 − 12	0	$0/3 = 0.00$
22 − 20	4	$4/20 = 0.20$
6 − 8	4	$4/8 = 0.50$
6 − 13	49	$49/13 = 3.77$
25 − 23	4	$4/23 = 0.17$
14 − 9	25	$25/9 = 2.77$
		$22.50 = \chi^2$

4. Comparison:

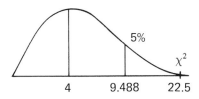

5%

χ^2

4   9.488   22.5

5. Conclusion: actual χ^2 outside confidence interval; $\therefore$ there is a statistically significant difference; $\therefore$ there is a relationship and classifications not independent (i.e., the amount of bacon purchased relates to the size of the eggs).

Concepts behind Statistical Testing

The problems presented in the past few pages have involved some unfamiliar terms. It is the purpose of this section to attempt to explain these terms more fully.

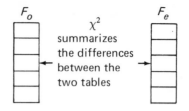

F_o

χ^2
summarizes
the differences
between the
two tables

F_e

Figure 11·14
Chi-Square

What Is Chi-Square?

The easiest way to think of *chi-square* is as a summary of the differences between the observed and the expected classification tables (fig. 11·14).

The *chi-square distribution* is a distribution of the differences (scatter) we would expect even if there were no fundamental difference in the underlying distributions that generated the two tables (fig. 11·15). That is, even if we drew both distributions from the same pile, we would still expect to see some differences between the arrangement of the values in the two classification tables (fig. 11·16). The distribution of these differences is given by the chi-square tables in the back of the book.

The *chi-square test* looks at the amount of difference (as summarized by the chi-square statistic) that exists between the two classification tables. If the value of chi-square is low, then it is concluded that the two classification tables could have come from the same underlying distribution (fig. 11·17).

On the other hand, if the difference in the two tables is large, then the conclusion is that the tables must have come from different places; that is, the observed frequency distribution could not have come from

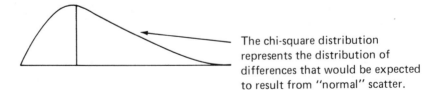

The chi-square distribution represents the distribution of differences that would be expected to result from "normal" scatter.

Figure 11·15
Chi-Square Distribution

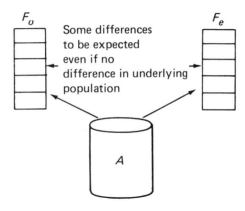

Figure 11·16
Both Distributions from the Same Source

the same source that generated the expected frequency distribution (fig. 11·18).

Note that no statement is made concerning the source of the observed classification table, nor is any statement made about the nature of the population that generated this observed classification table. The only statement the statistical test will make is that the difference seems so great that the observed distribution must have come from somewhere else. Hence, although the null hypothesis is rejected, the alternative hypothesis states only that the observed frequencies and the expected frequencies are not equal.

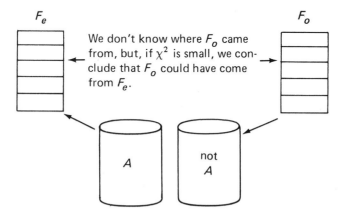

Figure 11·17
Low Chi-Square Value

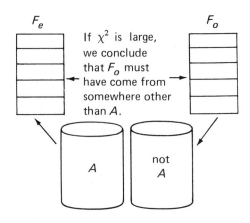

Figure 11·18
Large Chi-Square Value

The Concept behind Cutoff Points

As explained in the discussion of the theoretical chi-square distribution, the values in the chi-square table are computed for the various degrees of freedom under the assumption that there will be *no difference* between the observed and expected distributions. That is to say, the cutoff values of chi-square obtained from the table represent the differences expected from the *normal* scatter of sample estimates, the scatter caused by sampling error. When we choose a 95 percent cutoff value, we are saying that *if there is no difference,* then 95 percent of that time the scatter between those two frequency distributions will be less than that cutoff.

Type 1 and Type 2 Errors

Suppose that we compute a given chi-square value, and the value is outside the 95 percent cutoff value. What does that show? Well, the value could be outside the cutoff for one of two reasons:

1. The chi-square in question is one of the 5 percent expected to fall outside that 95 percent cutoff (even though the populations are still basically the same);

2. The populations that generated those frequency distributions are not the same. The "true" difference is not zero.

Since hypothesis testing is a mathematical procedure, it tries to play the odds by opting for the second reason. In doing so, it recognizes that 5 percent of the time an incorrect decision will be made; that is, a difference will have been claimed when in fact there is none. For this reason, another way of speaking of a 95 percent confidence level is to say that *alpha* (α) — the symbol used to designate the probability of making that particular type of error — is being set at 5 percent. Likewise, a 99 percent confidence interval would require an alpha of 1 percent, or 0.01. Making the mistake of saying that a difference exists between two populations, when there really is none is called the type 1 error.

There is another type of error, which is the decision not to reject the idea of a difference, when actually there is some real difference between the populations. This is called a type 2 error, and the probability of making this error is termed *beta* (β). Unfortunately, the mechanics of computing beta are beyond the scope of this book.

Of Rejecting, Accepting, and Not Rejecting

Technically, it is not proper to say that a given chi-square test has shown that there is no difference; we can say only that we have failed to demonstrate that there is a difference. Many students are confused by the fact that "accept" is not the same as "fail to reject." The reason for this seeming anomaly lies in the nature of the statistical test. The classification tables that are compared in the chi-square test are seldom, if ever, truly equal, and thus it would be improper to say that two classification tables with some actual differences have "proved" that the underlying distributions are equal. Rather, all we can say is that the tables have failed to demonstrate that the distributions are not equal.

MARKETING IMPLICATIONS OF NONREJECTION

Although nonrejection is really but an inconclusive result, in many actual situations the marketing researcher is not allowed the luxury of "no decision." If two brands are competing and a decision has to be made to cancel one and retain the other, that decision must be made whether the results are statistically significant or not. In such a situation it really may not make much sense to compute the significance at all. The real world demands a decision, and so the businessman goes with his best and hopes that it is good enough.

Note also that in performing a statistical test and declaring there to be a "significant" difference, the researcher is pointing out a *statistic-*

ally significant difference. And it is a difference tested against the idea of *absolutely zero difference*. As discussed previously, the ability to "prove" this difference is a function of sample size and is a matter of the relative size of the difference. The absolute size and the importance are of no concern, statistically. However, such matters are of great concern to the businessperson. For instance, suppose a tire manufacturer developed a tire that for approximately double the cost would roll five hundred miles further than the standard tire. The formulas would soon show a statistical difference, a significant difference; but the average motorist would probably not perceive any difference, and he certainly would not be willing to pay twice the price.

In view of the previous discussion of the applicability of statistical tests and the inconclusiveness of nonrejection, you may be wondering what the value of a test like this really is. Its value is that, by determining the range of normal scatter, the range of sampling error, we are sometimes able to realize that what had previously appeared to be a noteworthy difference between two values was actually completely within the range of normal sampling error. In other words, the differences we observed are really (or possibly) illusionary; they may have been caused simply by the normal scatter expected within all sample estimates.

The Effect of Sample Size on Chi-Square

Sample size definitely affects the researcher's confidence in sample estimates. Sample size also increases the precision of and the confidence that may be given to results of tests involving the chi-square distribution.

An Example Involving Sample Size

In fig. 11•19, three chi-square tables are presented. In each case the relative (percentage) breakdown of the items in the tables is the same, although the total number of items in the matrix (the sample size) goes from 12 to 120 to 1,200.

Notice that increasing the sample size has increased the precision of the estimate, thus allowing the null hypothesis to be rejected at a higher level of confidence. In the chi-square test, the value of the chi-square statistic increases proportionately with sample size. (Note: although increasing sample size always increases the precision of a test, the relationship is not always linear.)

H_0 Classifications are independent, voting patterns are not related to political party.

H_1 Classifications are not independent, voting patterns are related to political party.

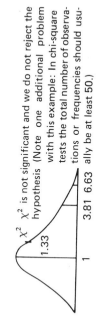

Dem. Rep.

	Dem.	Rep.
For	2	4
Against	4	2

total of 12 persons

$\chi^2 = 1.33$

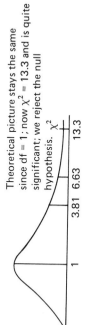

χ^2 is not significant and we do not reject the hypothesis (Note one additional problem with this example: In chi-square tests the total number of observations or frequencies should usually be at least 50.)

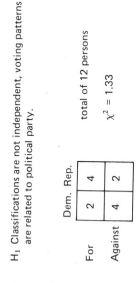

Dem. Rep.

	Dem.	Rep.
For	20	40
Against	40	20

total of 120 persons

$\chi^2 = 13.3$

Theoretical picture stays the same since df = 1; now $\chi^2 = 13.3$ and is quite significant; we reject the null hypothesis.

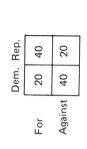

Dem. Rep.

	Dem.	Rep.
For	200	400
Against	400	200

total of 1,200 persons

$\chi^2 = 133.3$

Now χ^2 value is extremely significant.

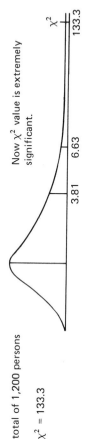

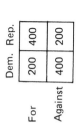

Figure 11·19
An Example Involving Sample Size

Summary

This chapter has tried to give some insight into the statistical considerations of sampling. In doing so, the first step was to examine sampling error, or that error which results from the natural scatter of sample estimates about the population value. This sampling error contrasts with nonsampling error, or that qualitative error which comes from bias in the way the sample is conducted.

There are four quantitative factors that influence the strength of our confidence in the conclusions we draw from a sample result: (1) the magnitude of the miss, (2) the sample size, (3) the dispersion of the sample values, and (4) the conditions affecting the test. Of these four, only number (2), the sample size, is under the control of the researcher. However, in this case, one is enough, because by properly manipulating the sample size, the researcher can achieve any level of precision desired. The central limit theorem tells the researcher that increases in the precision of the sample estimate will come as a function of increasing the sample size. If the researcher is willing to spend the money, results of negligible sampling error can be obtained; but because the sample size is increasing rapidly, increased precision can soon become prohibitively costly.

Furthermore, it must always be remembered that sampling error is only one kind of error that can be encountered in a survey. There is also nonsampling error to contend with, and whereas the sampling error can be both calculated and controlled, the nonsampling error cannot be. Because the possibility of significant amounts of nonsampling error exists with most marketing surveys, marketing researchers are often relatively unconcerned with obtaining the last decimal places of statistical precision. Most marketing researchers prefer to spend their money on a smaller sample of higher quality, rather than a larger sample of lower quality.

This chapter has also presented one statistical technique, the chi-square test. The chi-square technique is very useful in that it is designed to work with nominal data, such as the data in a frequency distribution or classification table. Since any type of data can be downgraded into nominal data, the chi-square is applicable to any type of data.

The chi-square test provides a method of determining whether a statistical difference exists between two frequency distributions. In looking for a statistical difference, we are testing whether the difference between the distributions is within that range attributable to "normal" scatter or whether the difference is so large that we can conclude that there must be some real difference between the distributions. It should be noted, however, that in saying that there is a "real" difference we are not saying how much difference. It is possible to have a statistical difference of such small absolute size that it is of no marketing significance.

Questions for Discussion

1. Distinguish between sampling error and nonsampling error.

2. Discuss the relationship between marketing and nonsampling error. Is nonsampling error a problem for researchers in all fields?

3. Someone has claimed that a drug has 60 percent effectiveness, and a sample has been taken to test this claim. In judging whether the sample results support or refute the claim, what four factors would you examine?

4. Of the various factors impinging upon the confidence we have in a sample estimate, which one is under the direct control of the researcher?

5. A sample is being made to estimate the percentage of minority students in a certain high school, where it is believed that approximately 20 percent of the students are from minorities. How many students would have to be sampled to be 95 percent sure that the estimate is within five percentage points?

6. The Nielsen Television Ratings used to estimate network shares around 30 percent are currently based upon a sample of about 1,100 homes. The Nielsen researchers are 95 percent certain that their results are within how many percentage points of the true population percentages? Why would the Nielsen researchers be reluctant to try to get that error down to 1 percent or less?

7. There are two candidates running for sheriff. One of the candidates takes a poll of two hundred people that shows him to have 51 percent of the vote, with the other candidate having 46 percent of the vote and 3 percent undecided. "I've got the election in the bag!" he crows; "even if my opponent gets all 3 percent of the undecided vote, he still can't catch me!" Does he have the election wrapped up? Discuss.

8. The theoretical chi-square distribution can be defined as a distribution of the chi-square values (which represent a summary of the differences between two classification tables) that would result as a consequence of normal scatter. Explain that statement.

9. What is meant by a chi-square goodness-of-fit test? What is meant by a chi-square independence-of-classification test? In the independence-of-classification test, the cell values for the expected frequency distribution are computed by the *method of marginal products*. Why is this method so called?

10. A certain college expects all its professors to grade on the following curve: A = 10% B = 20% C = 40% D = 20% F = 10%. Consider the curious case of Professor X. In a certain class of forty students, he gives the grades shown here. Are his grades within the range of acceptable deviation?

40 Students

	A	B	C	D	F
Observed	7	15	8	6	4
Expected	4	8	16	8	4

Suppose that he actually has two classes of forty students and maintains the same distribution shown for the first group over the entire group of eighty students. Use the chi-square to test again for significant difference.

80 Students

	A	B	C	D	F
Observed	14	30	16	12	8
Expected	8	16	32	16	8

11. On a certain basketball team the average per-game point totals of the starting five members of the team are: the center = 20 points; one forward = 20 points, the other forward = 10 points, one guard = 25 points, the other guard = 10 points. Test against the hypothesis that all members of the team are contributing equally.

12. Given this classification table showing the relationship between age and adult TV watching, test for significant differences in classification (i.e., relationship between age and TV watching).

F_o

Age Groups	TV Viewing Low	TV Viewing High
20–30	5	10
30–50	10	10
50–80	6	9

13. Given this classification table showing the relationship between classification in school and grades, test for independence of classification.

	A	B	C	D	F
Lowerclassmen	6	3	2	3	6
Upperclassmen	2	8	6	3	1

Chapter 12

The Research Report

THE MARKETING RESEARCH PROCESS BEGINS with exploratory research and problem definition. The final link in this process is the research report itself — the finished product — which is often the weakest link. This weakness stems from a communications failure, the inability of some researchers to communicate effectively the essence of their findings to an intended audience.

Exactly what is a research report? It is the concise, clear communication of the essential findings of a research study. This communication can be in written, oral, or visual (slides, overhead transparencies, and so on) form, or in a combination of all three.

Professional marketing researchers are not the only people confronted with the difficulties of preparing reports. Virtually all people in reponsible positions, including those in nearly every phase of business, education, or government, have to prepare research reports of one type or another at regular intervals throughout their careers. Graduation from college or university is no escape from report preparation. In fact, it is in challenging managerial positions that effective written and oral communication becomes most important.

It should be clearly recognized that a well-written and well-organized research report is the only truly effective way in which marketing researchers can communicate with top management. Even if all the steps and procedures in the marketing research process have been well executed up to this point, they are of little use if the research findings cannot be effectively communicated. You may now be asking yourself exactly how one prepares a marketing research report. Let us begin to answer this question by examining the principal types of research reports.

Types of Research Reports

Written research reports may vary in length, though it is advisable to keep them as short as possible. The short report is more likely than the long report to be read from cover to cover. One variation of the short report is the *executive summary report*, which may be used to complement the long report. It is, as the name implies, a management summary. As a much shorter version of the final report, the executive summary report presents the main findings, recommendations, and conclusions. Usually omitted are technical sections dealing with research methodology, statistical treatment, and data analyses. The executive summary report may be presented at the beginning of the research report or as a separate document. Usually, it is preferable to submit the executive summary at the very beginning of the final research report. This placement allows the reader to gain a quick overview of the full contents of the report without having to read all the material or to look for the final report if the two are not together. If the executive summary report and the final research report are presented as separate reports, one of the two is likely to be misplaced and not read.

We emphasize that because the report is a communications vehicle, it must be prepared and presented in a manner that will enable it to be favorably received and implemented. A major problem facing researchers is the quantity of data to include in the research report. Again, it is the characteristics of the intended audience that determine the answer to this question. These characteristics also determine which of two main types of reports will be drafted: the technical report or the popular report.

The Technical Report

Normally, technical reports are prepared by research specialists for other marketing research professionals. The technical report assumes that the reader is up-to-date on the background material relevant to the subject under consideration. Thus, the technical report usually concentrates upon detailed research methodology and the findings of the study. Appendixes may be attached to the technical report to present descriptions of the measuring instrument used (for example, a copy of the questionnaire) and computer print-outs of statistical analysis of variance. Because of its often highly technical nature, the *Journal of Marketing Research* is illustrative of the format for technical reports.

The highly quantitative structure of the technical report is permissible and expected when the audience consists of fellow researchers and others well versed in research jargon. These people, who are usually familiar with current research and theories, are equipped to cope with the technical report. Should the researcher have to present findings to both research specialists and a general audience, a popular report may be drawn up from the technical report and be presented to this latter audience separately.

In summary, there are five key criteria for technical reports to meet. They must be:

1. Complete
2. Arranged logically
3. Impersonal
4. Accurate
5. Brief

The Popular Report

A much less complicated instrument than the technical report, the popular report is intended for a more general audience. The popular report is shorter than the technical report; and whereas technical reports may go extensively into research methodology and data analysis techniques used, popular reports will concentrate on findings and recommendations.

The popular report is an executive report. That is, it is prepared for executive decision makers within the organization. Accordingly, it is very important that popular reports be written as clearly and simply as possible without sacrificing the essential contents. It is acceptable to omit extensive methodological details, since executives are more interested in applying the findings. Although no distortion of facts should enter into the popular report, it is necessary that it contain the researcher's conclusions and recommendations. Many researchers may be hesitant to risk their opinions, but research reports should make positive recommendations. On the other hand, researchers should not be surprised if their recommendations are not acted upon. This is all part of the game as it is played, not necessarily as it *should* be played.

Sometimes a popular report may begin with an executive summary. As noted earlier in this chapter, the executive summary is a brief report that summarizes the entire report within the scope of one or

Table 12•1
Comparison of Technical and Popular Report Styles

Technical Report Language

"Many if not most of the test-retest correlations presented in the advertising research literature as measures of the reliability of copy testing methodologies are subject to the kinds of ambiguities and limitations noted in the preceding examples. To illustrate, a finding often cited is the test-retest correlations of .67 obtained from an analysis of on-air recall scores for 106 commercials first reported by Clancy and Kweskin and discussed at greater length by Clancy and Ostlund. In describing the data on which this correlation is based, the latter authors note, 'The interval between test and retest for each commercial varied from one to eleven weeks.' Thus there were numerous and varied opportunities for the different test and retest samples to be affected by nonequivalent sets of influences and therefore it is not surprising to learn. 'The average difference between the test and retest score was ± 6.4 percentage points.' Because the variances of the test and retest scores are not reported, the test for their equality suggested heretofore could not be carried out." [a]

Popular Report Language

Findings from previous research studies into this area are inconsistent and do not give us a clear solution to the problem, because they are not all measuring exactly the same things.

[a] Alvin J. Silk, "Test-Retest Correlations and the Reliability of Copy Testing," *Journal of Marketing Research* 14 (November 1977): 483.

two pages. It is not expected to be a substitute for the full report, but merely a chance for busy executives to orient themselves quickly without having to read every word in the full report. The executive summary should be designed not only to convey the essential findings and recommendations of the report but to encourage the reader to follow through and read the full report.

Examine the contrast in writing styles between the technical and popular reports presented in table 12•1. The example of the technical report is drawn from the *Journal of Marketing Research*, a journal so technical that it is considered largely unreadable even by many research professionals. Nevertheless, it remains a highly valued publication outlet for research-oriented marketing academicians.

Contents of the Research Report

No universally accepted guide establishes the exact contents of marketing research reports. There is no standardized way of presenting either the popular or the technical report. The exact format of the report depends to a large extent on its nature and the audience for which it is intended. However, there are certain guidelines that can be used to establish the basic contents of any marketing research report. The following list is only a suggested guideline and need not be followed exactly in every report:

1. Title page
2. Table of contents
3. Executive summary
4. Introduction
5. Research methodology
6. Findings
7. Limitations
8. Conclusions and recommendations
9. Appendixes

Title Page. The title page is a covering page that should include the title of the report, the name or names of the researchers, for whom the report was prepared, the date of the report, and where it was prepared. If the report is confidential, this restriction and the names of the intended recipients should be clearly identified.

Table of Contents. A table of contents is necessary for all but the shortest of reports. It should list the page numbers of all major sections, subsections, charts, tables, and appendixes (in short reports only the major sections need be identified).

Summary. The summary, often called the executive summary, is usually the most important part of the research report. Many executives do not have the time to read the full report and will read only the summary. Thus, it is very important for the summary to provide the essential information, so that the reader will not miss important details. Though the summary should be no longer than one or two pages, it should be able to stand by itself.

It should be noted that not every research report requires a summary. In general, very short reports, which can be read in a brief period of time, and reports intended for in-depth reading by a select group of executives do not require summaries.

Introduction. This part of the report presents the background and objectives of the research and gives the reader a view of the overall problem and a justification for the study. It is appropriate in the introduction to cite similar studies conducted in the past and explain how they relate to the present project.

All reports require some introduction. The length of the introduction section is dependent upon the reader's familiarity with the subject and the length of the report. Generally speaking, the wider the distribution of the report, the more extensive the introduction required.[1]

Research Methodology. In this section the research design used in conducting the research project should be described. All research reports should contain a description of the research methodology used, but some may give greater attention to this section than others. Technical reports usually have much more detailed methodological sections than do popular reports.

Included in the research methodology section should be not only a description of the research design but an explanation *why* that particular design was chosen. A discussion of *how* and *why* secondary or primary data were used is appropriate. The section should also cover sampling frame, sample size, and confidence intervals obtained in the sample. Again, the degree of detail is highly dependent upon the background of the audience; in all cases, lengthy technical charts and graphs are best left for the appendixes.

Findings. The findings constitute the major portion of the report. It is here that the results of the study are presented to the reader. The principal difficulty in presenting findings is deciding which are relevant and should be included and which are irrelevant and should be left out altogether or reserved for a technical appendix. It is here that the good judgment of the researcher is called upon. Every research project generates a mass of findings, most of which are not especially relevant and should be omitted in the final report.

Limitations. Research professionals recognize there is no such thing as the "perfect" study. Every research report has some qualifications that limit the extent to which the results can be generalized. For example, it would be difficult to apply generalizations from a study of consumer attitudes in the Dallas-Fort Worth area toward purchase of automobile air-conditioning units to a group of similar consumers living in the Seattle area.

At the same time, the researcher must not overemphasize the limitations of the report. It is the researcher's job to sell the report, not to undersell it. The limitations section should therefore be balanced to

[1] Gilbert A. Churchill, Jr., *Marketing Research: Methodological Foundations* (Hinsdale, Ill.: Dryden Press, 1976), p. 597.

give the reader a clear idea how far the results of the study can be applied to other situations.

Conclusions and Recommendations. All reports should contain both conclusions and recommendations, which are not the same thing. A *conclusion* is a deduction based on the findings, whereas a *recommendation* is a suggested course of action. In other words, the researcher may conclude that there is not a potentially profitable market for a new product and then recommend that the product not be introduced. Unfortunately, this is usually the most neglected segment of the research report. Many people prefer to avoid making unpopular decisions or risky recommendations, preferring instead to let readers draw their own conclusions and make decisions without any recommendations. The argument against making recommendations is the researcher does not have the full picture and therefore should not be advising higher management. Although recommendations may not be popular and may not be acted upon, it is still the duty of the research specialist to suggest a specific course of action unless instructed to the contrary.

Appendixes. Material too detailed or too complex to be placed in the text of the report may be inserted in an appendix, with a reference in the text stating, for example, "A copy of the questionnaire is included in Appendix A." This reference allows the reader to examine the questionnaire at that time or at the end of the report. Included in the appendixes might be, in addition to a copy of the questionnaire, detailed charts or graphs, relevant computer print-outs, names and addresses of respondents, and any detailed mathematical calculations.

The value of the appendix is that it allows important material to be added without interrupting the text of the report. As a general rule, if there is any question whether something should be included in the report or in the appendix, it is best reserved for the appendix.

Presenting the Report

The Oral Report

As well as preparing a written report to be read by top management, the marketing researcher may be called upon to make an oral presentation before a group of company executives. This oral presentation does *not* replace, but merely supplements, the written report.

There are several reasons for making oral presentations. First, an oral report allows the researcher a second chance to present the findings of the study, thereby increasing the exposure given to the report and the likelihood of its findings being acted upon. Second, the oral report, like the executive summary report, gives a busy executive, who may not have time to read the full report, a quick view of the research project. Third, the oral presentation is an ideal occasion for executives to ask questions for further clarification and for the researcher to explain points that may not have been evident in the written report.

The importance of preparation for an oral presentation should not be overlooked. If you have only forty-five minutes to explain four months' work, you will need to be efficient in your explanation. The presentation should be rehearsed, several times if necessary, before it is given formally. When making an oral presentation, the researcher should try to make maximum use of visual aids — using transparent slides, an overhead projector, charts, and chalk boards. On these, as in the written report itself, the results can be graphically presented. Pictures, charts, maps, and diagrams are essential visual aids for successful oral presentations. These charts are the most important component in presenting research results, whether in oral or written form.

Using Visual Presentations

Any number of different charts can be used by researchers to make effective report presentations. Three of the most important are: (1) bar charts, (2) pie charts, and (3) line charts. The value of good charts is they add significantly to the audience's ability to understand and follow the report. On the other hand, poor graphic presentation is no help at all.

Although tables are important aids in graphic presentation, researchers usually prefer charts over tables, because a chart is more easily comprehended by the viewer. The chart's graphic presentation is more quickly grasped, without sacrificing quality.

PIE CHARTS

Probably the favorite chart for researchers is the *pie chart*, so named because, like a pie, it is a circle divided into slices or sections. It is especially effective for visually conveying comparative figures on market share or other breakdowns totaling 100 percent because the different sizes of the slices are readily apparent. A pie chart may be used to supplement a table: compare, for example, table 12•2 and figure 12•1. Though both the table and the pie chart are presenting the same data, the percentage figures are much more easily and quickly

Table 12•2
Full-Time Undergraduate Enrollment at Utopia University in 1979

COLLEGE	NUMBER	PERCENTAGE
Arts	3,249	37
Business	2,586	30
Science	1,154	13
Engineering	915	10
Fine arts	839	10
Total	8,743	100

grasped in the pie chart. This is the principal advantage of the pie chart: it permits the quick and easy understanding of relative percentages, or divisions of the whole.

BAR CHARTS

Another very popular way in which research findings are presented is through the use of bar charts. A *bar chart* presents the data through a series of bars, either horizontal or vertical, the height or length of which is used to measure some variable. The data presented in table 12•2 could have been presented using a bar chart, with bars representing student enrollment in each of the five colleges in Utopia University.

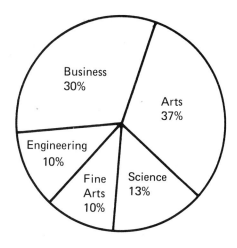

Figure 12•1
Full-Time Undergraduate Enrollment at Utopia University in 1979

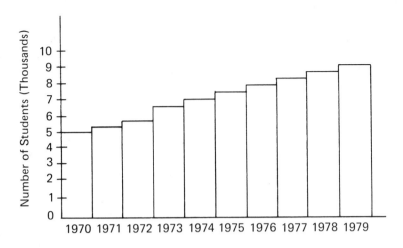

Figure 12•2
Bar Chart Showing Growth in Number of Full-Time Students at Utopia University for the Period 1970–79

However, the bar chart is best and most often used to make comparative representations over time, with changes shown by the length of the bars. Figure 12•2 provides an example of a vertical bar chart showing changes over time. Notice that this material could have been presented in a horizontal bar chart; either method is acceptable.

LINE CHARTS

In addition to pie charts and bar charts, research reports often incorporate line charts. A *line chart* is a two-dimensional chart that also represents changes or trends over time but is most useful for extrapolations or forecasts. Forecasting is commonly done using the straight line formula $Y_c = a + bX$, which is covered in the sales forecasting section in Chapter 16. Other advantages of a line chart are its ability to compare several series on one chart, to illustrate the movement of the data when the time period is a lengthy one, and to illustrate the trends of a frequency distribution.

Look at figure 12•3. This example of a line chart, showing changes over time, incorporates the same data presented in figure 12•2, a vertical bar chart. It really does not make too much difference which type is used in this instance. However, had we been attempting to *forecast* changes, say for the years 1980 to 1985, then the line chart would have been the better of the two charts. This is because a line can readily be extrapolated to indicate future expected trends.

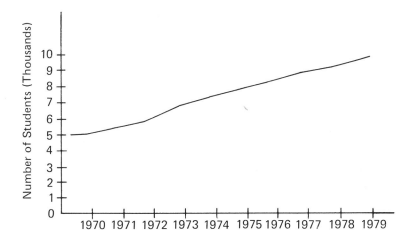

Figure 12·3
Line Chart Showing Growth in Number of Full-Time Students
at Utopia University for the Period 1970–79

One danger in using line charts to predict the future is over-reliance upon historical data. We tend to assume that what has happened in the past will happen in the future: a company that has had regular annual sales increases of 15 percent for the past ten years may well assume that this increase will continue in the future. The fact is that there is no guarantee that what has happened in the past will continue to happen in the future. However, in the absence of other marketing information, trend forecasts derived from line chart data have an enormous allure for forecasters.

Is the Researcher a Decision Maker?

Earlier in this chapter we noted the importance of including the researcher's recommendations and conclusions in the research report. Despite arguments and tendencies to the contrary, research professionals are obliged to provide management with clear conclusions and recommendations, though their advice will not always be followed.

Conflict between executives and research professionals may result from the researcher's suggestions. In explaining the basis for this conflict, Joseph Newman writes: "Executives rise to power either by making correct assumptions about uncertainty or by persuading others that they have done so. Typically, there are few checks on their judgments. If an executive thinks that others regard him as a good business artist, he can hardly be expected to welcome research which, in effect, challenges both the adequacy and the quality of his skills." [2]

At the beginning of this text we noted that the changing nature of the marketing research function recognizes the increasing importance and complexity of research in most organizations. Though the role of the marketing research specialist is rapidly changing, research directors retain essentially a staff function in most organizations; accordingly, they have limited influence on line managers, who make the key decisions.

In examining the role of researchers as decision makers, Robert J. Small and Larry J. Rosenberg discovered a number of policy implications for top executives who work with marketing research personnel:

> *Top Management* Top management would be well advised to recognize the marketing research department as a reservoir of managerial talent. Research revealed little evidence that marketing researchers typically avoid decision responsibility. On the contrary, many researchers were seen to be highly decision oriented. Thus, it would seem reasonable to consider lifting traditional barriers that prevent research personnel from entering line positions that require decision-making skills.
>
> *Research Directors* Research directors should neither discourage subordinates from assuming decision responsibility nor hold back recommending them for nonresearch positions. Research directors should also provide career paths for researchers who are more interested in research techniques than decision responsibility, even at the risk of losing these "career researchers" to higher-echelon marketing research departments. Otherwise, departmental morale is likely to decline and, in time, the department itself may be perceived by management as a stagnant area in which no talent — research or management — is likely to be found.
>
> *Middle Management* Middle management must firmly commit itself to developing and maintaining good working relationships with marketing researchers. In this study, researchers were seen to communicate in a manner acceptable to marketing managers and to respect the equality of subjective executive judgment with objective research techniques. Therefore, it seems reasonable to suggest that product, sales, and other marketing managers should reinforce their understanding of the marketing research process. Opportunities for this achievement may be found in more manager-initiated contact with researchers in areas involving line responsibility and in the incorporation of periodic stints in the marketing research department into the management training program.

The effectiveness and efficiency of marketing decisions is largely

[2] "Put Research into Marketing Decisions," *Harvard Business Review* 40 (March-April 1962): 108.

contingent upon how well the marketing researcher participates in the managerial process. How well he can perform this role depends in part upon the satisfaction he derives from his job and the minimization of friction with managers. As a means of achieving these benefits, companies should consider the enlargement of decision responsibility for the researcher.[3]

Evaluating Research Reports

We have stressed from the beginning of this text the need for all managers to have some basic understanding of the marketing research process, regardless of whether they are ever involved in research activities themselves. We emphasize this point because *all* managers have to make decisions under conditions of uncertainty, and many will require research information in order to reduce that uncertainty.

However, not all research is done in an objective and professional manner. Certainly, research reports vary drastically in quality, ranging from excellent to worthless. How then is a manager able to judge the quality and hence the dependability of a research report?

Several guidelines are available to assist managers in evaluating research findings. Quoted here is a listing of common-sense guidelines for evaluating research studies:

1. *The purpose of the research, or the problem involved, should be clearly defined and sharply delineated in terms as unambiguous as possible.*

The statement of the research problem should include analysis into its simplest elements, its scope and limitations, and precise specifications of the meanings of all words significant to the researcher. Failure of the researcher to do this adequately may raise legitimate doubts in the minds of readers as to whether the researcher has sufficient understanding of the problem to make a sound attack upon it.

2. *The research procedures used should be described in sufficient detail to permit another researcher to repeat the research.*

Excepting when secrecy is imposed in the national interest, research reports should reveal with candor the sources of data and the means by which they were obtained. Omission of significant procedural details makes it difficult or impossible to estimate the validity and reliability of the data and justifiably weakens the confidence of the reader in the research.

3. *The procedural design of the research should be carefully planned to yield results that are as objective as possible.*

[3] "The Marketing Researcher as a Decision Maker: Myth or Reality?" *Journal of Marketing* 39 (January 1975): 7.

When a sampling of a population is involved, the report should include evidence concerning the degree of representativeness of the sample. A questionnaire ought not to be used when more reliable evidence is available from documentary sources or by direct observation. Bibliographic searches should be as thorough and complete as possible. Experiments should have satisfactory controls. Direct observations should be recorded in writing as soon as possible after the event. Efforts should be made to minimize the influence of personal bias in selecting and recording data.

4. *The researcher should report, with complete frankness, flaws in the procedural design and estimate their effect upon the findings.*

There are very few perfect research designs. Some of the imperfections may have little effect upon the validity and reliability of the data; others may invalidate them entirely. A competent researcher should be sensitive to the effects of imperfect design and his experience in analyzing the data should give him a basis for estimating their influence.

5. *Analysis of the data should be sufficiently adequate to reveal its significance; and the methods of analysis used should be appropriate.*

The extent to which this criterion is met is frequently a good measure of the competence of the researcher. Twenty years of experience in guiding the research of graduate students leads the writer to conclude that adequate analysis of the data is the most difficult phase of research for the novice.

The validity and reliability of data should be checked carefully. The data should be classified in ways that assist the researcher to reach pertinent conclusions. When statistical methods are used, the probability of error should be estimated and the criteria of statistical significance applied.

6. *Conclusions should be confined to those justified by the data of the research and limited to those for which the data provides an adequate basis.*

Researchers are often tempted to broaden the bases of inductions by including personal experiences not subject to the controls under which the research data were gathered. This tends to decrease the objectivity of the research and weaken confidence in the findings.

Equally undesirable is the all-too-frequent practice of drawing conclusions from study of a limited population and applying them universally. Good researchers specify the conditions under which their conclusions seem to be valid. Failure to do so justifiably weakens confidence in the research.

7. *Greater confidence in the research is warranted if the researcher is experienced, has a good reputation in research, and is a person of integrity.*

Were it possible for the reader of a research report to obtain sufficient information about the researcher, this criterion perhaps would be one of the best bases for judging the degree of confidence a piece of research warrants. For this reason, the research report should be accompanied by more information about the qualifications of the researcher than is the usual practice.

Some evidence pertinent to estimates of the competence and integrity of the researcher may be found in the report itself. Language that is restrained, clear, and precise; assertions that are carefully drawn and hedged with appropriate reservation; and an apparent effort to achieve maximum objectivity tend to leave a favorable impression of the researcher. On the other hand, generalizations that outrun the evidence upon which they are based, exaggerations, and unnecessary verbiage tend to leave an unfavorable impression.[4]

The foregoing criteria are general and require good judgment to be used in their application. Nevertheless, they can be useful guidelines for the evaluation of research reports.

Summary

The focus of this chapter has been upon the *research report*, the means by which the essential findings of a research study are communicated to the intended audience. The report should be viewed as a communications vehicle, in which the researcher should be communicating findings to top management in as complete and concise a manner as possible. Although the report is the end link in the research process, it is often the weakest one because of communications failure resulting from poor preparation, and not from any weakness in any of the prior steps.

Depending on the level of the audience to whom the report is addressed, the research report may take either of two forms: technical or popular. The *technical report* is a detailed report prepared for professionals in the field who are well versed in research methodology and in previous studies. A *popular report* is geared for a more general audience and gives greater relative importance to findings than to methodology. A combination of the two report styles is appropriate when the audience contains a mixture of specialists and generalists. In every case the format of the report is dependent upon the characteristics of the audience.

Contents for a research report are not standardized. The length of the project and audience characteristics dictate not only the basic content but also the extent of treatment given each of the topic areas.

---

[4] James Harold Fox, "Criteria of Good Research," *Phi Delta Kappan* 39 (March 1958): 285–86.

Guidelines for writing research reports have been presented here. The single largest part of any research report is the findings section, where the results from the research project are reported. Conclusions and recommendations should always be included.

Report presentations are made much more understandable to the audience through charts and other visual aids. Three major types of charts are (1) the *pie chart*, (2) the *bar chart*, and (3) the *line chart*. Pie charts are best for reporting breakdowns that total 100 percent; the line chart is best for making forecasts into the future. A combination of visual aids will make report presentation much more effective.

The question is often asked, is the researcher a decision maker? The answer is no — at least not in the classic sense. Marketing researchers fulfill essentially staff functions and cannot make line decisions. For example, the researcher should recommend whether to launch a new product but cannot make the final decision, which remains a line management prerogative. However, all managers need a basic understanding of the research function, even if they are not directly involved in it. Several criteria for the evaluation of research studies, designed to help managers determine which ones they may trust, have been presented here.

Questions for Discussion

1. You, the researcher, are asked by the sales manager to make a market share forecast presentation to your company's sales department.

   a. Will you prepare a technical or a popular report? Why?

   b. What type(s) of charts will you use?

   c. What recommendations might be important?

2. Describe a situation in which each of the following charts would be most appropriate: (a) bar chart, (b) line chart, and (c) pie chart.

3. For your report to the vice-president of marketing, you have a detailed calculation of sample size and confidence intervals used in a survey of consumer attitudes toward your firm's proposed new product offering. Where in the report will you place these calculations?

4. Research reports must be both complete and concise. How can a report be both at the same time?

5. When would you use an executive summary, and where in your report would it go?

6. What is the single most important factor in determining the type of research report format to use?

7. How could marketing researchers become more actively involved in the decision-making process?

8. Carefully evaluate and then criticize the guidelines presented in this chapter for evaluating research findings. How would you modify them?

9. What part of the research report format is most often neglected by researchers? Why?

10. What is the purpose of the limitations section in a research report?

CASE 2·1

SAM'S SNAPPY SUPERMARKETS (B)

Sam Snodgrass, Jr., a recent marketing graduate of State University, has just joined the management team of his father's business, Sam's Snappy Supermarkets. Annual gross sales are approximately $75 million. Net profits after taxes are $750,000. The chain has twenty-five stores with a total of three hundred employees.

A careful review of the operating data has revealed that the growth rate has been tapering off and profit margins narrowing over the past three years.

Three problems are particularly bothering Sam, Jr.:

1. One store in a remotely located area has experienced a deficit every month for the past two and a half years. Sam, Jr., suspects there has been a shift in the population of the town, a rise in unemployment, or a drop in average income. Alternatively, the problem may lie with store management. Therefore, Sam, Jr., would also like to know which departments in the store have been hardest hit and which products consumers are buying.

2. After reviewing the inventory listings, Sam, Jr., has become concerned about stock turnover and how it compares to that of competitors. He wonders where he can get this information.

3. In order better to acquaint himself with the industry, Sam, Jr., would like to draw an industry profile of several large publicly owned competitors. He needs to obtain the following information: gross margin on sales, net profit after taxes, earnings per share, and stock prices over the last three years. He hopes to find individual articles on some of the larger stores, industry marketing trends, and management innovations.

Questions

1. What specific data sources would you suggest that Sam, Jr., consult?

2. Where is the best place for Sam, Jr., to locate these sources?

DONNY'S PANCAKE HOUSES, INC.

Donny's Pancake Houses, Inc., is a chain of forty-eight restaurants located in metropolitan Boston and surrounding cities. The company was founded in the early 1960s when pancake houses became popular in the Northeast. Corporate strategy included research into location and potential market. As a result, most of the pancake houses were situated in shopping centers or next door to hotels along well-traveled freeways.

In order to attract customers, the company frequently ran special promotions with cents-off coupons in local papers and served free coffee several times a week. During the evening, hamburgers, steaks, and sandwiches were also available.

Throughout the first ten years of operations, the company made average earnings. However, in the early 1970s, increases in the prices of coffee and food, compounded by labor problems, caused the profit picture to darken. Nevertheless, Donny's weathered the storm and profits picked up again in 1975–76. Although 1977 began well, management noticed a decided decline in business by midsummer. Some customers complained about price and the limited menu. Management was well aware that cheaper breakfasts could be had at some of the fast-food outlets that were just breaking into this market. In addition, these franchises were springing up so fast, and were so reasonably priced, that the owners suspected that they were affecting midday and evening business as well. Obviously, the competition had some benefits that Donny's Pancake Houses, Inc., did not offer.

As of 1977, market research had been limited to secondary sources and internally generated sales and profit data. Management decided it was time to approach customers directly in order to determine their needs and obtain suggestions for improvement.

The vice-president of sales and an assistant developed a question-naire and decided to conduct a two-day survey on a Saturday and Sunday. Each waitress was instructed to distribute the questionnaire to customers waiting to be served. There was no obligation to answer the questions, because management did not wish to inconvenience diners. The survey was conducted simultaneously at the five locations with the most dramatic sales decline in the preceding six months. Here is the questionnaire:

Questions

1. Evaluate the marketing survey technique devised by the vice-president of sales. How could the plan be improved?

2. Criticize the questionnaire. What kind of bias has been introduced? How could it have been avoided?

THE MERCHANTS' AND
CONSUMERS' BANK (B)

The Merchants' and Consumers' Bank is the oldest and second largest bank in California, with three hundred branches statewide. Recently it began investigating the possibility of offering low-cost banking services to senior citizens. The bulk of the research is presently being handled by Ellen Walett of the marketing research department. (See Case 1·2 for additional details.)

The bank has never been interested in actively promoting banking services for senior citizens but has, instead, always taken these customers for granted. Realizing that little banking information was available on senior citizens, except for some demographic statistics collected in previous surveys, Walett decided first to collect some primary data on this potential target market.

Her first step was to call Beverley Baker, manager of a small branch on the outskirts of Los Angeles. Baker's bank is located near a prominent upper-income senior citizens' residence, and consequently, she is familiar with this customer segment.

From her experience as a branch manager, Baker produced the following observations about the banking patterns and attitudes of senior citizens:

• Senior citizens purchase more money orders than the average population because they like to have a copy of all payments made.

• Many senior citizens are holders of government savings bonds. They store their coupons in safekeeping or in safety deposit boxes, and often they forget to clip coupons. For this reason, a coupon clipping service offered at a reasonable price would probably be appreciated.

• Many senior citizens, desiring security and liquidity above all, keep money in high-interest savings accounts rather than investing it more profitably.

• Retired people want to have money coming in on a regular basis, the way it did when they were working. If their savings are invested, they live off the yearly dividends. Therefore, they must budget the lump sums on a monthly basis. Therefore, the bank might offer senior citizens a deposit account that would pay interest on a monthly basis.

Walett found Baker's comments relevant and recommended that the bank include some of them in the final package.

Next, Walett spoke to the president of the Golden Age Association and to other people involved in social agencies dealing with senior citizens. The general consensus was that retired persons would be very interested in such services and would even switch banks to apply for them.

During this preliminary investigation, four people have become involved in a debate on primary data-collection methods:

Walett is a strong believer in testing new services. She has proposed that a questionnaire be mailed directly to seniors selected randomly from lists of various social organizations, on the assumption that active members of these clubs will be more likely than other seniors to make use of the new bank services.

Peter Graham thinks individual door-to-door interviews would provide better insight into the specific needs of seniors. They would give feedback on the usefulness of the package and would uncover new ideas that could be promoted. He is sure that seniors will readily accept such a package, because it will offer them useful specialized services at a very low cost. Knowing that older people tire easily and often have hearing problems, he opposes group interviews. Furthermore, he fears that wealthy seniors might monopolize financial discussions, inhibiting their less-well-off peers.

Bill Bossy, director of marketing, has also become involved. Prior to taking his current job at the bank, he was president of his own marketing consultant firm. Bossy contends that door-to-door interviewing would be too time-consuming and expensive. He expects the competition to introduce similar plans within six months of the launching of the new program at Merchants' Bank. Bossy favors telephone surveys: he wants to formulate the plan, test it, and implement it within as short a time as possible.

Frank Daley, a consultant who has done a good deal of research for the bank in the past five years, has also been contacted. He proposes a series of focus group interviews consisting of financially homogeneous seniors. The interviews could be held in several areas of the state to allow for regional differences. Daley rejects door-to-door interviewing as too costly and too slow. Senior citizens comprise a relatively small proportion of the population, and many of them are disabled and would be unwilling to open their doors to strangers to discuss financial matters. Daley estimates that over two thousand contacts would have to be made to obtain two hundred completed interviews.

The director of marketing research wants Walett to submit a report by the end of the week outlining the method of primary data collection to be used.

Questions

1. Evaluate each of the four proposed primary data-collection methods. Which method would you recommend if you were Ellen Walett?

2. What specific information should be gathered in the study?

CASE 2·4

THE McLAURIE COMPANY

The McLaurie Company is a well-known manufacturer of candies, chocolate bars, biscuits, and similar food products. Because of thorough market research, high quality, and heavy advertising campaigns, the company is rapidly becoming a leader in its field.

Its newest innovation is Choco, instant hot chocolate powder to which only boiling water has to be added. Laboratory and in-home use tests have indicated that Choco should be a success. The next step is test marketing in a medium-sized city. The company has obtained the A. C. Nielsen reports and consumer purchase diary panel data for this city. Nielsen monitors sales at the retail level; the consumer diary panel estimates the number of repeat purchases. The data should enable McLaurie's to measure the success of its test market.

Free samples of Choco have been distributed on a random basis to half of the households in the test city. Advertising and promotion are being carried out on a regular basis. A follow-up personal interview is planned for the end of the test period.

Question

1. Design a follow-up questionnaire that will measure the effectiveness of the free sample. Your questionnaire should indicate the extent of awareness, trial, and adoption of Choco in households that received the sample, compared to those that did not. In addition, be sure the questionnaire highlights which market segments were influenced by the free sample (i.e., income group, family size, age, educational background).

CASE 2·5

THE HOME STUDY INSTITUTE

The Home Study Institute (H.S.I.) is a large correspondence school with its head office in Detroit, Michigan. When it was founded in the 1940s, the school offered strictly academic subjects that fulfilled the requirements of the surrounding states for the completion of high school.

The institute relies heavily on newspaper and radio advertising. Potential students either phone in for more information after radio announcements or send in their names on information coupons clipped from the company's newspaper ads.

Once the name of a prospective customer is received, it is given to a district salesperson, who visits the client and sells the course of studies. If the respondent lives in an area outside the range of the sales office, which is the case almost 20 percent of the time, enrollment is completed through the mail. Students are required to study one course at a time, sending in exams to be corrected after every two or three chapters of the text. At the end of their studies, high school diplomas are issued.

After World War II a large percentage of enrollments were war veterans who had dropped out of high school to join the armed forces. At present, 30 percent of the students are immigrants with a limited knowledge of English; 50 percent are young adults over seventeen who want to complete their high school educations in order to get better jobs; and the remainder are middle-aged adults who dropped out of school and now want a chance to finish their educations. The school enrolls about twenty-three thousand students a year.

In 1971 the institute introduced several courses that were career-oriented rather than academic. These included Bookkeeping and Accounting, Typing, How to Become a Medical Secretary, How to Become a Legal Secretary, Business English for Secretaries, and Business Law. The courses proved very popular. Within two years the institute put together a complete business program offering a Diploma of Business Administration to high school graduates who completed ten specific courses. Sales increased substantially as this new market area was tapped. Many of the institute's graduates reenlisted to take the new program.

In fall 1978 the institute decided to investigate adding a data-processing program to its curriculum. Investment would be high, since the firm would have to purchase or rent a computer for its students.

The market research firm of R. A. Golden Consultants was contacted to undertake a study to estimate the expected student body. Ray Golden, who worked for five years at a medium-sized research firm before setting up his own company, devised the following plan to determine the market potential for the Diploma of Data Processing.

Each of the institute's six sales managers was given a specific number of questionnaires — twelve for each salesperson — to be administered to the next twelve prospective clients each salesperson visited. Salespeople were given three weeks to complete this process, although the institute knew that some would make twelve calls in one week or less. At the end of the three-week period, salespeople were to send in all the forms directly to Golden Consultants, who would tabulate the results and report to H.S.I. No editing was done until the questionnaires reached Golden.

Exhibit 1
Home Study Institute Survey for the Diploma of Data Processing

Please read the following paragraph to your client, and then answer the questions with him or her: "A survey is being conducted to determine your interest in a Diploma of Data Processing course. Thank you for taking the time to complete this questionnaire. All answers will be kept confidential."

1. Name _____
   Address _____

   Please check one:
   Age: under 21 _____
          21–29 _____
          30–39 _____
        over 40 _____
   Sex: Male _____
        Female _____
   Marital status: Single _____
                     Married _____

2. Please indicate present line of work:
   Technical _____   Managerial _____
   Clerical _____   Crafts _____
   Sales _____   Other _____
   If other please describe: _____

3. Has the client ever taken any courses at the Home Study Institute?
   Yes _____   No _____
   If "yes," please indicate which ones:
   Grade 7 _____   Grade 11 _____
   Grade 8 _____   Grade 12 _____
   Grade 9 _____   Business Program _____
   Grade 10 _____
   In what year were the courses completed? _____

4. Please indicate the client's last year of education:
   Grade 7 _____   Grade 11 _____
   Grade 8 _____   Grade 12 _____
   Grade 9 _____   Business Program _____
   Grade 10 _____

5. Is the client interested in data-processing courses? Yes _____
   No _____ If "no," go to question 10. If "yes," please continue.

6. Would the client take the full ten-course program? Yes _____
   No _____

Exhibit 1—*Continued*

---

7. If "no," how many courses would he or she be willing to take?
   1–2 _____
   3–4 _____
   5–6 _____
   7–8 _____

8. If "yes," what is the maximum price he or she would be willing to pay for the Diploma of Data Processing program?
   $ 800 _____
   $1,000 _____
   $1,200 _____
   $1,500 _____

9. For those interested in the full ten-course program: Will the client be able to come to the Detroit Data Center to use the computer? Yes _____ No _____ (Approximately five two-hour sessions with the computer will be necessary. They can be arranged at the client's convenience.)

10. For those who answered "no" to question 5, please indicate why the client is not interested in data processing:
    Only wants high school program _____
    Data processing not connected to line of work _____
    Dislikes data processing _____

Exhibit 2
Summary of Survey Results

Territory	Number of Salesmen	Incomplete Questionnaires	Total Usable Questionnaires	Total Number of Questionnaires Distributed
1	21	198	54	252
2	16	0	192	192
3	18	142	74	216
4	15	125	55	180
5	9	72	36	108
6	13	156	0	156
Totals	92	693	411	1,104

Notes to Exhibit 2

1. In Territory 2 all forms appear to have been completed in the same handwriting.

2. The sales manager in Territory 6 disagreed with the method of presentation of the survey. Salespeople were told to give the prospect the form and ask the prospect to return it by mail to the institute if he or she wished to help with the survey. It is doubtful that any clients were given the survey form.

3. Many salespeople stopped at question 5. If they did so, results were disregarded.

Exhibit 3
Summary of Responses
(This material is based on Exhibit 2, Total Usable Questionnaires).

	%
1. Age: under 21	38
21–29	24
30–39	22
over 40	16
	100
Sex: Male	64
Female	36
	100
Marital Status: Single	32
Married	68
	100
2. Present line of work:	
Technical	27
Clerical	31
Sales	5
Managerial	2
Crafts	16
Other	19
	100
Breakdown of "other" category:	
	%
Shipping	2
Driving	3
Armed forces	6
Restaurant work	2
Self-employment	6
	19

Exhibit 3—*Continued*

3. Has the client ever taken any courses at the Home Study Institute?   Yes

   No

	%
Yes	4
No	96
	100

   The result indicates that 16 people have taken courses at H.S.I.; last years completed are as follows:
   Grade 9 — 5 people
   Grade 10 — 4 people
   Grade 11 — 6 people
   Grade 12 — 1 person
   All have completed courses between 1961 and 1977. None has taken the Business Program.

4. Client's last year of education

Grade 7	6
Grade 8	16
Grade 9	20
Grade 10	28
Grade 11	24
Grade 12	4
Business Program	0
Other	2
	100

   Note: "Other" category: 2 percent of respondents indicated they have begun university studies and are interested in the Business Program. They also indicated an interest in the Data-Processing Program.

5. Is the client interested in data-processing courses?

	%
Yes	51
No	49
	100

6. Would the client take the full ten-course program?

Yes	12
No	88
	100

7. If "no," how many courses would he or she be willing to take?

1–2 courses	51
3–4 courses	25
5–6 courses	18
7–8 courses	6
	100

Exhibit 3—*Continued*

8. If "yes," what is the maximum price he or she would
   be willing to pay for the Diploma of Data Processing
   program?

$ 800	96
1,000	4
1,200	0
1,500	0
	100

   Note: Several salespeople indicated that the client
   would be willing to pay $500–$600 maximum.

9. For those interested in the full ten-course program:
   Will the client be able to come to the Detroit Data
   Center to use the computer?

Yes	95
No	5
	100

10. For those who answered "no" to question 5, please
    indicate why the client is not interested in data pro-
    cessing:

Only wants high school program	37
Data processing not connected to line of work	21
Dislikes data processing	22
	90

    Note: Several salespeople filled in other reasons, in-
    cluding "Foreign student — does not know what data
    processing is" and "Client is only in grade 8 —
    would not qualify."

Questions

1. a. Critically analyze the questionnaire.

   b. What problems do you foresee with its administration?

   c. Suggest a better method of obtaining the information.

   d. Rewrite the questionnaire with full instructions for completion.

2. a. Suggest ways for making the sample design more efficient.

   b. How would you interpret the data in Exhibits 2 and 3?

CASE 2·6

HUDSON DEPARTMENT STORES

Hudson Department Stores, a New York City based firm, has three-hundred thousand users of its credit card throughout New York, New Jersey, Pennsylvania, and Massachusetts. The stores are located mostly in the downtown areas of New York City, Trenton, Philadelphia, and Boston; besides the main downtown stores, there are also branches in surrounding suburban shopping centers and a few in outlying areas.

Hudson is interested in determining whether the socioeconomic characteristics of its card holders have an impact on their spending habits. For example, do upper-income customers use store credit only for major purchases, such as stoves or refrigerators, or also for minor purchases? Is their consumer behavior the same as that of card holders in lower-income brackets?

Question

1. What type of sampling should be used to obtain this information — simple random, stratified random, or cluster sampling? Why? Show how each type of sample could be used.

CASE 2·7

O.K. SUPER DRUG MART

O.K. Super Drug Mart, a large discount drug chain, is planning to enter the Miami market. Management would like to estimate the average square feet of selling space of competing drug stores in the Miami area. A stratified sample of these yielded the following data:

Size of Store	Total Number in Miami	Total Number in Sample	Mean Size of Stores (Sq. Ft.) in Sample	Standard Deviation of Stores (Sq. Ft.) in Sample
Large	200	6	20,000	3,000
Medium	500	15	10,000	2,000
Small	900	20	2,000	1,000

Question

1. What is the average size of discount drug stores in Miami? Find the 95 percent confidence interval around that size.

CASE 2·8

THE DR. BAKER DOG FOOD COMPANY

The Dr. Baker Dog Food Company has conducted a survey of dog owners to determine if there is a difference between dog food consumed by show dogs and that consumed by all other dogs. The data in Exhibit 1 have been obtained.

Exhibit 1
Dog Food Consumption of Show Dogs versus All Other Dogs

Brand	Numbers of Dogs Being Fed		
	Show Dogs	All Other Dogs	Total
A	50	270	320
B	30	160	190
C	40	50	90
All other brands	80	320	400
Totals	200	800	1,000

Questions

1. Calculate the chi-square statistic for this set of data.

2. How many degrees of freedom are there in this example?

3. If there is a probability of 0.01 that a value of χ^2 larger than 11.34 will occur as a result of random variations, what can we infer about the data?

Part 3

Applications

Chapter 13

Consumer Behavior and Motivational Research

THE PRECEDING CHAPTERS have dealt with "nose-counting" research — that is, research directed at finding the answer to a specific question, or even the number that answers a specific question. Thus, the focus of the book has been upon such questions as *"How many* of *which* demographic types buy *which* products?"* To questions like these the exact answer is assumed to be attainable; the only problem is to get that answer in an efficient and unbiased manner.

In this chapter, a different type of problem is presented. We are now trying to look into the thought process of the consumer in an effort to determine not just what he has bought but *why* he has bought it. We are going from a very objective, quantitative process to a situation that by its very nature is highly subjective and often totally qualitative.

Consumer Behavior

The purpose of motivational research in marketing is to answer the question *why*, to discover the reasons why people will favor one brand over another, why they will buy Ford rather than Chevrolet, why they will consistently prefer Schlitz over Bud, and so forth. And yet, although marketers seek to determine the reasons for the purchase of their individual products, the overall process of consumer behavior is a virtual mystery. It is as if the oil companies were spending millions of dollars to increase the octane of their gasolines, while scientists remained unaware that the basic combustion process requires fuel, air,

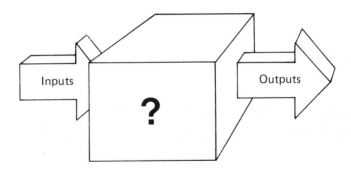

Figure 13•1
The Human Mind as a Black Box

and heat. Many writers and investigators pay homage to this ignorance in labeling the human decision process a "black box" (fig. 13•1). The image behind this name is the human mind as a totally opaque box. We can see various inputs going into the box, and we can see various results coming out of the box, but what happens inside the box remains a complete mystery. In the case of consumer behavior, we see inputs, most notably advertising, and we see outputs, most notably purchases, but why one advertisement seems to work while another one fails is primarily a matter of speculation.

And yet, every purchase is made for a reason. The reason may not be apparent — in fact, even the purchaser may be unaware of the true reason for that purchase — yet there is a reason. Every purchase we make says something about us; it is a very vital way in which we express the totality of our personalities and of our thought processes. To this end, note what one motivational researcher has to say about the purchase of Pet Rocks:

> Re Pet Rocks, may I note that such humorous products may also have a serious side. While such products, by their unmitigated absurdity, may have the potential for tapping people's funny bones (and pocketbooks), they may also represent something a little less funny.
>
> Past depth research done by our company indicates that the kinds of pets people have tend to be related to the kinds of people that they are, and the kinds of relationships they seek and can tolerate. For instance, the time and emotional demands involved in caring for goldfish tend to be less than those involved in caring for a dog and are some indication of the degree of involvement people want or can stand.
>
> Without making too big a deal out of it, I submit that beneath the humorous smoke of such products as Pet Rocks and Trained

Sticks, there is the fire of a wry recognition of the extent to which the depersonalization of people and relationships in our society may be taking place.[1]

Factors Affecting the Consumer Decision Process

Although there is no generally accepted theory explaining exactly what goes on within that wonderous region we call the human brain, researchers have been able to propose and show evidence of a variety of factors at work within the human decision process. Some researchers have postulated that the purchase of a single product may be influenced by upwards of six hundred different motives; [2] this chapter, however, will attempt to discuss only a handful of motives under three general subgroups.

ECONOMIC FACTORS

One of the oldest and best-known models of purchasing behavior is that of "economic man." According to this type of analysis, consumers are motivated to purchase and to make purchase decisions among products upon economic grounds. The economic man theory suggests that the consumer rationally computes the marginal utility of each purchase dollar and spends his money upon those products with the highest marginal utility. Although this analysis does provide a quantitative, comprehensive theory of purchasing, and although it is true that price is often important as a buying factor, this theory still leaves much to be desired from the standpoint of the marketing manager. Most notably, it does not indicate how the consumer determines those marginal utilities. It is easy enough to say that consumers who buy Cadillacs do so because they think that the happiness they will get from Cadillacs will exceed the happiness they could get from any other use of their money, but the marketing researcher is still left with the fundamental question of *why* they feel that way. Correspondingly, the economic man theory leaves unanswered the question why one person would feel that his money was best used with the purchase of a Cadillac, whereas another would choose to purchase a Continental, and yet a third would purchase a Volkswagen and leave the remainder of her money in the bank.

Nevertheless, it remains true that price is a very sensitive marketing variable. Though the theory of economic man does not explain

[1] John Kishler; quoted in *Advertising Age*, 8 March 1977, p. 65.

[2] Joseph Clawson, "The Coming Break-Throughs in Motivational Research," *Cost and Profit Outlook* 11, nos. 5 and 6 (May-June 1958) : 1.

everything, many marketing phenomena can be explained by the effect of prices and the law of supply and demand. Thus, whereas price tends to fail as an explanatory variable, it is quite valuable as an operational variable. We know, for instance, that if we cut prices sales will probably increase, and much research is done by companies to determine the price elasticity, the price sensitivity, of their products. (Note, however, that this type of descriptive, operations-oriented research falls within the domain of traditional "nose-counting" research and not within the domain of motivational research.)

PERSONALITY FACTORS

Consumer personality factors represent an important segmentation variable for the marketing efforts of most companies. Virtually all products have a distinctive personality profile, and, accordingly, they appeal to persons who either have or want to manifest that particular profile. For illustration, consider the personality dimensions presented in table 13•1 and the products that generally emphasize those dimensions in their appeals.

Although table 13•1 is exhaustive neither of personality dimensions nor of those products utilizing a specific type of appeal, it does indicate that a given product may make very strong appeals to several personality dimensions. Marketers actively study these personality dimensions and attempt to construct the personality profile of both the product and the type of person to which that product appeals. This investigation of the psychological dimensions of the consumer is called *psychographics*, as compared with *demographics*, which involves such standard "nose-counting" variables as age, income, sex, education, and so forth.

Although marketing researchers have difficulty in relating per-

Table 13•1
Personality Factors in Marketing

PERSONALITY DIMENSION	TYPE OF PRODUCT APPEALING TO THAT DIMENSION
guilt	life insurance, tires, religion, charities
love	jewelry, cosmetics, clothes, florists
machismo	beer, cigarettes, sports, fashion, exercise
vanity	clothes, cosmetics, health and beauty aids
fear	disinfectant cleansers, smoke alarms, religion
snobbery	yachts, luxury cars, exclusive restaurants
excitement	motorcycles, ski equipment, scuba gear

sonality considerations to other buying motives, and they have additional trouble in handling the multitude of personality variables that may impinge upon a single purchase decision, this remains a very viable and important area of marketing research. Personality characteristics are probably the major factor determining the selection of one commodity product rather than another. By *commodity product* we are referring not only to "true" commodity products, such as eggs, potatoes, and flour, but also to that wide range of consumer products among classes of which the consumer cannot discern any distinguishable difference under average usage conditions. The number of products that fit within this definition of *commodity* is enormous, including, in truth, virtually every product sold. Consider almost any product — gasoline, cereals, hand lotions, automobiles, televisions, canned corn, and so on — and you will find scarcely any difference in actual product performance among the various brands within a given generic division and within a given price range. No less an expert than advertising great David Ogilvy has said:

> I am astonished to find how many advertising men, even among the new generation, believe that consumers can be persuaded by logic and argument to buy one brand in preference to another, even when the two brands concerned are technically identical. . . . The greater the similarity between products, the less part reason really plays in brand selection. There really isn't any significant difference between the various brands of whisky or the various cigarettes or the various brands of beer. They are all about the same. And so are the cake mixes and the detergents and the automobiles.[3]

In actual tests, the average consumer can usually tell the difference between different generic products, as between cola and lemon-lime soft drinks (although you would be surprised how many people cannot tell such differences in blind taste tests). Other persons can distinguish between a high-priced and a lower-priced brand — for example, between Coke and a house-brand cola (although, here again, many people cannot tell the difference: in most studies, people pick the name-brand cola no more often than the house-brand; in other words, they cannot tell the difference). But even of those consumers who can distinguish between product types and between high-priced and low-priced brands, the number who can distinguish between two brands at the same price level, such as between Coke and Pepsi, is almost infinitesimal. And yet it is precisely at this level that the most avid brand loyalty occurs, indicating the importance of the psychological dimension in purchase

[3] David Ogilvy; quoted in Vance Packard, *The Hidden Persuaders* (New York: Pocket Books, 1957), p. 17.

behavior. Thus, in psychographic research, the psychological, or personality, variables are investigated. Much attention is given to brand image and product image, and the attitudes of consumers are tested for a large number of both tangible and intangible attributes.

EXTERNAL FACTORS

Another set of factors that researchers investigate in their studies of consumer behavior are those which are external to the individual, yet which still provide input into the individual decision process. For convenience of discussion, we will divide these factors into two groups, marketing-controlled variables and nonmarketing-controlled variables.

Nonmarketing-Controlled Variables. By *nonmarketing-controlled variables*, we are referring to various economic, social, and cultural forces that are outside the control of the individual firm and are often referred to as *external factors*.

Economic factors are extremely important in consumer buying. One of the most critical determinants of buying proclivity is the economic strength of the region, which includes not only the amount of total overall income but also the distribution of that income among the citizens. The buying patterns of a region are further affected by the stability, or lack of stability, of that income flow. Even where total dollar amounts are similar, workers in highly seasonal, "boom-or-bust" types of industries show a markedly different spending pattern from workers in industries with a more stable cash flow.

Social factors include such things as population age distribution, family formation patterns and family size, and average education levels. As persons and families mature, they need different product assortments. The shifts in buying habits that accompany these changes can be anticipated by watching the shifts in the underlying population distribution. In this spirit, many marketers are predicting a shift away from the young consumer, whose image has been in vogue among marketers for the last few years, toward an older, more affluent, more conservative consumer. Similarly, changes in family formation and family size (such as we have seen recently in the United States, where couples are waiting longer to get married and are having fewer children) have a tremendous impact upon the products being bought, as consumers spend less on "family" items, such as food, housing, clothes, toys, and lawn equipment, and more on discretionary items, such as stereos, motorcycles, entertainment, and vacations. Education and social class levels are also beyond the control of the individual firm, but they, too, must be researched and integrated into the marketing plans, since many buying patterns revolve around these variables. Even when family size and family income are the same, blue-collar and white-collar workers will buy different assortments of goods.

The receptiveness of a country and its consumers is also affected by various cultural factors, most notably religion and politics. For instance, in certain nations and within certain sections of this country, there are prohibitions against specific types of products (liquor being the most obvious), which affect the sales for those products. Yet, short of legal restrictions, there will be marked differences between countries and regions in the enthusiasm with which consumers will embrace a given offering. The same item, using the same promotion and marketed toward ostensibly similar consumers, may meet with noticeably different degrees of success.

Marketing-Controlled Variables. Marketing-controlled factors are those elements influential to consumer decisions that are under the control of the company. These elements include all the variables in the marketing mix of both the individual company and its competitors. Thus, the consumer's purchase decision is affected by the combination of prices, products, promotions, distribution availabilities, and services which she is exposed to in the marketplace.

In the larger, more progressive firms, all these elements are tested through marketing research in order to develop the best marketing approach. Different product versions are tested, different packages are tested, different package designs are tested, different ads are tested, different promotions are tested, different prices are tested, different store displays are tested, and so on, in a never-ceasing effort to attain higher profitability.

Most of this testing can be done by relatively straightforward experimental designs ("nose-counting" research). For instance, a firm might want to test the relative effectiveness of two promotional displays. For this test the firm could select a small number of stores, putting one display in half the stores and the other display in the other half, rotating the displays once a week, and keeping careful records of the actual sales in each store. If one display is more effective, it will surely become obvious within a very few weeks.

Comprehensive Theories of Consumer Behavior

In the preceding sections, an attempt has been made to trace some of the influences on the human decision process. Here these influences have been divided into three basic sets: economic factors, personality factors, and external, or environmental, factors. Although there have been many attempts to develop comprehensive theories of consumer behavior, most of these attempts, though perhaps conceptually enlightening, have been operationally useless. The result of trying to mesh together this enormous mass of competing influences is an unworkable mishmash that is hopelessly vague. Ultimately, despite all our research into decision processes, all we can conclude is that different people will indeed prefer different things.

The Importance of Consumer Behavior Studies

After the foregoing description of the multitude of difficulties and imponderables involved in the study of consumer motivation, you may be wondering why companies even bother with such an endeavor. The reason is simple: the companies *need* this information. Even if consumer behavior is just a simple matter of varying appeal, companies still need to know which things appeal to which people. Furthermore, if the advertisers and marketers are ever going to develop truly effective advertising scientifically, they need to know *why* different consumers perceive the same stimuli in different manners.

A company needs to know exactly what its image is, and it needs to know the image of its competitors. It needs to know the personality profiles of its customers and of its competitors. Only from this information can a valid marketing strategy emerge. Deliberate efforts can then be made to market the product appropriately for its consumers. Advertising campaigns can be developed to stress the precise image the company is seeking to cultivate. Various demographic and psychographic information can be used in order to select the specific media combination for the target audience. The simple fact of the matter is that all modern marketing strategy — target market, marketing mix, market segmentation, and so on — depends upon an accurate assessment of the images of the product, the customers, the competitors, and the individual brand.

Motivational Research

The Nature of Motivational Research

As noted in the opening pages of this chapter, motivational research by its very nature is different from traditional, or "nose-counting" research. So far in this chapter we have already touched on some of these differences, such as the subjective nature of motivational research. But motivational research is more than just different; in many ways it is much more difficult.

One reason for the extreme difficulty of motivational research has been discussed previously: the tremendous number of factors that can influence a consumer decision; but there are several other factors making consumer motivational research a difficult, yet at the same time a highly interesting, task. The biggest problem in motivational research is that direct approaches generally do not work. The researcher cannot simply go up to a consumer and ask her *why* she prefers one product over another and expect to get the correct answer. Generally, direct questioning does not give correct answers for one of two reasons: either the consumer *does not know* her true reasons or she knows but is *unwilling to tell* them to you.

THE CONSUMER DOES NOT KNOW

Most people, especially those without exposure to the methods and findings of motivational research, are surprised to learn that consumers are generally unaware of their own "true" reasons for specific brand and product selections. For instance, beer drinkers are often extremely brand-loyal, and if you ask them why they prefer specific brands they will answer, without hesitation, "Taste!" Unfortunately, this answer does not square with the well-documented fact that the average consumer is unable to distinguish among various bottles of unlabeled beer. (If you don't believe it, try it for yourself: select several brands of beer, including your favorite, and have someone pour them into unmarked glasses. The odds are that you will identify your brand no more often than if you were guessing at random.) The beer drinker is brand-loyal, but only to a specific beer image, not to a specific beer taste. Thus, if you want to discover why someone is brand-loyal to a particular beer (or almost any similar product), you cannot ask him directly; you must investigate his attitudes toward the various brands and thereby determine the various images, the various personality profiles for the different brands and the consumers of those brands.

Another reason that consumers do not know their true reasons for purchasing, and thereby fail to give accurate answers to direct questioning, is that, regardless of the specifics of the purchase situation, they tend to parrot the answers that have been conditioned by the advertising. Thus, if you ask someone what he likes about the taste of Schlitz, he probably will reply, "The gusto." Consumers can also become confused about what brand they actually bought, because of the influence of heavy product identification with a single brand: hence, all facial tissue is Kleenex®, all soup is Campbell's®, all soft drink is Coke®, all photocopiers are Xerox®, and so forth. From the standpoint of the major manufacturer, this heavy brand-product identification can be viewed as either a blessing or a curse, depending upon the management's objectives. But from the standpoint of the marketing researcher, it is a total disaster. In response to direct questioning concerning purchase behavior, all the researcher gets are major brand names — even when the consumer is buying "off brands."

THE CONSUMER WILL NOT TELL

Another reason for incorrect answers lies in the choice, made by many consumers, not to tell the correct answer even if they know it. Generally speaking, it can be assumed that a significant amount of deliberate misrepresentation will occur any time the subject area is either *morally sensitive* or *status-related*. Thus, people tend to overestimate their income, their charitable giving, and their purchases of name-brand items; and they tend to underestimate their drinking, their smoking, their adultery, and their purchases of house-brand items. Respondents will also modify their answers in an attempt to appear logical and intelligent. For instance, the purchaser of a new Cadillac may know that the reason she bought such an expensive car was to show it off to her friends and relatives, but it is doubtful she will say so to the interviewer. Rather, she will talk of the outstanding safety and good resale value of the car. Her true reasons can be discerned only through use of the relatively indirect methods of motivational research.

ILLOGICAL REASONS

The reasons for consumer preference are seldom logical. The researcher who approaches the question in a direct, logical, straightforward manner will often obtain very misleading results. Whereas some motivational research can be conducted in a relatively direct fashion, in other cases valid results can be obtained only from very indirect and seemingly roundabout methods. Furthermore, since the nature of the investigation is subjective, the conclusions produced are often highly speculative and will vary greatly with the person performing the research.

Motivational Research Techniques

In this section we will present a variety of motivational research techniques under four basic headings: (1) attitude research, (2) depth research, (3) projective research, and (4) miscellaneous techniques. In this order of presentation, the various techniques move from fairly direct to extremely indirect, from the relatively objective to the totally subjective.

ATTITUDE RESEARCH

In attitude research, measurement of the attitudes consumers hold is generally obtained in a relatively direct fashion through the use of some type of attitudinal scale. In this method a fairly direct question is given, and respondents reflect the strength and direction of their attitudes by their responses, as measured upon carefully designed scales.

Problems in Attitude Surveying. It is worth noting at this point that even the collection of "objective" data from highly structured questions is a process fraught with uncertainty and a variety of subjective judgments. There is the question of the neutral point on the scale: should the researcher allow the respondents the luxury of no decision, or should he force them to choose one side or the other? Likewise, there is the problem of the number of response choices. The greater the number of points on the scale, that is, the greater the number of response choices, the greater the precision of the scale (just as a ruler marked off in thirty-seconds of an inch is more precise than one marked off in fourths). However, this does not mean that a scale can or should be divided indefinitely: there is a very serious question just how precisely individual respondents can conceptually divide their opinions. Should the scale, for example, express positive feelings simply as "agree" and "strongly agree," or can respondents meaningfully differentiate among "extremely strongly agree," "very strongly agree," "strongly agree," "somewhat strongly agree," "definitely agree," "agree," "somewhat agree," and "only mildly agree"? Then, too, there is the problem of reporting. In the final analysis, most decision makers want an overall summary: how many "for" and how many "against"? Therefore, a large number of response choices on a scale will eventually be collapsed into somewhat fewer and more comprehensive categories. This being the case, it makes little sense to incur the extra confusion, coding expense, and tabulating expense inherent in a larger number of categories, not to mention the possible bias from improperly collapsing responses. It makes much more sense to use broader categories from the onset.

A brief discussion of some of the more popular types of attitude scales follows here.

The Likert Scale. Probably the most common type of attitudinal scale is the Likert scale (after Rensis Likert). This scale involves a proposition with which the respondent can either agree or disagree. The normative form of the Likert scale offers exactly five choices, ranging from "strongly agree" to "strongly disagree," with a neutral position in the middle, for example:

Q. I like sardines.

A.	strongly agree	agree	neutral	disagree	strongly disagree
probable coding	5	4	3	2	1
alternate coding (less desirable)	+2	+1	0	−1	−2

The formation of the actual questions to be used in a questionnaire involving a Likert scale is technically a very structured process. Many variations of the questions are postulated, and scores from all the questions are averaged. The individual questions are then examined to see which discriminated best between those respondents who tended to score high and those who tended to score low on the questions. Only those questions shown to be good discriminators are included in the final questionnaire. Questions are also checked to see if they show a good balance or distribution over the points on the scale.

Although the construction of Likert scales is carefully defined from a technical standpoint, from a practical standpoint virtually any scale that features response choices ranging from "agree" to "disagree" will often be called a Likert scale. Furthermore, scales with greater than five or fewer than five response choices are often seen, and they, too, are usually referred to as Likert scales.

The Error Choice Scale. Another type of scale that can be used to detect respondents' attitudes (this time in a slightly more indirect way) is the error choice scale. In this scale a respondent is given a question and is then asked to pick from a series of answers. The trick behind this attitude scale is that, in most cases, the respondent will have very little factual information. In other words, her choice will be primarily a function of her *attitude* toward the situation and only secondarily a function of her true knowledge of the situation. In this example:

Q. Sears's average net profit margin on sales is:

A. 4% 8% 12% 16% 20% 24% 28% 32% 36% 40%

the correct answer is 4 percent, with the magnitude of the miss indicative of the strength of the respondents' antibusiness feelings.

The Semantic Differential Scale. **One** of the most interesting scales, as well as one of the simplest to use, is the semantic differential. In this scale, respondents express their feelings on a given concept according to a set of matched pairs of antonyms, for example:

Belch Beer

Happy	— — — — — — —	Sad
Rich	— — — — — — —	Poor
Light	— — — — — — —	Dark
Smart	— — — — — — —	Dumb
Fast	— — — — — — —	Slow
Young	— — — — — — —	Old

Despite the seeming inapplicability of some of the adjectives used in the matched pairs, it is amazing how quickly a distinct product or brand image begins to emerge. Consumers really do differentiate between the brands, even upon the dimensions that seem nonsensical. In the usual studies involving use of the semantic differential, at least two brands are tested with the same series of words; the replies for all respondents are averaged for each question; and then the averages are plotted as a personality profile, or image analysis, of the two competing brands. As can be seen from the two profiles shown in figure 13·2, Sudsy Beer seems to have the much lighter image, the much younger image, the much more alive image, and, given the current marketing thrust toward the eighteen to thirty-five-year-old market, the much "better" image. The marketing strategy for Sudsy Beer would seem to be fairly

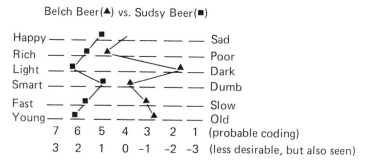

Belch Beer(▲) vs. Sudsy Beer(■)

7 6 5 4 3 2 1 (probable coding)

3 2 1 0 -1 -2 -3 (less desirable, but also seen)

Figure 13·2
The Semantic Differential Scale

clear: continue to build on this youthful, lively image. The strategy for Belch Beer is a bit more uncertain. On the one hand, the company could try to give the beer a younger, livelier image; the survey does show that it has weaknesses in that respect. Or the company could try to "play from strength," emphasizing the rich, strong flavor and heritage of the beer and hoping that the younger consumers (the eighteen to thirty-five market) grow to appreciate that image. Generally speaking, most firms (over the last few years, at least) have emphasized the youth appeal, which helps account for the tremendous similarity among advertising campaigns.

Semantic differential scales generally consist of a range of seven response choices, although such scales with more or fewer than seven positions are often seen. The semantic differential, because of its ease of construction, the simplicity of answering and coding, the density of information (information on a wide variety of dimensions is given in a relatively small amount of space on the questionnaire), and its obvious applicability to marketing and advertising problems, is one of the most popular scales used in marketing.

Ranking Scales. Another type of scale that can be used to measure attitudes in marketing is the ranking scale. Most of us are familiar with scales asking us to rank several objects according to some criterion, specific or otewise, for example:

Criterion Indefinite
Rank these soft drinks in terms of preference: Coke, Royal Crown Cola, Pepsi

Criterion Specific
Rank these soft drinks according to tartness: Coke, Royal Crown Cola, Pepsi

With this scale, as with the error choice scale discussed earlier, the respondent probably does not have any objective information on the subject. If someone asked you, for instance, to rank Ford, Chevrolet, and Chrysler according to resale value, you would probably be able to give only your opinion on their resale values. Neither you nor most other respondents would be likely to own a copy of the book that lists these values for each year and every make.

Forced Choice Bias. One of the problems with the ranking scale (and with some of the other types of scales as well) is that it may distort the results by forcing the respondent to rank one choice higher than another when the actual difference may be quite small. This is another version of the problem, previously discussed, of the neutral position on the scale. Some researchers prefer to force respondents to commit themselves to one side or the other, and others feel that doing so can create a bias. For instance, in the example used above, many people will probably have very weak feelings regarding the three soft drinks. They perceive little real difference and do not mind which of the three they are served. One way to get around this problem is through the use of the *total points technique* (also called the *constant sum technique*). In this method, the respondent is given a certain number of points, which he is to divide among the various choices. The number of points is arbitrary, but in this case six would be a viable number. By dividing the points in various manners, a variety of opinion structures can be expressed:

No Difference	Equal Differences	Extreme Brand Loyalty
Coke = 2	Coke = 3	Coke = 6
RC = 2	RC = 2	RC = 0
Pepsi = 2	Pepsi = 1	Pepsi = 0

Types of Data. Before leaving the topic of scales and attitude measurements from scales, it should be mentioned that care must always be taken to keep the usage of the data obtained from such scales consistent with their strength. Look back at the discussion of the different types of data (nominal, ordinal, interval, and ratio) in the chapter on data analysis: you will see that most of the data produced by the types of scales that have been discussed are probably ordinal (nonmetric). If we stretch things a bit (and most researchers do), the data can be claimed to be interval, but certainly not any better. The important thing to realize is that, though the answers from ranking scales and other attitudinal scales may look quite "solid," a closer look shows that these numbers are not suitable for all types of numeric calculation. When dealing with data from attitudinal scales, the precision of the calculations (the output) may easily outrun the precision of the questions (the input). Care must be taken to avoid upgrading the findings into an exactness and precision not warranted by the original input.

DEPTH RESEARCH

Attitude research assumes that the respondent will be able to respond meaningfully to fairly direct questioning. As we move into a consideration of depth research, we begin to investigate techniques that can produce valuable results even when the respondent is unwilling or unable to respond meaningfully to a direct question.

The idea, taken from the psychoanalysts' couch, of Freudian fame, is to get consumers to talk, at length, about all their feelings concerning a product and the "pleasures, joys, enthusiasms, agonies, nightmares, deceptions and apprehensions" the use of that product brings to mind.[4] The rationale behind this technique is that consumers will be able to express their true (hidden) feelings regarding the product if the discussion lasts long enough. So the consumer and the analyst (most motivational researchers who perform this technique are trained in psychology, not marketing) sit down together and begin talking. Though the analyst tries to keep the discussion pointed roughly toward the product and its use, a rambling conversation ensues, which may last several hours or more for each consumer.

Several things about this method should be immediately apparent. First of all, the entire process is *extremely* subjective. The direction the conversation takes is subjective (and highly dependent upon the interviewer-respondent relationship). Likewise, the conclusion the interviewer draws from these ramblings are also highly subjective. Different interviewers may come to vastly different conclusions about the significance (if any) of a given statement and about what should be done in response.

Finally, it should be noted that this process has a very high per-unit cost ratio. In other words, each interview is extremely expensive, as highly trained analysts must spend great lengths of time interviewing and then analyzing the results from each interview. For this reason, sample sizes in motivational research depth studies tend to be frighteningly small, perhaps as few as eight or ten people. Therefore, conclusions about the perceptions and feelings of an entire nation are based upon a mere handful of people. Because of the uncertainties brought on by the small sample size and the highly subjective nature of the process, depth research is used primarily as an exploratory technique. Research directions obtained from the depth interviews can be explored more fully by more exhaustive and exacting quantitative surveys.

The Focus Group. This discussion of depth interviewing has assumed that one consumer is interviewed by one analyst. In the focus group, however, several consumers participate in the discussion at the same time. There are various reasons why the focus group is gaining in popularity over the single-person depth interview. Most importantly, focus groups provide cost savings, in that a larger sample size can be interviewed for the same cost. An additional advantage is that

---

[4] George Smith; quoted in Packard, *The Hidden Persuaders*, p. 31.

the larger number of people interviewed tends to make the research less dependent upon the interaction of a single interviewer-respondent pair; hence, it is not quite as subjective a process. And finally, the group setting encourages some respondents to talk more freely, as they find that other people share many of their problems and feelings (sometimes the research team will plant one of its own members in the group to act as a catalyst for the group — to be the first to broach taboo topics and so forth).

Usually, the focus group meets in a comfortable, homelike room, and the conversation is recorded on hidden tape recorders and often on hidden cameras as well. When these tapes are played for a group of creative thinkers, many good ideas for product design, new product usage, and advertising campaign strategy may emerge. Therefore, the use of focus groups has become a very important tool of marketing and advertising strategists.

Projective Techniques

Projective techniques are a still more indirect group of motivational research methods: they can provide insight into the thinking of consumers even when consumers are deliberately trying to misrepresent their feelings. For attitude research and depth interviewing, it is assumed that the consumers' true feelings will immediately or eventually emerge. But what can be done to discover these true feelings when the respondent is intentionally giving answers that "look better"?

The answer to that question lies in the use of projective techniques, which employ a stimulus that is usually quite vague. Because of this vagueness, the respondent is forced to use his imagination to make it truly meaningful. In doing so, he *projects* himself and his personality into the situation.

Probably the most famous use of this technique in marketing is the Mason Haire Nescafé study.[5] The problem prompting this research was that instant coffee, at the time of its introduction, was terribly unpopular. The reason given by housewives was that they (or their husbands) did not like the taste, yet blind taste tests consistently revealed that there was no discernible difference. In an effort to get at the true reason for the dislike of instant coffee, Haire formulated two grocery shopping lists that were identical except that one contained instant coffee and the other, ground coffee. Housewives were then asked to describe the shopper who had bought each basket of groceries. Evaluations of the housewife who bought the regular ground

[5] Mason Haire, "Projective Techniques in Marketing Research," *Journal of Marketing* 14 (April 1950): 649–56.

coffee were consistently good: the woman was seen as thoughtful, efficient, and loving. On the other hand, the shopping list with the instant coffee produced many negative descriptions. The Nescafé instant coffee housewife was seen by many as lazy, wasteful, a poor planner, and a bad wife. The problem here was not the taste; it was the image. The ritual of preparing the coffee was an integral part of the way in which many wives showed their affection for their husbands, and the claim of "bad taste" was just an excuse, given by both husbands and wives, for insisting upon the maintenance of this ritual. (Note that this research took place in the early 1950s; attitudes toward instant coffee and toward the institution of marriage have obviously changed markedly since then.) With this information in hand, the instant coffee industry took a different advertising tack. No longer did the ads stress ease and convenience (which are obvious). Instead, the quality and taste were emphasized, and to assuage any lingering guilt, some ads featured the solicitous wife hovering affectionately around the family members at the dining table, while the voice-over cooed, "Gives you more time to be with your family."

Projective techniques can range from quite objective and structured to quite subjective and unstructured. The projective techniques presented here are given in order of increasing subjectivity.

Word Association. In word association, which has been used by analysts for over a century, the interviewer calls out a series of words and the respondent quickly replies with the first word that enters her mind. For instance, what is the first word that pops into your mind for each of these products: oatmeal, coal, prunes, beer, crystal, wool? If your answers were dull, strike, laxative, belch, break, and itch, then those products may be facing some image problems that need to be addressed in their advertising.

Sentence Completion. Sentence completion is like word association, except that the respondent completes an unfinished sentence, for example: "I don't like to eat bananas because . . . ," "People who go to Palm Beach are . . . ," "Some people don't like to fly because . . ." Notice that the last two examples involve *double projection*, in that the respondent projects herself not only into an unfinished sentence but also into the person of someone else. By answering for someone else, the respondent can say things she would be embarrassed to say if they were directly concerned with herself. For instance, if asked about *who* goes to Palm Beach, she might reply, "The rich and famous," whereas if asked why *she* doesn't go to Palm Beach, she might say, "Because there are too many pushy slobs." In other words, what is going on in her mind is that she really would like to go to Palm Beach but is too poor. So rather than admit that she is a poor, unknown clod, she gives another reason.

To the question on flying, the respondent might reply that many people are afraid of flying; whereas if asked directly if *he* were afraid of flying, he would bravely say "no."

Story Completion. In story completion, the respondent supplies the end of a story, for example: "John and Mary recently bought a new Ford. After about two months and 1,400 miles, the transmission began knocking violently. The mechanic at the local filling station said that it sounded like the whole transmission was about to give out. John and Mary took the car back to the dealer from whom they had bought it and . . ." As you can see, the attitudes toward both that specific make and car warranties in general will be vigorously expressed as respondents complete the story.

The Rosenweig Picture Frustration Test. In the Rosenweig Picture Frustration Test, the respondent is shown a cartoon-type drawing, usually involving two characters. One of the caption balloons is completed, but the other is blank and the respondent must fill it in. Consider the situation in figure 13·3. It seems probable that many women and more than a few men would guess that the woman is making a negative comment, such as, "Ugh, who wants to look at an old boat?" or, "Yeah, a boat so that he and his cronies can go drinking and 'fishing.' " This sort of response would indicate that boating advertisers need to address some effort to the cultivation of enthusiasm among women, in addition to their regular advertising in male-ori-

Figure 13·3
A Rosenweig Picture Frustration Test

Figure 13•4
A Thematic Apperception Test

ented magazines. For instance, the advertiser might place ads in women's or general interest magazines showing a happy family out on a fishing or camping trip, with the wife beaming, "Our family hasn't had this much fun in years . . . and our new Evinrude motorboat made it all possible."

The Thematic Apperception Test. The Thematic Apperception Test is a picture frustration cartoon-type test with none of the balloons supplied. The respondent is asked to tell what is happening in the picture. For instance, the picture frustration test in figure 13•4 could be used to determine true attitudes of racial prejudice. In the picture a white policeman is facing a black man; nothing else is known about the situation. Maybe the black man is asking for directions; maybe they are two friends who have run into each other; maybe the black man is an undercover or off-duty policeman. But if white respondents immediately jump to the conclusion that the policeman is arresting a lawbreaker, or if black respondents jump to the conclusion that a brother is getting hassled by a "pig," then they give strong evidence of deep-seated racial prejudice, prejudice that could have been easily hidden had the question been of a direct nature.

Rorschach Tests. Although their use in marketing is limited, no discussion of projective techniques is complete without at least a mention of the famous Rorschach or ink-blot tests. Most of us have seen examples of these tests (see fig. 13•5). The Rorschach test expresses in a classic way the rationale behind all projective tests: that is, in filling in the missing parts of a vague and incomplete stimulus, the respondent projects himself and his personality into the picture.

Figure 13•5
A Rorschach Ink-Blot Test

Finally we come to a grab bag of miscellaneous techniques that researchers sometimes use for the investigation of marketing problems. In this section we will look at two different kinds of techniques: *physiographic* and *espionage*.

Physiographic Techniques. Physiographic techniques make an effort to measure physically some bodily process as an indication of the consumer's interest and involvement in the advertising or marketing effort. These methods include the use of galvanometers (or psychogalvanometers) and various eye response measuring devices. Some of these techniques are also discussed in Chapter 15 as they relate to advertising research.

Galvanometers (or, as generally called, lie detectors) measure the galvanic skin response that is believed to be a measure of the interest and excitement a respondent is feeling. In the usual marketing application (which in itself is not very common), a respondent is connected to one of these lie detectors and shown a series of commercials. The galvanometer then provides a scientific measurement of her "true" interest in each commercial. Aside from the fact that the reading of

the galvanic responses requires no small amount of subjective interpretation, there is the larger problem of the applicability and validity
of such an obviously artificial viewing situation: probably all commercials could have fairly strong impact if the advertisers were able
to strap the viewers into chairs wired with all kinds of electronic
equipment and then force them to watch each commercial intently.

There are several devices that measure the response of the eye to
various stimuli. The perceptoscope measures the dilation of the pupils
of the eyes. Research has shown that the greater the interest, the
greater the dilation; hence, commercials that produce the greatest dilation are judged the most interesting.

Eye cameras, or *oculometers*, measure the ocular movement of
the eye; in other words, they measure and trace the exact point of focus
of the eye. The eye does not see an entire magazine page or television
screen at once. At any given instant, the eye is actually focusing on a
very tiny section of only a few square inches. The purpose of the oculometer is to trace the movement of the eye as it travels over a page or
screen. To what parts does the eye first move? The headline? The picture? Are there parts of the ad that seem to attract virtually no attention? These and other such questions can be answered with the oculometer.

There are *eye-blink* cameras, which measure the respondent's rate
of eye-blinking. According to researchers, a person normally blinks
about thirty times a minute. As the person's tension increases, his eye-
blink rate will increase accordingly; and if he is very relaxed, his
eye-blink rate will decrease. By monitoring eye-blink, researchers can
identify commercials that are more exciting to the viewer. Note, however, that interpretation of results is quite subjective. As with the galvanometer and the pupilometer, increased "interest" may be good or
bad: mechanical measurements of interest will increase with either
anger or happiness. Then, too, there is the ever-present problem that
no clear relationship connects interest and sales. The presence of a
beautiful or scantily clad young woman in an advertisement will increase the interest level among males for that ad (which explains
why many ads feature beautiful, provocatively dressed young women).
What is debatable is whether the presence of the young woman helps
sell the product. Since an ad has to be seen before it has any chance
for effectiveness, some advertisers continue to utilize these sexist
models. However, it is entirely probable that their use may actually
be dysfunctional, in that it alienates an ever-growing group of people.

Yet another research technique involving the eye is the *tachisto-*

scope, a machine that can flash images at extremely high rates of speed, so fast in fact that in some cases the eye does not consciously see anything at all. The tachistoscope is most commonly used in marketing to measure the impact of various package designs. Subjects are shown a variety of package designs at extremely high speed and then asked questions concerning each of the designs. How, you may ask, can respondents comment meaningfully upon a package they hardly even saw? The answer is that, although the image went by so fast that their conscious minds could not assimilate it, the image was still taken in by the subconscious minds through what is called subliminal or sub-threshold effects. The subconscious mind may not recognize the package for what it actually is, that is, a package with a name brand and a great deal of description on the front, but will probably perceive it as an entire image or pattern, as a gestalt or conceptual whole. If the package is loaded with hidden meanings — sexual images, death images, happy images, and so forth — these meanings will penetrate the subconscious and be revealed in subsequent testing. Packages are also tested on quality dimensions: some combinations of colors and designs just tend to connote higher quality. Finally, packages are tested for recognition, to determine which can be most quickly recognized as containing a specific product and which are most easily identified with a particular brand. It is very startling to see the way in which the use of the tachistoscope can reveal significant differences between relatively similar-looking packages.

Espionage Techniques. A final way in which researchers can gain information about respondents, even those who are unwilling or unable to provide the information directly, is to adopt some type of espionage or spying strategem. Although these methods may seem inelegant, unscientific, and even unethical, they represent the only way in which information can be gleaned under some types of circumstances.

One such technique is the use of *hidden recorders,* such as hidden tape recorders, hidden cameras, and hidden observers to watch consumers as they purchase and consume various items, in order to gain insight into their buying behavior. Researchers will, for instance, watch shoppers in grocery stores to observe at least the outward mechanics of their decision processes. They can in this manner investigate how consumers' eyes move over the shelves, how long they take to make brand decisions, how many different brands they compare, whether they read the labels, whether they make use of unit pricing if it is available, and so forth. Sometimes the researchers will unobtrusively observe a shopper making a selection, and then, after the selection is made, quickly approach the shopper and ask why he bought that particular item. Information from this type of analysis can be valuable in designing packages and store promotions.

Another type of espionage activity is involved in the *rubbish research* that many sociologists, as well as motivational researchers, conduct. In rubbish research, researchers sift through the garbage of individuals or groups to record patterns of consumption, waste, and brand preference. Although this practice may at first appear blatantly ridiculous, it must be realized that estimates for the consumption of many products (liquor, cigarettes, medicines and drugs, hygiene products, contraceptive products, sex-related products and magazines, and so on) cannot be accurately obtained through direct questioning. For instance, by polling garbage cans rather than consumers, researchers have determined that people drink two and a half times as much liquor as they tell interviewers they do. One of the key attributes of good researchers is that they will do whatever is necessary to come up with the correct answer. And while on the subject of rubbish research and its relationship to true marketing research, the following anecdote is appropriate:

Let me begin by reviewing briefly the roots of marketing research.

As you may know, modern marketing research began with Charles Coolidge Parlin at Curtis Publishing Co. In these days of concern about ecology, you will surely recognize Parlin's methods.

It is written on a plaque on the wall of a National Guard unit in Philadelphia that Charles Parlin once rented the place. He had a prosaic problem: How to prove to a large potential advertiser, Campbell Soup Company, that the wives of blue-collar workers bought soup in that newfangled invention called the can. In those days before the wonder of television, the mass medium was *The Saturday Evening Post.*

Campbell Soup Co. told Parlin that the *Post* was read mainly by blue-collar workers. And, Campbell said, the wives of blue-collar workers made soup from scratch.

To disprove that notion, Parlin made arrangements to count garbage. That's right. He drew a scientific sample of garbage routes from all over the city. He then had the contents of the carts dumped on the floor of the armory. And he counted the number of soup cans in each pile of garbage.

The record showed that Campbell Soup was wrong. It was the rich that had bought no soup as it was servants who made soup from scratch. The poor made soup from cans, one of the earliest convenience products for the busy woman.

That scientific count of cans convinced Campbell Soup, and the company became a regular advertiser in the Post.[6]

As Charles Parlin knew, in marketing research it is not the methods that count, it is the bottom line, the results.

Summary

The purpose of this chapter has been to consider some of the methods by which researchers investigate the psychology of consumers, to discover not only what, but *why*, they buy. The study of consumer motivations is vastly different from the traditional, "nose-counting" type of research discussed in other sections of this book. Motivational research is much more subjective and much less direct than traditional research. Often, the researcher will be trying to find the reasons for consumers' behavior when they, themselves, do not know the reasons. In other situations, the researcher will be trying to obtain valid, accurate information when respondents are deliberately misrepresenting their feelings.

In probing respondents, the researcher is proceeding under the assumption that there is a reason behind every purchase. Although the phenomenon of consumer behavior is terribly complex, and no comprehensive theories of consumer behavior are operationally applicable to marketing, many influential factors can be isolated. This chapter has discussed three sets of factors: economic, personality, and external.

This chapter has also examined a variety of motivational research techniques, under four headings: attitude research, depth techniques, projective techniques, and miscellaneous techniques.

In attitude research, the attitudes of the respondents are measured by recording their responses to direct questions upon a carefully constructed attitudinal scale. The scales used include: Likert scales, error choice scales, semantic differential scales, and ranking scales.

The depth approach employs a rambling, in-depth conversation between a respondent and a trained analyst or, in the case of a focus group, between a group of respondents and a trained analyst. This

[6] Kenneth Hollander, "Audacious Audi Ad Echoes Parlin's Iconoclasm," *Marketing News* 11, no. 15 (27 January 1978): 17.

method is highly subjective and is used primarily for exploratory studies.

Whereas attitude and depth research assume that respondents can and will give truthful answers to direct questions, the projective technique assumes that the respondents either cannot or will not be able to provide correct answers. Accordingly, indirect questioning is used: the respondent is given a vague stimulus and must fill in missing parts of the picture to make a meaningful situation. In filling in these missing parts, he *projects* himself and his personality into the situation. Projective techniques discussed here include word association, sentence completion, story completion, Rosenweig Picture Frustration Tests, Thematic Apperception Tests, and Rorschach tests.

Among the miscellaneous techniques considered here are physiological measuring devices, such as galvanometers, perceptoscopes, oculometers, tachistoscopes, and eye-blink cameras, and espionage techniques, such as hidden observers and rubbish research. Although the relationship between the information provided by these techniques and the sales of the product is often tenuous and subjective, such is the nature of motivational research. Motivational research is seen primarily as an exploratory or hypothesis-generating procedure; research directions that emerge from these efforts can be investigated at greater lengths by more quantitative methods.

Questions for Discussion

1. Compare and contrast traditional research and motivational research. Why is traditional research referred to as "nose-counting" research?

2. Discuss the three factors listed in the chapter as influential upon consumer choice.

3. Why is it difficult to obtain answers through direct questioning concerning respondents' reasons for various purchases?

4. Give an example of a question appropriate for each of these attitudinal scales: Likert, error choice, semantic differential, and ranking.

5. What is forced choice bias? How can the total points technique help to reduce forced choice bias?

6. What is depth interviewing? What are the advantages of focus groups over individual depth interviews? Why are focus groups popular with marketing and advertising strategists?

7. What is the rationale behind projective tests? How do they work? Why are they needed?

8. Give an example of the Rosenweig Picture Frustration Test. Why is it used in marketing research?

9. What is a tachistoscope and how is it used in marketing?

Chapter 14

Product Research

PRODUCT RESEARCH IS the application of research techniques to business problems in the development of new products and the modification of existing products in order to satisfy consumers and make profits. Good product research, like good marketing, always incorporates the marketing concept by combining customer satisfaction with profitable sales.

The dimensions of product research can best be understood by examining the meaning of the word *product*. A product may be defined as "a complex of tangible and intangible attributes, including packaging, color, price, manufacturer's prestige, retailer's prestige, and manufacturer's and retailer's services, which the buyer may accept as offering satisfaction of wants or needs."[1]

From this definition, it should be apparent that product research involves much more than a laboratory testing of the physical characteristics of a product. Involved also are a host of intangible attributes, such as price and color appeal, which must be carefully tested and evaluated by the researcher. As most consumer products are purchased to satisfy customer wants, the alert firm will promote product benefits rather than just the physical product itself and will use product research as an aid in this effort, by learning what benefits consumers expect to derive from various products and the extent to which these expectations are being satisfied. Surveys indicate that approximately 75 percent of all large consumer goods manufacturers are engaged in conducting some type of product research.[2]

[1] William J. Stanton, *Fundamentals of Marketing*, 3rd ed. (New York: McGraw-Hill, 1971), p. 192.

[2] Dik Warren Twedt, ed., *1973 Survey of Marketing Research* (Chicago: American Marketing Association, 1973), p. 41.

The Importance of Product Research

Successful new products are the lifeblood of a profitable firm. Fickle consumers with ever-changing tastes dictate that corporations provide a steady stream of new products. In complying with consumer demand (or aggravating it, as some critics charge) for new products, marketing-oriented firms are increasingly aware of the growing importance of product research in developing product lines and expanding their product mixes.

A *product line* is a group of products with similar characteristics (thus, DuPont produces a line of paints), whereas *product mix* describes all the products produced by a firm (DuPont's entire production), whether the products are related or not. A firm may have several product lines, but it can have only one product mix. Product line and product mix are the same in a case where a firm produces only one product or one group of related products.

Consumer products firms, such as Procter and Gamble, Warner-Lambert, Gillette, and General Foods, are but a scant few of the many companies bent on satisfying consumer demands for new products in the marketplace. Increased consumer affluence and faster-changing consumer tastes have enabled these firms to maintain a rapid growth rate in their quest to satisfy what has been called "the consumer's insatiable thirst for new products." [3]

The Reasons for the Importance of New Product Research

The importance of product research can best be demonstrated by analyzing events and conditions that have caused, and are presently causing, product research to assume a position of greater concern to firms. The three main factors are (1) the cost of new products, (2) the new product failure rate, and (3) the product life cycle concept.

The *cost of new products* continues to soar and is now one of a firm's major expenditures. During the 1960s, the amount spent by American companies on research and development more than doubled, reaching a total of approximately $19 billion in 1969. [4] One example of this soaring rise in the cost of new products has occurred in the U.S. pharmaceutical industry, where "tighter Food and Drug Administration restrictions have doubled the average costs and development time of new drugs to $9 million and nine years in just a decade, causing the

[3] "The Spectacular Rise of the Consumer Company," *Business Week*, 21 July 1973, p. 48.

[4] "Inflation Ups the R&D Ante," *Business Week*, 17 May 1969, p. 78.

pharmaceutical manufacturers to look for new fields."[5] Large companies spend millions of dollars every year on research and development of new products: Procter and Gamble alone spends well over $100 million a year on new product research.

The principal reasons for the high cost of new products include inflation, additional governmental restrictions requiring more research and testing, and the increasing cost of business decisions, stemming from larger operations designed to reach bigger markets in order to achieve economies of scale in manufacturing and distribution. This increasing cost of new products becomes still greater when considered in light of the new product failure rate.

The *new product failure rate* is a second major factor contributing to the increased importance of product research. Though estimates concerning the failure rate vary, the overwhelming majority of all new products are failures. The new product failure rate has been estimated at anywhere from 50 to 90 percent, depending upon how far back the product development process is analyzed. Table 14·1 lists the major reasons for new product failure. Note that the most important one, inadequate market analysis, stems directly from lack of adequate research.

A major goal in product research is to reduce the new product failure rate through extensive research and testing before a product's full-scale introduction to the market. Reduction of this failure rate has been achieved by large consumer goods firms that are engaged in extensive product research; still, even these firms have product failures. For example, new product failures for Heinz (best known for ketchup)

Table 14·1
Reasons for New Product Failure

REASON	PERCENTAGE OF OCCURRENCE
1. Inadequate market analysis	32%
2. Product defects	23
3. Higher costs than anticipated	14
4. Poor timing	10
5. Competition reaction	8
6. Inadequate marketing effort	13
TOTAL	100%

Source: Betty Cochran and G. Thompson, "Why New Products Fail," *National Industrial Conference Board Record* 1 (October 1964): 11–18.

[5] *Business Week,* 21 July 1973, p. 51.

324 • **Marketing Research**

include Great American soup, Happy soup, Heinz salad dressings, and Help fruit drink.[6]

Few new product failures are as spectacular as the failure of the Edsel or the maxi dress. The reason is product research, which results in new product offerings that tend to be in tune with consumer wants.

The third main factor contributing to the importance of product research is the *product life cycle concept*. This concept recognizes that products go through stages of introduction, growth, and maturity and then into decline and possible abandonment by manufacturers.

Figure 14•1 shows that the life cycle for a typical product begins with an introductory period where both sales and profits are low. Profits and sales climb during the growth period at a rapid rate. Profits typically peak in the market growth stage, whereas sales may continue climbing into the maturity stage, when profits are actually declining. This seeming paradox of falling profits during a period of rising sales occurs primarily because of intense price competition among manufacturers.

Management of this product life cycle requires product research in forecasting sales and profit curves, timing the introduction of new products, and making decisions to modify or abandon existing products. Product research is necessary if management is to know when to make the product elimination decision. The challenge facing new product research for consumer goods manufacturers has been summarized in this way:

Left unchanged, a packaged product will tend to increase its market share for a few years after it is introduced, hit a peak, and then sink

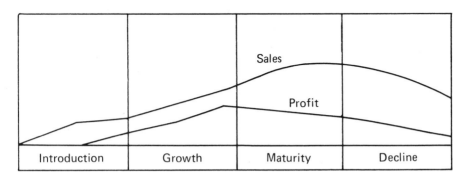

Figure 14•1
Product Life Cycle for a Typical Product

[6] *Marketing News* 10 (19 November 1976).

into decline. Though no one knows for sure, many marketing men believe these product life cycles are becoming shorter. A study by the A. C. Nielsen Co. concludes that 85 percent of all new brands can expect less than three years of success before their market shares start declining rapidly. While manufacturers can try to lengthen the life cycle by launching a new advertising campaign or redesigning a package, they don't always succeed. And when they do succeed, the study says, they revive the brand for only an average of fifteen months before it sinks once again.[7]

The result of shorter product life cycles is that manufacturers are spending less time in developing new products. One example of this trend is the shampoo industry: a new shampoo appears on the market nearly every three months and competes with all existing brands. This trend places additional pressure on product researchers to compress the time devoted to new product development.

Product Testing

Product testing is a valuable tool in marketing research. Before launching a new product on the market, a manufacturer wants to know what consumers think about it. Product testing minimizes the risk in marketing new products; which may take two forms: first, a new product risks failing from lack of sales; and second, a new product may require extensive and costly redesigning if it is introduced to the market without first having been extensively tested. By product testing, manufacturers hope to place a stable and acceptable product on the market. Extensive product testing enables them to offer sound warranty policies and avoid false or misleading claims in advertising product benefits.

Figure 14•2 presents an overview of product testing. Fundamentally, there are two main ways in which new products may be tested: (1) technical testing and (2) consumer testing.[8]

Technical Testing

Technical testing is conducted by the manufacturer or by an independent testing laboratory. Technical testing aids the manufacturer in determining how his product compares with competitors' products in composition and performance.

[7] Peter Vanderwicken, "P & G's Secret Ingredient," *Fortune*, July 1974, p. 79. (Chapter 14 relies heavily on this article.)

[8] D. Maynard Phelps and J. Howard Westing, *Marketing Management*, 3rd ed. (Homewood, Ill.: Richard D. Irwin, 1968), pp. 99–120.

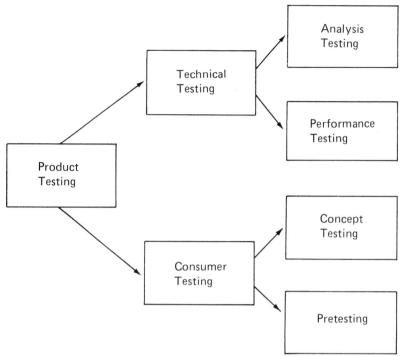

Figure 14•2
Overview of Product Testing

There are basically two phases of technical testing: analysis testing and performance testing. *Analysis testing* tells what a product *is* and may be accomplished by analyzing the composition of a product to see what raw materials were used or exactly how it was assembled. Analysis testing is undertaken in order to determine the composition of new competing products. *Performance testing* is conducted in order to find out what a product will *do* and involves simulating use conditions. Extensive performance testing is carried out by Detroit automakers. All new automobile models are tested by professional drivers under almost every imaginable road condition and hazard. The industry desperately wants to avoid expensive product recalls, such as the General Motors recall of nearly five million Corvairs to check for safety defects — a move that cost an estimated $50 million, as well as bad publicity.[9]

Virtually all major manufacturers are involved in technical testing, as are numerous other organizations. One such organization is

---

[9] George Fisk, "Guidelines for Warranty Service after Sale," *Journal of Marketing* 34 (January 1970): 63.

Consumers Union, which publishes *Consumer Reports* (in Canada known as the *Canadian Consumer*). Consumers Union extensively tests a wide range of consumer products through analysis and performance tests and then publishes the results, much to the concern of manufacturers whose products receive poor ratings. *Good Housekeeping*, a well-known women's magazine, maintains laboratory facilities for testing advertisers' products. If a product successfully passes the tests, it is then advertised with the *Good Housekeeping* "Seal of Approval."

The question is often asked, should technical testing be conducted by the manufacturer or by an independent testing laboratory? Although there are many aspects to the answer, one clear advantage of the independent testing laboratory is objectivity. Consumers are more likely to believe claims if they have been verified through an independent testing laboratory than if tests have been conducted on the manufacturer's premises and under the manufacturer's supervision. Even so, some manufacturers have been known to distort and misrepresent independent testing data in advertising campaigns. The case of Detroit automakers using Environmental Protection Agency (EPA) data in support of superior gasoline mileage claims provides an excellent example of abuse of independent testing laboratory data. The objectivity of these independent testing agencies is also subject to question: some, like *Good Housekeeping*'s agency, are financially dependent on manufacturers for fees or advertising revenue.

Consumer Testing

Consumer testing is undertaken to determine consumer attitudes toward a product or product idea. The underlying basis for consumer testing is the expectation that favorable consumer attitudes toward a product, or product concept, will be translated into sales in the marketplace. The fact that this may not always occur represents the most significant limitation of consumer test data.

Consumer testing usually takes place under controlled conditions that may inadequately represent normal market conditions. Testing by consumers is of two main types: *concept testing* and *pretesting*.

CONCEPT TESTING

Concept testing represents an attempt to measure consumers' reactions to a new product concept or idea. That is, concept testing seeks to learn what buyers' probable reactions will be before the product's

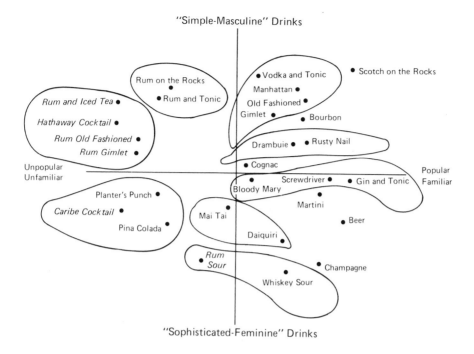

"Simple-Masculine" Drinks

- Scotch on the Rocks
- Vodka and Tonic
- Manhattan
- Old Fashioned
- Gimlet
- Bourbon
Rum on the Rocks
- Rum and Tonic
- Rum and Iced Tea
- Hathaway Cocktail
- Rum Old Fashioned
- Rum Gimlet

- Drambuie
- Rusty Nail

Unpopular
Unfamiliar

- Cognac

Popular
Familiar

- Screwdriver
- Gin and Tonic
- Bloody Mary
- Planter's Punch
- Martini
- Caribe Cocktail
- Mai Tai
- Pina Colada
- Beer
- Daiquiri

- Rum Sour
- Champagne
- Whiskey Sour

"Sophisticated-Feminine" Drinks

Figure 14·3

Application of Concept Testing Using Two-Dimensional Configuration of Twenty-two Alcoholic Drinks and Six New Rum Concepts

Reprinted, by permission from Yoram Wind, "A New Procedure for Concept Evaluation," *Journal of Marketing* 37 (October 1973): 2.

actual development. In order to measure interest in a product that has not yet been developed, researchers normally use pictures or drawings to help describe the proposed product. Though concept testing has broad applications, its primary utility is as a preliminary screening device for evaluating completely new concepts or product ideas.

Multidimensional scaling is one analytical procedure that may be employed in the concept-testing data analyses. Figure 14·3 shows an example of this method involving a hypothetical rum manufacturer who wishes to measure reaction to some new rum drink mixes.[10] The six rum drink concepts (rum old-fashioned, rum sour, Hathaway cocktail, Caribe cocktail, rum and iced tea, and rum gimlet) are described and then tested, along with twenty-two other drinks included for con-

[10] Yoram Wind, "A New Procedure for Concept Evaluation," *Journal of Marketing* 37 (October 1973): 2–11.

trol purposes. By analyzing this perceptual map of clusters drawn around groupings of drinks, the researcher concluded that a manufacturer interested in a new rum drink concept should promote a rum sour over any of the other five new rum drinks, since it was found that the other five concepts all competed with existing rum drinks, whereas the rum sour competed only with the whisky sour.

PRETESTING

If a product idea successfully passes the concept-testing state, the manufacturer may then choose to begin producing it in limited quantities for pretesting. *Pretesting*, the second main form of consumer testing, is done before introducing a product on the market; accordingly, it is the experimental use of products by a sample of potential consumers.[11]

Pretesting presents a manufacturer the opportunity to learn consumer reactions to a new product before market introduction. Still, although the time and expense of entering test markets are avoided at this stage, there are problems in consumer pretesting. Four main problems encountered by the researcher are:

1. *The sample.* Perhaps the major problem encountered is getting a sample of prospective consumers that is representative, chosen without bias, and large enough to be statistically significant. Since most firms are unable to overcome this limitation in their pretesting, the sample is the main problem in evaluating test data.

2. *Supervision and control.* If pretesting of products takes place in the homes of sample members, there is little opportunity for supervision and control over conditions of use. Another problem in the area of supervision and control concerns the product itself: should brands, labels, and other distinguishing marks be removed, so that the manufacturer's name or advertising claims cannot influence consumers? If labels are removed, then the question of the realism of the pretesting process arises, since labels and distinguishing marks constitute part of the product; but the labels themselves may bias the results, because the manufacturer's name may distort consumer response.

3. *Accurate responses.* As with all research involving consumer responses, there is a problem of securing accurate replies. If company employees are utilized in pretesting, will their perceptions of the firm's products be unbiased? Care must be taken to prevent the use of leading questions that will influence test results. The firm must be

[11] Phelps and Westing, *Marketing Management*, p. 107.

willing to spend necessary funds to hire trained interviewers capable of securing accurate replies from the sample.

4. *Measurement.* The fourth and final main problem faced by researchers in the pretesting process is one of measurement. As pretesting involves the measurement of consumer reactions to a new product, it is necessary to develop accurate methods of measuring these reactions. How does one measure the taste or smell of a food product? What do the words "like" or "dislike" really mean? Can they be translated into "buy" or "would not buy"? [12]

These problems illustrate limitations inherent in the pretesting process and show why manufacturers of consumer goods normally follow pretesting with test marketing, before attempting full-scale distribution of a new product. Despite these limitations, many firms make extensive and successful use of employees for pretesting new products. Consider the example of Procter and Gamble's pretesting process, which uses the firm's own employees:

> In the company's Hair Care Evaluation Center, women have half their hair washed with a new shampoo, and half with their regular brand as a control. To analyze detergent performance, technicians in a Proctor & Gamble laboratory wash the laundry of five hundred employees every week. Some tests become a little bizarre. Employees sampling a new toothpaste or mouthwash, for example, enter a laboratory where they breathe through a hole in the wall. A researcher on the other side sniffs their breath to judge the product's effectiveness. A new deodorant is tested similarly, by a professional armpit-sniffer.[13]

The Use of Panels as a Method of Product Testing

The use of panels in product testing is especially popular among the larger manufacturers of consumer convenience goods. A panel is a semipermanent group of people, which should be representative of a manufacturer's potential customers and which has the task of evaluating products and product ideas. Panels may be used for concept testing and pretesting in the product-testing process. However, panel members are not qualified to engage in technical testing of new products, which must be left to people with appropriate expertise.

Different types of panels are used in marketing research, depending on the type of data sought from the panel members. Market Facts,

[12] Phelps and Westing, *Marketing Management*, pp. 108–10.
[13] Vanderwicken, "P & G's Secret Ingredient," p. 77.

Inc., has the Consumer Mail Panels (CPM) division, which consists of forty-five-thousand households used in mail surveys. The A. C. Nielsen Company uses a panel of approximately eleven hundred homes where the Nielsen Audimeter is attached to television sets; the resulting data are used in compiling the famous Nielsen Ratings of television programs.

Problems in Panel Testing

Panel usage in product research presents several problems. First, panel membership must be representative of prospective customers for the product. Second, the researchers need to establish some degree of control over conditions of use by panel members in order to get needed feedback on consumer attitudes toward the product. Third, researchers may need to disguise the identity of the product's manufacturer in order to eliminate preconceived attitudes about the firm or its products. Fourth, researchers must deal with nonresponse bias, which occurs if some panel members drop out.

After a new product has been pretested by the firm's employees, it may then be sent to a panel for final consumer-use testing before being placed in test markets. At Procter and Gamble, panels constitute another hurdle that must be successfully passed before a product can be test marketed. Peter Vanderwicken, writing in *Fortune* magazine, has reported: "If the product passes its tests by employees (who tend to be overly critical, the testers say), Procter & Gamble presents it to panels of consumers picked at random. In all Procter & Gamble queries 250,000 consumers a year (church groups are a favorite target), asking whether this or that product fills their needs and whether they would buy it. To be considered for introduction, the product must win the votes of a majority of consumers in tests against each major competing brand." [14]

Test Marketing of New Products

A consumer goods firm that has done solid product research will be relatively sure of product success even before going to a test market. Nevertheless, before a new product is distributed nationwide, it is usually tested in one or more cities that demographically represent the full national market. Costs of test marketing vary with time and the number of cities used, but $250,000 for a two-city test market is typical.

[14] "P & G's Secret Ingredient," p. 77.

The decison to test market a product before a full-scale nation-wide push represents a cautious and usually prudent step. Test marketing assumes that results gathered from the test-market cities can be projected nationwide; this assumption may be questionable, however, since conditions in test markets may differ from those in national markets.

There are two principal benefits to be gained by a firm from market testing.[15] The primary benefit is learning more about the product's potential sales. The firm wants to know whether the product's sales potential is large enough to justify full-scale market introduction; if sales are insufficient, the product is considered a failure at this stage and joins the ranks of the "might have beens."

A secondary benefit derived from test markets is the opportunity to pretest alternative marketing strategies. This procedure can involve using different media and promotional mixes in various test-market cities. The marketing strategy associated with the best sales results in the test markets will then be the one used in the national introduction of the product. Not only does test marketing provide the benefit of pretesting promotional strategy, it also allows the firm a final chance to test its product, pricing, and distribution strategies before introduction. A case in point is Procter and Gamble's Pampers, which initially failed in test markets through low sales; further testing of alternative marketing strategies changed results drastically:

> One product that was not discarded after initial failure went on to become a huge success: Pampers which now rivals Tide as P & G's best-selling brand. On its first market test, Pampers bombed. The product was priced too high — about 10 cents each, which was more than the cost of buying a cloth diaper and washing it. By simplifying the package, speeding up the assembly lines, and using less costly components, the company gradually got the price down to 6 cents.
>
> As the price dropped, each of the subsequent tests over four years indicated a bigger potential market. So management progressively reduced the profit-margin target and raised the volume target. By the fourth test, the price was right and Pampers took off.[16]

Finding test cities that are demographically representative of national or even regional markets can be difficult, since no one city perfectly represents the entire nation. Some test-market cities include Dayton, Ohio; Syracuse, New York; and Portland, Oregon. In Canada the cities of London and Peterborough are considered representative

[15] Philip Kotler, *Marketing Management*, 2nd. ed. (Englewood Cliffs, N.J.: Prentice-Hall, 1972), pp. 497–98.

[16] Vanderwicken, "P & G's Secret Ingredient," p. 78.

of Ontario, whereas Sherbrooke is a favorite test city in Quebec. Still, demographic composition of test cities is a factor, and regional test-market cities are necessary for products with regional appeal. For example, Austin, Texas, a popular test-market city, would be ideal for test marketing a new line of Mexican food because of its large Mexican-American population and the popularity of Mexican food in the city.

Regarding test marketing of new food products, the *Wall Street Journal* reports: "This isn't an exact science, but it's close. People in coastal cities, marketers have found, tend to accept nearly all new products quickly. Those who live in the Middle West, however, seem to reject most of them. Thus, it is that Syracuse, New York, which is neither coastal nor Midwestern, is considered to be the ideal test market, researchers say." [17]

The length of time a product may remain in a test market presents a problem to researchers. The longer a product is in a test market, the more time the manufacturer has for ironing out problems before the product is introduced nationally. Sometimes test-market times have been lengthy. When General Foods Corporation first brought out its new freeze-dried coffee, Maxim, the firm kept Maxim in test markets for several years before opting for full market introduction. However, firms are under increasing pressure to reduce the time new products are in test markets, for two reasons: (1) shrinking product life cycles and (2) competitive pressures. Shrinking product life cycles, resulting from consumers' never-ending quest for new products, force manufacturers to bring out a constant succession of new products, which intensely compete with one another, even though they are produced by the same manufacturer. A prime example of this *multibrand* strategy is the heavy-duty detergent industry. In 1975 the detergent market was controlled by three manufacturers — Procter and Gamble, Lever Brothers, and Colgate Palmolive. These three firms produced twenty-three different detergent brands, all in competition with one another for a total of 94 percent of the market.[18] This relationship is shown in table 14·2. Are all these brands still on the market today?

Competitive pressures force manufacturers to limit the length of time a new product can remain in test markets because of the fear that competitors will learn of it and attempt to beat the firm to the market with a similar product. When Lever Brothers took a year test marketing its Mrs. Butterworth pancake syrup concept, General Foods, manu-

[17] "Food Marketers Spend Billions Persuading Us to Buy Their Products," *Wall Street Journal*, 24 June 1977, p. 24.

[18] *Advertising Age*, September–October 1975.

Table 14·2
Overview of Product Testing

HEAVY-DUTY LAUNDRY DETERGENTS	RETAIL MARKETING SHARE
P&G	
Tide	28.0%
Cheer	9.5
Bold	3.0
Gain	3.0
Dash	3.0
Oxydol	2.8
Duz	0.7
Bonus	0.7
Salvo	0.5
Era	5.0
TOTAL	56.2
Lever Brothers	
All	8.5
Wisk	9.0
Breeze	1.2
Drive	1.3
Rinso	1.0
Surf	0.1
Silver Dust	0.3
TOTAL	21.4
Colgate-Palmolive	
Fab	4.7
Cold Power	4.3
Ajax	2.8
Dynamo	3.0
Punch	0.8
Burst	1.0
TOTAL	16.6
SUBTOTAL	94.2
All others	5.8
	100 %

Source: *Advertising Age*, September–October 1975.

facturer of Log Cabin syrup, monitored Lever's sales in Indianapolis and Cleveland. General Foods then managed to introduce buttered syrup at the same time nationally, thus substantially reducing from projected levels the sales of Mrs. Butterworth's syrup.

Test marketing is designed to reduce risk to manufacturers by increasing the certainty that products will be successful in general distribution. However, success in test markets is no guarantee of nationwide produce acceptance. Consider the case of the Procter and Gamble Company: "In the last ten years, P & G failed in an attempt to extend a brand beyond its test market on three occasions. Hidden Magic, a hair spray, turned out to have no magic at all. Stardust, a dry bleach, failed to convert housewives from the customary liquid. Cinch, a spray household cleaner, just never caught on, and the men at Procter & Gamble still haven't figured out why." [19]

Consumer-Use Tests

In cases where a manufacturer wishes to have consumers evaluate the merits of his product as opposed to his competitors' products under "real" conditions, product researchers will utilize *consumer-use* tests. The consumer-use test enables a manufacturer of consumer products to have his product objectively compared with competing products by consumers under conditions of actual use. Consumer-use tests may be conducted using commercial panels in a laboratory setting, by manufacturers' own employees on company premises, or by independent consumers in their own homes. Consumer-use tests are a form of product testing by consumers but are separate and distinct from concept testing and pretesting.

In order to meet the criteria of objectivity, consumer-use tests must be "masked," or "blind." A blind test is one in which all identifying labels or marks are removed from the product to be tested. Labels are removed from otherwise identical beer bottles, and competing brands of cigarettes are masked to avoid recognition. Not only is the blind test effective in obtaining unbiased perceptions of relative merits of competing products, it is also an important tool for measuring brand loyalty among customers. Numerous research studies using blind tests have shown that fiercely brand-loyal customers have often been unable to distinguish between their favorite (and supposedly superior) brands and those of competitors. This has been found to be particularly true among brand-loyal beer drinkers, a fact that encourages heavy advertising expenditures among firms in that industry. In establishing a market share for its new Lite beer, the Miller Brewing Company used a $10 million advertising blitz campaign. This expenditure amounted to an estimated $6.50 per barrel of beer, as opposed to an industrywide average of $1 per barrel, and was considered a key in-

[19] Vanderwicken, "P & G's Secret Ingredient," p. 78.

gredient in the initial market success of Miller Lite.[20] This raises the issue of advertising effectiveness, which we shall examine in the next chapter.

Two basic consumer-use tests are paired comparison placement tests and staggered comparison tests.[21] Both of these are normally blind tests, where consumers test products under conditions of actual use.

Paired comparison placement tests, also known as *side-by-side* tests, derive their name from the way in which the tests are conducted. Typically, two masked products are placed side by side in front of consumers, who are asked to use and compare the two products and then pick the one preferred. In cases where the manufacturer desires comparisons among more than two products, comparisons are still made in pairs, in order to establish consumer preferences clearly. If three products, X, Y, and Z, were compared all together, instead of in pairs, consumers might give the following preferences:

Product	Consumer Preference
X	42%
Y	38%
Z	20%
TOTAL	100%

Without paired comparison tests it might be assumed that X is the product most preferred. However, what if the 20 percent of respondents preferring product Z also preferred product Y over product X? Product Y would then be a 58 to 42 percent preferential choice over product X. Therefore, it is necessary to run paired comparison tests, comparing X with Y, X with Z, and Y with Z, in order to have completely accurate results.

Staggered comparison tests differ from paired comparison tests only in their timing. Whereas paired comparison tests involve simultaneous use of products, staggered comparison tests require consumers to use the products at different times. Respondents are given two products several days or weeks apart. The respondents may be divided into two groups, with one group given product X first and the other given product Y first, in order to eliminate any bias from having tried one product first, and to make the test more realistic, since consumers seldom use two competing products at the same time.

[20] "How Miller Won Market Slot for Lite Beer," *Business Week*, 13 October 1975, p. 116.

[21] Harper W. Boyd, Ralph Westfall, and Stanley F. Stasch, *Marketing Research*, 4th ed. (Homewood, Ill.: Richard D. Irwin, 1977), pp. 590–91.

Consumer-use tests have the admirable goal of attempting to create as realistic an atmosphere as possible, but these blind tests do not fully represent actual market conditions, and the validity of the research findings is therefore questionable. Still, consumer-use tests are important in obtaining unbiased information about consumer product preferences and in measuring the bases for brand loyalty.

Despite the most sophisticated new product research techniques, firms are unable to avoid some market failures among new products. Like marketing research in general, new product research cannot guarantee marketplace success. However, it is an important aid in making sound decisions, as uncertainty can be *reduced* and the probability of success *increased*.

Summary

Product research is the application of marketing research techniques and the marketing concept to problems in developing new products and modifying existing ones. About 75 percent of all large consumer goods manufacturing firms conduct some product research. Today, U.S. firms spend over $20 billion a year on research and development.

In attempting to satisfy consumer thirst for new products, firms have expanded product lines and enlarged their product mixes. Understanding and managing the product life cycle is necessary to help reduce product failures.

Product testing involves both technical testing and testing by consumers. Technical testing is conducted in order to find out what a product is (analysis testing) and what it will do (performance testing). Consumer testing measures consumer attitudes toward a new product or product idea; it includes concept testing — an attempt to determine consumer attitudes toward a yet undeveloped product — and pretesting, which involves the experimental use of a new product by a sample of potential customers. Pretesting presents problems with sample selection, supervision and control, accurate responses, and measurement.

Panels are widely used in product research for testing new products and concepts. A panel is a semipermanent group of people, which should be representative of potential customers and which has the task of evaluating new products or concepts. Despite their wide use, panels are not always ideal testing instruments.

Before a new product is introduced to full nationwide distribution, it is nearly always placed in test markets that demographically represent the national market. Test marketing enables the firm to gather information regarding the product's potential sales and allows the pretesting of alternative marketing strategies. Shrinking product life cycles and competitive pressures have, however, forced many firms to limit their test marketing efforts.

Manufacturers may wish respondents to compare and evaluate competing products in consumer-use tests, where all identifying marks have been removed from the products. These blind, or masked, tests may be paired comparison placement tests, in which the two products are placed side by side and evaluated at the same time, or they may be staggered comparison tests, in which the two products are evaluated several days or even weeks apart in order more nearly to duplicate actual market conditions. Results indicate little if any difference between these two types of tests.

Questions for Discussion

1. Why should a consumer goods firm engage in product research?

2. What is the relationship between product research and the marketing concept? Can a firm practice the marketing concept without engaging in product research?

3. What do you think is the most important part of product research? Why?

4. Why should product research be concerned with the product life cycle concept? Is there a connection between the two?

5. Some people say that concept testing is unrealistic. What do you think about the validity of concept testing? What is the purpose of concept testing?

6. Are the firm's own employees the best testers or should professional panels be used? Why?

7. What is test marketing? Why would a firm wish to test market a product?

8. What effect do shrinking product life cycles have on test marketing?

9. Develop a product research plan for a new mouthwash. What steps will you follow?

10. Why would it be important to use a blind test if you were trying to determine whether consumers can actually tell the difference between Coke, Pepsi, and RC?

Chapter 15

Advertising Research

Throughout North America, advertising is a multibillion dollar and ever-present force that is generally considered, whether for good or evil, to exert tremendous influence over consumer buying habits. In damning advertising as economically wasteful, one critic has written: "Overall, it is difficult for anyone to gain more than temporarily from large advertising outlays in an economy in which counter-advertising is general. The overall effect of advertising, on which we spent $14 billion in 1965, is to devote these productive resources (men, ink, billboards, and so forth) to producing advertising rather than to producing other goods and services." [1]

Though the ethics and effectiveness of advertising are both highly controversial subjects, the fact remains that advertising expenditures constitute major corporate expenses. For example, Procter and Gamble, the world's leading firm in advertising expenditures, spent approximately $360 million on advertising in 1975 alone. The basic task facing the researcher is evaluation of the effectiveness of advertising for the firm. This problem has been summarized as follows:

> Today, the money spent on advertising resembles tribute laid on the altar of some savage and arbitrary god.
>
> If you don't advertise, you're dead. If you do, you still may be. The unknowable deity must be appeased. But it's costing too much. Advertisers are rebelling.
>
> They can't stop advertising: they don't want to. But they want to know what they are getting for their money.
>
> So the time of the researcher is at hand. Formulas, concepts, sys-

[1] George L. Bach, *Economics*, 5th ed. (Englewood Cliffs, N.J.: Prentice-Hall, 1966), p. 437.

tems of management are being invoked. But the answers are confusing, often irrelevant. What should be measured—"exposure," "readership," "awareness," what else? And how? Through a box attached to the TV set, or a personal interview, or by measuring dilation and contraction of the pupils?

If the V.P. of Sales or Marketing could measure anything he wanted, chances are he would say: Measure advertising's relationship to sales and profits. Tell me how much it costs.[2]

What Is Advertising Research?

Advertising research is one of the most important segments of marketing research, employing research techniques and concepts covered in previous chapters. The American Marketing Association has defined advertising as "any paid form of non-personal presentation and promotion of ideas, goods, or services by an identified sponsor."[3] Advertising research is designed to measure advertising *effectiveness* and improve advertising *efficiency*. In this context, *effectiveness* is defined as how well an advertisement or advertising campaign accomplishes its objectives; *efficiency* is defined as the most optimum use of the advertising budget and media mix in implementing an advertising campaign. Since the fundamental goal in advertising is to sell something (whether it is a good, a service, or an idea), the ultimate goal in advertising research is to try to measure advertising's impact or influence on sales. However, as it is almost impossible to measure advertising's effect on sales directly, most advertising research involves copy and media research. Hence, it is advertising efficiency rather than advertising effectiveness that is most often studied.

Advertising research involves three principal aspects of advertising: (1) the *message*, (2) the *media*, and (3) the *results* of the advertisement. An evaluation of the message itself, the medium that carries the message, and the results of the advertisement are interrelated factors with all of which the researcher must be concerned.

An advertising message carried on the medium of television may appeal to different audiences and produce different results from a similar message carried over another medium. For example, advertising messages for liquor are usually conveyed through magazines and billboards; soap powders are advertised on television and in magazines.

[2] A. J. Vogl, "Advertising Research," *Sales Management* 91, no. 10 (1 November 1963): 40.

[3] "Report of the Definitions Committee," *Journal of Marketing* 12 (October 1948): 202.

This interrelationship of message, media, and results is a focal point that cannot be ignored.

Why Is Advertising Research Important?

Advertising research has become an area of increasing importance to businessmen as total advertising expenditures continue to rise and as techniques for measuring advertising effectiveness continue to improve.

In the United States, which has the highest per capita advertising expenditure in the world, there is the greatest economic incentive for advertising research. In 1972, the U.S. per capita advertising outlay was $110.78, more than twice the per capita spending in Canada and in sharp contrast to the two cents a person spent on advertising in Ethiopia that year.[4] Advertising expenditures in the United States have been steadily climbing and in 1976 were in excess of $32 billion.[5] However, total dollar outlays fail to tell the full story. In many consumer goods companies, advertising expenditures are disproportionately high and may exceed 10 percent of sales, though the average firm allots only about 1.5 percent of sales to advertising.

Thus, it becomes critically important for an advertiser to know if the money allocated to advertising has been well spent. Only through advertising research can it be determined if efficiency in expenditures and effectiveness in results are being obtained.

Methods of Advertising Evaluation

The researcher may wish to evaluate an advertisement before it has been run (pretesting), or he may wish to evaluate it after it has been run (posttesting). In some cases it may be desirable to both pretest and posttest the advertisement, in order to evaluate the testing procedures being used.

Pretesting the Advertisement

Pretesting is used more commonly than posttesting, because it is much more important to measure advertising effectiveness *before* an advertisement has been run than afterward. Therefore, pretesting should be viewed as a means of saving money, whereas posttesting is often de-

[4] *Wall Street Journal,* 24 February 1975, p. 6.
[5] *Advertising Age,* 5 July 1976.

voted to finding out what went wrong. Many of the techniques used in pretesting may also be used in posttesting, and vice versa. Two of the most common pretesting techniques are consumer jury tests and laboratory tests.

CONSUMER JURY TESTS

Consumer jury tests are a useful method for evaluating an advertisement's effectiveness before it is run. A "jury" composed of hypothetical customers is asked to evaluate an advertisement. The number of prospective customers on the jury may range from a dozen to several hundred. The test may take a number of forms. Jurors may evaluate one advertisement or many; they may view advertisements individually or collectively; and the evaluation process may take place at home or under controlled conditions.

One variation used on consumer jury tests is the *mock magazine*. *New Canadian World*, distributed to a random sample of consumers by Young and Rubicam, is a mock magazine that allows firms to have new advertisements tested and compared with advertisements for competing products.

Both television commercials and print advertisements may be evaluated through the use of consumer jury testing methods. In either case, the normal method is to have jurors look at several advertisements in order to determine which receives the best rating. The two main procedures for evaluation are (1) order of merit and (2) paired comparisons.

Order of merit involves having each respondent rank several advertisements in order of preference. It is usually inadvisable to ask respondents to rank more than six advertisements at once, since the average consumer can rarely work with more than six with any degree of accuracy.

The *paired comparison* method is especially advantageous when the researcher wishes to have jurors evaluate more than six advertisements. In this method, respondents compare two advertisements at a time, so that only two are being considered at any one time. Each advertisement is compared with every other advertisement in the group. The winner in each comparison is noted on a score card, and at the end, the number of times each ad "won" is totaled.

A major advantage of the paired comparison method over the order of merit method is that it enables the researcher to obtain advertisement ratings of greater consistency and accuracy. It also allows the evaluation of a larger number of advertisements; however, this advantage can disappear if the number of advertisements to be evaluated becomes too large. The number of advertisements being evaluated should not exceed ten; otherwise, the procedure becomes too tedious. Use of the formula

$$\frac{n(n-1)}{2},$$

where n equals the number of advertisements being evaluated, permits calculation of the number of comparisons to be made.[6] For example, in a case where respondents were asked to rank eight advertisements in the paired comparison method, a total of twenty-eight comparisons would be involved:

$$\frac{n(n-1)}{2} = \frac{8(8-1)}{2} = \frac{8(7)}{2} = \frac{56}{2} = 28.$$

Evaluation of Consumer Jury Tests. Though jury tests are considered useful and have wide application, there are certain fundamental difficulties inherent in their usage, which include:

1. Sample selection problems. Here the difficulty lies in getting a jury that accurately reflects the market.

2. Measurement criteria problems. On what basis is the advertisement being evaluated? What is the definition of "effective?" Does "effective" mean respondents like the ad best, find it most believable, or think it is the most interesting one?

3. Respondent control problems. Unless respondents evaluate advertisements under controlled conditions, there is no guarantee that the evaluation process is being done properly. In group evaluations some respondents may influence others.

4. Artificial nature of the test. The most serious weakness of the consumer jury test is that it tends to be unrealistic. Since it is only a test, the conditions are not what they would be in the actual marketplace, and jurors' answers are only hypothetical.

Despite these weaknesses, the jury test remains a popular method for pretesting advertisements. This method allows the researcher to get an evaluation in a relatively brief period of time and at a much lower cost than if the advertisement had been run through the mass media.

[6] C. H. Sandage and Vernon Fryburger, *Advertising Theory and Practice*, 8th ed. (Homewood, Ill.: Richard D. Irwin, 1971), pp. 560–64.

As a method of pretesting advertisements, respondents' physiological reactions to advertisements may be measured in the laboratory through the use of mechanical devices. Three principal measuring devices utilized in such testing are: (1) the eye camera, (2) the psychogalvanometer, and (3) the perceptoscope.[7] Additional information on these and other techniques is found in chapter 13.

The *eye camera*, or *oculometer*, as it is also known, was first developed about 1890, but it was not used in advertising research until 1938, when results of its use were reported by *Look* magazine. In an eye camera test, the respondent views an advertisement while the camera records how long and on what area of the advertisement the reader's attention is focused. Though the eye camera has the advantage of accurately measuring what part of the advertisement the respondent's eye focuses on, it does not measure interest in the advertisement. It is an instrument of questionable usefulness, despite its objectivity.

Perception Research Services, a subsidiary of the Interpublic Group, uses eye movement cameras to measure respondent interest to each part of an advertisement. Interviewers then question respondents further about both the advertisement and the product. The firm has found this research most useful when creative work is still in process.[8]

The *psychogalvanometer* (or *galvanometer*) is another mechanical device used for pretesting advertisements under laboratory conditions. This instrument, similar to a lie detector, has been used by psychologists to measure respondent reactions and emotions. Emotional changes in respondents are recorded by measuring, through electronic impulses, perspiration changes in the palm of the hand. Presumably, an increase in perspiration indicates a reaction to a given advertisement. However, left unanswered is the question whether a favorable or an unfavorable reaction is being recorded. The measurement of galvanic skin responses is an extremely questionable technique in advertising research, useful mainly for advertisements of a sensitive nature.

A third laboratory measuring device, the *perceptoscope*, also is intended to measure respondent arousal or interest in a particular advertisement. This instrument records changes in the pupil size of the respondent's eye. The principle involved is that pupil dilation is indicative of interest and pupil contraction indicative of lack of interest in what is being viewed. Though the perceptoscope is an instru-

[7] Maurice I. Mandell, *Advertising* (Englewood Cliffs, N.J., Prentice-Hall, 1968), pp. 569–70.

[8] *Advertising Age*, 15 July 1975, p. 23.

ment of great potential for measuring respondent interest in advertisements, it does not directly measure advertising effectiveness.

These laboratory testing devices remain instruments of limited utility to the advertising researcher. However, with proper use by qualified experts, such devices can play a worthwhile role as aids in the pretesting process.

Posttesting the Advertisement

If advertising pretesting were an established science of great precision, there would be little need for posttesting advertisements. Unfortunately, pretesting is primarily a screening device, which, it is hoped, will enable the researcher to eliminate the least effective advertisements.

Posttesting is designed not only to measure effectiveness (or lack of effectiveness) of advertisements after they have already been run, but to find out the reasons *why* an advertisement was effective or ineffective.

Since it is generally assumed that one significant and measurable factor is respondent memory of an advertisement, posttesting techniques are often concerned with measuring what (if anything) the respondent remembers about the advertisement. Two standard techniques used in posttesting are (1) recognition tests and (2) recall tests.

RECOGNITION TESTS

Recognition tests, also known as *readership tests*, are designed to find out which advertisements respondents have read. Accordingly, the recognition test measures market penetration. The best-known and most widely used recognition tests are the Starch Advertisement Readership Ratings, which have been conducted by the Daniel Starch organization since 1932. In the Starch readership tests, respondents are shown issues of magazines that they claim to have read, and results are tabulated for three categories of readership: (1) "noted" (N) — the percentage of readers having seen the advertisement; (2) "seen–associated" (A) — the percentage of readers associating the advertisement with the product or advertiser; and (3) "read most" (RM) — the percentage of readers having read over half the advertisement. From these data a calculation of the readers per dollar can be determined, using the following formula:

$$\frac{\text{Percent noted} \times \text{magazine primary readers}}{\text{space cost}} = \text{Readers per dollar}$$

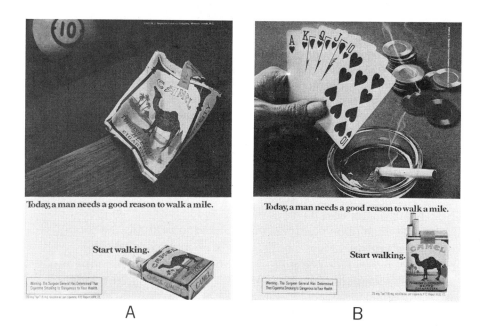

Figure 15•1
Which Ad Attracted More Readers?

Reprinted with permission from the April 22, 1974 issue of *Advertising Age*. Copyright 1974 by Crain Communications, Inc.

Consider figure 15•1. These two ads for Camel cigarettes appeared in *Playboy* magazine in September 1972 and March 1973. Advertisement *B*, the poker hand, received a much higher score on actual readership tests conducted by the Daniel Starch organization. Test results were reported in *Advertising Age* (see figure 15•2) and the differences were explained as follows:

	N	A	RM	HEADLINE
Ad (B) poker	54%	46%	14%	23%
Ad (A) pool	31	26	2	8

Reprinted with permission from the April 22, 1974 issue of *Advertising Age*. Copyright 1974 by Crain Communications, Inc.

Figure 15•2
Starch Readership Scores of the Ads

There may be research which indicated the relative incidence among Playboy readers of poker players vs. those who played billiards or shoot pool. Even without research, however, it would seem more logical for a poker player to go along with the headline idea and heed the copy injunction and be willing to "walk a mile" for a royal flush, than it would be for a cue artist to get that excited about a chance at a single ten-ball. The negative appeal of an empty cigarette pack did little to help the situation.

The royal flush, of course, appeals to a much larger audience than just the poker players; those five honors in hearts are going to grab the attention of every bridge player in the crowd, too.[9]

Recognition tests have the advantage of simplicity and have proved to be a valid measurement of reader interest and awareness of advertisements. On the other hand, there is no proved direct positive correlation between recognition of advertisements and sales of the product advertised. Additionally, researchers must cope with respondents' claims to have seen more advertisements than they could have seen, which necessitate the insertion of dummy advertisements in order to cross-check reader claims.

Recall Tests

Recall tests, like recognition tests, also measure market penetration of advertisements. The respondent is asked what she recalls or remembers about an advertisement. The recall test differs from the recognition test in that the respondent in the recall test is not shown the advertisement in advance.

There are three main types of recall tests: (1) "unaided recall," in which the respondent is given no help whatsoever by the interviewer; (2) "aided recall," in which the respondent is given cues; and (3) the "triple associate test," in which the interviewer seeks to measure the respondent's recall in associating product, brand name, and copy theme. The triple associate test is useful when the researcher wishes to find out if an advertising campaign is successful in promoting consumer awareness of a product through the brand name and copy theme. Thus, respondents could be asked, "What gasoline [product] advertises that it will put a tiger in your tank [copy theme]?" If the reply is "Exxon," then the association with the brand name has been successful.

Recall tests effectively tell how successful an ad has been in penetrating the respondent's memory. The scores "reflect the advertiser's

---

[9] *Advertising Age*, 22 April 1974, p. 56.

ability to register the sponsor's name, and to deliver a meaningful message to the consumer." [10] However, a high recall score does not necessarily mean that consumers will buy the product; it means only that consumers remember the advertisement.

Recall and readership (or recognition) tests are normally used in posttesting advertisements. However, they may sometimes be used in pretesting *split-runs*, where two variations of an advertisement are inserted into two otherwise identical press runs of a magazine. Since this technique involves varying only the advertisement, the researcher has a controlled experiment in which the effectiveness of advertisements *A* and *B* can be measured. Even in split-run tests, this technique has limited application. In describing the problem, Martin Mayer has written: "The comparative ratings of the two ads on all three tests (aided, unaided recall, and readership) will guide the agency in deciding which advertisements to run, but the test is most useful in deciding technical questions — such as, shall we use one big picture of a cake made with Betty Crocker mix or two small pictures of two goodies made with two different kinds of mix?" [11]

Media Research

Another goal of the advertiser is to select the most desirable medium or media combination to reach potential customers with the advertising message. Thus, decisions must be made regarding media selection and media mix. *Media mix* refers to the combination of media types used by the advertiser. Should television, radio, or newspapers be used for advertising? Would some combination of all three be best?

Obviously, these and other related questions cannot all be answered without an investigation into the relative strengths and weaknesses of each medium. Table 15•1 presents in summary form the aggregate spending totals for all major types of media in the United States for 1970 and 1976. From the table, it can be seen that in total dollar expenditures, newspapers remain the most important advertising medium. However, it should be noted that newspapers are primarily a vehicle for *local* advertising, whereas television is the most important medium for *national* advertising.

[10] William D. Wells, "Recognition, Recall, and Rating Scales," *Journal of Advertising Research* 4, no. 3 (September 1964): 8.

[11] *Madison Avenue, U.S.A.* (New York: Harper and Row, 1958), p. 279.

Table 15·1

Advertising Expenditures in the United States in 1970 and 1976

| | 1970 | | 1976 | |
MEDIUM	MILLIONS	PERCENT	MILLIONS	PERCENT
Newspapers	$ 5,850	29.9	9,910	29.4
Television	3,585	18.3	6,721	19.9
Direct Mail	2,680	13.7	4,813	14.3
Radio	1,270	6.5	2,330	6.9
Magazines	1,375	7.0	1,789	5.3
Business Papers	720	3.7	1,035	3.1
Outdoor	206	1.0	383	1.1
Farm Publications	33	0.2	86	0.3
Miscellaneous	3,846	19.7	6,653	19.7
TOTAL	$19,565	100.0	33,720	100.0

Source: *Advertising Age,* January 9, 1978.

Problems in Media Selection

The selection of the appropriate advertising media involves three basic steps or decisions.[12] First, which general category or categories of media shall be used? Should newspapers, magazines, radio, or some combination be utilized? Second, which media class within a particular medium type would be best? That is, if the firm opts for television advertising, would network or spot be better? Third, which particular medium should be selected? In the case of weekly magazines, would *Time, Newsweek,* or *Business Week* be best? If network television is decided upon, should it be CBS, ABC, or NBC?

Media research is conducted by the media, advertisers, independent market research firms, and advertising agencies. Media researchers, buyers, and sellers are all concerned with obtaining accurate and reliable figures regarding size and demographic characteristics of media audiences. In both print and broadcast media, audience size is a factor of particular importance in calculating media ratings, cost per advertisement, and cost per prospect reached by the advertisement.

PRINT MEDIA

Newspapers and magazines are heavily (and sometimes exclusively) dependent upon advertising revenue. As circulation increases, so does the attractiveness of a newspaper or magazine to an advertiser,

[12] Mandell, *Advertising,* p. 284.

and the medium can raise its advertising rates. In the past, this situation has encouraged some unethical publications to claim a much higher circulation than really existed.

In order to protect the print media industry against unreliable circulation figures, the Audit Bureau of Circulations was established in 1914. The A.B.C. is sponsored by advertisers, agencies, and print media publishers. The purpose of the A.B.C. is to provide "a reliable standard for reporting the quantity, quality, and distribution of circulation."[13] Two other audit bureaus, the Traffic Audit Bureau and the Business Publications Audit of Circulation, provide similar services. These two audit bureaus provide a valuable service to advertisers and are intended to guarantee accurate circulation figures.

However, circulation is sometimes a poor way to measure the total audience for a newspaper or magazine, though it is still a better indicator than "press run," which might be much enlarged by unsold copies. A better (though more difficult) way to measure a publication's real distribution impact is through measuring its *readership*, or *total audience*.

Readership measurement was pioneered by Alfred Politz in work done for *Life* magazine. Through the use of recall and recognition methods, the size of audience for a given publication is estimated. This method takes into account that a single copy of many publications may be read by several people.

Media buyers need accurate circulation and readership figures to compare costs among various publications that reach similar audiences. In the case of magazines, the formula for the cost per page per thousand circulation is

$$\frac{\text{page rate} \times 1{,}000}{\text{circulation}} = \text{cost per page per thousand circulation.}$$

For example, if the rate for magazine A is forty-five thousand dollars for a one-page four-color advertisement, and magazine B's rate is fifty thousand dollars for the same thing, it would appear that magazine A represents the better media buy. However, if the circulation of A is fifteen million and that of B is twenty million, then, as the formula shows, magazine B reaches more people for less money than magazine A. For magazine A,

$$\frac{\$45{,}000 \times 1{,}000}{15{,}000{,}000} = \$3 \text{ cost per page per thousand;}$$

[13] S. Watson Dunn and Arnold M. Barban, *Advertising*, 3rd ed. (Hinsdale, Ill.: Dryden Press, 1974), p. 469.

for magazine B,

$$\frac{\$50{,}000 \times 1{,}000}{20{,}000{,}000} = \$2.50 \text{ cost per page per thousand.}$$

Newspaper advertising rates can be compared by using the milline rate (cost per line per million circulation) formula:

$$\frac{1{,}000{,}000 \times \text{line rate}}{\text{circulation}} = \text{milline rate.}$$

In the case of two newspapers, X and Z, having different advertising line rates and different circulations, the milline rate allows effective comparison. If newspaper X has a daily circulation of 500,000 with a rate of $1 per agate line, and newspaper Z has a circulation of 800,000 with a line rate of $1.60, which is the better buy? For newspaper X,

$$\frac{1{,}000{,}000 \times \$1}{500{,}000} = \$2 \text{ milline rate;}$$

and for newspaper Z,

$$\frac{1{,}000{,}000 \times \$1.60}{800{,}000} = \$2 \text{ milline rate.}$$

In this case, it would make no difference in which newspaper the ad was placed (all other things being equal), as the milline rate is the same for both papers.

Unfortunately, audience and circulation figures published by the advertising researcher may not always be accurate. The reliability of magazine research has been seriously questioned. In a celebrated case, two research firms, W. R. Simmons and Associates Research and Target Group Index (TGI), came up with major differences in total audience figures for numerous magazines surveyed by both firms. Table 15·2 shows some of the differences. These contrasting figures, which point out the difficulty of media research into audience or readership measurement, resulted in lawsuits and demands for a serious investigation into the research methodologies involved. Unfortunately, this problem exists and controversy about research statistics continues.

Whereas total readership is considered important, it is also of vital importance to measure the demographic characteristics of the audience. Advertisers want to know if this particular medium has a

Table 15·2
How Some Research Figures Switched

		TOTAL ADULT AUDIENCE (MILLIONS)			
	CIRCULATION	TGI 1974	SIMMONS 1973	SIMMONS 1974	PERCENT DIFFERENCE
Time	4.6	18.6	22.5	19.4	−13%
Newsweek	3.0	17.0	15.1	19.0	+26
Sport	1.4	4.5	5.8	3.6	−37
Sports Afield	1.4	5.6	5.0	5.8	+14

Source: *Business Week*, 27 January 1975, p. 68.

readership containing a high proportion of potential customers. *Playboy* magazine's audience contains an extremely high number of relatively young, affluent single men, making this magazine a particularly attractive advertising medium for manufacturers of high-quality colognes, stereos, liquors, and clothing.

Table 15·3 presents a leisure-time profile of the *Business Week* subscriber developed from a 1976 research study conducted by the magazine. How might the marketing managers of Anhauser-Busch and the Joseph Schlitz Company react to these research statistics in making a decision to advertise in *Business Week*?

A broader question revolves around the issue of whether readership figures are meaningful: "there are those in the industry who claim that the rises and falls in total audience are meaningless. One such detractor of the Simmons reports is S. Spencer Grin, publisher of *Saturday Review*. 'The whole idea of a pass-along readership is a spurious thing,' Mr. Grin says. 'The real measure of a magazine is the guy who plunks his money down to buy the thing and reads it carefully from cover to cover, not the guy in a barbershop who may flip through a few pages.' "[14]

BROADCAST MEDIA

The broadcast media are television and radio. The task of measuring audience size for these media is considerably different from that of measuring print media audiences. Measuring total audience is more complex for broadcast media than for print media because of the intangible nature of the message. Also, several people may listen to a

[14] *Wall Street Journal*, 10 March 1975, p. 28.

Table 15•3
Leisure Time Profile and Alcoholic Beverage Preference of the *Business Week* Subscriber

Most popular leisure activities: golf, listening to stereo, fishing, photography, boating and tennis

Leisure time: The *Business Week* subscriber participates in a variety of activities during his leisure time:

Activity	Percent Participating
Listening to Stereo Equipment	46%
Golf	43
Tennis	40
Fishing	34
Photography	31
Boating	28
Cycling	28
Bowling	22
Skiing (snow)	21
Camping	20
Hunting	16
Paddle tennis	8
Flying a plane	7
Home care (gardening, remodeling)	6
Hobbies	5
Other activities, team sports	5
Reading	5

(Activities not shown for those with less than 5%)

Four out of five traveled for pleasure in the past year

Pleasure trips: 85% of Business Week's subscribers traveled for pleasure within the past year. Of them, 62% traveled by air, and 82% traveled by auto.

Subscribers averaged two business and/or pleasure trips outside the continental U.S. in the past year

Travel outside U.S.: Aside from his frequent traveling throughout the United States, the Business Week subscriber often leaves the country for business or pleasure. In the past year, 35% have taken trips outside the continental U.S., averaging two trips.

Table 15•3—*Continued*

Almost nine out of ten subscribers serve alcoholic beverages at home; average monthly expenditure about $42

Alcoholic beverages: 89% of all Business Week subscribers serve some sort of alcoholic beverage at home. Average monthly expense of $42.40 is divided as follows: liquor $22.30, wine $12.10, beer and/or ale $8.

PREFERENCES	PERCENT OF THOSE SERVING ALCOHOLIC BEVERAGES AT HOME
Beer & ale	73%
Scotch	73
Wine	73
Vodka	63
Gin	60
Straight bourbon	46
Canadian	41
Vermouth	35
Cognac & brandy	29
Rum	29
Cordials	28
Blends	21
Bonded bourbon	17
Rye	6

FAVORITE BRANDS AMONG DRINKERS OF:

Beer/Ale:	Budweiser (25%), Coors (16%), Miller (12%), Michelob (10%)
Scotch:	J&B (24%), Cutty Sark (19%), Johnnie Walker (14%), Chivas Regal (13%), Dewars (White Label) (13%)
Wine:	Gallo (11%), Almaden (8%), Paul Masson (5%), Taylor (5%)
Vodka:	Smirnoff (34%), Gordon's (8%), Wolfschmidt (6%), Gilbey's (4%)
Gin:	Beefeater (24%), Gilbey's (20%), Gordon's (18%)
Straight bourbon:	Jack Daniel's (25%), Jim Beam (16%), Early Times (11%), Wild Turkey (6%), Old Crow (4%), Old Grand Dad (4%)
Canadian:	Canadian Club (48%), Seagram's V.O. (29%), Crown Royal (5%)
Vermouth:	Martini & Rossi (28%), Noilly Prat (10%), Stock (8%), Tribuno (7%)

Table 15·3—_Continued_

Cognac/brandy:	Courvoisier (18%), Christian Brothers (15%), Hennessy (11%), Remy Martin (10%)
Rum:	Bacardi (42%), Ronrico (12%)
Cordials:	Drambuie (13%), Grand Marnier (11%), Kahlua (11%), B & B (10%), Tia Maria (7%), Amarreto (5%), Galliano (5%)
Blends:	Seagram's 7 Crown (40%), Calvert (6%), Imperial (6%), Four Roses (5%)
Bonded bourbon:	Old Grand-Dad (17%), Bonded Beam (7%), I. W. Harper (5%), J. W. Dant (4%), Hiram Walker (3%), Old Forester (3%)
Rye:	Old Overholt (18%)

Source: Reprinted with permission from the 1976 Business Week Executive Profile Summary. Copyright 1976, McGraw-Hill, Inc., 1221 Avenue of the Americas, New York, N.Y. All rights reserved.

single radio or watch one television set at the same time or for varying lengths of time.

Despite the difficulties peculiar to these particular media, researchers have developed four basic methods for measuring radio and television audience size and characteristics: (1) the roster-recall method, (2) the coincidental method, (3) the Audimeter, and (4) the diary method.

Developed by Pulse, Inc., a broadcast media research firm, the _roster-recall_ method incorporates a form of the aided recall method in personal interviews of a sample of households. Respondents are shown a roster, or list, of programs broadcast the previous day, and the interviewer checks those the respondent claims to have seen or heard.

The roster-recall method enables researchers to obtain detailed information concerning audience composition, as well as audience size. However, the chief disadvantage of the roster-recall method is that it depends on the respondent's memory, an often unreliable factor in research.

A second way in which audience size for broadcast media can be measured is through the _coincidental_ method. In this method a random sample of homes is selected to be telephoned by interviewers during broadcasting hours. Respondents are asked what program they are watching or listening to at that particular time and what sponsor or product is being advertised.

Trendex, Inc., is one example of a firm that uses this method. Trendex administers coincidental telephone interviews for programs broadcast by the three major television networks in the United States. These interviews, conducted simultaneously in twenty-six markets, make it possible to measure the popularity of new programs quickly. Advantages of the coincidental method include speed and economy in gathering data; and the main weakness in the roster-recall method — having to depend on respondent memory — is avoided. The coincidental method has two limitations: it is restricted to homes having telephones; and, because homes can only be called during certain broadcasting hours, this method cannot measure broadcasts late at night or early in the morning.

Probably the best known of all techniques in broadcast measurement is the *Audimeter* used by the A. C. Nielsen Company (see figure 15•3). This device, the famous Nielsen black box, is attached to television and radio sets in a random sample of eleven hundred homes scattered throughout the United States. The Audimeter electronically records on a magnetic tape "a continuous record of set usage and station

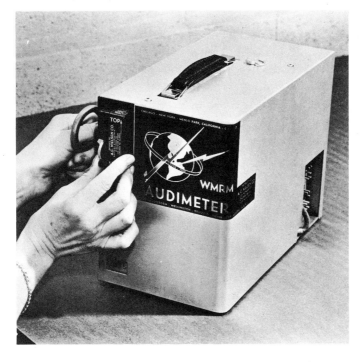

Figure 15•3
The Audimeter

Used with permission of A. C. Nielsen Company

tuning."[15] With the aid of the Audimeter, the well-known Nielsen Ratings of television programs are developed and then published in the Nielsen Television Index twice every month.

Though the Audimeter has the advantage of accurately measuring "sets in use" from a valid sample, it does not indicate who is watching the set or whether the set is being watched at all. All the Audimeter does is record that the set is turned on to a particular channel; it tells nothing about the audience.

In order to avoid some of the more obvious limitations inherent in using the Audimeter as the sole broadcast measuring device, Nielsen and other media research firms also utilize the *diary* method. This method, used by Nielsen in conjunction with the Audimeter, involves having a representative sample of respondents record their broadcast listening or viewing habits in a diary supplied by the research firm. This method obtains individual listening and viewing data on every household member. However, the diary method suffers from the limitation of the human element: it assumes that respondents will faithfully and accurately record their household viewing habits in the diary. Human nature being what it is, this is a questionable assumption indeed.

None of these four techniques used in measuring broadcast media audiences is without significant flaws or limitations. As a result, measurements derived from these techniques, such as the Nielsen Ratings, will undoubtedly continue to be subject to criticism from both experts and laymen. Criticism is to be expected, especially in light of the "life and death" power the Nielsen Ratings exercise over television programs.

Despite these limitations, measurements of broadcast media audiences are necessary, so that program sponsors have some idea whether their messages are reaching the people they want to reach and whether the money they are paying the media is being well spent. On the other hand, none of these four media measuring techniques evaluates the relative efficiency of the various types of media. Left unanswered is the question whether television or magazines constitute the most efficient medium for presenting advertising messages. Answers to this type of question can be determined only through a case-by-case approach, taking into account a number of factors (such as cost, product, target audience, and type of message).

[15] Mandell, *Advertising*, p. 356.

Difficulties in Advertising Research

Measuring the effectiveness of advertising is a particularly difficult task, which may frustrate the three parties having an interest:

1. Advertisers, who want to know if the money they are spending is producing worthwhile results;

2. Advertising agencies, who must prove to advertisers that their creative efforts can produce desired results;

3. Advertising media, each of which wants to demonstrate that its medium is the most effective vehicle for carrying the advertiser's message to prospective customers.

Despite the complementary and conflicting interests at hand among these three parties, all have an interest in accurate advertising research. Unfortunately, though, precise research in advertising effectiveness is a matter of great difficulty, because of three main factors: the problematic effect of advertising on sales, time and cost considerations, and weaknesses in research methodology and interpretation.

First, and most important, is the problem of isolating and measuring the effect advertising has in producing sales. In a laboratory experiment, one factor can be allowed to vary while all other variables are held constant. This procedure is not possible in the business world where advertising operates: the business world is not a laboratory, and there are many factors operating at the same time that may affect sales, only one of which is advertising. For example, do beer sales rise in summer because of extra advertising, or because of hot weather? This problem has been summarized by Alfred R. Oxenfeldt and Carroll Swan:

> . . . it is almost necessarily impossible to measure precisely the effectiveness of advertising upon sales, profits, or even attitudes and preferences. The main reason is that one cannot completely isolate advertising's effects from the many other effects that operate concurrently. Another reason is that advertising's effects are spread out over time so that what happens now reflects past advertising, as well as recent advertising; and today's advertising will yield benefits in the future.[16]

Consider the actual case of Marlboro cigarettes: when Marlboro introduced the flip-top box in packaging and the famous "Marlboro man"

[16] *Management of the Advertising Function* (Belmont, Calif.: Wadsworth Publishing Co., 1964), pp. 77–78.

theme in advertising, sales soared from 300,000 cigarettes in 1955 to 1.3 billion in 1957. Was this dramatic sales increase caused by advertising, packaging, a combination of the two, or other unknown factors? The essence of the problem is how to isolate the effects of advertising upon sales. That consumers like or read an advertisement offers no guarantee they will buy the product. The almost impossible complexity involved in isolating advertising's effect on sales causes researchers to concentrate on the more measurable factors of recognition and recall.

Test markets are sometimes used to study the effects of specific changes in advertising strategy. One firm, E. I. duPont de Nemours and Company, has used test markets in measuring media effectiveness "by sealing off comparable markets and then purposely varying the media in each market — while other marketing conditions remain the same." [17] Sales are then analyzed in both markets to assess the effectiveness of the media mixes used. There are serious deficiencies in this method. As Oxenfeldt and Swan have written, ". . . this kind of controlled experiment is often not possible. It has to be carried on under somewhat artificial conditions of marketing in a local area, using local media only. And it does not take into account the long-range results of advertising; to judge advertising effectiveness only by immediate sales may be misleading." [18]

Time and cost factors present a second problem in advertising research. Good advertising research is both expensive and time-consuming. It cannot be done on a shoestring budget, and problems therefore arise when top executives want quick answers concerning the anticipated effectiveness of a proposed advertising campaign. Often, research considerations become secondary to those of time and economy. As a result, advertisements are sometimes rushed through the pretesting process and introduced to the market without proper screening.

Third, there are weaknesses in the research methodology itself and in interpreting results. Researchers themselves exhibit considerable disagreement over the validity of the different methods of measuring audiences. Research methods are subject to abuse, and results are subject to misinterpretation and misrepresentation.

Facing the researcher are such questions as: is aided recall or unaided recall best? Are consumer jury tests realistic? Should people who casually leaf through magazines in a doctor's office be included in the total audience for that publication? Are the readership figures themselves accurate?

[17] Oxenfeldt and Swan, *The Advertising Function*, p. 76.
[18] *The Advertising Function*, p. 77.

Overcoming these difficulties in advertising research is a matter of legitimate concern to the advertising researcher, though considerable progress has been made in this direction in recent years. However, until a great deal more progress has been made, advertising research will remain a highly inexact process, and researchers will continue to experience great difficulty in attempting to perform the central task of measuring the effectiveness of advertising.

One recent experiment in measuring advertising effectiveness was an attempt to get consumers to read advertisements with greater care by testing them with questions next to the ads and then rewarding them for correct answers.[19] This approach, developed by Newmedia Marketing Company, involved the creation of *Shopper's Voice*, a magazine consisting only of ads, which was mailed to several million consumers. It was financed by $600,000 each from the manufacturers of Alpo, Taster's Choice, Ajax Cleanser, and several other products.

Next to each advertisement was a questionnaire designed to test the reader's comprehension of the product story. The completed questionnaire was worth 100 free trading stamps and a chance to win 200,000 more in a drawing. The theory behind this unique approach was that it could "break through the clutter of more than 1,500 advertising impressions that assault the average consumer each day . . . by offering a reward in return for close attention to a specific ad." [20]

Did this approach work? Apparently it did. When a panel of *Shopper's Voice* recipients was compared with a panel of consumers who had not seen the magazine, the results were impressive. *Shopper's Voice* readers were found to have increased their buying of Renuzit Air freshener by 31.9%, Bufferin by 32.1%, Seven Seas Salad Dressing by 20.1%, Visine by 34.9%, and Ajax by 19.9%.

Summary

Advertising research is designed to measure the effectiveness and improve the efficiency of advertising. To accomplish these tasks, the researcher evaluates (1) the message, (2) the media, and (3) the results of the advertisement.

Because of the rapid growth in total advertising expenditures and improved research techniques, advertising research has assumed a position of increasing importance: advertisers want to know if their ad-

[19] "Reinforcing the Impact of TV Commercials," *Business Week*, 18 July 1977, pp. 40–41.

[20] "Reinforcing the Impact of TV Commercials," p. 40.

vertising dollars have been well spent. Still, advertising research faces three main problems: (1) isolating and measuring the effect of advertising on sales, (2) time and cost factors, and (3) abuses and weaknesses in advertising research methodology. The result is that most advertising research concentrates on measuring advertising effectiveness via copy testing and media research.

In evaluating the copy, or message, of an advertisement, two main testing methods are used: pretesting and posttesting. Pretesting, testing an advertisement *before* it has been run, may involve the use of (1) consumer jury tests or (2) laboratory tests. Consumer juries evaluate advertising messages by order of merit or paired comparison methods. Laboratory tests include use of eye cameras, psychogalvanometers, and perceptoscopes. Posttesting, testing advertising copy *after* it has been run, involves the use of recall and recognition, or readership, tests. The split-run technique allows comparison of two different advertising messages in two otherwise identical press runs of a magazine.

The goal in media research is to select the most desirable medium or media combination to reach the most potential customers at the lowest cost. In total dollar expenditures, newspapers are the number-one advertising vehicle in the United States, though they are used primarily for local advertising; television is the most important medium for national advertising. A central problem in evaluating media is the measurement of readership, or total audience.

Media research techniques differ for print and broadcast media. Since advertising rates and circulation vary among print media, magazine advertising costs are measured according to the cost per page per thousand circulation, and newspaper advertising costs are compared according to the milline rate. Broadcast media research may use one or a combination of four main methods: (1) roster-recall, (2) coincidental, (3) Audimeter, and (4) diaries. Despite the existence of these and other techniques, media research remains an extremely controversial and inexact function.

Questions for Discussion

1. Is it possible to measure the effect of advertising on a firm's sales? Why or why not?

2. What are the principal differences between order of merit and paired comparison jury tests?

3. Do you think consumer "awareness" or "interest"' in an advertisement is a valid measurement of the effectiveness of that advertisement? Explain.

4. What are three laboratory techniques used for pretesting advertisements? Are they realistic?

5. What is the difference between pretesting and posttesting advertisements? Which is better?

6. What are the main differences between recognition and recall tests? Which is also called a readership test?

7. What type of recall test question might be asked in the following manner: "What cigarette advertises that it 'tastes good like a cigarette should'?"

8. What is the purpose of media research? What is a media mix?

9. What is the Audit Bureau of Circulations? Why was it necessary to create the A.B.C.?

10. What is the total audience concept in media research? How does it differ from press run?

11. a. *Time* magazine, with a *readership* of 19.4 million in 1974 (according to W. R. Simmons and Associates Research) charges $46,460 for a one-time, one-page, four-color ad, whereas *Newsweek,* with a *readership* of 19 million, charges $32,565 for the same ad. What is the cost per page per thousand for each magazine?

b. *Circulation* figures for *Newsweek* are 3 million, whereas *Time's* are 4.6 million. On the basis of circulation figures, using the ad rates just given, which magazine is the better media buy?

12. What are the four main techniques used to measure size and characteristics of broadcast media audiences? Why is it so important to have accurate media audience figures?

13. Which newspaper represents the better media buy?

Newspaper	Line Rate	Circulation
A	$0.08	50,000
B	0.10	60,000

14. Prepare a paired comparison test for eight automobile advertisements appearing in current magazines. (Note: This test can then be administered in class as an exercise.)

Chapter 16

Sales Estimation and Sales Forecasting

Introduction

ONE OF THE MAJOR MISCONCEPTIONS fostered by the average college business curriculum is the notion that marketing is a glamorous job and that selling is the exclusive province of "peddlers," like the "Fuller Brush man." In actuality, the two jobs of selling and marketing merge in the thoroughly professional world of corporate sales. Although TV and motion picture writers make much sport over the "lowly" salesperson, the big blowhard with the corny pitch, every businessperson knows that those "lowly blowhards" are actually highly trained, highly paid, very professional people — the people upon which a company depends. Not only does the company rely upon the success of its sales force for its very existence, every *operating* aspect of the company is determined by the nature and level of the company's sales; every facet — procurement, purchasing, production, warehousing, shipping, personnel, accounting, and so forth, right down the line — depends upon the level and type of company sales.

Sales Forecasting: A Major Activity

Although the job of sales estimation and sales forecasting may sound mundane in comparison to other topics, such as consumer surveys for new product development, consumer motivation, and so forth, the job of estimating sales potential and developing sales forecasts is one of the most critical the marketing research department is asked to handle.

And in many firms, sales estimation represents virtually the entire effort of the market research department. Furthermore, it is a job that becomes more important with each passing year: as shipping costs, warehousing costs, and distribution costs continue to climb, the accuracy of the sales forecast (which is used to schedule production) becomes more critical. These forecasts are made even more critical by the decentralized nature of most modern businesses. No longer is it a simple matter of the proprietor individually deciding to start, stop, speed up, or slow down his production to the pace of the market. All these planning decisions must now be made in a decentralized environment, which involves the coordinated effort of many departments often scattered over several different areas of the country. In addition, the larger scale of production also entails a longer lead time and implies that the forecast must remain valid for a longer period of time if the investment is to be recovered. Because of the tremendous importance of these sales estimates to the entire corporate operation, they are often quite sophisticated, and great care and expense is lavished on their preparation. However, the casual corporate observer is usually unaware of the intensity of this effort: much of it is conducted in virtual secrecy, since these forecasts would be of almost equal value to a competitor.

Problems in Estimating Market and Sales Potential

One of the primary reasons why sales forecasts require such effort and such sophistication is that the estimation of future events is an extremely *complex* task. Whereas schoolroom examples usually involve the very neat interaction of only one or two clearly defined variables, real-world estimation requires the juggling of dozens of poorly defined, yet nevertheless influential, factors that are interconnected in a spaghettilike maze.

The estimation of the sales potential of an area is dependent upon a host of factors, some obvious and some not so obvious. Obvious factors would be things like population size and population density. Also important would be the income of the area, both total and per capita. Even in locales with the same per capita income, differences in the *distribution* of those incomes might make a tremendous difference in the buying habits of the two regions. See, for example, figure 16•1.

Then, too, regional needs and preferences may also have a large effect. For instance, even if the income and population of an area in Minnesota and an area in Florida were the same, the area in Minnesota would have more sales potential for heavy winter outerwear than the area in Florida. Though this is a blatantly obvious example, the fact

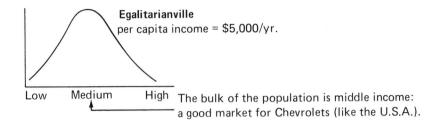

Egalitarianville
per capita income = $5,000/yr.

Low   Medium   High   The bulk of the population is middle income:
                         a good market for Chevrolets (like the U.S.A.).

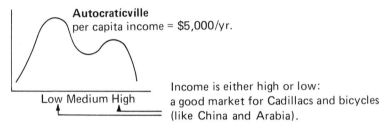

Autocraticville
per capita income = $5,000/yr.

Low Medium High   Income is either high or low:
                  a good market for Cadillacs and bicycles
                  (like China and Arabia).

Figure 16·1
Sales Forecasting for Two Towns with the Same Total Regional and Per Capita Income

remains that *each* area of the country has its own preferences and its own specific demand schedule for each product.

The Buying Power Index

Because of the importance of population, income, and previous buying habits, and because of the ready accessibility of figures for these categories, they are often used as guidelines to the sales potential of various areas. One of the better-known adaptations of such figures is the Buying Power Index published by *Sales Management* magazine. In this index, each section of the country is rated in comparison to the U.S. average. The values of population, income, and last year's retail sales are figured into a formula that weights the income factor as 50 percent, the retail sales factor as 30 percent, and the population factor as 20 percent. Without going into the mechanics of exactly how these figures are obtained and utilized, we hope you can see that there is no such thing as a truly objective estimate. Every estimate is prepared according to certain assumptions, assumptions that may be quite reasonable but are nevertheless subjective in nature. In the Buying Power Index, the assignment of the weights of 50 percent, 30 percent, and 20 percent is a subjective decision; if the assignment of the weights is changed, so are the values of the index computed. A firm that sells a very expensive product might want the income factor rated at 90 percent, whereas a firm selling some inexpensive commodity product, such as soap or potatoes, might want the population factor rated at 90 percent.

In addition, such general estimators, although useful, do not allow for the dynamics of the market. They do not make allowance for changing market conditions, like those observed in the home insulation business: previous demand schedules for insulation have gone out the window, and insulation producers have gone to double and triple shifts to keep pace with the still-growing demand. Nor do these general estimators anticipate changes in the overall level of economic activity, such as a nationwide recession. Most significantly, they fail to differentiate between overall retail demand for all products as opposed to specific demand for individual products. As noted previously, the demand for each product varies markedly between regions.

Finally, and probably of greatest importance, these overall composite indices fail to differentiate between the market potential of a given area and the sales potential of a given company. The market potential is the total amount of sales that should occur in that area for all brands of that product. The sales potential is the amount of sales a specific company should make. The obvious factor of note in this case is the amount and strength of the competition. A firm may find itself looking at a market of high market potential, but one already dominated by strong competitors. In this case, although the market potential is very high, the sales potential to the firm is quite low. The firm may find higher sales potential in a smaller market where there is less competition. This has been the strategy of the Gibson chain of discount stores. Gibson has pressed expansion into small towns overlooked by the larger discount chains. Its thinking is that, although the market potential is relatively low, there will probably be enough business to support one discount house. Therefore, Gibson's objective has been to get in first and thereby to seal off these markets. Because the markets are so small, Gibson will probably have little competition in the foreseeable future.

Although we are about to discuss various methods by which sales estimates and forecasts can be made, it is important at this juncture to realize the subjective nature of such forecasting. As we have just seen, estimates of sales potential vary with a host of factors, some objective, some subjective, some quantitative, some qualitative. Thus, any sales estimate must examine not only quantitative aspects, such as the number of people, their income, and their product and brand preferences as shown by previous spending habits, but also less quantitative factors, such as general economic forecasts, consumer trends, and demographic shifts. It also must attempt to gauge the strength of the company's own competitive stance, as well that of the competition in the market, for the upcoming year. Aside from being difficult and sometimes impossible to measure, the competitive efforts of both the individual firm and competitors can be quite volatile. Although market share positions usually tend toward stability over time, they can fluctuate rapidly, especially during periods of transition, such as the entry of new competitors into the market, old competitors dropping out, or new management teams. Unfortunately for the modern-day forecaster, all these situations are happening with ever-increasing frequency. New firms — especially international and foreign competitors — are entering the market as never before. Old firms are dropping out, as managements become more finance-conscious and prune lagging divisions from the corporate tree. And there is more management shake-up, as the trend toward diversification through merger and acquisition continues. Every time a large firm acquires a subsidiary, there will be inevitable changes in the competitive posture of that firm. All these aspects make the art of forecasting at least one part luck for each part skill.

Sales Forecasting Techniques

In this section we will investigate three methods of sales forecasting: subjective techniques, market surveys, and objective extrapolation.

Subjective Techniques

"Subjective predictions" is but a fancy name for guesses, hunches, and opinions. Accordingly, these predictions are quite personal and often highly erratic. It might be noted, however, that the most famous economic prediction in history was made by just such subjective analysis (or perhaps inspired analysis). This prediction would be Joseph's fourteen year economic-forecast made to the Egyptian Pharoah in Genesis 41, which reportedly took place nearly four thousand years ago. Astrologers, oracles, fortune tellers, and other such forecasters have abounded throughout history and are with us today.

Such subjective sources should not be ignored as a source of forecasting input. In a rapidly changing environment, they are often the best guide (and sometimes the only guide) to future events. The firm's use of subjective forecasts usually takes one of two forms: executive jury or sales force estimates.

EXECUTIVE JURY

In the executive jury, also called the jury of executive opinion, managers, executives and other decision makers in the company are probed for their predictions of the future (this method could just as well be called "executive estimates"). An extended version of this basic technique is known as the Delphi method (after the oracle at Delphi). In the Delphi technique, estimates are first obtained from all executives. These estimates are averaged, distributions are computed, and then the averages are returned to the executives, who reestimate the events with the advantage of the collective wisdom expressed by the group. These new estimates are averaged, and the process begins again. Of course, what will happen is obvious: all those persons with extreme predictions will quickly become embarrassed and pull their estimates back in line with the group average. This is one reason why so many economic forecasts are both dull and wrong. People don't like to stick their necks out, to go out on a limb by themselves; it is much safer to go with the group. One of the sad things about corporate (and governmental) life is that it is seen as better to be wrong with a group than to be correct by oneself. Then, too, a large consensus tends to have a bandwagon effect, which creates a self-fulfilling prophecy. If "everyone" is predicting a slight decline in the economy, and businesspeople believe those predictions and act upon them, then businesspeople will begin to pursue more conservative policies, to "batten down the hatches." These conservative policies (deferring capital investment, reducing inventories, and so forth) will then result in the very slowdown that was predicted. This is one reason why government forecasts are always optimistic: for political reasons, the government is constantly in the position of trying to boost public and corporate confidence, so that business, bankers, and consumers will continue to enlarge their operations through more expansive policies.

SALES FORCE ESTIMATES

The use of the sales force for sales forecasting, sometimes referred to as the poll of sales force opinion, proceeds exactly like the use of the executive jury. The only and obvious difference is that salespeople, rather than executives, are questioned.

Talking to the sales force can be advantageous in several ways. First, because the salespersons are closer to the ultimate customers, they may have a better feel for the market. Studies comparing estimates of manufacturers and wholesalers and of manufacturers and retailers show that retailers tend to do better than wholesalers, and wholesalers tend to predict more accurately than manufacturers. This finding implies that the closer one is to the ultimate consumers, the better one's forecasting will be. Another advantage of sales force estimates is that, by making the salespeople feel like a part of the management team, these estimates often improve relations between management and the sales staff.

Dealing with the sales force can have drawbacks, however. One of the most serious problems involves the question of sales quotas. Often the sales forecast becomes the basis for the sales quota, which in turn will be used to monitor the salespeople's selling efforts and ultimately to determine their commissions and bonuses. Thus, salespersons may be motivated to underestimate the sales potential of their areas significantly, in hopes of getting low quotas, which, when exceeded, will in turn provide them with healthy bonuses.

Another drawback to the use of the sales force in producing these estimates is that the time spent on such "management" duties subtracts from the time they can devote to actual selling. As with so many other areas in the management of a business enterprise, there is a trade-off between the amount of time directly devoted to a task and the efficiency of the effort devoted to it. These sales estimates are made in the hope that the business will run more efficiently, but though such efforts to improve efficiency are important, they are not, in and of themselves, productive. They do not manufacture, they do not sell, they do not transport. Although many firms do suffer from inefficiency caused by undermanagement, there are other firms that suffer from lethargy brought on by a top-heavy management.

Market Surveys

Another way to gauge the vigor of a market is through the use of some type of market survey, either a survey of consumer intentions or a market test. These methods are especially applicable to a new product, where the firm does not have a previous track record to use as a basis for estimates.

CONSUMER INTENTIONS

Surveys of consumer intentions test consumers' responsiveness to a product. Sometimes just the product concept is tested; at other times, samples of the product are produced and distributed to a sample of consumers (often the consumer mail panels). On the basis of the response of these consumers, management decides whether to push ahead with the project, to rework the product, or to drop it completely. The major disadvantage with this method is that it involves a rather artificial marketing environment. To say to a consumer, "Would you like to buy a pair of heavy-duty kitchen scissors for $2.49?" is much different from fighting to gain market distribution and then persuading that shopper actually to select the product from competing items on the shelf and to pay for it from the cash in her purse.

TEST MARKETING

To gain a measure of how the product would fare in the more exacting light of the real-world marketplace, complete with apathetic consumers, reluctant middlemen, and hostile competitors, the next step is usually test marketing. In this case, one or more cities are selected for market testing of the product. Sales are carefully monitored, especially the rate of repeat sales, since the novelty of the product, along with the introductory specials, will bring in a number of one-time-only trial users. With a few notable exceptions (such as vasectomies and burial caskets), the key to the success of most products is in the repeat business. By graphing the relationship between introductory and repeat purchases as shown in figure 16•2, the firm can ascertain within two or three purchase cycles whether the product is going to be a success.

Objective Extrapolation

The techniques of subjective estimation or of market surveys could be used to estimate either ongoing products or entirely new products. The more common problem, and in most respects the more simple task, is the estimation of the future sales of a product that is already in production and has a sales history — a sales history that gives a starting point for estimates.

Although the use of objective data in a forecast can remove some

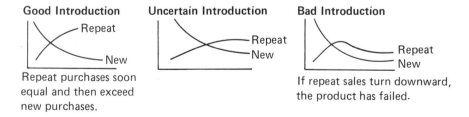

Good Introduction
Repeat purchases soon equal and then exceed new purchases.

Uncertain Introduction

Bad Introduction
If repeat sales turn downward, the product has failed.

Figure 16•2
Relationships Between Introductory and Repeat Purchases

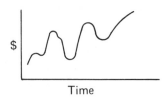

Figure 16·3
Time Series Analysis

of the guesswork encountered in subjective estimates and in market surveys, predicting the future is still fraught with danger. Thus, forecasting from objective data is analogous to driving a car by looking in the rear view mirror: you still don't have any real idea where you are going, only where you have been. Most importantly, such past data will fail at precisely that point where it is needed the most. If the road were straight and level, with no traffic or other such obstacles to encounter, you actually could drive a car with reasonable safety by looking out the rear view mirror. However, if there were a sharp curve in the road, you might never realize it until it was too late. Likewise, in business, as long as everything continues as usual, there is no real need for a prediction at all; the business can continue just as usual. Forecasting is a sort of Catch-22: when you need it you can't get it, and when you don't need it, it is easy to obtain.

Nevertheless, some information is better than none at all, so objective forecasting continues to be used more widely as a business tool. Here we will take a brief look at the forecasting technique of time series analysis and at the use of economic indicators.

TIME SERIES

The basic rationale of time series analysis is that certain economic activities are said to vary with time, which has the same effect mathematically as saying that the change in economic activity is caused by the change in time (see fig. 16·3). Though things do of course, change over time, it must be remembered it is not time itself that is causing the changes. Thus, time series efforts are almost invariably doomed to results that fall short of the success envisioned by the statistical analysts. Yet, because all planning must be done over time, the study of time series remains a lively topic.

Time Series Extrapolation by Scatter Diagram. The easiest, fastest, and sometimes most meaningful way to extrapolate time series data is through use of a scatter diagram. As illustrated in figure 16·4, a scatter

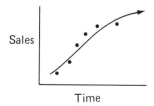

Figure 16·4
A Scatter Diagram

diagram is but a rough plot of the relevant data through which the researcher has sketched a curve summarizing the data. Although this method lacks precision and objectivity, it compensates for those lacks by being inexpensive to perform and simple to understand. In addition, because the user can adjust the curve to conform with her subjective evaluation of the situation, there are instances in which the simple scatter diagram can quite accurately predict the future. A mathematically derived straight line regression produces the graph in figure 16·5. However, it seems obvious that the last two time periods represent a vastly different operating situation, and hence, the prediction from this graph would seem very improbable. The prediction given by the scatter diagram in figure 16·6 seems much more probable.

Time Series Extrapolation by Short-Cut Formula. A simple formula for predicting next year's sales uses the percent of sales increase or decrease of this year compared to last year:

$$\text{next year's sales} = (\text{this year's sales}) \times \left(\frac{\text{this year's sales}}{\text{last year's sales}}\right).$$

Thus, if sales this year were eight million and last year were six million, the prediction of sales for next year would be

$$\text{next year's sales} = 8 \times (8/6) = 10.67 \text{ (round to 10.7)}.$$

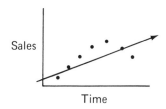

Figure 16·5
A Straight Line Regression

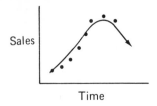

Figure 16·6
The Comparable Scatter Diagram

Although this method is easy to use and simple to understand, it does have two drawbacks that should be mentioned. First of all, it takes only two time periods into account, this year and last year. If there is anything unusual about either of those two periods, estimates made from this method will be highly suspect. A second problem is that this formula assumes that the increase or decrease for next year will be of exactly the same magnitude as the increase or decrease this year. In the real world, such constant (logarithmic) changes are very hard to sustain for any length of time.

Time Series Extrapolation by Linear Regression. If data are plotted in the manner discussed in the scatter diagram section, with time along the X axis and sales along the Y axis, then time series analysis becomes a regression problem with time as the independent variable. To perform this regression analysis, we will utilize a technique known as simple, least-squares, linear regression. In other words, we will compute a regression equation (or the equation for a line through the given set of data points) that incorporates only *one* independent variable, time, as a predictor of one dependent variable (simple regression) and that graphs as a straight line (linear regression). Furthermore this line will be computed in such a way that the sum of the squares of the deviations from the various data points to the line will be a minimum (least squares).

The ultimate result of least-squares analysis is the formation of the equation

$$Y_c = a + bX,$$

where X and Y are the variables and a and b are the regression coefficients.

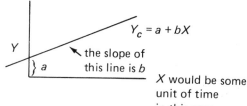

$Y_c = a + bX$

the slope of
this line is b

X would be some
unit of time
in this case.

b = the slope, the rate of increase or decrease

$$b = \frac{\Sigma XY}{\Sigma X^2}$$

a = the Y intercept, the value of Y when $X = 0$ (or the point where the line crosses the Y axis)

$$a = \frac{\Sigma Y}{\eta}$$

We are trying to use time series regression analysis to estimate the probable sales for 1980. Taking the relevant information from the graph, we can compute the formula $Y_c = a + bX$ in the following sample problems.

Sample Problem 1: Forecast sales for 1980 using the least squares method (even number of years).

Years	Sales (Y)	X*	X²	XY
1975	97	−3	9	−291
1976	99	−1	1	− 99
1977	100	+1	1	+100
1978	101	+3	9	+303
	$\Sigma Y = 397$		$\Sigma X^2 = 20$	$\Sigma XY = + 13$

$$a = \frac{\Sigma Y}{\eta} = \frac{397}{4} = 99.25$$

$$b = \frac{\Sigma XY}{\Sigma X^2} = \frac{13}{20} = .65$$

$Y_c = a + bX$
$= 99.25 + .65 \ (7)$
$= 99.25 + 4.55$
$= 103.80$

Thus, the sales forecast for 1980 is 103.80.

* *Note:* The sum of X should always be 0. In an even number of years, it is computed as −1, −3, −5, etc. With an odd number of years, the middle year is 0 and we number −1, −2, etc. The value for X in our equation $Y_c = a + bX$ is the year for which we are forecasting — in the above example, it is 7 for 1980 sales. The number of years is η.

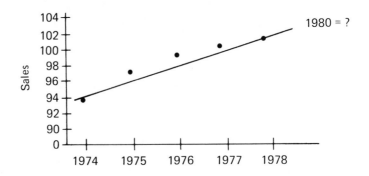

Figure 16·7
Data for Time Series Regression Analysis

Sample Problem 2: Forecast sales for 1980 using the least squares method (odd number of years).

Years	Sales (Y)	X	X²	XY
1974	94	−2	4	− 188
1975	97	−1	1	− 97
1976	99	0	0	0
1977	100	+1	1	+100
1978	101	+2	4	+202
	$\Sigma Y = 491$		$\Sigma X^2 = 10$	$\Sigma XY = + 17$

Again, using our formulas from the previous example:

$$a = \frac{\Sigma Y}{\eta} = \frac{491}{5} = 98.2$$

$$b = \frac{\Sigma XY}{\Sigma X^2} = \frac{17}{10} = 1.7$$

$$\begin{aligned} Y_c &= a + bX \\ &= 98.2 + 1.7(4) \\ &= 98.2 + 6.8 \\ &= 105 \end{aligned}$$

Thus, our sales forecast for 1980 is 105. Note again that the value for X is 4, the number of years we are forecasting for away from the midpoint.

It is important to note that although least squares linear regression is extremely popular in sales forecasting, it suffers from one fundamental weakness: the method assumes that the future is a function of the past. In our examples of forecasting for 1980, the method showed that sales would increase as they had through the years 1974–78. This may not be the case. For example, during the 1960s when university enrollments were growing, universities responded by rapidly increasing physical facilities and number of faculty. Today many universities have regretted their optimism.

Components of Time Series. Researchers have also noted that variation of data over time may be a function of several different factors, all of which seem to be varying over time. These factors, usually referred to as the *four components of time series*, are *trend* and *cyclical*, *seasonal*, and *erratic* variation. We explain and illustrate these four components in order of duration, from the longest to the shortest.

Trend is the long-term rise or fall in the data. In working the time series problems, we computed the trend equation, $Y_c = a + bX$. Trend answers the question "When examined as a whole, is the variable of interest rising or falling?" In analyzing time series data, trend is usually viewed as representing time periods of from ten to twenty years. For example, automobile manufacturers in the United States discontinued the production of convertibles because the sales *trend* had been downward for many years.

The most important component of the time series data is the *cyclical* fluctuation associated with the basic health of the economy, or more simply, the business cycle. Usually from two to ten years in duration, the business cycle is the focus of constant study. However, despite intensive effort, mathematical attempts to plot and predict the cycle over time usually do not work well, because the cyclical variations are caused not by time but rather by political and scientific activity at home and abroad. For example, because of the energy crisis and the subsequent recession, automobile sales were down in the period 1974–76. With the upturn in the economy, however, automobile sales went up in 1977–78.

Much of the variation in time-related data shows regular periodic patterns and may be *seasonal*. Seasonal variation includes both changes dictated by the seasons of the year (such things as Christmas, summer travel, and winter heating) and changes of shorter duration (such as bigger grocery bills at the first of the month, when people have their pay checks, movie attendance on weekends, and so forth). For example, the automobile industry usually experiences a flurry of activity during late summer and early fall, as the models from the previous season are closed out and those for the new season are brought in. Noting this annual sales spurt, manufacturers of other products, such as washers and refrigerators, have tried to introduce the model year concept to their products, although with only limited success.

Erratic variation is fluctuation of very short term that is totally unpredictable. For example, car sales in Buffalo were no doubt way below normal for the month of January 1977, for the simple reason that, because of the blizzard, no one could get out to shop for cars.

Adjusting for Seasonal or Cyclical Variation through the Use of Indicators

In considering a piece of economic data, one must keep in mind the effects of the components of time series and adjust the data accordingly when necessary. Suppose that a new salesman is boasting of the superiority of his sales record over that of his predecessor. Now, of course, it is quite possible that he is indeed a better salesman. It is also quite possible, however, that his increases are only cosmetic. Perhaps he arrived at the start of the best selling season, and he is comparing his sales record during the peak season with his predecessor's record during the worst selling season; or perhaps he has been employed during a very good year, whereas his predecessor was employed during a very bad one. We can adjust for the effects of these variations through the use of *indicators*.

A seasonal or cyclical indicator is formed basically by comparing the activity in the time period to be tested with the activity in the base time period. Thus, a seasonal indicator gives the relative amount of activity to be expected in a given season in comparison to the average activity expected throughout the year. A cyclical indicator is a ratio of economic activity during one period, perhaps one year, to economic activity in past periods or years. The use of cyclical indicators has become so prevalent that they are usually called, simply, *business indicators*.

Using Business Indicators. The government as well as many private sources, collects great volumes of data on literally thousands of facets of economic activity — things such as volume of production, lineage of help-wanted advertising, unemployment figures, inventory backlogs, building permits, and so on. Over time, some of these facets have revealed unique and distinctive relationships to the overall economy. These relationships take a variety of forms. Sometimes the individual activity will tend to precede the movement of the overall economy and can therefore be used as a *leading indicator*. Other times the individual facet tends to move behind the overall economy, thus forming a *lagging indicator*. Leading indicators are the most desired, and the government publishes regular reports of them. The Commerce Department even compiles an index of nine such factors: stock prices, consumer installment debt, average workweek, new durable goods orders, plant and equipment orders, ratio of price to unit labor costs, industrial material prices, building permits, and initial claims for unemployment insurance. By studying these various indexes, firms can often anticipate changes in market activity. For instance, the recession of 1974–75 was forewarned by the tremendous buildup of manufacturers' inventories during the 1972–73 period. Whereas activity during 1973 seemed very brisk, much of it was artificial, in that it was going into the manufacturers' inventories as a hedge against inflation and not into final sales. The 1974–75 period saw a slowdown in manufacturing as businesses sold off their inventories.

Factors Used in the Assignment of Sales Territories

As noted earlier, one of the main applications of sales estimates and forecasts is development of sales quotas and assignment of sales territories. Hence, one of the main activities of many marketing research departments is assisting in the development of these sales territories. The objective of the assignment of the territories is, obviously, to equalize the load among salespeople, while providing sales goals and quotas that are fair to both the company and the individual salesperson. Although this may seem like a simple task, it should be realized that, once again, there are a host of interconnected factors, all of which must be considered. The factors listed here illustrate their diversity, but it should be realized that this list is *only* illustrative and not exhaustive.

- *Dollar Sales Volume.* The most obvious breakdown of sales territories is by dollar sales volume. A company wants its salespersons to operate in areas of approximately equal sales potential, so that commissions resulting from sales will be roughly equal. Yet, in addition to total dolar volume, care must also be given to balancing the number of sales; it would be highly inequitable to give one salesperson two huge accounts, from which she could earn a handsome income with only two calls a week, whereas another salesperson might have to call on two hundred small accounts to make the same salary.

- *Geography.* Another factor to be considered is geography. The ideal is to create contiguous territories of approximately equal size. Discrepancy in size frequently creates friction between the "rural" sales force and the "urban" sales force. The salesperson calling upon small accounts in scattered towns may spend much of his "selling time" driving between accounts and may be on the road virtually every night of the week. On the other hand, his counterpart in a large city, in addition to having the advantage of concentrated territories, may be home for supper every night. Many people have the idea that corporate selling involves a great deal of traveling. Of course, some selling positions do involve travel away from home, but much business selling is done in concentrated territories within a few minutes driving time of one another. For instance, Armour-Dial, which manufactures Armour meats and the Dial line of soaps and other cosmetic products, has six sales territories *within* the city of Atlanta.

•   *The Product Line*. In some firms, the emphasis is upon assigning territories by product. One salesperson will have exclusive responsibility for only one of the product lines his company makes, and if the customer wants a different product from the same company, a different salesperson will be called in. IBM, for example, has some salespeople that sell nothing but typewriters, others that sell nothing but small business computers, and others that sell nothing but the large computers. The advantage of this method is that the salesperson becomes quite knowledgeable within the area of her specialty.

•   *The Customer*. In yet other firms, the assignment of selling responsibility will be done on the basis of customers, and the salesperson will have selling responsibility for every product in the company catalog. The advantage of this system is that the salesperson develops greater rapport through the intensity of his association with the customer. The company may also save on selling expenses, in that only one salesperson, rather than several, will call upon the customer.

•   *The Competition*. Still other factors that must be considered are the nature of the competition, the market potential, and the sales potential. The competitive strategy of the firm will have a bearing upon how the territories are staffed and assigned. If the market and sales potential are believed to be high, a very intensive selling effort may be chosen, with each salesperson having only a small number of accounts. On the other hand, if the potential is considered to be low, then the selling effort may be minimized.

The purpose of reviewing these factors has been to illustrate the complexity of the problem of the assignment of selling territories. To divide the territories by a single factor, such as total sales dollar or total traveling time, would be relatively simple. However, to divide the territories by total sales dollar, while simultaneously dividing them by travel time, by the number of accounts, by product line, and by customer, can become an enormous task for the research department. And since the efforts and the pay of the sales force are dependent upon the equity of these divisions, any inequities, real or imaginary, are sure to be speedily brought to the attention of the supervisors. As with so many types of business analysis, the mathematics of the analysis are not terribly sophisticated. But what is lacking in mathematical sophistication is more than offset by the *complexity* caused by the multitude of factors impinging upon the situation and by the *importance* of these factors: business decisions are not made lightly, because frighteningly large amounts of money are often at stake.

Sales Analysis

One vital element of any good sales management program will be a comprehensive program of sales analysis. Sales analysis means literally just that: *who* bought *how much* of *what* for *how much, where, when,* and *who* sold it? In sales analysis, the company tries to break its sales down by customer (what are the demographics of the customers?), by product (what items are the best sellers? the worst?), by quantity (who are the big customers?), by price (how sensitive is the product to price competition and price-related dealing?), by area (where is the corporate strength concentrated?), and by salesperson (who are the best performers and why? the worst performers and why?).

Although this may seem like a mammoth task, it is actually easier to accomplish than one might think. For one thing, most of the data that will be desired have already been collected and are available for processing. All the information discussed above is contained on the order invoice: "customer name," "customer address," "date," "product," "quantity," "price," "terms," and "salesperson." All that remains to be done is to organize this bulk of data into a source of management information. This organization, too, can be easily accomplished, especially if the information is already being coded into computer-readable form as a part of the accounting and inventory systems. In this analysis process, data that were generated as a normal by-product of the selling operation are reviewed from a management perspective. This review is often referred to as a management information system. Although it would be possible to perform such an analysis on any type of business, at any time, management information systems usually involve the computer, the use of which generally and certainly historically has implied a firm of some size and sophistication. These systems involve the computer because they are most easily developed in firms that already have most of their records computerized. If sales data are being coded into machine-readable format as a normal part of the accounting procedures, to glean the required management information from the records is quite simple.

The impetus to install a management information system comes from the nature of profit contributions existing in most markets. The pattern for most companies is a very skewed sales distribution: in other words, some customers buy a great deal and others very little; likewise, some products sell very well, and others sell very poorly. In fact, many marketing books summarize this relationship in what is known as the "20–80 rule," which says that for most products, approximately 20 percent of the customers will provide 80 percent of the sales and profits. Given this kind of distribution, it is imperative that management isolate and identify these top performers. These, whether they be products, customers, territories, or salespersons, represent the heart of any company's business, and their health and cultivation should be the primary focus of management concern.

It should be added that most sales analysis is structured around what information is available — not necessarily what is desired. Sales analysis may take its cue from the information collected as standard procedure on the sales invoice or from the various standardized data sources, such as Nielsen retail sales figures, SAMI (Sales Areas — Marketing Incorporated) warehouse sales figures, the purchase series data available from the consumer panels, and, of course, the *very* standardized data available in the various government publications. Many companies organize their product analysis along the lines of the S.I.C. (Standard Industrial Classification) system used by the federal government in its collection of production and sales statistics. Likewise, many geographic planning decisions must be made with the sometimes unwieldy "county" designation, since many federal statistics on selling and trading areas are collected by counties (counties are used because, unlike city or SMSA (Standard Metropolitan Statistical Area) delineations, counties cover *all* the land area without overlap).

Distribution, or Profit, Analysis

One piece of sales information that is desired by the company is not available from the sales invoice: namely, the profit of the sale. Although the selling price will be prominently displayed, the profit, especially the true profit, is much harder to determine.

Use of the term *true profit* underscores the fact that the real profit a firm makes upon a sale is not the simple difference between buying price and selling price, that is, the product markup. The true profit is the amount of profit after *all* the costs have been taken from the selling price. These include not only the cost of the merchandise (the buying price, or cost of goods) but also the costs of selling, handling, shipping, warehousing, returns, and adjustments, as well as allocations for corporate overhead. In short, everything involved in selling the product to the customer is included. The usual name for determination of true profits is *distribution analysis.*

Because of the tremendous difficulty of performing it, distribution analysis has been underutilized as a management tool. However, as companies have become larger and as more sophisticated mathematical techniques and computational tools have become available, an increasing number of firms have turned to distribution analysis in an effort to improve the efficiency of their operations. For instance, distribution analysis may show that many of the products carried in the product line are simply not making any money. They are indeed being sold at prices above their costs of production, but when the entire distribution costs are added, the items are actually losing money. In a classic case, the Nicholson File Company recently dropped *90 percent* of its product line and achieved an increase in both sales and profits!

A word of caution: distribution analysis does not work for all firms. It works best when the direct costs of production represent a large percentage of the selling price. Conversely, as the percentage of indirect costs (overhead) becomes larger, distribution analysis becomes progressively more difficult to perform. For industries and products in which indirect costs are extremely high, such as transportation or heavy industry, distribution analysis may be virtually impossible. For instance, how would you figure the profit margin on a single airline ticket? Some of the costs are direct, such as the fuel, the food, the pilots, and so forth, but how do you allocate the cost of the plane or the cost of the airport terminal? The obvious answer is to take the total value of these various indirect costs (or joint costs, or overhead costs) and to divide that figure by the total number of passengers that plane or facility is expected to handle. The only problem here is that this approach leaves unanswered the question of the number of passengers expected. The price of a given airline seat is based not upon the costs associated with that passenger, but rather on the basis of an estimate of all the passengers that are expected. High indirect costs are the reason why many industries, such as transportation, steel, chemicals, and so forth, will sometimes sell at very low margins: they are willing to take any business, just as long as it helps to pay for the overhead.

Sales Estimation and Sales Forecasting • 383

Location Analysis: A Special Research Need of Retailers

Thus far this chapter has proceeded from the viewpoint of a manufacturer attempting to estimate the sales of a given product. A conceptually similar, although mechanically different, situation is faced by the retailer who attempts to estimate the probable sales for a given retail location. The estimation of such sales has given rise to a slightly different kind of forecasting known as *location analysis.*

Location analysis is a hybrid of marketing and real estate that concerns itself with the investigation of various sites (both present and future) and with a determination of the probable profitabilities of those locations. Accordingly, a site investigation will include not only such marketing factors as population density, traffic counts, and zoning restrictions but also real estate factors, such as site availability and cost.

As always, there are also a host of qualitative factors to consider. One such factor would be the *competition.* Someone opening a Chinese restaurant in a town of fifty thousand would not want to be located next door to another Chinese restaurant; the town is too small to support two restaurants so close together. And yet that is just what happened in Athens, Georgia, when two Chinese restaurants (there were two others in town already) opened within a block of each other. Of course, this duplication was probably not deliberate; very likely the two owners signed leases, both unaware that the other was moving into the next block. Perhaps the situation illustrates a case of insufficient market research: had the owners of the restaurants been more thorough in their investigations, they might have avoided this problem.

In other cases, however, a business will welcome its competitors because they strengthen the trading area. When the first shopping malls were built, they usually contained only one large department store, because the department stores were wary of sharing their business with competitors. Yet, over time, the department stores realized from experience that malls could draw many more customers if several department stores were located in each. Thus, shopping malls being constructed today usually feature at least two and often three or more large department stores.

Another factor to be considered is the *traffic count.* Generally, a high traffic count is considered good, but there are cases in which the traffic count is so fierce that it actually blocks potential customers. Then, too, traffic poses a parking problem. Stores that require quick access and parking within a close proximity, such as grocery stores, drug stores, and liquor stores, are therefore usually located in shopping centers, whereas stores that are more suited to browsing, such as fashion and craft shops, are located in either shopping malls or downtown shopping districts.

Subjective evaluations must also be made of the neighborhood and the relationship between its image and the image the store is trying to present. Furthermore, it must be remembered that the establishment of a store location is usually a proposition of at least twenty years, and, accordingly, expectations of the direction and character of neighborhood change must be considered.

Summary

This chapter has reviewed some of the major problems and techniques in sales estimation and sales forecasting. The responsibility for these estimates is usually assigned to the marketing research department and often constitutes the bulk of its effort. Sales estimation is an area of great importance to the firm because of the tremendous number of operating plans directly determined by the level of the estimates. Furthermore, the calculation of these estimates continues to grow both in importance and in difficulty as the scope of business activities widens and the pace of business life accelerates.

Three techniques for the development of sales forecasts are subjective techniques, market surveys, and objective extrapolation. *Subjective techniques*, which are essentially guesses, are often provided by company executives, as well as by the company sales force. The use of *market surveys* usually begins with consumer concept testing and may continue through full-scale market tests. *Objective extrapolation* involves the use of previous sales data for the forecast of future sales. The use of scatter diagrams, shortcut formulas, and linear regression time series analysis, as well as the use of seasonal and cyclical indicators, have been discussed as methods of producing estimates through objective extrapolation.

The assignment of sales territories is a critical subject. Setting sales quotas is a very delicate and sensitive issue to the sales staff, and many factors, both quantitative and qualitative, must be figured into their calculation.

Sales analysis involves study of the sales records to determine what product is sold, where, when, to whom, at what price, by whom, and in what quantities. The objective of sales analysis is to isolate and identify those areas of corporate strength that can be emphasized and those areas of corporate weakness that can be either improved or discarded.

Distribution analysis is an extension of sales analysis in which the objective is to determine the profitability of a given sale. This task is a very difficult one, in which all the costs involved in the manufacture, sale, distribution, and servicing of an account are computed to find the true profit represented in the sale. Although never easy, distribution analysis becomes progressively more difficult as the proportion of indirect costs involved in the selling of an item increases.

Location analysis represents an extension of the concepts of sales forecasting from a single product to a retail location. Location analysis is a hybrid between marketing analysis and real estate, as both the sales potential and the real estate costs must be considered.

Questions for Discussion

1. Why is sales estimation growing more important to both the individual firm and the economy?

2. Despite new sophisticated tools and techniques, sales estimation and forecasting are becoming progressively more difficult. Why?

3. What are the three techniques of sales forecasting discussed in this chapter?

4. Why is the use of the sales force to produce the sales forecast sometimes risky?

5. Given the following sales data:

Year	Sales
1974	$3,000
1975	$4,000
1976	$6,000
1977	$6,000

find the estimate for sales in 1978 by the technique of least-squares regression.

6. What is the major assumption in objective extrapolation? What dangers are present in that assumption? Discuss that assumption in relation to the estimate of 1978 sales produced in problem 5.

7. What are the components of time series? Discuss.

8. Discuss, compare, and contrast distribution analysis and sales analysis. Under what industry and product conditions is distribution analysis especially difficult?

9. What are leading indicators? Discuss their use.

10. What is the difference between location analysis and sales analysis? What is the difference between location analysis and real estate? Under what conditions can a location be less good than it seems?

Chapter 17

The Future of Marketing Research

THE PURPOSE OF THIS CHAPTER is to examine the nature of present trends in the marketing research industry and to speculate upon developments that the industry may be experiencing within the near future.

Marketing Research Is Big Business

Marketing research has been growing both in dollar volume and in the amount of actual utilization since its formal inception in 1911 by the Curtis Publishing Company. With the development of the computer and other related tools of data analysis, its growth has been even stronger. In 1976 the research revenue of the twenty largest research firms in the country was approximately $420 million, and total research efforts of all firms (including in-house work) are believed to earn well over a billion dollars a year. Market research is usually thought of as an informational adjunct to an established or prospective business, but, as you can see from these figures, marketing research is big business itself!

Why Marketing Research Is Sure to Grow

Not only is marketing research a large and important activity presently, it is sure to grow even larger over the foreseeable future. There are several reasons why market research utilization seems certain to increase, primarily the increased size of businesses and the growing sophistication of research.

Larger Businesses

One of the clear trends of business development over the past century is the move toward larger and larger operating units. This trend has become extremely pronounced as the industrialized nations of the world have moved toward national and even international markets.[1] Everywhere, the move is toward large, standardized operating units. A person could travel across the country in a car rented from Hertz, stay in Holiday Inns, eat at McDonald's (or Burger King, or Pizza Hut, or Kentucky Fried Chicken), buy shirts at Sears, fill up with Exxon, watch Johnnie Carson before bed while drinking Cokes, before brushing with Crest and retiring on Serta mattresses. This large scale of operation forces an increased utilization of marketing research, for several reasons.

COST EFFECTIVENESS

One of the major reasons for increased use of marketing research is the large scale of modern corporate operations, which makes the research effort justifiable from a cost/benefit standpoint. For instance, if you were the owner of a small, local drug store, it probably would not be cost effective for you to perform an exhaustive study of store and shelf layout. The cost of performing the survey, which would probably increase sales by only a few percent, could not be repaid from the sales of a single, small store. However, such a study could easily be repaid if it could increase the sales by a few percent in each of dozens of stores. Because of the enormous scale of modern business, research efforts that produce increases of only a fraction of a percent are cost justifiable, and as the scale and scope of business continue to grow, the volume of research is certain to grow right along with them.

INFORMATION FLOW

As the size of any organization grows, the ability of a single person, or even a single group of persons, to effectively manage it becomes jeopardized. The decision makers are separated from the producers, the producers from the distributors, the salespeople from the distribu-

---

[1] Of the 1976 revenue of the A. C. Nielsen Company, 45 percent ($78.4 million) came from research conducted outside the United States.

tors, and the customers from everybody! All these people cannot possibly keep in touch with one another personally. Hence, the organization must synchronize its operations through information flows. For instance, information is needed by product designers on consumer needs and desires, and therefore market surveys and product tests are conducted. The *results* of these studies are communicated to designers and decision makers, who, on the strength of those results and those results alone (they themselves will attempt no survey work), make their decisions. Likewise, the production department schedules its efforts around sales trends and sales forecasts and the advertising department evaluates campaign and media strategy around various measures of advertising effectiveness. Because of the size of the enterprise, no individual can secure all the information: it is necessary to rely upon information flows from other units. Generally speaking, most of these information flows will involve some type of marketing research, either internal or external.

LONGER LEAD TIME REQUIRED

The longer lead time caused by the enlarged scale of production means that the value of research information is greater than in the past. It also means that the accuracy of the information is more critical; hence, more research time and effort are invested, to ensure that decisions are based upon the best, most accurate information available.

Increasing Sophistication

The use of computers by market researchers is a comparatively recent development. For many years, there was a feeling of mistrust toward marketing research and its tools: marketing research, it was reasoned, was nothing but fancy mumbo jumbo using computers to produce a lot of funny looking numbers, but very little else. Corporate personnel from the president to the salesperson to the janitor did not understand and did not trust researchers or their findings. But that was twenty years ago. Today most companies are quite comfortable with the use of the computer and marketing research. They have seen it in operation, they understand it, they know how and why it works, and, most importantly, they know that it *does* work. As this sophistication grows — and it continues to grow, as each group of new employees is more receptive than the preceding one toward sophisticated research, because of increased emphasis upon such research at the college level — then the use of marketing research will continue to grow also.

Overall Trends in Market Research

More Realistic Goals

One change in the nature of the research effort has been toward a smaller, more definite, more modest analysis. When the computer, along with newly devised mathematical techniques, first came onto the business scene twenty years ago, analysts envisioned these techniques as grand and almost omnipotent. There was talk of total corporate integration and management resource optimization. Entire companies would be cybernetically linked into synergistic systems that would provide for logistical and informational optimization. Well, so much for the jargon of the sixties. The buzz-words flew thick and fast in the early days of the computers and the newly developed management research, but today both buyers and sellers are more modest in their claims and in their objectives. Technical sophistication continues to grow, but the promises are more realistic. Research proceeds more often on a case-by-case basis, and researchers, rather than claiming to know everything about everything, have become more specialized, claiming real expertise in only a small section of the overall research spectrum.

Splintering

The changes in research and in the direction of research appear to be but another manifestation of the splintering process that seems to be taking place in many areas of our society. For instance, *Life* and *Look* magazines were founded and flourished for twenty to thirty years, and then the magazine market splintered. More magazines, and more different magazines, are being sold, but the "consensus" magazine no longer exists. Likewise, there is no consensus technique in marketing research. From the mere handful of techniques available just twenty years ago, literally scores of marketing research techniques have been developed.

By the same token, attitudes toward quantitative and technological innovation have also splintered, just as they have done throughout society as a whole. Twenty years ago, most Americans were solidly behind technology: rockets, jets, cars, nuclear power, household gadgets — the more the better. Whereas some Americans continue to favor technology, a growing group says that technology has gone too far; many even take the drastic action of forsaking such conventional technological items as televisions and dishwashers and elect to go "back to the land." Likewise, marketing research has seen a division of opinion over the value of mathematical sophistication. In the early days of market research, all developments in methodological and computational analysis were hailed as steps of progress for a growing discipline. Today, however, many people question some of the more sophisticated techniques and advocate a simpler treatment. As some segments of society are buying microwave ovens and videodisc recorders, while other segments strive to get back to the land, in marketing some groups are pushing mathematical sophistication to mind-boggling lengths, and others intentionally return to older, more simple forms of analysis.

REASONS FOR INCREASED SOPHISTICATION

The reasons for the use of increasingly sophisticated techniques are twofold. First, the techniques seem to be providing answers to pressing questions, and secondly, and probably more importantly, it is now possible to compute these answers very easily. A bit more elaboration on each of these points is in order.

In pondering such techniques as multiple discriminant analysis or canonical analysis, and the tremendous amount of mathematical sophistication behind them, the first question that enters the mind is, "Why?" Why is such an unwieldy piece of mathematics necessary? These various techniques that seem so irrelevant and obscure are actually the mathematical response to some very relevant and obvious questions. In the course of this book (and perhaps in some basic statistics book), you may have encountered some of these techniques in their more simple, single-variate forms. Most of the more sophisticated techniques are but an attempt to answer these same types of questions in their more realistic, multivariate forms. That is, they attempt to answer these questions in the real-world environment where many independent (predictor) variables have a simultaneous effect upon both the dependent (criterion) variable of interest and each other. Listed here are some of the more common techniques and their objectives (the answers they give, the questions they answer).

• *Regression analysis* is used to describe the nature of a relationship and to make predictions. Simple regression has one predictor variable predicting one criterion variable, whereas multiple regression has two or more independent variables predicting one dependent variable.

• *Correlation analysis* measures the amount of association between variables. Simple correlation measures the association between one variable and another. Multiple correlation measures the association between one variable and a set of others.

- *Canonical analysis* measures the association between two sets of variables, multiple variables associated with multiple variables.

- *Chi-square* looks for significant differences between cell values in a cross-classification table.

- The *Z test* and *t test* look for significant differences between the averages of two groups.

- *Analysis of variance* looks for significant differences between the averages of two or more groups.

- *Discriminant analysis* attempts to discriminate among members of a group. It answers the question which variables are the best discriminators — separators — among the various members of the group.

- *Factor analysis* is a technique that tries to take a large number of variables and break them into a smaller group of factors. The factors may represent the combined "influence" of several discrete variables.

- *Cluster analysis* is a technique that uses the scores of the group members on several variables to break the group into smaller subgroups or clusters (analogous to market segments).

- *Conjoint analysis*, often referred to as *trade-off analysis*, measures the relative importance of the various product benefits or attributes and tries to determine how much of one attribute must be given in exchange for an increase in one of the others.

- *Multidimensional scaling* maps the perceptions of subjects on various items or attributes in multidimensional space. It can show how one brand is perceived in relation to the others.

- *Stochastic techniques* are a fancy name for probabilities. They are generally used to predict brand share or repeat purchasing behavior, subject to some probability model.

This list of techniques and their uses is meant to be illustrative, not exhaustive. There are more techniques than those listed above, and most of the techniques have more uses than the ones listed. As a matter of fact, almost any single technique can be used to answer a variety of questions, since most of the techniques have a common source: they all work in some manner with the variation or scatter observed among the variables. Most of them have a common basis in the theory of matrix algebra and are thereby conceptually interrelated.

As the list shows, the questions the techniques answer are the very questions that are of direct relevance to marketers. Techniques, such as conjoint analysis, that can show which product attributes are viewed as most important and how much of one attribute can be traded against how much of another are of obvious value to a product designer or a promotion strategist.

However, these techniques are extremely difficult to understand conceptually and almost impossible to compute by hand. Hence, even though they have been known to mathematicians for many years, they had for a long time little popularity and even less utilization. Real utilization would wait until the development of the computer and the canned program. With these two items, anybody who could keypunch could use the most sophisticated techniques available, and that is exactly what has happened. With large-scale computers and the canned computer libraries, it is as easy to run sophisticated analyses as it is to run averages and standard deviations. The wide use of these techniques is directly attributable to the simple fact that it is so easy to use them. It is as if you could become a musician by turning on the radio: nowadays, you can become an analyst by calling up a series of computer programs.

Reasons for Decreased Sophistication

Despite the ease with which this sophisticated analysis can be utilized, many researchers decline to take advantage of it — and for some very good reasons, as we shall see.

Surely the main reason why some researchers validly shy away from the more advanced techniques is that such techniques are simply too sophisticated; they are too much of a good thing. The problem is that researchers can get so bogged down in minutia that they miss the important factors, in the old "can't see the forest for the trees" syndrome. To be slightly more specific, the use of extremely complicated techniques is like looking at a picture in a newspaper with a magnifying glass. You want to see more detail, but instead all you see is dots. In other words, there is a certain level of detail that newspaper pictures can convey, and attempts to carry your investigation beyond that level are fruitless.

Likewise, when we investigate consumer behavior, there is a certain level of precision beyond which we cannot carry the analysis. The complex techniques are trying to milk a great deal of precision and certainty from a situation that by its very nature is quite imprecise and very uncertain. Many researchers feel that almost any analysis beyond the most superficial is too much, that the results should be reported in rather vague generalities because, in truth, vague generalizations are about all we really can say about consumers and their behavior. In fact, despite the efforts of the researchers, sometimes the output of a very sophisticated analysis is nothing more than a loose generality. During one presentation, for example, a very prominent researcher detailed the results of an elaborate cluster analysis his company had performed on several hundred consumers. Cluster analysis is a natural for marketing research, in that it groups consumers into homogeneous clusters highly analogous to market segments. Researchers can cluster consumers to discover which types of consumers buy which products, what media schedules they prefer, and so forth. At any rate, his findings showed five distinct clusters. Unfortunately, the clusters were nothing more than five obvious white, Anglo-Saxon, Protestant stereotypes. The five types were young blue-collar, young white-collar, older blue-collar, older white-collar, and retired limited income. In other words, a tremendous amount of statistical firepower was expended to discover what were already well-known stereotypes.

Another problem along the same lines is that most research is strategic in nature, not operational. That is, the researcher can say that from the perspective of the research done at that time, it seems that such and such would be a good strategy. However, this approach ignores two very important factors. For one, it does not take into account the *dynamic* nature of the marketplace. A person has one opinion this week, but he may have a different opinion next week. Thus, to spend great amounts of time and money to make a sophisticated analysis of consumers at one point in time may be senseless, in that within a few weeks the situation (and all those numbers) will have changed.

Another thing the analysis ignores is the element of *execution*. In the real world, what counts most is execution, not strategy. For instance, suppose that after meticulous research involving a well-executed experimental design, it was determined that the company's products were price elastic and that a price cut of 10 percent would increase company *profits* by 5 percent. Even assuming that the results of the small experimental survey could in fact be generalized to the entire marketing environment, such a small survey could not account for the possible effects of competition and execution. The firm might discover that a nationwide price cut was immediately matched by all competitors, setting off a price war that drove profits down to almost nothing (the price cuts in the small number of stores used in the experiment were not matched, probably not even noticed). Likewise, the package that looked good in testing may meet with dismal success if competitors run a vigorous advertising campaign or a heavy coupon blitz, or if distribution is spotty and the product is not available on the shelf. In short, the marketplace is full of changes and uncertainties that no amount of research can overcome. As one writer on the subject has sagely advised: "If sophisticated calculations are necessary to justify an investment, don't do it!" [2]

There are yet other reasons why sophisticated analysis is often inadvisable. For one, such analysis is very powerful, and as such it should be used only by those qualified to use it. In this respect it is like laser brain surgery: just because the technique is wonderful does not mean that everyone should try it; in the wrong hands, or in unskilled hands, the results would be disastrous. In the same manner, many of these newly developed research techniques are actually quite difficult to use properly. Of course, with canned computer programs, anybody can get answers from them, but to use them properly the researcher has to know what she is doing. There are many assumptions and requirements regarding the way in which the data are collected and entered that can affect the results. In addition, the output from many of these more sophisticated techniques requires a great deal of subjective analysis before it can be understood. Used properly, the techniques can be excellent diagnostic tools. Unfortunately, the number of people who are truly qualified to use them is still relatively small, and their use by the unqualified can lead to trouble.

Yet another problem with the canned programs and the esoteric forms of analysis they bring is that their use tends to reverse the proper sequence of the research process. In the preferred sequence, research starts with an idea or hypothesis. On the basis of that idea, certain data are gathered and certain analysis is performed. From the results of the analysis, a conclusion is drawn about the original idea.

The existence of these marvelous programs tends to reverse the process by encouraging researchers to perform the analysis first and then think of the hypotheses second. When the analysis was difficult to perform, the researcher would be very selective about which variables he wished to analyze and which techniques he would employ. Nowadays, however, it is just as easy to compute the correlations among forty variables as it is to compute those between two variables. Therefore, the researcher is tempted to use the computer and the canned programs like a gigantic sand sifter at the beach. He throws in all the data, turns on the programs, and lets the programs find his answers. The problem with this approach is that the results of such analysis are often quite nonsensical. They are fun and sometimes enlightening to look at, but they may not fit into a workable marketing strategy. *If there is a single*

[2] Robert Heller, *The Great Executive Dream* (New York: Dell Publishing Co., 1972), p. 345.

problem upon which most research failures can be blamed, it would be the failure to define the problem and the objectives adequately at the beginning of the research effort. The existence of canned programs that make formerly exhaustive analysis easy only adds to the temptation to hurry over these first steps in a haste to begin the analysis of the data.

Still another problem has to do with the implications of the more advanced types of segmentation research. When research first began to be used, marketers were aiming at the mass market. Hence, techniques such as simple averages and percentage breakdowns could be used to develop the best product for the "average" consumer.

As we moved into the sixties and seventies, marketing strategy moved from a mass appeal to a more selective appeal. The emphasis today is on market segmentation, on the cultivation of a product variation that more exactly suits the needs and tastes of a smaller target market. Therefore, many of the techniques that have become popular over the last decade are precisely suited to solving the problems inherent in the isolation and identification of target markets. These techniques include cluster analysis, discriminant analysis, multidimensional scaling, and conjoint analysis, to mention just a few examples.

However, as the splintering of the market continues to accelerate, will new and more powerful techniques continue to be developed? Possibly, but maybe not. In the process of continuing to splinter the market in a desire to produce "something for everyone," we are elevating the status and the pertinency of "mother-in-law" research, which is a name for the idea that if your mother-in-law likes some product, then there are many others who would like it, too. When dealing with a country as large as the United States, even a small percentage of the market may add up to a large number of customers; hence, many variations of a product can be produced. One way to determine those variations is through various types of sophisticated numerical analysis, but an easier and faster way is through mother-in-law research.

A final drawback to the use of sophisticated research is that it can create a variety of legal headaches. In other words, if you are using numerical calculations as a basis for making some decision, then you need to be very sure that those numbers are correct, because if they are not, you may find yourself sued. (If you did not utilize research techniques at all, but instead relied upon judgment, probably you would not be sued for a judgmental error, although you might get sued for having failed to consult such techniques at all.)

In our legalistic society, researchers are finding themselves sued with increasing regularity for their findings. Magazine publishers have been taking readership survey companies to court over readership studies showing declines in their magazine readerships. And one really can't blame the magazines: advertisers are highly influenced by the results of these studies, and a reported decline in readership can easily cost millions of dollars of advertising for a large-circulation magazine. That is a great deal of money to lose just because the survey company made a mistake.

Along the same lines, one researcher reports having to go to court on more than one occasion to justify the use of a certain statistical test.[3] From the standpoint of the marketing manager operating in the dynamic and competitive marketplace, such distinctions are of no operational importance. If, however, two products are competing on a contract and, upon the basis of the tests, one of the products is accepted and one is rejected, then an improperly done test might mean a world of difference.

As a consequence, some researchers are beginning to shy away from the more involved types of analysis in situations that look touchy, choosing instead to perform very simple analyses with which no one can argue. As mentioned before, the more complicated the technique, the more assumptions will be involved, and the more subjective the interpretation will be. In such situations it is easy to get honest differences of opinion (even from trained experts) on what the proper method of analysis should actually be.

Future Developments and Predictions

Survey Research

Personal interviewing is probably on the decline, especially door-to-door personal interviewing. That method is being beset by a variety of problems, including rapidly rising costs, decreasing effectiveness, and legal restrictions. Costs have been rising for several reasons, including application of minimum wage guidelines and a depletion of the primary pool of interviewing talent, married women with school-age children, as many of these women return to work full-time. Costs, as well as effectiveness, have been adversely affected by the increasing difficulty researchers face in trying to contact respondents. Larger numbers of working women, larger numbers of broken households, more active lifestyles that embrace more out-of-the-home dining and entertainment,

---

[3] B. Venkatesh, "Unthinking Data Interpretation Can Destroy Value of Research," *Marketing News* 11, no. 15 (27 January 1978): 9.

along with a population that is moving and relocating constantly, make the job of contacting respondents more difficult and costly. And when prospective respondents are finally contacted, the increasing reluctance of many of them to submit to interviews makes the task more difficult and more costly still.

In comparison, and partly in response, the use of telephone interviewing is on the increase. Respondents generally have less fear about talking on the phone, and advances in interviewing techniques have made longer telephone interviews more feasible. In addition, telephone charges for many types of service have actually decreased in some situations, making the use of the telephone a relative bargain, especially in these times of rising travel costs. One problem faced by both telephone and personal interviewing is the possibility of legal restrictions upon these techniques. What many consumers feel is undue harassment from both legitimate survey researchers and those who are actually trying to sell under the guise of taking surveys has led to pressure to ban most types of direct in-home solicitation. Although marketing researchers are lobbying vigorously in Washington and other places to ensure that legitimate survey research does not get banned along with the various selling tactics, from the standpoint of the home-owner the interruption and irritation of a survey is probably virtually indistinguishable from that of the salesperson.[4]

Those who depend primarily upon mail surveys are also worried. Rising postage costs, as well as possible bans on this type of direct solicitation, make the future somewhat cloudy.

One area that seems to be holding the promise of tremendous growth and potential is interactive surveying. Such systems are now being actively installed; there is, for example, a system called Qube in Columbus, Ohio, and one called Viewdata in England. These interactive systems work in conjunction with an advanced cable TV system. The "viewer" is furnished with a small keyboard much like a touch-tone phone, which is hooked up to his television. With this system the viewer can select from a wide variety of programs, and even news editing and news selection possibilities are envisioned (for instance, someone could request just state news, or just Washington news, or just news concerning events in the Middle East).

Marketers are envisioning a series of exciting possibilities for these interactive systems. Live action catalogs would be possible: the viewer could request certain items from certain catalogs to be displayed on the

---

[4] In fact, the survey is probably more irritating. After all, people may want to buy the salesperson's wares; many women eagerly await the Avon saleswoman, for example. Few, if any, welcome and await the survey taker.

screen and could even order the merchandise and be billed for it through the proper sequence of commands. Surveyors likewise relish the possibility of instantaneous surveys. Since this system will probably be charged on a per-program cost basis, survey companies could offer to provide the next program free if viewers would agree to watch a certain commercial, or respond to a series of questions, or even respond to questions about a commercial. The possibilities are endless, and the technology for implementation is already available; it is only a matter of getting the cost down low enough to prompt viewer acceptance. If the past record of cost reductions in the electronics industry are a valid guide for this new electronic technology, then we should see significant cost reductions in the very near future. Many experts predict that such systems will be as common in homes ten years from now as color TV is today.

Physiographic Research

Another area that seems to be aided in part by newly developed technology is physiographic measurement. Several new devices seem quite promising. One of the most promising (or perhaps frightening) developments is the Voice Pitch Analyzer, or Truth Detector. Also known as the Psychological Stress Evaluator, the voice analyzer works like a conventional lie detector, in that it measures the amount of stress a person registers when she makes a statement. As with the lie detector, the greater the stress, the more likely that a falsehood has been told. The advantage (or perhaps disadvantage) is that the voice analyzer is totally unobtrusive. Unlike the lie detector, which must be strapped to the respondent, the voice analyzer needs only to hear what is being said. Thus, it can give a "truth reading" from a tape playback, over a telephone, from a TV set, and so forth. Based upon current developments in electronic microcircuitry, it may be possible to develop a unit no larger or more costly than a transistor radio. Although this possibility is seen as a boon to market researchers trying to get at respondents' "true" feelings, widespread use of such devices may herald a new era in human and social relations. Most marriages, business relationships, and political associations thrive on a variety of lies and half-truths. What will happen, for example, when the newsmen at a presidential news conference all have truth analyzers in their laps and begin to guffaw loudly as their meters zoom off the scale?

Other technological developments in physiographic research may deal with various types of messages the body gives off through assorted electromagnetic fields, which, although invisible to the naked eye, can nevertheless be detected with certain types of instruments. Brain wave measurement is but one of the developments in this area.

Computer-Related Advances

Most of the changes in marketing research envisioned in this section are technology-dependent, and the changes likely to come from advancing computer technology are no exception.

One probable thrust in the foreseeable future is the continuing and accelerating usage of the computer as an active business participant. This increased utilization will be especially noticeable as it affects small business: the cost of computing power has gone down so dramatically that all businesses, however small, will have the opportunity to use the computer in business operation and planning. The existence of small, affordable machines, along with canned programs to handle payroll, inventory, and tax charges, may allow small businesspersons to be as managerially sophisticated as their larger competitors. As energy costs rise, and managerial sophistication evens out, we may see a decline of the large production and shopping facilities and the rebirth of more localized production and distribution sites.

Legal and Regulatory Implications

The last area of marketing research predictions involves a variety of legal implications. Marketing research, like every other industry, is going to find itself increasingly involved in legal and regulatory matters. This increasingly legalistic environment is coming from several sources.

The main legal problem researchers will be facing over the next few years may come from the privacy-related legislation being discussed in Washington and throughout the country. In an effort to ensure more domestic privacy for the citizenry, laws are being proposed that would ban door-to-door selling, door-to-door fundraising, and door-to-door surveying. Other proposed laws would ban telephone selling and/or telephone surveying. Other laws banning mail-order selling and mail surveying have also been proposed. Though none of these laws have yet been passed, the desire for such legislation is growing.

Another aspect of the general concern for privacy is the question of information dossiers. Will marketers be allowed to collect information on individually identifiable persons, and, if so, what safeguards will ensure the protection and anonymity of the records? As more and more personal information is placed upon these files, the possibility of serious misuse increases. As the ability to transmit, exchange, and duplicate these files continues to grow with technology, the threat to the individual also grows. As Senator Sam Ervin has poignantly remarked:

> Once a vast information gathering and processing program is put to work, it will take years to undo the harm done or to trace the flow of data on an individual in order to destroy files and microfilm.
>
> Furthermore, it is my belief that while the Recording Angel drops a tear occasionally to wash out the record of our human iniquities, there is no such compassion to be found in computers. Nor is it to be found in all the new instruments for measuring man which the behavioral sciences and the New Technology hold out to us. In other words, a computer has a most remarkable memory, it never forgets anything. But it has no heart and no forgiveness.[5]

Because of the grave dangers these systems impose, it is possible that all respondent-identifiable survey efforts may be forbidden in the foreseeable future.

Another concern may increase the amount of marketing research performed. Lately we have seen an increasing number of stockholder suits against corporate management for a variety of reasons, including just plain poor management. If the number of these suits continues to increase, we may see more managers using research to justify their actions. At that point, the researcher would be employed not essentially as a researcher but as part of the legal defense effort. The researcher, rather than acting as an operational problem solver, may be functioning in the same way as a lawyer on retainer, who gives periodic advice and testifies in court cases.

Along this same line, we are going to see increasing pressure on the firms that perform survey research. If management loses money on the basis of an incorrect decision based in some manner upon a research effort, then management may sue the research company. The research company is in an especially precarious position, because there is no such thing as a perfect survey. All surveys have weaknesses, and all analysis is subject to certain assumptions. A trained researcher can always point out possible areas of weakness in any survey, though this is not to say that the critic could have done a better job. As has already happened with advertising claims, weaker research is the result, as firms attempt to hedge behind vague generalities and liberal use of probabilities: rather than recommending a certain course of action,

[5] Sam Ervin, *The Wisdom of Sam Ervin*, ed. Bill Wise (New York: Ballantine Books) , p. 63.

the research firm will instead say that a certain course of action has a 60 percent chance of success, whereas the alternative action has a 40 percent chance.

Summary

This chapter has reviewed current trends and developments in marketing research and has speculated upon the future of marketing research.

The use of market research has climbed steadily over the last few years, and the prospects for future growth look good. One of the main reasons for this growth is growth in the size of the business unit. Larger operating units encourage the use of marketing research for several reasons: the larger size makes the research more cost effective, in that the benefits of the research effort will be applied to a larger operation; the larger, more dispersed organization depends more heavily upon information and research flows in order to coordinate its operations; and, finally, larger units need longer lead times, which dictate the need for better forecasting. Another reason why the research function is growing, apart from the larger operating size, is that management is becoming more sophisticated, more trusting of the research, and more knowledgeable about its uses.

As are most fields, marketing research is experiencing a splintering, with specialization becoming the norm. Like other specialists, marketing researchers are finding themselves knowing more and more about less and less. In addition, there is an increasing polarization: some researchers are advocating the use of numerical techniques of increasing sophistication, whereas others are arguing against the use of these complicated analytical techniques.

The impetus for increased numerical sophistication comes from two sources. First, these techniques appear to be the exact mathematical answer to many of the pertinent questions of marketing. Secondly, and probably more importantly, the use of these programs has been greatly simplified in recent years by the development of computer program libraries, which eliminate the need for the user to have mathematical or programming ability.

Those arguing for the decreased use of these techniques point to several problems, such as the ability of various techniques to carry the precision of the output past the precision of the input. In addition, many of the techniques are quite sophisticated, and it is easy to misuse and misinterpret the results. Some researchers claim that emphasis upon the analysis tends to get overblown, with too much attention given to the methods and not enough to the problem definition. A final argument is the increased danger of legal action concerning the validity and interpretation of a given piece of numerical analysis.

In the foreseeable future, technology will have a major part in the reshaping of marketing research. Technological developments such as interactive interviewing, Voice Pitch Analysis, computer retrieval systems, and generally increased computer utilization at all levels of business planning seem imminent and will have major impacts on the techniques and uses of marketing research.

By the same token, human-dependent operations, such as personal door-to-door surveying, personal in-depth interviewing, and hand-calculated store audits, seem certain to decline in usage.

If there is a single element of concern and danger to the market research industry, it lies in the drive toward various kinds of legislation designed to ensure citizen privacy and respondent safety and anonymity. The field of marketing research, like medicine, law, and manufacturing, is going to see an increasing amount of time relegated to legislative, regulatory, and legalistic concerns.

Questions for Discussion

1. Why does the growth of the fast food franchises portend an increased use of marketing research by the food industry?

2. "Marketing research has splintered as a discipline." Discuss this statement. How do the trends in marketing research relate to the trends of society as a whole?

3. What are the two reasons given here for the increased use of sophisticated numerical analysis? Why is it difficult to find any researcher who is qualified in all areas of marketing research?

4. Explain the purpose of each of the following techniques and give an example of how each could be used in a marketing or sales-related application: regression analysis, correlation analysis, cluster analysis, conjoint analysis, multidimensional scaling, stochastic modeling.

5. Why did author Robert Heller say: "If sophisticated calculations are necessary to justify an investment, don't do it!"? Explain the significance of his statement to marketing.

6. What is the largest single problem with most marketing research studies? Why does the existence of the computer and sophisticated computer program libraries aggravate this problem?

7. Survey research utilizes a variety of techniques. What seem to be the probable trends in the use of personal surveys? of telephone surveys?

What is meant by interactive surveying? How will it affect marketing re-search?

8. What is Voice Pitch Analysis? How could it be used in marketing research? How do you feel personally about the use of such a device by marketers?

9. Why are marketing researchers concerned about privacy legislation? What can marketing researchers do to protect their future?

CASE 3·1

FISHER CIGARETTES (A)

Fisher Cigarettes, one of several brands made by the Dominion Tobacco Company, have experienced a 3 percent drop in market share over the past 2 years. Fishers are made from a special blend of dark tobacco that give them a taste similar to European cigarettes. Parker, Malloy and Company (P.M. and Co.), the advertising agency that handles all Dominion Tobacco's ads, uses the motto "A Strong Cigarette for a Strong Taste" when describing Fisher.

The cigarette's image has remained unchanged for the past twenty-two years. It has been generally believed by Dominion Tobacco executives that smokers of Fishers are extremely brand-loyal. Until now, market share statistics seemed to bear out this conclusion. In a recent effort to improve a deteriorating sales situation, Fisher's brand manager asked permission to switch advertising agencies. He decided to go with Boyle, Bane, and Associates (B & B), who as he knew, turned around another sinking brand of cigarettes a few years ago.

B & B wanted to conduct a research investigation in order to determine people's image of Fisher Cigarettes. The former agency used a backdrop of a fishing village, with a fisherman pulling in his boat and lighting up a Fisher afterward. Other ads focused on a ship's captain sitting alone in his cabin smoking a Fisher. Much newspaper and outdoor advertising showed only the Fisher logo (a fisherman) and the motto.

The first part of the B & B investigation included sentence completions, which were judged the easiest way to determine the cigarette's image. The results of the survey are as follows:

1. "The fisherman in the Fisher commercial is a good example of the type of man who . . ."

lives in a small town	12%
enjoys smoking	10
is lazy	6
is tough	12
smokes Fisher	11
is hardworking	24
drinks a lot	15
is a loner	5
has no education	1
is poor	4
	100%

2. "A fishing village is the type of place . . ."

I would like to visit	19%
that is picturesque	12
I would like to live in	4
that is quiet	23
I would not want to live in	11
that is dying out	3
that is boring	7
that is poor	9
where fisherman live	8
that is on the ocean	4
	100%

3. "Fisher has a _____ tar and nicotine count."

high	74%
average	26%
	100%

(Responses varied, but most fell into these two categories. None said "low." Some said "acceptable." Several respondents indicated that they "couldn't care less about tar and nicotine content.")

4. "People who smoke Fisher smoke them because . . ."

they like the strong taste	41%
they like them	24
they taste good	18
other cigarettes are too mild	10
they want to be different	5
no one will ask for one	2
	100%

5. "The type of person most likely to smoke Fisher . . ."

is an individualist	23%
likes strong cigarettes	34
is strong	13
lives in the country	12
works in a factory	8
smokes too much	4
is a man, not a woman	6
	100%

6. "The type of person who smokes Fisher has a _____ income."

high	5%
average	35
low	41
steady	19
	100%

7. "The type of person who smokes Fisher works . . ."

at an office	24%
at a factory	27
at manual labor	13
as an artist	21
is unemployed	8
outdoors	5
hard	2
	100%

8. "The type of person who smokes Fisher feels that sports are . . ."

fun to watch	28%
good exercise	22
unnecessary	38
something other people do	12
	100%

9. "Persons who smoke Fisher are most likely to engage in _____ sports."

no	55%
dangerous	5
team	12
active	4
outdoor	3
individual	19
miscellaneous	2
	100%

(Miscellaneous sports named that did not fit the categories above were chess, flying, fishing, boxing.)

10. "People who smoke Fisher are _____ sociable."

not very	71%
very	29
	100%

Questions

1. Interpret the findings of the sentence completion test.

2. Suggest other methods of obtaining the same information. Which is the best method? What problems would B & B have with the method used?

3. Set up a semantic differential scale comparing Fisher to any other brand of cigarettes.

CASE 3·2

FISHER CIGARETTES (B)

Boyle, Bane, and Associates (B & B), a large advertising firm, has recently acquired the account of Dominion Tobacco Company's Fisher Cigarettes. The brand lost 3 percent of its market share during the past 2 years, probably because of poor advertising. (See Case 3·1 for more information.)

The team of copy writers at B & B working on the new ad image for Fisher have developed two sets of ads. Each set consists of four ads, which, if successful, can be built on in the future. The ads will be run in general interest magazines such as *Time* and *Newsweek*, as well as in the more specialized *Sports Illustrated, Popular Mechanics, Field and Stream,* and so on. Extensive newspaper campaigns in major cities are also anticipated.

Question

1. Should the firm use pretesting or posttesting of the ads? Discuss the various methods of each. Which method would you recommend that B & B try?

CASE 3·3

THE AUSTIN REGIONAL SAVINGS AND LOAN CORPORATION

Louis Sullivan has just been promoted to assistant manager of the Austin Regional Savings and Loan Corporation. Sullivan has noted that the company has been losing customers steadily to neighboring banks and to other S & L branches in the city. He suspects that the changes are caused by poor service. This is one area that has been sadly neglected by the present manager, who, being near retirement age, is content to leave the situation to his successor.

Question

1. Design a Likert scale attitudinal test to measure service at the savings and loan corporation. Your test should cover such aspects as service, location, hours, interest rates, and so on.

CASE 3·4

HANRAHAN LIFE INSURANCE COMPANY

Hanrahan Life Insurance of New York is one of the Lee Yung Advertising Agency's largest clients. Recently, Jane Macdonald, director of marketing for Hanrahan, approached Yung regarding a new target market for life insurance — professional women. Macdonald informed Yung that she had seen competitors' ads directed at these women and that Hanrahan was presently formulating several packages for this new market segment. The company intended to hire several women to sell a program appealing to women. Macdonald said that she was counting on Yung to devise a clever advertising campaign to support the company's efforts.

Yung did not anticipate any problems with advertising copy to attract professional women. However, he wanted the media mix of the Hanrahan campaign to reach the maximum number of potential clients per advertising dollar spent. For this reason, he arranged a meeting with Gerry Regan, who had been assigned to the Hanrahan campaign. The following conversation took place:

> *Yung*: Gerry, you know as much about Hanrahan as I do. They've been in business 40 years — founded in Buffalo and moved the head office here to New York City twenty years ago. Now they operate in the Northeast, South, and Midwest. We've had no

trouble with the account so far, but I am concerned about this project. Since professional women are a new market for Hanrahan Life, I want to be sure we zero in on the right advertising media to reach this segment.

Regan: I know what you mean, Lee. I figure that we're aiming at upper-income women, probably with $25,000 or more household income. Jane Macdonald told me that she thinks most of these women work full-time, are married with children, and live in large cities and surrounding suburbs. The women who would be interested in life insurance are college-educated, professionals or managers earning over $20,000. Jane also mentioned that the largest number of purchasers of life insurance are between the ages of twenty-five and forty-four. The women we want to reach probably own a home worth $50,000 or more.

Yung: As you know, Gerry, Macdonald wants to go with a print media campaign. She vetoed television as being too expensive. Besides the usual local newspapers where we always place Hanrahan ads, Jane wants to try a national magazine. She can get a budget of $100,000–$150,000 for three one-time black-and-white ads in any magazine. The question is, which one?

Regan: I was speaking to the sales representative of *Time* last week. He quoted a rate of $34,300 for a one-time black-and-white full-page ad. He also said *Time* is geared toward college graduates.

Yung: I looked into *Reader's Digest* myself. It has one of the largest readerships of any magazine in North America. It charges $55,100 for one full-page black-and-white ad. If we place the Hanrahan ad in *Reader's Digest*, we will be reaching the biggest audience.

Regan: The other alternative we might consider is *Woman's Day*. Women would be more likely to read that magazine than *Time* or *Reader's Digest*. Maybe we should try the feminine approach. *Woman's Day* charges only $33,500 for a black-and-white one-page ad.

Yung: You have a copy of the Simmons Audience Report for Adult Women. Why don't you look into it and let me know?

Regan: OK, Lee. We also have the Target Group Index. I'll check them both and get back to you Monday.

Exhibit 1
1976/1977 Simmons: Average Issue Audience of Three Selected Magazines

ITEM NUMBER	DEMOGRAPHIC CHARACTERISTICS	READER'S DIGEST (000)	TIME (000)	WOMAN'S DAY (000)
1	Adult women	23,441	9,182	17,058
2	18–24 years	3,669	1,973	2,946
3	25–34 years	4,288	2,345	4,017
4	35–44 years	3,737	1,512	2,905
5	45–54 years	4,094	1,569	2,928

Exhibit 1—*Continued*

Item Number	Demographic Characteristics	Reader's Digest (000)	Time (000)	Woman's Day (000)
6	55–64 years	3,835	913	2,290
7	65 years or older	3,818	870	1,972
8	Graduated college	2,802	2,241	1,963
9	Attended college or better	6,562	4,528	5,101
10	$25,000 or more HHI[a]	3,522	2,383	2,593
11	$20,000 or more HHI	6,105	3,648	5,057
12	$15,000 or more HHI	9,992	5,079	7,987
13	$20,000 or more IEI[b]	198[c]	144[c]	162[c]
14	$15,000 or more IEI	571	447	363
15	$10,000 or more IEI	2,518	1,641	1,883
16	Professional, technical	2,049	1,496	1,575
17	Managers, administrators	687	391	508
18	Total professional/managerial	2,736	1,887	2,083
19	Metro central city	6,873	3,170	4,746
20	Metro suburban	9,908	4,395	7,281
21	Total metro area	16,781	7,565	12,027
22	Own home	17,355	6,072	12,402
23	Value $40,000+	5,697	2,946	4,262
24	Value $30,000+	9,516	4,329	7,079
25	Married	15,792	5,650	11,785
26	Children HH under 18	10,552	4,322	8,563
27	Northeast	5,332	2,593	4,656
28	Central	6,860	2,260	5,662
29	South	7,056	2,477	3,995
30	West	4,193	1,853	2,745
31	County size A	8,169	4,423	6,323
32	County size A & B	15,054	6,974	11,316
33	Employed	10,738	4,908	8,250
34	Full Time	7,603	3,556	5,947
35	Part Time	3,135	1,352	2,303

[a] HHI = household income.
[b] IEI = individual earned income.
[c] Projection relatively unstable because of small sample base — Use with caution.

Exhibit 2
Fall 1976 Target Group Index: Average Issue Audience of Three
Selected Magazines

ITEM NUMBER	DEMOGRAPHIC CHARACTERISTICS	READER'S DIGEST (000)	TIME (000)	WOMAN'S DAY (000)
1	Adult women	23,266	7,797	18,428
2	18–24 years	3,280	1,699	2,670
3	25–34 years	4,534	1,892	4,335
4	35–44 years	4,073	1,257	3,403
5	45–54 years	4,102	1,331	3,553
6	55–64 years	3,665	934	2,628
7	65 years or older	3,612	682	1,839
8	Graduated college	3,175	2,009	2,632
9	Attended college or better	7,428	3,886	6,029
10	$25,000 or more household income	2,963	1,734	2,455
11	$20,000 or more household income	5,156	2,606	4,586
12	$15,000 or more household income	9,995	4,146	8,748
13	$20,000 or more IEI[a]	62[b]	81[b]	71[b]
14	$15,000 or more IEI	288	271	378
15	$10,000 or more IEI	2,044	1,146	1,970
16	Professional, technical	2,405	1,375	2,123
17	Managers, officials, proprietors	677	359	537
18	Total professional, managerial	3,082	1,734	2,660
19	Metro central city	7,552	3,078	6,040
20	Metro suburban	9,151	3,192	7,574
21	Total metro area	16,703	6,270	13,614
22	Own home	17,741	5,419	13,947
23	Valued $50,000+	2,937	1,507	2,277
24	Valued $25,000+	11,476	4,148	9,356
25	Married	15,824	4,875	12,646
26	Children in household under 18	10,864	3,672	9,372
27	Northeast	5,852	2,262	5,362
28	Central	6,692	2,335	5,726
29	South	5,993	1,742	4,045
30	West	4,729	1,457	3,294
31	County size A	8,965	3,879	7,431
32	County size A & B	15,725	6,047	13,308
33	Employed	10,572	4,297	9,117
34	Full time	7,476	3,121	6,326
35	Part time	3,096	1,176	2,791

a IEI = individual earned income.
b Either projected number based on less than approximately 50 unweighted respondents or percent under 0.05% or index of selectivity under 0.5.

Questions

1. Calculate the cost per page per thousand circulation for each of the three magazines, using both the Target Group Index and the W. R. Simmons Report for:

a. Total adult women readership;

b. Adult women ages twenty-five to thirty-four years;

c. Adult women ages thirty-five to forty-four years;

d. Adult women who graduated college;

e. Total adult women in professional and managerial capacities. Which magazine represents the best media buy?

2. Is there any significant difference between the two sets of data calculated above? If so, what would account for it? What should the Lee Yung Advertising Agency do about it?

3. What factors are used in calculating audience measurement?

CASE 3.5

JOHN DILLON, INC.

John Dillon, Inc., is a franchised distributor of automotive parts throughout the Eastern seaboard. The dealerships purchase their stock from the parent company, J-D Manufacturing, which makes spark plugs, batteries, gaskets, fan belts, headlights, and other car parts. In addition, the outlets carry other brands of the same items, as well as tires, car paint, tools, and related products. The franchises sell to small industries that make auto repairs, such as gas stations, truck companies, taxi companies, factories, and body repair shops. Usually, the customers are businesses located nearby. Individuals may also purchase automotive parts over the counter.

The company is conducting a survey to determine where it should locate new franchises. Previous research studies indicate that sales are a function of location, the number of gas stations within the territory, and the number of car dealerships in the area. Exhibit 1 shows the results of the latest company survey.

Exhibit 1
Selected Data for John Dillon, Inc.

TERRITORY	SALES FOR 1977 (000,000)	NUMBER FRANCHISES IN TERRITORY	LOCATION OF FRANCHISES[a]	NUMBER GAS STATIONS IN TERRITORY	NUMBER CAR DEALERSHIPS IN TERRITORY
1	$12	2	S	150	12
2	14	3	M	200	16
3	10	1	O	100	8
4	18	5	M	280	22
5	16	4	M	210	19

[a] Location of franchises:
M — metropolitan area with over 500,000 population;
S — smaller city with population 100,000–500,000;
O — small town that also serves outlying rural areas.

Questions

1. Draw scatter diagrams to indicate the relationship between (a) sales and the number of franchises in the territory; (b) sales and the number of gas stations in the territory; and (c) sales and the number of car dealerships in the territory.

2. Using regression analysis, calculate the relationship between sales and the number of franchises in the territory. From the regression equation, predict what sales will be if the company adds two more franchises to territory 4.

3. Do the territories appear to have been divided equally? What factors should be taken into consideration if the salespeople at John Dillon, Inc., are on commission?

CASE 3·6

JAISON CORPORATION

The Jaison Corporation, established in 1967, is a Canadian manufacturer of men's toiletries. Originally, the company manufactured only shaving cream and soap, but soon it began to introduce some new products in the market, like shampoo and after-shave lotion.

The annual sales of the Jaison Corporation averaged about $2,500,000 in the period 1974–77 (see exhibit 1 for a record of sales). Of this amount, approximately 40 percent was represented by sales of shaving cream, 10 percent by soap, 15 percent by shampoo and 35 percent by after-shave lotion.

The growth policy of the company was implemented by introducing new products to the market, and toward the end of 1977, Charles Davis, the company's president, was planning to introduce deodorants.

On 26 January 1978, Davis received a report from the marketing research department, saying, "According to the results of the survey conducted by our department, the strong antiperspirant effect is the most important attribute the consumer looks for in a deodorant."

With this information, Davis advised Henry Smith, product research director for the company, to make up some samples of antiperspirant deodorants.

In May, Smith walked into Davis's office with two containers and said: "Here I have the results of our extensive research, and both have the same desired effect sought by the market. The experimental deodorant in container A has a better fragrance than B, but the latter one is drier than the former."

Davis then called upon David Green, the marketing research manager, and asked him to perform a product test.

On 15 November 1978, after looking at the findings of the product test, Davis called a general meeting. He invited Nancy Jones, the marketing vice-president, David Green, and Geoffrey Deneuve, the production vice-president; they were asked to analyze the advantages and disadvantages of each product in order to decide which one should be test marketed.

The meeting proceeded in the following manner:

Davis: Ladies and gentlemen, in order to implement the company's growth policy, I think this is the right time for us to introduce a new product to widen our actual product mix.

On examining the results of the research done by our marketing research department, we find that there is a good opening for a new deodorant whose main attribute is to be a strong antiperspirant.

We are gathered here today to discuss these two fine samples developed by our chemical laboratory. The results of today's meeting should help us to decide which one should be test marketed.

Green: The two samples received from the chemical laboratory were sent out for a consumer survey through a national mail consumer panel, just as we have done with our previous products. We chose Montreal, Toronto, and Vancouver as representative of the entire deodorant market of Canada.

At random, 120 regular users of deodorant were chosen as a representative sample of the whole Canadian market.

As before, we restricted ourselves to the following two product test techniques:

1. The paired comparison blind product test. Here men receiving the two deodorants were asked to use one of them for the first week and the second for the following week. The products in the paired comparison blind test were identified only by code letters.

2. The independent blind product test. In this test situation the men received just one of our deodorants to test and evaluate against the current brands they are using. In testing the two products by the independent blind product test, it was obviously necessary to employ two separate panels, one for each test product.

The results of the survey can be found in exhibits 2, 3, 4, 5, and 6 on the memo provided by our department.

Davis: But, Mr. Green, don't you think that your findings are contradictory? At one stage you suggest that deodorant *A* is preferred to *B*, whereas at the second you suggest that deodorant *B* is preferred to *A*.

Green: This is the best I could do with the limited time and budget provided for the survey. My associates are still working on the figures, and I am hoping to have the results before the end of the meeting.

Davis: Mr. Deneuve, could we have your view on the production of these deodorants?

Deneuve: Well, Mr. Davis, I think the marketing research department has provided you with all its findings. As far as the production is concerned, my best estimate is we would incur an extra fixed cost toward the purchase of an additional machine worth $80,000 in order to produce deodorant *B*.

My comparative production cost estimate is shown in exhibit 7 in the memo.

Davis: Based on Mr. Deneuve's estimates, deodorant *A* should be preferred over *B*, unless Ms. Jones has something to add.

Jones: At this level of discussion, we should agree on one of the findings of the marketing research department, that is, both deodorants *A* and *B* are definitely scoring over the existing brands.

So, my conclusion lies in the paired comparison blind product test, which says deodorant *A* should perform better than deoodorant *B* in the market.

Looking at the prices of the existing brands, I recommend that our deodorant be priced not more than $1.05.

While the meeting was in progress, one of Green's associates walked in with the analysis of the survey data and handed it over to him.

Davis: Well, ladies and gentlemen, I think we have everything we need for our decision-making process.

Exhibit 1
Breakdown of the Annual Sales

Year	Sales Volume ($)
1974	2,100,000
1975	2,400,000
1976	2,900,000
1977	2,600,000

Exhibit 2
Gross Returns from the Mail Test

	Total Number Mailed	Gross Returns	
		Number	Percent
Paired Comparison (*A* and *B*)	300	120	40
Independent (*A*)	300	123	41
Independent (*B*)	300	117	39
Total	900	360	

Exhibit 3
Age of Respondents Used in Test

Age	Number	Percent
Under 20	10	2.8
20 to 25	54	15.0
26 to 30	49	13.6
31 to 35	30	8.3
36 to 40	42	11.7
41 to 45	35	9.7
46 and over	140	38.9
Total	360	100.0

Exhibit 4
Test Preferences for Deodorants A and B Using the Paired Comparison Technique

	Prefer Deodorant A %	Prefer Deodorant B %	No Preference %
Which had the better fragrance?	64	32	4
Which felt more comfortable to the skin?	43	38	19
Which had the more powerful antiperspirant?	47	50	3
Which did you prefer for its dryness?	37	58	5
Which did you prefer?	32	28	40

Exhibit 5
Test Preferences for Deodorant A and Deodorant Used by Respondents at Time of Test

	Prefer Deodorant A %	Prefer Brand Used %	No Preference %
Which had the better fragrance?	74	19	7
Which felt more comfortable to the skin?	81	14	5
Which had the more powerful antiperspirant?	61	28	11
Which did you prefer for its dryness?	88	9	3
Which did you prefer?	77	21	2

Exhibit 6

Test Preferences for Deodorant B and Deodorant Used by Respondents at Time of Test

	PREFER DEODORANT B %	PREFER BRAND USED %	No PREFERENCE %
Which had the better fragrance?	62	33	5
Which felt more comfortable to the skin?	73	14	13
Which had the more powerful antiperspirant?	91	5	4
Which did you prefer for its dryness?	76	6	18
Which did you prefer?	89	9	2

Exhibit 7

Estimation of Production Costs

COST ITEM	DEODORANT A	DEODORANT B
Direct material[a]	$ 0.20	$ 0.15
Direct labor[a]	0.30	0.25
Variable factory overhead[a]	0.15	0.15
Fixed factory overhead	$120,000.00	$200,000.00

[a] Direct material, direct labor, and variable factory overhead costs are expressed on a unit basis.

Questions

1. Using hypothesis testing (discussed in Chapter 11, calculate with 95 percent confidence whether deodorant B is preferred to deodorant A as indicated in the independent tests shown in exhibits 5 and 6.

2. Another decision criterion to be used by Jaison Corporation is the cost-volume-profit relationship. Calculate the break-even points for product A and product B. If the demand forecast is 1,200,000 units, which deodorant should be produced? If it is only 700,000 units, which product would you recommend be marketed?

Appendix A

Chi-Square Distribution

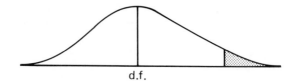

d.f.

The table below shows the shaded area.

	CHI-SQUARE VALUES			
DEGREES OF FREEDOM (d.f.)	PROBABILITY (P)			
	.10	.05	.02	.01
1	2.706	3.841	5.412	6.635
2	4.605	5.991	7.824	9.210
3	6.251	7.815	9.837	11.345
4	7.779	9.488	11.668	13.277
5	9.236	11.070	13.388	15.086
6	10.645	12.592	15.033	16.812
7	12.017	14.067	16.622	18.475
8	13.362	15.507	18.168	20.090
9	14.684	16.919	19.679	21.666
10	15.987	18.307	21.161	23.209
11	17.275	19.675	22.618	24.725
12	18.549	21.026	24.054	26.217
13	19.812	22.362	25.472	27.688
14	21.064	23.685	26.873	29.141
15	22.307	24.996	28.259	30.578
16	23.542	26.296	29.633	32.000
17	24.769	27.587	30.995	33.409
18	25.989	28.869	32.346	34.805
19	27.204	30.144	33.687	36.191
20	28.412	31.410	35.020	37.566
21	29.615	32.671	36.343	38.932
22	30.813	33.924	37.659	40.289
23	32.007	35.172	38.968	41.638
24	33.196	36.415	40.270	42.980
25	34.382	37.652	41.566	44.314
26	35.563	38.885	42.856	45.642
27	36.741	40.113	44.140	46.963
28	37.916	41.337	45.419	48.278
29	39.087	42.557	46.693	49.588
30	40.256	43.773	47.962	50.892

Reprinted from Table III of R. A. Fisher: *Statistical Methods for Research Workers*, published by Oliver and Boyd, Ltd. Edinburgh and London, 1936, p. 173.

Appendix B

Normal Curve Areas*

z	.00	.01	.02	.03	.04	.05	.06	.07	.08	.09
0.0	.0000	.0040	.0080	.0120	.0160	.0199	.0239	.0279	.0319	.0359
0.1	.0398	.0438	.0478	.0517	.0557	.0596	.0636	.0675	.0714	.0753
0.2	.0793	.0832	.0871	.0910	.0948	.0987	.1026	.1064	.1103	.1141
0.3	.1179	.1217	.1255	.1293	.1331	.1368	.1406	.1443	.1480	.1517
0.4	.1554	.1591	.1628	.1664	.1700	.1736	.1772	.1808	.1844	.1879
0.5	.1915	.1950	.1985	.2019	.2054	.2088	.2123	.2157	.2190	.2224
0.6	.2257	.2291	.2324	.2357	.2389	.2422	.2454	.2486	.2517	.2549
0.7	.2580	.2611	.2642	.2673	.2704	.2734	.2764	.2794	.2823	.2852
0.8	.2881	.2910	.2939	.2967	.2995	.3023	.3051	.3078	.3106	.3133
0.9	.3159	.3186	.3212	.3238	.3264	.3289	.3315	.3340	.3365	.3389
1.0	.3413	.3438	.3461	.3485	.3508	.3531	.3554	.3577	.3599	.3261
1.1	.3643	.3665	.3686	.3708	.3729	.3749	.3770	.3790	.3810	.3830
1.2	.3849	.3869	.3888	.3907	.3925	.3944	.3962	.3980	.3997	.4015
1.3	.4032	.4049	.4066	.4082	.4099	.4115	.4131	.4147	.4162	.4177
1.4	.4192	.4207	.4222	.4236	.4251	.4265	.4279	.4292	.4306	.4319
1.5	.4332	.4345	.4357	.4370	.4382	.4394	.4406	.4418	.4429	.4441
1.6	.4452	.4463	.4474	.4484	.4495	.4505	.4515	.4525	.4535	.4545
1.7	.4554	.4564	.4573	.4582	.4591	.4599	.4608	.4616	.4625	.4633
1.8	.4641	.4649	.4656	.4664	.4671	.4678	.4686	.4693	.4699	.4706
1.9	.4713	.4719	.4726	.4732	.4738	.4744	.4750	.4756	.4761	.4767
2.0	.4772	.4778	.4783	.4788	.4793	.4798	.4803	.4808	.4812	.4817
2.1	.4821	.4826	.4830	.4834	.4838	.4842	.4846	.4850	.4854	.4857
2.2	.4861	.4864	.4868	.4871	.4875	.4878	.4881	.4884	.4887	.4890
2.3	.4893	.4896	.4898	.4901	.4904	.4906	.4909	.4911	.4913	.4916
2.4	.4918	.4920	.4922	.4925	.4927	.4929	.4931	.4932	.4934	.4936
2.5	.4938	.4040	.4941	.4943	.4945	.4946	.4948	.4949	.4951	.4952
2.6	.4953	.4955	.4956	.4957	.4959	.4960	.4961	.4962	.4963	.4964
2.7	.4965	.4966	.4967	.4968	.4969	.4970	.4971	.4972	.4973	.4974
2.8	.4974	.4975	.4976	.4977	.4977	.4978	.4979	.4979	.4980	.4981
2.9	.4981	.4982	.4982	.4983	.4984	.4984	.4985	.4985	.4986	.4986
3.0	.4987	.4987	.4987	.4988	.4988	.4989	.4989	.4989	.4990	.4990

* Percentage figures are obtained by doubling. Example: if z is 1.96, double .4744 for the 95% confidence interval.

Index

S

Sales analysis, 381–82
Sales Areas—Marketing Incorporated (SAMI), 383
Sales force estimates, 369–70
Sales forecasting, 364–86
  market surveys, 370–71
    consumer intention, 370–71
    test marketing, 371
  objective extrapolation, time series, 371–79
    by linear regression, 374–77
    by scatter diagram, 372–73
    by short-cut formula, 373–74
    components of, 377–78
    use of indicators, 378
  subjective techniques, 368–70
    executive jury, 369
    sales force estimates, 369–70
Sales Management, Annual Survey of Buying Power, 107, 366–68
Sales territories, assignment of, 379–81
Sample, 188
  size, 233, 236, 254–55
  types
    area, 198
    cluster, 198–200
    convenience, 202–203
    judgment, 203–204
    nonprobability, 202
    probability, 194–202
    quota, 204–205
    simple random, 195–97
    stratified, 197–98
    systematic, 200–202
Sampling
  area, 198–99
  versus census, 192
  cluster, 192, 201
  control, 133, 167
  distribution, 231
  error, 193, 228
  frame, 167, 192, 198
  nonprobability, 202–205
  plan, 27
  probability, 194–202
  problems, 192–94, 228
  simple random, 195–97
  size of sample, 233–36, 254
  stratified random, 197–98
  systematic, 200
Scales
  error choice, 306
  forced choice bias, 308
  Likert, 306
  ranking, 308
  semantic differential, 307–308
Scatter diagrams, 371–72
Scientific method, 30, 40–57
  in marketing, 42
  in marketing research, 47–51
  steps in, 45–46
Seasonal variation, 377
Secondary data, 95–119
  government agencies, 100–104
  library use, 109–14
  miscellaneous published sources, 107–109
  sources, 96–100
  syndicated commercial information, 104–106
  trade and professional associations, 106–107
Semantics, in questionnaires, 175
Sentence completion technique, 312
Side-by-side tests, 337
Significant differences. *See* Analysis, collected data
Simmons, W. R., and Associates Research, 352, 353
Simple correlation, 391
Simple regression, 374–77
Skewed distribution, 217–18, 239
Social distance, 172
Specificity, of primary data, 140
Split-run tests, 349

Spurious precision, 219–20
Staggered comparison tests, 337
Standard and Poor's, 37, 104–105
Standard deviation, 222, 223, 231
Standard Industrial Classification (SIC), 382
Standard Metropolitan Statistical Area (SMSA), 102, 382
Standard Rate and Data Service, 37
Starch Advertisement Readership Ratings, 346, 347
Statistics, summary
  measures of central tendency, 217–18
  measures of dispersion, 221–22, 231
Stochastic techniques, 392
Store location research, 384–85
Story completion technique, 313
Stratified random sampling, 197–98
Substitution, 184
Survey administration, 166–87. *See also* Survey research
Survey of Buying Power (*Sales Management*), 41, 107, 366–67
Survey of Current Business and Business Cycle Developments, 104
Survey of Marketing Research, 37, 109, 179, 180, 321
Survey research, 65–67, 128, 398–99
  accuracy of data, 130
  administration, 166–87
  administrative control, 134
  amount of data gathered, 132
  buyer intentions, 123, 370–71
  control, 133
  cost, 67
  comparison of survey types, 135
  criteria for selecting survey type, 130
  flexibility, 133
  interview control, 133
  limitations of, 67
  mail survey, 129

nonresponse error, 177–81, 183–85
personal interviews, 129
response error, 174–76
response rate, 132
sample control, 133
speed, 130
telephone survey, 69, 129, 132, 398
Survey Research Center (University of Michigan), 123
Survey response rate, 181, 182, 183
Syndicated commercial information, 104
Systematic sampling, 200–202

T

Tabulation of data, 145, 214–26
Tachistoscope, 316–17
Target Group Index (TGI), 352
Technical reports, 260–61
Technical testing, 326–28
  analysis testing, 326
  performance testing, 327
Telephone interviews, 69, 129, 132, 398
Television audience measurement, 31, 50, 68, 70–71, 105, 138, 332, 357–58
Test marketing, 72, 332–36, 371
Thematic Apperception Test, 314
Thurstone scale, 49
Time series analysis, 372–79
  components, 377–78
  methods, 372–77
  use of indicators, 378
Traffic Audit Bureau, 351
Traffic count, 384
Training interviewers, 169–70
Trend projections, 377
Trendix, Inc., 357
Triple associate test, 348
True profit, 383
T-test, 392

Type I error, 252–53
Type II error, 252–53

U

Unaided recall tests, 348
Uncertainty, 43
Universe, 188
Universities, 37
Unstructured questionnaires, 145,
    147–48

V

Validity, 78
Variables
    marketing-controlled, 301

nonmarketing-controlled, 300
Variance, 222
    analysis of, 392
Variation of data, 377–78
Voice Pitch Analyzer, 399

W

Weighted mean, 217
Weighting response, 184
Word association, 312

Z

Z-test, 392